A SOURCE BOOK OF ANCIENT CHINESE BRONZE INSCRIPTIONS

Revised Edition

Early China Special Monograph Series, No. 8

Series editors:

Sarah Allan and Andrew Meyer

A SOURCE BOOK OF ANCIENT CHINESE BRONZE INSCRIPTIONS

Revised Edition

Edited by

Constance A. Cook

Paul R. Goldin

The Society for the Study of Early China

Berkeley, California

2020

© 2020 by The Society for the Study of Early China

All rights reserved. No part of this publication may be reproduced, stored in a retrieval system, or transmitted in any form or by any means, electronic, mechanical, photocopying, recording, or otherwise, without the prior permission of the publisher.

Cover by C.A. Cook, K.T. Stein, M. Poli and A. Panato

Library of Congress Control Number: 2020931588
ISBN 978-0-9969440-1-4 (pbk. : alk. paper)

Names: Cook, Constance A., editor. | Goldin, Paul Rakita, 1972- editor.
Title: A Source Book of Ancient Chinese Bronze Inscriptions (Revised Edition) / edited by Constance A. Cook and Paul R. Goldin. Revisions by Maddalena Poli and Alice Panato.
Description: Berkeley, California : The Society for the Study of Early China, 2020. | Series: Early China Special Monograph Series; No. 8 | Chinese and English. | "The Revised Edition of A Source Book of Ancient Chinese Bronze Inscriptions offers English translations of eighty-two of the most important bronze inscriptions, ranging in date from approximately 1200 B.C.E. to 200 C.E., with critical corrections to the first edition. The translations and discussions are a collaborative effort of expert scholars, including Constance A. Cook, Wolfgang Behr, Robert Eno, Paul R. Goldin, Martin Kern, Maria Khayutina, David W. Pankenier, David Sena, Laura Skosey, and Yan Sun. For each inscription, authors offer a brief overview of the provenance and historical context of the bronze, followed by a transcription in modern Chinese graphs, an idiomatic translation, and a list of further readings." | Includes bibliographical references.
Subjects: LCSH: Inscriptions, Chinese. | Bronzes--China--Inscriptions.
Classification: LCC CN1160 .S68 2020 | DDC 495.11/1--dc23
LC record available at https://lccn.loc.gov/2020931588

THE EDITORS DEDICATE THIS BOOK TO THE MEMORY OF

GILBERT L. MATTOS.

We acknowledge the support of the University of Pennsylvania Provost and the Society for the Study of Early China.

We thank Zhao Lu for his help with the bibliography.

For the revised edition, we are grateful to David P. Branner for a list of corrigenda, and deeply appreciate the corrections, suggestions, and technical expertise furnished by Maddalena Poli and Alice Panato.

TABLE OF CONTENTS

Foreword
    The Aims of This Book   *xi*

Introduction: Essays and Guides   *xvi*
    Bronzes and Sacrifice   *xix*
    Ceremony and the Creation of the Text   *xlix*
    The Legacy of Bronzes and Bronze Inscriptions in
        Early Chinese Literature   *lv*
    Tables
    Chronology   *lxv*
    The Sexagenary Cycle   *lxvi*
    Conventions and Abbreviations   *lxvii*

Inscriptions: Numbers 1-82   *1*

1.	*Er Si Bi Qi* you	二祀邲其卣	*3*
2.	*Zi Huang* zun	子黃尊	*5*
3.	*Wo* fangding	我方鼎	*8*
4.	*Li* gui	利簋	*10*
5.	*Tian Wang* gui	天亡簋	*13*
6.	*He* zun	何尊	*16*
7.	*Ke* he and *Ke* lei	克盉 克罍	*19*
8.	*Yan Hou Zhi* ding	匽侯旨鼎	*21*
9.	*Yi Hou Ze* gui	宜侯夨簋	*23*
10.	*Jing Hou* gui	井侯簋	*28*
11.	*Da Yu* ding	大盂鼎	*30*
12.	*Shenzi Ta* guigai	沈子它簋蓋	*36*
13.	*Geng Ying* you and *Geng Ying* ding	庚嬴卣 庚嬴鼎	*39*
14.	*Zuoce Mai* fangzun	作冊麥方尊	*42*
15.	*Zuoce Ling* fangyi	作冊令方彝	*45*
16.	*Yu* ding	旟鼎	*49*
17.	*Zuoce Huan* you	作冊睘卣	*51*
18.	*Zhong* xian	中甗	*53*
19.	*Jing* gui	靜簋	*55*
20.	*Shi Qi* ding	師旂鼎	*57*
21.	*Ban* gui	班簋	*60*
22.	*Dong* gui and *Lu Bo Dong* gui	㝬簋 彔伯㝬簋	*64*

23. *Qi* gui	趞簋	72
24. *Hu* guigai	虎簋蓋	74
25. *Shi Wang* ding	師望鼎	77
26. *Li* fangzun and *Li* juzun	盠方尊 盠駒尊	80
27. *Qiu Wei* he *Wusi Wei* ding and *Jiunian Wei* ding	裘衛盉 五祀衛鼎 九年衛鼎	84
28. *Shi Qiang* pan	史墻盤	93
29. *Shi Zai* ding	師𩛥鼎	101
30. *Shi Yong* yu	師永盂	105
31. *Xun* gui and *Shi You* gui	詢簋 師酉簋	108
32. *Shi Xun* gui	師詢簋	112
33. *Xing* zhong	癲鐘 and Related Inscriptions	115
34. *Yin Ji* ding and *Gong Ji* li	尹姞鼎 公姞鬲	126
35. *Hu* ding	曶鼎	129
36. *Ying* yi and *Ying* yigai	𠁁匜 𠁁匜蓋	136
37. *Fifth-year Diao Sheng* gui and *Sixth-year Diao Sheng* gui	五年琱生簋 六年琱生簋	139
38. *Shi Mi* gui	史密簋	144
39. *Hu* gui and *Hu* zhong	㝬簋 㝬鐘	147
40. *Yu* ding	禹鼎	154
41. *Duo You* ding	多友鼎	157
42. *Guai Bo* gui	乖伯簋	160
43. *Guo You Bi* ding and *Guo You Bi* guigai	鬲攸比鼎 鬲攸比簋蓋	163
44. *Guo Shu Lü* zhong	虢叔旅鐘	166
45. *Sanshi* pan	散氏盤	168
46. *Da Ke* ding	大克鼎 and Related Inscriptions	172
47. *Shi Song* gui	史頌簋 and Related Inscriptions	181
48. *Xi Jia* pan	兮甲盤	184
49. *Guo Ji Zibai* pan	虢季子白盤	187
50. *Buqi* guigai	不娶簋蓋	190
51. *Ying Hou Jiangong* zhong	應侯見工鐘	192
52. *Ju Fu* xugai	駒父盨蓋	195
53. *Bin Gong* xu	燹(豳)公盨	197
54. *Wu Hu* ding	吳虎鼎	201
55. *Mao Gong* ding	毛公鼎	204

TABLE OF CONTENTS

56. *Shanfu Shan* ding	膳夫山鼎	*210*
57. *Jin Hou Su* zhong	晉侯穌(蘇)鐘	*213*
58. *Kunbi Wang* zhong	昆疕王鐘	*219*
59. *Chu Gong Jia* zhong	楚公豪鐘	*221*
60. *Jing Ren Ning* zhong	井人妄鐘	*223*
61. *Ni* zhong	逆鐘	*225*
62. *Liang Qi* zhong	沙(梁)其鐘	*227*
63. *Qiu (Lai)* pan	逑(速)盤	*231*
64. *Shan Bo Hao Sheng* zhong	單伯昊生鐘	*241*
65. *Zha* zhong	柞鐘	*243*
66. *Qin Gong* bo *Qin Gong* gui and *Qin Gong* yongzhong	秦公鎛 秦公簋 秦公甬鐘	*245*
67. *Rong Sheng* bianzhong	戎生編鐘	*251*
68. *Jin Jiang* ding	晉姜鼎	*255*
69. *Shu Yi* bo and *Shu Yi* zhong	叔夷鎛 叔夷鐘	*258*
70. *Zifan* bianzhong	子軛(犯)編鐘	*265*
71. *Lü Qi* zhong	郘黛鐘	*268*
72. *Wangsun Yizhe* zhong	王孫遺者鐘	*270*
73. *Wangzi Wu* ding	王子午鼎	*274*
74. *Cai Hou Shen* pan and *Cai Hou Shen* zun	蔡侯申盤 蔡侯申尊	*277*
75. *Wu Wang Guang* jian	吳王光鑒	*280*
76. *Guo Zuo* dan	國佐鐕	*282*
77. *Dishi* hu	杕氏壺	*285*
78. *Gongyu taizi Gu-fa-X-fan* jian	工獻大子姑發胥反劍	*287*
79. *Piao Qiang* zhong	鷹羌鐘	*290*
80. *Zhongshan Wang Cuo* ding	中山王譽鼎	*294*
81. *Chu Wang Yin Han* ding	楚王酓悍鼎	*301*
82. *Shuo ren* jing	碩人鏡	*303*

Glossary *309*

Bibliography *321*

Index *351*

TABLE OF CONTENTS

CONTRIBUTORS

CAC	*Constance A. Cook, Lehigh University*
DMS	*David M. Sena, Harvard University*
DWP	*David W. Pankenier, Lehigh University, Emeritus*
LAS	*Laura A. Skosey, University of Chicago*
MKe	*Martin Kern, Princeton University*
MKh	*Maria Khayutina, Ludwig Maximilian University of Munich*
MP	*Maddalena Poli, University of Pennsylvania*
PRG	*Paul R. Goldin, University of Pennsylvania*
RE	*Robert Eno, Indiana University, Emeritus*
WB	*Wolfgang Behr, University of Zurich*
YS	*Yan Sun, Gettysburg College*

Foreword

The Aims of This Book

Bronze inscriptions are among the most important sources for the study of ancient China, yet they remain largely unappreciated because few scholars, including historians of China, are familiar with them, mostly because they are inherently difficult to read. They are written in an archaic form of the Chinese script that can be mastered only after years of epigraphic study (and is still not completely understood); in addition, they are composed in a terse and formulaic style that sometimes baffles even the most advanced researchers. The highly specialized nature of research on Chinese bronze inscriptions has discouraged general readers from examining them.

A Source Book of Ancient Chinese Bronze Inscriptions is intended to redress that deficiency by offering English translations of eighty-two of the most important bronze inscriptions, ranging in date from approximately 1200 B.C.E. to 200 C.E. Preceding the inscriptions is an introduction outlining the nature and significance of bronze inscriptions, along with summary discussions of specific issues, such as the changing ritual milieu in which bronzes were used, as well as the rhetoric and intended audience of the inscriptions cast and incised on them. The editors have decided that a collaborative effort involving several expert scholars would best represent the range both of the extant inscriptional literature and of the leading modern approaches to it. In order to keep this book within a reasonable length, we present only the following for each inscription: a brief overview of its provenance and historical importance, followed by a transcription in modern Chinese graphs, an accurate but idiomatic translation, and a list of further readings for those who wish to study the sources in more detail. (The transcription may not mean much to readers who do not command Chinese, but is nevertheless crucial because it lays out the translator's interpretation of each graph of the original.)

It is important to state at the outset that, in one sense, the inscriptions included in this source book are not *representative* because most known bronze inscriptions are very short. Many of them mention only a name and a vessel type: "Tripod for Ancestor So-and-so." (In these cases, the name, which might take the form "Father Bing-Day" 父丙, is understood to refer to a dead ancestor because it includes the day of the ten-day week when the spirit was scheduled to receive sacrifices.) Thus it would be senseless to translate the many thousands of attested inscriptions of this type, since they offer scant information about their context. Rather, the inscriptions we have chosen come from among the most *informative* ones, those that shed the most light on the culture that created and cherished them.

At the same time, we have chosen certain typical inscriptions so that readers will acquire a sense of what standard inscriptions look like. For example, one important class consists of so-called "appointment inscriptions," in which a person who has just received a noteworthy reward—usually, but not always, from a king—commemorates the occasion by means of a bronze inscription recounting his merit and his superior's recompense.[1] Appointment inscriptions generally conform to the following pattern.[2] A date is given first. This date may be absolute ("It was in such-and-such year of King So-and-so's reign"), but usually it is relative ("It was at the time when the King did such-and-such/was in such-and-such place")—and our ability to pin down such dates is obviously limited unless they are associated with specific events that we happen to know from other sources. The rare inscriptions that are furnished with unambiguous absolute dates can serve today as benchmarks for similar inscriptions (or for inscriptions on similar vessels) with less certain dates, and have become canonical for precisely this reason.

Next might come a narration of the achievements that warranted the award, but this information, invaluable as it may be to modern readers, does not always appear; instead, the inscription might take the reader immediately to the award ceremony itself, sometimes naming the persons who accompanied the awardee to his audience or who took part in the ceremony. (Scholars have profitably mined such oblique references for the purpose of reconstructing kinship and other networks in Bronze-Age China.) Finally the King will speak, announcing the reasons for the award in grandiloquent language that may have been taken from a document prepared specifically for this event. Often the awardee will be asked to succeed his honored father or ancestor in some important office, or, for specific acts

---

[1] Appointment inscriptions are defined more fully by Li Feng in the following three publications: "'Feudalism,'" *Landscape and Power*, and *Bureaucracy and the State*; they are also discussed below by Martin Kern, who translates a representative set of them, namely the Shi Song *gui* 史頌簋 and related inscriptions (no. 47). See also Kane, "Aspects of Western Zhou Appointment Inscriptions."

[2] Cf. Shaughnessy, *Sources of Western Zhou History*, 76–85.

FOREWORD   xiii

of loyalty or bravery, he will be lauded and granted lands, titles, or both. The King may sometimes preface his charge with an assertion of his ancestral right to rule, conspicuously mirroring the awardee's succession to his own ancestor's position.

Then we are usually given a list of ancillary gifts granted by the superior; these tend to be ritual paraphernalia, including ceremonial vestments (like colored kneepads) and equestrian furnishings. Some of these gifts must have been extremely valuable because few appear to have been given on any single occasion. While hundreds of people and families may be transferred to the awardee's control without further comment, only a handful of such ritual items appear in the list of gifts.[3] One can only infer that they were made of the finest materials by the King's own craftsmen.

The awardee then typically "extols in response" (*duiyang* 對揚) the King's virtue and grace, often with kowtows and similar ritual gestures. At the end, the inscription contains a *guci* 嘏辭, or "benediction": the awardee states that he is commemorating the felicitous event by commissioning the vessel on which the inscription appears, which he prays that his descendants will eternally use and treasure.

As Lothar von Falkenhausen has observed, this commonplace sequence also yields "a straightforward past-present-future pattern":[4] the announcement of merit referring to the past, the account of the award ceremony referring to the present, and the formal benediction referring to the future.

Not all bronze inscriptions are appointment inscriptions—for example, some vessels were cast for women as part of their dowries, while other inscriptions served as records of legal decisions—but the overwhelming majority of the inscriptions in this book are commemorative in some respect. Why did the ancient Chinese elite choose to commemorate accomplishments by casting inscribed vessels? In order to answer this question, we need to look at how ritual vessels were used in ancient Chinese society.

Bronze inscriptions from several dynasties are represented in this book: Shang (ca. 1500–1045? B.C.E.), Western Zhou (1045?–771 B.C.E.), Eastern Zhou (771–256 B.C.E.), and Han (206 B.C.E.–220 C.E.). But the heyday was the Western Zhou, when bronzes were commissioned by priv-

---

[3] For a recent exploration of such awards, see Huang Shengzhang, "Xi Zhou tongqi zhong fushi shangci yu zhiguan ji ceming zhidu guanxi fafu"; also Cook, "Wealth and the Western Zhou."

[4] Falkenhausen, "Issues in Western Zhou Studies," 154.

ileged lineages for use in sacrifices to their ancestors that would have been conducted in private ritual precincts. Ritual bronzes were by no means unknown in earlier periods, but Shang bronzes were much less commonly inscribed. (This book includes the longest known Shang bronze inscription, namely the Ersi Bi Qi *you* 二祀𠨘其卣, no. 1, below.)

It was during the Western Zhou, when orderly sacrifices to ancestors must have been regarded as the most important religious ceremonies conducted in each lineage, that bronze inscriptions became common enough to encompass the various familiar types represented in this book. Though the bronzes would have been kept proudly within the lineage's estate, they were never intended for *public* display. This peculiar ritual context, combined with the recent observation that the inscriptions on Western Zhou bronzes are often placed in areas where it would have been difficult for anyone to read them, has led some scholars to suggest that inscriptions were intended not for human audiences, but for the spirits invoked at the sacred rituals in which the bronzes would have been used.[5] (I have witnessed a connoisseur struggling to make out the graphs cast on the inside wall of a vessel with a neck so narrow that it admitted virtually no light. For whose eyes could such an inscription have been intended?) According to this argument, the main purpose of the inscriptions is to inform the powerful spirits of their living descendants' achievements on earth. And their accounts need not have been perfectly true: bronze inscriptions often recount events with euphemious details that we know were not strictly accurate (such as the Shi Qiang *pan* 史墻盤, no. 28). Ritual codices were aware of this tendency, and indeed sanctioned it: "The principle of an inscription is to cite what is beautiful and not what is ugly" 銘之義，稱美而不稱惡 (*Liji* 禮記, "Jitong" 祭統 chapter).[6]

The most satisfying answer to the contentious question of the intended audience of the inscriptions may be gleaned from some of the *guci* themselves. Take, for example, the conclusion of the Geng Ying *you* 庚嬴卣 inscription (no. 13), which dates to the second half of the tenth century B.C.E. and commemorates a royal acknowledgment of Ying's merit: "Ying of Geng extolled in response the King's beneficence, wherefore she made

---

[5] For a judicious recent overview, see Olivier Venture, "Visibilité et lisibilité dans les inscriptions sur bronze de la China archaïque." The fullest discussion remains Falkenhausen, "Issues in Western Zhou Studies," e.g., 152.

[6] Cf. Shaughnessy, *Sources of Western Zhou History*, 176.

a treasured and revered vessel for her cultivated aunt; may her sons and grandsons eternally use and treasure it for myriad years" 庚嬴對揚王休，用作厥文姑寶尊彝，其子子孫孫萬年永寶用. These straightforward lines permit several important inferences. First, since Ying was probably female, it is worth noting that the assertive act of commissioning a commemorative bronze could be performed by powerful women as well as men (and that, just like men, women could be rewarded by the king for their merit).[7] No less importantly, the concluding benediction shows that the inscription was intended not just for Lady Ying's deceased ancestors, but for all generations of the lineage extending backwards to the beginning and forwards to the end of time. Just as lineage rituals united generations past, present, and future, the inscriptions on ritual vessels were intended *both* as proud announcements to the ancestral spirits *and* as brazen admonitions to future generations not to forget the achievements of their forebears. For Lady Ying could scarcely have been unaware, while she was thinking about how her inscription should be phrased, that one day she would become an ancestral spirit herself, cultivated and adored by descendants yet unborn.

But times changed. The grand aristocratic lineages that fueled the burgeoning of bronze inscriptions in the Western Zhou dynasty were gradually destroyed over the course of the following period, the Eastern Zhou, by monarchs who regarded them as impediments to centralized rule.[8] Bereft of their ritual context, bronze inscriptions came to express personal pretensions (often with diction that has been aptly characterized as "self-panegyrical")[9] more than the intergenerational continuity of the lineage—not "I was rewarded for doing such-and-such, wherefore I made this vessel in honor of my deceased ancestor; may my descendants eternally treasure it" and so on, but "I did such-and-such, and it redounds to my glory." References to ancestors and their spirits also became less and less prominent.

The Chen Zhang *fanghu* 陳璋方壺 is a good example.[10] This originally uninscribed vessel, a shining treasure inlaid with malachite, was apparently

---

[7] For a recent study of women in bronze inscriptions, see Cao Zhaolan, *Jinwen yu Yin Zhou nüxing wenhua*.

[8] For a fine study in English, see Lewis, *Sanctioned Violence in Early China*, esp. chapter 2; more recently, Shelach and Pines, "Secondary State Formation and the Development of Local Identity," esp. 217–22.

[9] Mattos, "Eastern Zhou Bronze Inscriptions," 88.

[10] Not included in this source book, but see Mattos and Yang, "The Chen Zhang Fanghu."

manufactured in the northeastern state of Yan 燕, but was taken as booty by a general of Qi 齊 named Chen Zhang (known in the received literature as Tian Zhang 田章 or Kuang Zhang 匡章). The triumphant warrior then caused an inscription to be incised into the vessel, with a date corresponding to 315 B.C.E., and the boastful final line: "I, Chen Zhang, have brought back spoils from the attack on the states of Yan and Bo" 陳璋納伐燕亳邦之獲. Bronze inscriptions from the Eastern Zhou sometimes address the philosophical controversies of the time—such as whether it is virtue or birthright that authorizes a ruler to rule, a question discussed at length in the Zhongshan Wang Cuo *ding* 中山王譽鼎 inscription (no. 78). Earlier bronze inscriptions rarely broached such issues, as they were not relevant to the lineage cult.

Beneath their formulaic veneer, then, bronze inscriptions range over a remarkable diversity of topics, including fields that we today would call history, law, philosophy, and religion, but the authors and readers of Bronze-Age China naturally did not recognize such divisions. To them, the subject matter of bronze inscriptions consisted of everything worth commemorating in the present and transmitting to the future. Especially for the Western Zhou dynasty, a period from which few other documents survive, bronze inscriptions are among the best sources for understanding ancient Chinese society and culture. We hope this book will succeed in introducing these neglected texts to a wider readership.

PRG

INTRODUCTION
Essays and Guides

Bronzes and Sacrifice

Few other textual resources survive from the era when bronze inscriptions emerged as a primary literary form: from the second millennium B.C.E. through the eighth century B.C.E. We have only the information contained in the inscriptions and the archaeological contexts of the bronzes to provide hints as to their cultural function. Bone divination texts preserved from the late Shang and early Zhou periods are even more cryptic than the formulaic bronze texts. Transmitted histories, documents, and odes that claim to describe this period were all edited and compiled hundreds, if not a thousand, years later. It is important to understand not only that ancient people cast bronze inscriptions into vessels and bells as records of significant cultural events, but also that these vessels and bells played roles in sacrificial feasts and were each parts of an assemblage of ritual objects used in mortuary worship to particular ancestral spirits.[11]

The vessels, bells, and texts function as independent and interdependent ritual symbols and processes within early Chinese ceremonies. That is, texts were at once part of the sacrificial ritual in which the bronze was used but also transmitted independently (orally and on bamboo records). Variations in the bronze types and numbers in assemblages discovered in tombs and caches reflect changing social dynamics, just as variations in the formulaic rhetoric and contents reflect changes in the lives of the individuals who owned the vessels. In addition, we see the rise of musical instruments cast in bronze at the same time that onomatopoeia and rhymed sections of text also increase, suggesting the importance of music to the ceremonies in which the inscribed text was formed and the vessel eventually used. The change in emphasis in the numbers of vessels used for rituals involving drinking concomitant with a rise in food vessels suggests a cultural shift to a society that values agriculture and hunting. At the same, we note that the varieties of inscribed texts increase, with some involving governmental charges, or lineage documents getting longer and longer. This reveals an increasingly sophisticated state and a spreading literacy.[12] It also confirms an expansion of the ritual space beyond ancestor worship into the political

---

[11] For general studies of feasts in ancient China, see Sterckx, ed., *Of Tripod and Palate*, and Sterckx, *Food, Sacrifice, and Sagehood in Early China*.

[12] See the studies on the spread of literacy in ancient China in Li and Branner, *Literacy*.

sphere, one in which separate lineage houses are bound to each other and to a central ancestral lineage represented by the ruler.[13] Thus it is essential that modern readers of ancient bronze inscriptions have some knowledge of what bronzes meant to the ancient people who used them before attempting to interpret their texts.

Metal (*jin* 金) represented power and magic among the ancient peoples of the Yellow River valley—the East Asian heartland. Bronze, in particular, which required the mixing of alloys and an incipient state-level organization to produce in large numbers, was highly valued. For thousands of years, bronze ownership, particularly in the form of sacrificial vessels, represented wealth, social rank, and access to the reigning network of ancestral gods. The Chinese Bronze Age rose during the late third millennium B.C.E. and declined during the first millennium C.E., but the peak of cultural signification in terms of text was during the Zhou dynasty, a time traditionally associated with the golden age of early Chinese government and the establishment of Chinese ritual law.[14] Bronze-making began first with incidental items, such as trinkets, knives, and mirrors in the upper Yellow River valley, but evolved during the late second and early first millennium B.C.E. into complementary sets of weapons, vessels, and eventually bells.[15]

Yellow River cultures existed in complex interlinked agricultural, pastoral, and hunting-and-gathering communities with a hierarchical social and political system that extended through ancestor worship into an equally complex supernatural world, one based in the natural world of earth, sky, and the four directions.[16] Metal was a tool for communication between the

---

[13] See discussions by Falkenhausen, "Royal Audience and Its Reflections," Li, "Literacy and Social Contexts," and Cook, "Education and the Way of the Former Kings."

[14] See Chang, K.C., and Xu Pingfang, *et al.*, *The Formation of Chinese Civilization*. For the rise of the Bronze Age, see also Thorp, *China in the Early Bronze Age*. For a statistical study of mortuary evidence during this time period, see Falkenhausen, *Chinese Society in the Age of Confucius*. For comprehensive discussions of material culture and funeral practices, see Thote, "Shang and Zhou Funeral Practices"; also Loewe and Shaughnessy, *The Cambridge History of Ancient China: From the Origins of Civilization to 221 B.C.* For detailed analysis of bronze styles, see Bagley, *Shang Ritual Bronzes in the Arthur M. Sackler Collections*; Rawson, *Western Zhou Ritual Bronzes from the Arthur M. Sackler Collections*; and So, *Eastern Zhou Ritual Bronzes from the Arthur M. Sackler Collections*.

[15] Linduff, *et al.*, *The Beginnings of Metallurgy in China*.

[16] Allan, *The Shape of the Turtle*; Keightley, *The Ancestral Landscape*. For earth rituals, see Kominami, "Rituals for the Earth." See also the Yi Hou Ze *gui* inscription (no. 9).

human king (*wang* 王) and the Deity Above (*shangdi* 上帝),[17] who resided in the sky and sent messages through star patterns and cracks on bones.

Writing on oracle bones, evident by second millennium B.C.E., evolved as a method for compiling ritual records of this communication.[18] Zhou records, preserved primarily on bronze vessels, archived records of state sacrifices and actions of the king and members of his clan network, all of whom referred to him as the Son of Heaven (*tianzi* 天子). Heaven, for the Zhou, was both the sky and a supernatural power equivalent to the Deity Above.[19] The supernatural world was divided between the spirits above and below (*shangxia* 上下). According to the inscriptions preserved on bronzes, the Zhou ancestral spirits who received the sacrifices were associated with the sky, even though their personal bronzes were buried with them in underground tombs. Bronze-Age political systems grew up around the control of agriculture, metal resources, and the manufacture of prestige goods, such as bronzes and jades, cultural artifacts that represented social status. These goods generally represented social roles in ritual or warfare and included items such as weapons, vessels, and bells, whose intertwined functions helped to provide meat or sacrificial victims for the sacrifices and to communicate prayers or receive blessings "sent down" (*jiang* 降) from above. Certain aspects of these items, such as their sizes, shapes, décor, and assemblages, represented social power. At first, this power was focused in the hands of Yellow River valley cultures, but by the end of the eighth century B.C.E., the centralized theocracy had disintegrated into a world of competing kings and other local gods. Tales of founders and kings of the Bronze Age were organized by later writers as a record of an idealized age known as the Three Eras (*sandai* 三代), i.e. the Xia 夏, Shang, and Zhou. Archaeological evidence reveals periods of great technological advance and political complexity in geographical regions roughly associated with each of these cultures. While there is no longer any question as to the reality of the Shang and Zhou, the Xia remains elusive, and the middle Yellow River valley-type site of Erlitou 二里頭 (c. 1900–1500 B.C.E.) is no more than a candidate for its identity.[20] The subsequent political center in Erligang 二里崗 culture (c. 1600–1250 B.C.E.), located farther east in old Shang

---

[17] This phrase can also be construed as "The Supreme Deity."
[18] See Keightley, *Sources of Shang History*; Allan, *The Shape of the Turtle*.
[19] Allan, "T'ien and Shang Ti in Pre-Han China"; Luo Xinhui, "Zhoudai tianming guannian."
[20] Thorp, "Erlitou and the Search for the Xia"; Allan, "The Myth of the Xia Dynasty."

territory, may or may not have belonged to Shang ancestors, but there is no question regarding the political identity of the literate establishment at present-day Anyang 安陽, Henan Province (occupied from roughly 1300 to 1046 B.C.E.). The Shang, clearly named as such in the oracle bones, were the first to apply writing to durable objects such as bone and bronze. The Shang political network included the early Zhou, located to the west, perhaps in the old Xia region.[21] Zhou-period archaeological culture took on its own characteristics as it arose in the Wei River valley, a western tributary of the middle Yellow River.

Artisans crafted bones and bronze vessels for purposes of sacrifice and divination rituals.[22] Inscribed records are found on the scapulae and thighbones of wild animals, cattle, humans, as well as the plastrons of tortoises, a tribute good from the south. Early artisans cast insignia or emblems (traditionally called "clan signs," *zuhui* 族徽) onto the hafts of dagger axe blades and under the handles of drinking vessels (see nos. 1, 2, and 3) to dedicate the item for use in sacrifice to a particular ancestral spirit. Bronze inscriptions evolved during the three hundred years of the Western Zhou (1046–771 B.C.E.) from simple ritual records to long manifestos (see no. 55), but, after the Zhou royal family was chased away from their ancestral burial grounds in the eighth century B.C.E., shorter local adaptations of Zhou-style texts and prayer texts began to predominate during what is known as the Eastern Zhou (770–221 B.C.E.). Only in the northeastern region did the tradition of longer texts on bronze remain (see nos. 69 and 78), despite the spread of literacy and growing trend for texts to circulate on bamboo strips sewn together into rolls or books. By the end of the third century B.C.E., bamboo and silk had completely replaced bronze as the medium for ritual records,[23] and in less than five hundred years, paper would be common. The category of "metal objects" by then had also grown to include iron and composite metal tools and weapons; bronze in the imperial age no longer functioned as the primary mode of communication with the gods above. Indeed, the emperor, who was called the "Brilliant Deity" (*huangdi* 皇帝), a title adapted from ancient epithets for

---

[21] See Underhill and Fang, "Early State Economic Systems in China."

[22] For a recent discussion of Shang state religion, see Eno, "Shang State Religion and the Pantheon of the Oracle Texts."

[23] See studies in Cook, *Death in Ancient China*; Li and Branner, *Literacy*.

royal ancestral spirits, was more concerned with balancing natural forces, a system in which the highest spirit and sky god was called "Grand Unity" (Taiyi 太一).[24] Ancestor worship was now a private affair, not a bond that held together a politicized network as during the Zhou period. Bronze too had been devalued by then to be used for quotidian objects such as coins and measures. Like other metals (such as copper, silver, and gold, which previously was limited to use as inlays in bronzes or for personal trinkets), bronze was no longer a symbol of political and religious power. When used to make religious statues, incense burners, mirrors, or bells, it was simply a shiny and durable metal.

Ritual Sets: Bronzes and Social Evolution

The Erlitou period witnessed the emergence of the earliest bronze ritual vessels, and it is during this time that we first can discuss a ritual assemblage of vessels used in sacrifice. Vessels were made of an alloy of copper, tin, and lead, and cast with clay molds, using a method called piece-mold casting—a method that would remain the primary casting method throughout most of the Bronze Age. As prestige goods, bronzes were placed along with finely worked jade, ceramic, and bone items in the tombs of the powerful elites, a tradition that would also persist through time. The first assemblages were simple drinking vessels (called *jue* 爵) along with vessels for heating and pouring liquids (*jia* 斝, *he* 盉) or cauldrons (*ding* 鼎) for cooking and serving meat stews.[25] The *jue*, used for drinking alcoholic beverages, dominated the ritual sets through early Zhou, but became obsolete by the seventh century B.C.E., as the Zhou focused more on food service vessels. The *ding* cauldron, on the other hand, would grow in importance and continue as a mainstay in ritual assemblages to the end of the Zhou period.

The Erligang culture dramatically expanded the number of vessel types cast in bronze. Many new shapes for cooking, steaming, storing liquids and

---

[24] For recent discussions, see Harper, "Warring States Natural Philosophy and Occult Thought"; Pankenier, *Astrology and Cosmology in Early China*, 83–117; Allan, "On the Identity of Shang Di 上帝 and the Origin of the Concept of a Celestial Mandate"; and Cook, "Ancestor Worship during the Eastern Zhou," 239.

[25] The names assigned to bronze vessel types by archaeologists are drawn from traditional Chinese texts, but the effort to classify bronze vessels systematically began during the Song 宋 dynasty (960–1279). Some of the names are found on oracle bone and bronze inscriptions. See Zhu Fenghan, *Gudai Zhongguo qingtongqi*, 59–229. For a list of common vessel types, see Glossary.

foods, bathing, and serving foods and drinks were cast in bronze, showing an increase in social status, personal or lineage wealth, and technology. Almost all of these vessel types would continue to be used throughout the Bronze Age, although the predominant decorative feature of the late Shang (second millennium B.C.E.), a symmetrical mask-like animal face (composed of unrelated animal parts and traditionally referred to as a *taotie* 饕餮) would devolve into more naturalistic sculpted animals or abstract geometric designs during the Zhou period. The mass production of bronze vessels and their distribution throughout the Yellow and parts of the Yangzi River valleys reflect the importance of bronze-vessel production in the reproduction of late Shang social norms as well as the expansion of Shang governmental control through trade and tribute networks.[26]

The wealthy interconnected clans allied under the Shang king populated the region around the royal burial ground in modern Anyang, making up a vast a city, known later as the "Ruins of Yin" (Yinxu 殷墟), after the Zhou name for this city and dynasty. Complexes of palaces, shrines, and workshops were overshadowed by the immense burial ground on the northern edge. Although most of the enormous royal tombs (distinguishable by their four large ramps) had been plundered over time, archaeologists in the 1970s discovered the tomb of a Shang queen named Fu Hao 婦好, who, according to oracle bone records, was both an official in Shang government and a wife of the powerful Shang King Wu Ding 武丁.[27] Her tomb was smaller than those believed to belong to kings, but even so it was furnished with 1,928 artifacts of all types, including 440 bronzes laid out as if for a huge underground ceremony. Besides sacrificial vessels (10 *yan* 甗 steamers, 31 *ding* cauldrons, and 5 *gui* 簋 tureens) there were also weapons, tools, bells, mirrors, serving implements (such as ladles), chariot paraphernalia, and dragonheaded staffs. The 195 bronze vessels were made up of twenty different types, but the 12 *jia* drinking vessels, 6 *he* pouring vessels, 40 *jue* drinking vessels and 53 *gu* drinking goblets—all vessels used in the heating, pouring, and consuming of alcohol—testify to a focus on drinking rituals at large feasts, a custom denounced in later Zhou writings as one of the causes for political failure (see the Da Yu *ding*, no. 11). Fu Hao's tomb revealed the innovation of square variants of many of the round ves-

---

[26] For a study of bronze as a symbol of power, see Chang, *Art, Myth, and Ritual*.
[27] *Yinxu Fu Hao mu*.

sel types seen in Erligang as well as new animal shaped vessels, featuring tigers, dragons, owls, rhinoceroses, and combined decorative animal motifs.

The inscriptions in Fu Hao's tomb consisted of emblems, an early form of inscription associated with Anyang bronze production. Anyang vessels included over four hundred different emblems, most of which were the names or titles of the owners or the ancestor spirit in whose name the bronze was used. Some names remain indecipherable. During the late Shang period, when writing became more common, inscriptions evolved from the simple emblems or name signs to longer records, including ancestor dedications and the documentation of awards including ritual items such as cowries, metal, or containers of precious alcoholic beverages. The basic syntax for each inscription consisted of a declaration of manufacture and dedication of the vessel to a spirit. Person A (a living person) "creates" (*zuo* 作) the vessel for Person B (an ancestral spirit).

The act of "creating" was part of a ritual process. First, the right to "create" a bronze derived from a reward for military or ritual support of the king. Second, the commission for the casting of the vessel had to be transmitted to the unnamed artisans in bronze workshop who actually crafted the vessel, although the awardee may have had some control over the text and the type of vessel. The name of Person A included a place name, social rank, and sometimes a personal name in that order. The ancestors' posthumous names consisted of two words, the first of which stated his or her lineage rank, such as "father" (*fu* 父), "mother" (*mu* 母), "male ancestor" (*zu* 祖) or "female ancestor" (*bi* 妣), and the second denoted the particular day (out of a cycle of ten "Heavenly Stem" days) that was associated with this ancestor.[28] Although the names varied in style over the course of the Bronze Age (and the use of specific ancestral names disappeared in the middle Western Zhou period—see Jiunian Wei *ding*, no. 27), this basic syntactic pattern persisted up to the end of the Zhou.

Also at the end of the Shang, the ritual records inscribed on bronze vessels began to record dates and sacrifices, both of which had to be determined through divination. Years were marked by the king's performance of an annual sacrifice called *si* 祀, which probably included all the ancestors, especially the lineage founder or a semi-mythical figure associated with the beginning of the dynasty, such as Cheng Tang 成湯 for the Shang.

---

[28] Allan, *The Shape of the Turtle*; Keightley, *The Ancestral Landscape*, 17–53.

The word *si* doubled as the Shang word for "year" and may have been similar to the annual *di* 禘 sacrifice celebrated by the Zhou (the Zhou would ordinarily use the word *nian* 年, with a graph depicting ripe grain, for "year"). During the Shang *si* sacrifice, the King and ritual officers offered up specially raised domestic animals such as cattle, sheep, goats, pigs, horses, dogs, and chickens, selected according to age, sex, and color.

Increasingly, inscriptions noted that the purpose of the bronze vessels was for the performance of memorial or mortuary feasts called *xiang* 享. By the end of the Western Zhou period, larger, more public, feasts were distinguished as *xiang* 饗 or *yan* 燕. In any case, mortuary feasts for royal ancestors and other state sacrifices were events that extended over many days in accordance with auspicious days of the ritual calendar.[29] For example, the square *yi* vessel commissioned by the scribe named Ling (Zuoce Li *fangyi*, no. 15) during the early Western Zhou period documents a sacrifice to his deceased father that took place over two days at three different places after the awards of governmental decrees. Feasts also sealed contracts, such as those recorded on the Qiu Wei vessels (see no. 27) dating to the middle Western Zhou period.

The Western Zhou: The Golden Age of Bronze Making

The use of ritual sets or assemblages of sacrificial vessels and bells became a hallmark of Zhou civilization. The Zhou made a number of radical changes to the Shang system that may have evolved from their greater contact with peoples farther west, north, and south than those belonging to the old Shang network in the east. The Zhou continued to worship the Shang deities and observed the cosmological scheme of the earth, sky, and the four directions, called the Four Regions (*sifang* 四方),[30] but they also made their own readings of astrological phenomena. In their understanding, Heaven could directly empower their own ancestors through a process of command or a "mandate" (*ming* 命) once the Shang had lost its authority (see the Li *gui*, no. 4). This Mandate of Heaven (*tianming* 天命) was the original source of the Zhou leader's right to rule as king over a decrepit Shang network of peoples and is associated in later texts with bird omens and

---

[29] For a study of twenty different Western Zhou sacrifices to ancestors and *shangdi* (seventeen of which were inherited from the Shang), see Liu Yu, "Xi Zhou jinwen zhong de jizu li." For Zhou style feasting rituals, see Cook, "Moonshine and Millet."

[30] Allan, *The Shape of the Turtle*, chapter 4; Keightley, *The Ancestral Landscape*, chapter 5.

planetary conjunctions (see the He *zun*, no. 6).³¹ Upholding the Mandate was the Zhou mission and involved enforcing through war the eventual shift of supernatural authority from the Shang to the Zhou founders and their descendants throughout the Four Regions (a term referring to both the visible and the supernatural worlds).

Heaven was the judge of all subsequent Zhou kings' right to rule. Rulers were required to "match" (*pei* 配) Heaven's pattern and divine will (see the Hu *gui*, no. 39). The power which Heaven passed down to the Zhou rulers was subrogated to Zhou allies through the gifting of the right to cast a bronze. The lineage rulers or patriarchs of these allies could then set up their own ancestral rites and gift bronze vessels as awards. The accumulation of awards by lineage representatives earned them the right to share the Zhou spiritual power called *de* 德. The attainment of *de* was valid only when acknowledged by the ancestors in rites (most likely involving musical performance and sacrifice). The spirits dispensed blessings of long life, fertility, and wealth in exchange for the prestige of lineage *de* and the sacrifices. After the end of the Western Zhou period and particularly after the fifth century B.C.E. with the collapse of the Zhou aristocratic network, the ancestors ceased to play a direct role in the accumulation of *de*, and eventually the cultivation of it through virtuous conduct as an innate and potential power (from a more natural Heaven, *tian* 天) became the sign of an educated person. The notion that the Zhou was visualized in later ages as a golden age of government was partly due to the legendary association of the Zhou founder kings, Wen and Wu, with initiating and spreading the spiritual quality of *de*.³²

Zhou Changes to the Shang Shapes, Decoration, and Rituals

Like Shang bronzes, the majority of Zhou bronzes were not inscribed, or else inscribed only with short dedications. Changes in the shape and décor of bronzes confirm the rise of a Zhou identity associated with royal ancestor worship evident in the inscriptions, one that gradually separated itself from Shang styles and reshaped the inherited ritual system into one

---

³¹ Pankenier, *Astrology and Cosmology in Early China*, 193–219.

³² See discussions by Kryukov, "Symbols of Power and Communication in Pre-Confucian China," and by Cook, "Wealth and the Western Zhou"; "Ancestor Worship in Eastern Zhou"; "Education and the Way of the Former Kings"; also Nivison, *The Ways of Confucianism*, 17–30.

with a Zhou imprint. The most significant change is the shift in emphasis from drinking to eating in the ancestor worship ceremonies. For example, the drinking beaker, the *gu* 觚, the most popular type of drinking vessel in Shang sacrifice, became less and less evident in Zhou tombs, despite the Zhou invention of a similarly slender but shorter beaker also with a wide, flared mouth. While traditional drinking vessels gradually disappeared, food vessels, such as cauldrons and tureens, became increasing popular. The Zhou focus on grain production is reflected in the popularity of new *gui* forms, such as one with a square box-like base (called *fangzuo gui* 方座簋) probably for keeping the dish warm over coals. Early examples with important inscriptions include the Li *gui* 利簋 and the Tian Wang *gui* 天亡簋 (nos. 4 and 5). Like the Shang beverage storage vessels, these were highly decorated and clearly meant for display. This type of vessel remained prominent in Zhou ritual until the middle Western Zhou period, when it was replaced by other forms. At the same time, the mask-like animal faces, which had so dominated Shang bronzes with their signature horns and eyes,[33] experienced a gradual decline on Western Zhou bronze vessels. Instead of covering the main surfaces of vessel bodies, small independent animal faces, with or without bodies, were subsumed into narrow bands of décor under the rim. These became increasingly abstract at the same time that Shang-style backgrounds, the square spirals for protruding decorative features, were modified or simply omitted. By the beginning of the middle Western Zhou period (around the end of the tenth century B.C.E.), the traditional Shang focus on dragons and tigers was overshadowed by the Zhou focus on birds, especially curlytailed birds—with crests, wings, and tails highlighted. By the end of the Late Western Zhou period, the diversity of vessel types and subtypes was significantly reduced and surface ornamentation was abstracted into geometric patterns such as wave- and scale-shaped motifs, with only the eyes of the animal motifs obvious, suggesting a decline in attention to bronze ornamentation. At the same time, the importance of preserving lineage chronicles and other texts increased. Many extremely long inscriptions appeared, often repeated on multiple vessels, or spanning a set of chime bells—also an increasingly popular medium for inscriptions. The reduction in ornament styles during this period

---

[33] See esp. Whitfield, ed., *The Problem of Meaning in Early Chinese Ritual Bronzes*; also Kesner, "The Taotie Reconsidered"; and Childs-Johnson, "The Metamorphic Image."

resulted in the production of only two standard types of *ding* and *gui* food (compare the styles of the Mao Gong *ding*, no. 55, and the Shi Song *ding* no. 47; as well as the Hu *gui*, no. 39, and the Shi Song *gui*, no. 47). In both *ding* and *gui* types we find the combination of abstraction and naturalism: abstract waves or rib-like patterns with naturalistic animal appendages, such as legs in the shape of elephant trunks. At the same time that traditional forms were being standardized, new food vessel types, such as the *xu* 盨 (an oblong shaped tureen) and *fu* 簠 (a *gui* vessel with a lid the same size as the vessel), were being adapted from southern bamboo or wood prototypes. While most old alcohol drinking and storage vessel types had become obsolete, the *hu* alcohol storage vessel increased in popularity and was cast in pairs with lids and so large (over 50 centimeters tall) that they would have towered above the other vessels in the sacrificial display, suggesting resurgence in an emphasis on drinking rituals. Examples from two recently excavated sites include one set that was found in a late Western Zhou hoard at Yangjiacun 楊家村, Meixian 眉縣, in the Wei River valley, and another set in the cemetery of the Jin 晉 rulers, in Qucun 曲村, Shanxi 山西 Province.[34] It is significant that some of the longest inscriptions in existence (a *pan* and two *ding*, see no. 63) were also discovered at Meixian. These, like the earlier Shi Qiang *pan* (no. 28), which was found in a hoard of slightly earlier date, revealed a narrative impulse to record lineage history on monumentally sized bronzes.[35] In each case, the history of the vessel owner's lineage began with the first ancestor to work for the Zhou kings and to support the Zhou plan of expansion into the Four Regions. The inscriptions detailed the merit of the Zhou kings who received *de* from Heaven and then passed it through the award of bronzes to the owner's founder-ancestor, and then down through each subsequent deserving generation until it reached the owner himself. (Award rituals for records of merit were called *mieli* 蔑歷; see nos. 22, 25, and 62.)[36] During the middle Western Zhou period, this ceremony required the king's presence, but this

---

[34] *Shaanxisheng kaogu yanjiusuo*, et al., "Shaanxi Meixian Yangjiacun Xi Zhou qingtongqi jiaocang fajue jianbao"; Ma, et al., "Shaanxi Meixian chutu jiaocang tongqi bitan." See also *Shengshi jijin*, 20–29; Zou Heng, *Tianma Qucun*; and *Jinguo qizhen*, 161.

[35] See Wu, *Monumentality in Early Chinese Art and Architecture*.

[36] For discussions, see Cook, "Wealth and Western Zhou," 278–79; and Li, *Bureaucracy and the State in Early China*, 226–29.

is not so obvious during the late period, suggesting a weakening of the links between the royal house, its allies, and bronze production.

Bronze Assemblage in Caches and Burials

The assembly of sets of different types of food or drinking vessels, and eventually musical instruments, reflects the styles of Zhou ritual performances that are described, if cryptically, in the inscriptions. The importance of grain agriculture to the Zhou is evident by the proliferation of the *gui*, particularly during the first half of the Western Zhou. Grain agriculture was celebrated by the Zhou—some believe that the ancient graph representing the Zhou was a depiction of fields with dots to represent grain crops—by their new graph for "year" (*nian* 年), which represented a grain stalk bending over heavy with seed and ready for harvest, and also by an annual harvest feast called *feng* 豊, which later came to mean "abundant" (see the *He zun*, no. 6).[37] At the harvest festival, the royal family and their retainers performed ritual archery on a boat in a large pond, shooting at birds and fish (see Tian Wang *gui*, Zuoce Mai *fangzun*, and Jing *gui*, nos. 5, 14, and 19). The production of clarified grain ale for use in sacrifice remained important particularly as a gift (such as the various types of fragrant millet ale, called *chang* 鬯,[38] mentioned in award lists). Although rarely mentioned in bronze inscriptions cast for human ancestral spirits, the founder spirit celebrated in Zhou odes was Lord Millet (Houji 后稷). Despite the continued interest in fine brews and the elegance of their service in large *hu*, the *ding* for meat dishes and the *gui* for grain dishes constituted the core of the Zhou bronze assemblage. Vessels such as the *pan* and the *he*, used for ritual bathing and the pouring of grain-infused liquids, also became standard by the middle Western Zhou.

During the middle Western Zhou (early ninth century B.C.E.), a new phenomenon occurred in the ritual sets—the introduction of series of similar vessels (called *lie* 列 by modern archaeologists).[39] The *lieding* and *liegui*

---

[37] For a discussion of the feast and the interpretation of the graph as *li* 醴, a fine ale, see Li Xueqin, *Xinchu qingtongqi yanjiu*, 69. Li notes that later descriptions of the feast involve the sharing of gifts of sacrificial meat.

[38] Millet ale possibly mixed with artemisia smoke when presented to the ancestral spirits; see Wu Zhenwu, "Shishi Xi Zhou X gui mingwen zhong de 'xin' zi."

sets were expanded to include multiple copies, usually identical in shape and decoration, but often descending in size. The two sets complemented each other in that *lieding* usually were composed of an even number of *ding*, and *liegui* with an odd number of *gui*. This practice was expanded with the addition of rows (also sometimes in descending size) of stone and bronze bell chime-sets. The impressive arrays reflected the high status of the owner; although these assemblages have been exclusively found in tombs, scholars assume that they also reflect the layout of sacrificial feasts in ancestral shrines above ground. Archaeological and textual evidence suggests these large banquets included relatives and guests lined up according to clan rank, with musical performances involving instrumentals, dance, and singing (see especially the Xing *zhong*, no. 33).[40] Another type of vessel introduced by the Zhou was "numinous implements," or *mingqi* 明器, a term first used by the late Eastern Zhou philosopher Xunzi 荀子 (c. 310–215 B.C.E.) to distinguish sacrificial objects used for the dead from those used by the living (*shengqi* 生器).[41] Vessels specifically made for use by the dead were typically made of low-fired pottery or roughly cast bronze and became extremely common during the Eastern Zhou period. Besides base economic considerations, perhaps their imperfections may have rendered the vessels as a ritual group less capable of transferring spiritual powers and hence useless to vengeful ghosts—a theory most viable in the case of the bent metal blades buried with the dead.[42]

In addition to evidence from tombs, bronzes from caches in the so-called Zhouyuan area provide another important line of evidence for the

---

[39] For major discussions of late Western Zhou ritual change, see Rawson, *Western Zhou Ritual Bronzes from the Arthur M. Sackler Collections*, II, 93–125; idem, "Western Zhou Archaeology"; Luo Tai, "Youguan Xi Zhou wanqi lizhi gaige ji Zhuangbai qingtongqi niandai de xin jiashuo"; and Cao Wei, *Zhouyuan yizhi yu Xi Zhou tongqi yanju*, 91–106. For a recent discussion of the *ding-gui* combination in tombs of high rank, see Zheng Wei, "Liang Zhou zhi jigao dengji guizu mu qingtongqi zuhe xintan."

[40] Falkenhausen, *Suspended Music*, esp. chapter 1; Cook, "Moonshine and Millet: Feasting and Purification Rituals in Ancient China."

[41] See Wu Hong, "'Mingqi' de lilun he shijian—Zhanguo shiqi liyi meishu zhong de guannianhua qingxiang"; Falkenhausen, *Chinese Society in the Age of Confucius*, 302–6; Cook, *Death in Ancient China*; Goldin, "Consciousness of the Dead."

[42] This theory was personally communicated to C. Cook by the now deceased Beijing University archaeologist Zou Heng 鄒衡 during a visit to the Jin burial grounds in Shanxi in the early 1990s.

installation of new ritual practices in the late Western Zhou. Since the caches all seem to date to the end of the Western Zhou period, some scholars speculate that these hoards represented wealth that the Zhou nobles could not carry east when they were forced to flee in 771 B.C.E.[43] From the lengthy inscriptions on the many fine vessels stored in them, we know that they represent lineage wealth collected over many generations. The caches were usually located near structures that may have been shrines or palaces.[44] The spatial relation between caches and buildings suggests that cached bronzes were originally displayed on ancestral altars and used for the ritual activities in lineage shrines before they were deposited in the ground. Bronzes from Pit 1 at Zhuangbai 莊白 in Fufeng and a hoard at Yangjiacun in Meixian are two famous examples from this period (see nos. 38, 43–44, 81–83). Pit 1 at Zhuangbai contained 103 bronzes commissioned by at least four generations of the Wei 微 family, whose founder-ancestor originally came from Shang to work as an archivist and ritual officer for the Zhou dynastic founder, King Wu.[45] The lineage heir and last owner of the hoard was an elder of Wei named Xing 㝬, who personally owned twenty-two bronzes, including identical sets of *gui*, *hu* 壺 vase-like alcohol storage vessels, *pen* 盆-style bathing vessels, *jue*, and *bi* 匕 scapulas. The preference was for simplicity and uniformity and for arrayed sets of vessels. The *gui* and *li* sets in this case were decorated with simple ridges encircled with bands of scale-like oval patterns, which were popular at this time.

Sets of *ding*-cauldrons were also popular. The recently discovered hoard in Yangjiacun contained twenty-seven magnificently cast bronze vessels, all carrying inscriptions, some quite lengthy.[46] A set of ten *lieding* commissioned by a certain Lai was fashioned in typical late Western Zhou style: wide and shallow bowls decorated with wave patterns and supported by three splayed legs. A band of abstract distorted dragon motifs encircled the vessels just below the rims. A bronze *pan* cast by Lai, like the *pan* of the earlier Wei family hoard, provided a lengthy lineage narrative that encapsulated the interconnections of the royal Zhou and Shan 單 lineage histories (see no. 63).

---

[43] Rawson, "Western Zhou Archaeology," 439.

[44] Cao Wei, *Zhouyuan chutu qingtongqi*, 1–27.

[45] "Shaanxi Fufeng Zhuangbai yihao Xi Zhou qingtongqi jiaocang fajue jianbao"; Falkenhausen, *Chinese Society in the Age of Confucius*, chapter 1.

[46] See *Shengshi jijin*.

The lineage narratives of the Wei and Shan families detail a glorified Zhou history that provided the roots for later mythologies. But as these records became longer and more complex, the connections between Zhou and its allies were actually weakening as the court became increasingly unable to defend itself against invaders and to maintain its economic control over local rulers in the face of famine. Northern aliens called Quan Rong 犬戎 eventually killed the Zhou king and occupied the ancestral lands (until chased out later by the forces of Qin 秦, who claimed their own right to the Mandate).[47] The remnants of the Zhou court migrated east to Chengzhou 成周 (in the same area as present-day Luoyang 洛陽) and set up a new king, but never recovered from the trauma of leaving the land of their ancestors. The next period of history is called the Eastern Zhou and is divided into two eras, the Spring and Autumn (722–481 B.C.E.), when former allies of the Zhou attempted (or pretended) to hold up the old Zhou framework as custodial rulers ("hegemons," *ba* 霸), and the Warring States (453–221 B.C.E.), when this pretense was given up and all-out war broke out between former allies and former tribute states, with states from cultures with no lineage connections to the Zhou, now taking the most prominent places on the political stage.

Western Zhou Bronze Rhetoric, Ceremony, and the Sacrifice

During the middle Western Zhou, when the vessel and bell sets became more standardized, so too did the formulaic rhetoric of certain types of inscriptions, such as those documenting award ceremonies.[48] This occurred at the same time that different types of inscriptions bloomed in response to a greater need to preserve a variety of documents, not all of them directly related to lineage ancestor-worship rituals, such as legal contracts (for example, see inscription nos. 27, 35, 36, 43 and 45) and lineage histories (for example, nos. 28 and 63). Since documentation of awards is among the most stylized and common, below we outline some of the basic rhetorical formulas—keeping in mind that variation in details is as common as standardization in overall format. We begin with the abbreviated award-ceremony rhetoric preserved in the Qi *gui* 趠簋 (no. 23).

---

[47] See Li, *Landscape and Power in Early China*.
[48] For studies of formulaic bronze rhetoric, see Cook, "Auspicious Metals"; Shaughnessy, "Sources of Western Zhou History"; and Falkenhausen, "Issues."

First is the dating phrase: "It was the third month when the King was at Zongzhou, on *wuyin* day [no. 15], that he arrived at the Grand Shrine" 唯三月王在宗周，戊寅王格于大朝（廟）. Many, but not all, inscriptions begin with a phrase that locates the event in time and place. In many examples, the date and place are listed separately and the date might begin with the year of the king's reign. This example reveals a variant; it leaves out the reign year and lists only the day (*wuyin*) when the King went to the main ancestral shrine in Zongzhou 宗周 in the Zhou homeland.

Next, the opening ceremony is recorded: "Once Mi Shu had guided Qi in from the right to take his position [in the center courtyard facing north and the King], the Inner Archivist gave the command [for award]" 密叔又（佑）趠即位，內史即命. This is an abbreviated version of the formula detailing the primary ceremonial participants' taking up their positions. Translators differ in their understanding as to whether the escort actually guided the awardee in from the right or simply took up his position to the right of the awardee. This simplified notation of the ritual is missing a common phrase explaining the positioning of the awardee with regard to the gift-giver's position. The Da Ke *ding* (no. 46) documents a complete record of the positions of the primary actors in the ceremony, but the statement occurs midway through the inscription, instead of the typical location at the beginning of the entire inscription, nor does it include year-month-day as part of the dating formula: "While the King was located at Zongzhou, at dawn, he went to the Mu Temple, and once having taken up his position, Shen *Li* guided Shanfu Ke in through the door from the right to stand in the center of the court facing north" 王在宗周，旦，王格穆廟，即位，申季佑膳夫克入門，立中廷，北嚮. (The King would normally face south.) Once all the main actors were properly positioned, the King asked the archivist or scribe to record the gift-giving and in some cases read out the awardee's record of merit.[49]

After the main actors were properly positioned, the awards were announced. The King or the primary archivist officer read out the awards. The awards often included a command regarding newly expected duties (or the reconfirmation of old duties) and new wealth associated with the duties, followed by gifts of ritual and/or military items: "The King, agreeing [to the award], said: 'Qi, I command you to act as Supreme Supervisor of Horses at

---

[49] See Glossary, celing.

Bin Encampment and [supervise] the officers matched by rank, including servants, archers, and elite youths. [I command you] to inquire about small and large [matters] and of colleagues and neighbors. Collect five measures of metal as pay. I award you crimson kneepads with a dark-colored belt and a pennant fringed with small bells for use in [military and ritual] service'" 王若曰：" 趩！命汝作豳師冢司馬，啻（適）官：僕、射、士，訊小大友鄰，取徵五鋝。賜汝赤市幽亢（衡）、鑾旂，用事。"

The types of ritual and military gifts vary to some degree. After the award announcements the awardee ultimately became the bronze owner, as he had received the right to cast a bronze as part of his award. He then performed a ritual of gratitude and the dedication of the vessel with prayers to the spirits: "I, Qi, clapped my hands together and knocked my head against the ground and in response extolled the King's grace. I took the opportunity to make for Ji Jiang [Jiang-lineage woman of the third birth-rank] a sacrificial vessel for expressing reverence. May [I have] sons of sons and grandsons of grandsons to treasure and use [it] for ten thousand years" 趩拜稽首，對揚王休，用作季姜尊彝，其子子孫孫邁（萬）年寶用。These formulaic phrases are generally found at the end of an award ceremony inscription.[50] Sometimes the final dedications are more elaborate, including speeches by the awardee extolling the gift-giver, both the gift-giver's and his own ancestral spirits, as well as the specific service to the Zhou court that merited the award. Towards the second half of the Western Zhou period, we find more and more inscriptions consisting of just these speeches by the awardees (see, for example, the Shi Qiang *pan* 史墻盤, no. 28). There is much variety in the length and style of the dedications and prayers at the end of inscriptions. In the Duo You *ding* 多友鼎 (no. 41), for example, we find: "Duo You dared to extol the grace of the Patriarch, and took the opportunity to make a cauldron to express reverence. (May he) use it to make companions and friends. May his descendants treasure it forever" 多友敢對揚公休，用作尊鼎。用朋用友，其子子孫永寶用。[51]

Versions of this award ceremony dominated the inscribed textual formats during the middle into the later era, but had largely disappeared by the end of the Western Zhou. However, the ritual itself persisted as a court

---

[50] For further details involving the awardee hanging a text on his belt and ceremoniously exiting and reentering the court, see the late Western Zhou Qiu inscriptions (no. 63) [CAC,YS]. On the expression *bai shou qi shou*, see Škrabal, "You tongqi mingwen de bianzuan jiaodu kan Xi-Zhou jinwen zhong 'bai shou qi shou' de xingzhi" [MP].

[51] See Glossary, *yong, yongzuo, gong, zisun.*

ceremony, as we find isolated records in the style of an award ceremony in transmitted texts from the Eastern Zhou period.

The Change of Bronze Tradition and Ritual Practice in the Eastern Zhou Period

During the Spring and Autumn, the states of Jin 晉 and Chu 楚, occupying regions to the north and south of the middle Yellow River valley, dominated the political landscape. Jin, in modern Shanxi, had an ancient connection to the Zhou court and considered itself a member of the extended Zhou mission of cultural and military domination. Chu, however, drew its strength from the Yangzi River valley, where it controlled access to mines and had a long non-Zhou religious tradition. The 左傳 *(The Zuo Commentary to the Springs and Autumns)* chronicles its battles for dominance over the old Zhou economic network. The collapse of Jin into three states run by local rulers and patriarchs of branch lineages in 475 B.C.E. is understood by later historians as the beginning of the Warring States. By this time, numerous smaller states had been absorbed by a handful of larger ones, dominated by Chu in the south, Qin 秦 in the west, and Qi 齊 in the northeast.

Despite the undertone of military aggression and the Zhou-like imperative to control the Four Regions as expressed in the inscriptions, trade and intermarriage between states, combined with diplomacy and a new culture of intellectual exchange, resulted in an explosion of cultural production. In addition, the collapse of the old network of interrelated and ranked clans connected to the Zhou royal house allowed for the rise of different types of power networks, particularly in the south. Thus old rituals that reinforced the Zhou hierarchy lost their meaning and dynamic changes occurred in all aspects of bronze design, casting technology, and ritual assemblage. Tomb structure changed, as did the styles and contents of the bronze inscriptions, which no longer glorified any connection to the Zhou past. Generally, basic changes and regional diversity are evident in all aspects of material culture, suggesting local practices,[52] although the essential use of bronzes for ancestor worship and social display remained.[53]

---

[52] Cf. Goldin, "Representations of Regional Diversity during the Eastern Zhou Dynasty."

[53] For a recent study of changes in Zhou ancestor worship, see Cook, "Ancestor Worship during the Eastern Zhou."

INTRODUCTION xxxvii

Continuation of Late Western Zhou Artistic and Ritual Traditions in the Territorial States during the Early Eastern Zhou

During the early Eastern Zhou, late Western Zhou styles persisted and some archaic features were even revived. Elite burials reveal that mortuary ritual practice was still centered on the use of *lieding* and *liegui*, sets of bell chimes, and *hu* alcohol storage vessels. This stylistic and ritual continuity is evident at the recently discovered Rui 芮 state cemetery in Hancheng 韓城, Shaanxi, on the western banks of the Yellow River.[54] Four ramped and richly furnished tombs were excavated at the cemetery, of which Tomb M27 was the richest.[55] The tomb, probably belonging to a lord of the small state of Rui, features a two-ramped burial chamber (an architectural form often used by royalty in the Shang and Western Zhou periods), an outer coffin and two inner coffins, and is furnished with an impressive number of burial goods of bronze, gold and jade. The tomb contained twenty-four bronze vessels in typical late Western Zhou styles, including seven *ding* and six *gui*. There were ten bronze musical instruments, including a set of eight suspended chime bells (*yongzhong* 甬鐘), one *zheng* 鉦 bell, and one *chunyu* 錞于 type bell.[56]

Curiously, older bronze styles and types—certainly considered antique by that time—were also included in the ritual display. This is particularly evident in a pair of identical square *hu* vessels that are similar to some found in earlier tombs at the Jin cemetery across the Yellow River from Rui. Each of the four registers on Rui *hu* was decorated with the bird motif popular over a hundred years earlier. Other vessels found in the Rui tombs associated with drinking may have been antiques preserved for hundreds of years. The use of archaic types of vessels to make up ritual sets in early Eastern Zhou tombs also occurred in a slightly early tomb of the small state of Guo in Shangcunling, Sanmenxia, Henan, farther south of Rui and Jin but still north of the Yellow River and within the old Zhou sphere of influence.[57] In the case of one Guo royal tomb, archaic types, also associated with drinking, were made as "numinous implements" (*mingqi*) rather

---

[54] Sun Bingjun, *Ruiguo Jinyu xuancui*.
[55] "Shaanxi Hancheng Liangdaicun yizhi M27 fajue jianbao."
[56] For the classification of bells, see Falkenhausen, *Suspended Music*, chapter 2.
[57] *Sanmenxia Guoguo mudi*, 15–228; Falkenhausen, *Chinese Society in the Age of Confucius*, chapter 2.

than being originally cast for display above ground. This suggests that the archaic types were associated with a historical sense of what might please ancestors.

Innovation during the Sixth Century B.C.E.

Political and cultural contacts between the Yellow and Yangzi River bronze cultures caused the most radical changes in ritual display.[58] Just as ideas and practices circulated throughout the states of the two great river valleys, bronze objects cast in regional styles also moved from court to court. They might have been presented as gifts or stolen as booty in wars as the ancestral shrines of destroyed states were looted. Tombs from the sixth century B.C.E. reflect the tendency to include objects from other places or mention in inscriptions that new bronzes were cast from "auspicious metal" (*jijin* 吉金) after battles. The new flexibility in bronze forms, styles, and assemblages used in mortuary displays and sacrifices shows that the old Zhou standards were being adapted to regional needs and new cultural influences. Local rulers began to see themselves as kings, and hence required a majestic display of bronzes associated with that rank.

A tomb belonging to an early sixth century B.C.E. ruler of the Zheng 鄭, discovered in Xinzheng 新鄭, Henan, clearly reflects the rising influence of southern culture in the sacrificial service. The food service included a pair of *zhan* 盞 (or *dui* 敦), a grain vessel type found typically in slightly later Chu tombs, such as those in the Xiasi 下寺 burial ground in western Henan.[59] For liquids, there was a large lidded *fou* 缶 jar for storing alcoholic beverages, two sets of elliptical drinking cups called *zhou* 舟, and a large basin for bathing called a *jian* 鑒. New block stamping techniques allowed certain patterns, such as the interlaced dragon motif called *panchi* 蟠螭, to be quickly and easily reproduced over the surface of a vessel. Sculptured dragon-like handles also became a signature for southern style. The numbers and types of *lieding* were also significantly expanded, suggesting a more sophisticated meat service.[60]

---

[58] For a discussion of contrasting regional variations and the expanding Zhou society, see Falkenhausen, *Chinese Society in the Age of Confucius*, chapters 5–6.

[59] *Xinzheng Zhenggong damu qingtongqi* and *Xichuan Xiasi Chunqiu Chu mu*.

[60] Guo Baojun, *Shang Zhou tongqiqun zonghe yanjiu*; Falkenhausen, *Chinese Society in the Age of Confucius*, 348–69.

The Rise of Regional Bronze and Sacrificial Tradition in the Middle and Late Spring and Autumn Period

The melding of old and new styles in bronze assemblages became common in both northern and southern tombs from the middle of the Spring and Autumn period onward. The expansion in food service vessels types reflects the emphasis on feasting mentioned in the inscriptions. The largest and earliest Chu examples (including inscriptions, see Wangzi Wu *ding*, no. 73) come from the elite burial ground at Xiasi, in western Henan, which is slightly later than the Xinzheng tomb discussed above.[61] Tomb Number 2 among nine large elite tombs reveals a typical Chu tendency towards animate vibrancy in style and excess in number. The fifty-two bronze vessels and many associated accessories and the set of twenty-six suspended bells dramatically show the blending of classical types with now locally inspired features. For example, as with the Xinzheng case above, the core of the sacrificial service used *lieding* for an elaborate meat service, suggesting a show of various preparation methods and animals. The nineteen *ding* of Tomb 2 included five different types with unique shapes and new self-styled names. Other vessels in the service reinforce the notion of new types of food service, using *zhan* and *fou* vessels (mixed with *gui* and *li*). The complete set for drinking and bathing by this time included the *yi* for storage, *he* for pouring, *zhou* for drinking and *pan* and *jian* style basins for ablution.

Animal appendages and open-work execution, a hallmark of Chu, are pervasive decorative features among Xiasi bronzes. Each of seven high-legged flat-bottomed *sheng-ding* 鼎, for instance, is fashioned with six stylized creeping dragon-like creatures around the rim. Copper, gold and turquoise inlays created a dazzling texture against the shining bronze background. The two *fou* and a *zhou*, for example, are copper inlaid with stylized animals and paired triangles. A large open-work altar table (131 × 67.6 cm) was cast using the newly developed lost-wax method. Altar tables had existed since at least the Shang period, but they were usually crafted out of wood and covered with painted lacquer designs. To cast one in bronze, taking an old shape and ornamenting it with new lost-wax technology,

---

[61] *Xichuan Xiasi Chunqiu Chumu*. See also Falkenhausen, *Chinese Society in the Age of Confucius*, 338–48.

was a clear step beyond the more staid altar sets belonging to the Western Zhou.⁶² The Chu table emphasized dramatic ornamentation: each side panel is composed of numerous small curves and curls in the openwork fashion and around the four panels are twelve creeping dragons similar to those seen on the highlegged *sheng-ding* vessels.

In north China, a new regional bronze tradition formed in the Jin territory in southern Shanxi. Jin rulers controlled a large bronze foundry in Houma 侯馬, near its burial ground at Qucun. The rising power of one of the Jin lineages, Zhao 趙, is obvious in a late Spring and Autumn or early Warring States period tomb.⁶³ The tomb contains twenty-seven *ding* of seven different types, suggesting numerous casting events, another display of wealth and power in addition to the varieties of meat service. Besides a large cauldron and four other graduated separate sets with seven, six, five, and four *lieding*, the assemblage included an array of fourteen *dou* 豆, a tall serving dish not typically cast in bronze. The Zhao tomb included three different types that would later become very popular. Eight *hu* of four types along with six *jian*-basins of two types display Zhao wealth at the feasts. The Zhao quest for political authority is further reflected in their incorporation of antique Zhou decorative features into the new bronze types.

Like bronze vessel shapes and decorations, the inscribed texts on Spring and Autumn period bronzes reflect the old and the new, as well as a tendency to emphasize display within local versions of mortuary sacrifices, focusing on bell music and extravagant feasts. Not surprisingly, the most conservative texts were those composed closer to the end of the Western Zhou period in the Zhou homeland occupied by the Qin (see the Qin Gong vessels, no. 66). But even these texts refrained from mentioning the failed Zhou kings, attributing the passing of the Mandate directly from Heaven to themselves. Surprising, however, is the fact that long texts involving speeches by the ruler, gift-giving, a new appointment, and a response by the awardee—completely missing in the Spring and Autumn re-

---

⁶² Actually, because lacquer does not preserve well in the north, its presence is mostly suggested by lacquer chips in tombs. The most famous is a Western Zhou bronze table from the Duan Fang collection now in the Metropolitan Museum of Art in New York. For bronze Shang examples, some of which also functioned as vessel lids when upside down, see Li Xueqin, ed., *Qingtongqi*, pl. 79, and Chase, *Ancient Chinese Bronze Art*, p. 49, no. 11b.
⁶³ Shanxisheng kaogu yanjiusuo and Taiyuanshi Wenwu guanli weiyuanhui, "Taiyuan Jinshengcun 251 hao Chunqiu damu ji chemakeng fajue jianbao."

cord of inscriptions in the middle Yellow River valley—reappeared towards the end of the period in the northeastern state of Qi (see the Shu Yi bells, no. 69). The three hundred years of the Western Zhou effort to dominate the old Shang network of polities and peoples deeply influenced coastal cultures. Even Yue 越, farther south, reveals in its inscriptions a familiarity with literature preserved now as the *Shijing* 詩經 (*Book of Odes*). The native coastal peoples, called Yi 夷, were a constant object of Zhou warfare, but it is clear that they were largely assimilated by the end of the Zhou era.

Music and song, already incorporated into Zhou mortuary ritual for over a hundred years as a mode of conveying prayers and ancestral blessings, became the dominant type of inscription on bells, many of which retain onomatopoeic strings of words representing bell sounds and meaning abundant fortune, phrases that have also been preserved in the Odes—suggesting an active musical culture during the Spring and Autumn that was shared with the authors or transcribers of those songs.[64] Food vessels with inscriptions describing the accomplishments of the owners continued, but in much fewer numbers and only as eulogies of self-worth.

One particularly striking change was the change in the phrase describing the "creating" (*zuo* 作). Except for an archaic Qi example (no. 69), inscribed vessels, bells, and weapons never attributed the authority to cast the bronze to a king, patriarch, or ruling patron of any kind. They were made instead on the sponsor's own authority (*zizuo* 自作). We see the pattern *wei X yong jijin, zi zuo* 隹（唯）X 用吉金，自乍（作）Y "Person X used auspicious metals to make of his own accord (i.e., outside of the Zhou giftgiving award structure) a Y type of vessel." Often the word "select" (*ze* 擇) supplanted the older word "use" (*yong* 用), further suggesting the increased agency of the owner (see no. 72, 73, and 75).

A typical inscription from this time period reveals both the shift in authority for casting inscriptions but also the shift to the use of the bronze (especially bells) in a feasting scenario in which an ancestral sacrifice is also the occasion for secularized self-aggrandizement while entertaining peers. Although the bell was still clearly used in ancestor worship, names of deities were not specified. A typical example is the Wangsun Yizhe *zhong* 王孫遺者鐘 (no. 72):

唯正月初吉丁亥，王孫遺者擇其吉金，自作龢鐘，終翰且揚，

---

[64] See Shaughnessy, *Before Confucius*, 181ff.; Falkenhausen, *Suspended Music*, 123, 199; Cook, "Education and the Former Kings."

元鳴孔皇，用享以孝，于我皇祖文考，用旂眉壽，余宏龏胡遲，畏忌翼翼，肅慎聖武，惠于政德，淑于威儀，誨猷丕飤，簡簡龢鐘，用宴以饍，用樂嘉賓、父兄、及我朋友。余念㠯心，延永余德，龢引民人，余敷昀于國，皇皇熙熙，萬年無期，世萬孫子，永保鼓之。

It was in the first month, *chuji*, on *dinghai* day [24]. I, Wangsun Yizhe, selected these auspicious metals and made for myself harmonious bells endlessly to let soar and to eulogize (the reputations of the ancestors) with primal sounds and resounding brilliance. I use the bells when presenting memorial feasts to express my piety to our Brilliant Ancestor and Accomplished Dead Father, and I use them to pray for extended long life. I behave with vast reverence and far-reaching equanimity, and, in awe and fear, step carefully, serious and attentive, sage and martial; I am benevolent with my governing power, skilled at my awesome decorum, amply providing sustenance with my strategies and plans—*kʕren?kʕren? (clang, clang), the harmonious bells! Use them when feasting and presenting fine ales; use them to entertain with music our fine guests, fathers, elder brothers, and our associates. Remembering them inside my heart, I can eternally extend my *de*, bringing the people into harmony. I spread [it] throughout the kingdom—Brilliant! Glistening!—may I have ten thousand years without limit and ten thousand generations of descendants to eternally protect and strike this bell.

The bronze-inscription record almost disappears during the subsequent Warring States period. This is probably due to the fact that bronzes not hidden in tombs in the ground were captured and melted down for weapons during the years of constant warfare. In many ways, the Zhou goal of conquering the Four Regions had been accomplished, with the Yellow River heartland divided into major Zhou-influenced states. The larger states quickly dominated nearby polities, creating regional, economically dependent networks. These major states included Qi in the lower Yellow River valley, Qin at the western end of the middle Yellow River valley, and Chu occupying over the course of the Warring States most of the area between the middle and eastern sections of the Yellow and the Yangzi Rivers.

The Warring States

Just as new trade and tribute networks rose along the Yellow and Yangzi River valleys, the need for an impressive public display intensified. Funeral rites and court feasts during the Spring and Autumn continued to act as stages for expressing one's power through knowledge of Zhou ritual. Yet by the end of the fifth century B.C.E., regional expression had overwhelmed tradition to the extent that, by the beginning of the imperial age in the third century B.C.E., Zhou-style bronze vessels were almost lost. New forms, such as red, yellow, and black lacquerware, with more accessible production sources, became *de rigueur* in ritual displays for shrines or courts. Bronze production also required steady control over metal and artisan resources as well as wealth, a reason why some states had to resort to melting down booty. Except for both large and inlaid examples in a handful of rich tombs,[65] bronze vessels buried in tombs became plainer over the course of the Warring States period, and the use of *mingqi* increased. Court and ritual records and prayers were increasingly included in longer texts written on bamboo books. Although many bronzes may have suffered destruction during the Warring States, those that survived suggest a reduction in the range of a vessel's purposes. Inscriptions once again became simple identifiers of ownership and function. The rise of a large variety of bamboo texts and the demise of bronze inscriptions placed in tombs suggest the need to display the accomplishments of the individual occupant rather than that of a representative of an old lineage.[66] The tombs of the elite became multi-chambered reflections of palaces, and, by imperial times, enormous mausoleums.[67]

Rich Tombs and Southern Culture

One of the most powerful economic networks belonged to Chu, based by this time north of upper-mid Yangzi River valley, just west of the lower Han River Valley. With access to bronze sources and controlling an everincreasing number of peoples to the north, east, and south, Chu supplanted the Zhou as the most influential cultural force. One rich tomb

---

[65] So, *Eastern Zhou Ritual Bronzes from the Arthur M. Sackler Collections*; idem, "Chu Art."
[66] See, e.g., Mittag, "The Qin Bamboo Annals of Shuihudi."
[67] Wu, "Art and Architecture of the Warring States Period"; *The Art of the Yellow Springs*.

dating to 433 B.C.E., located in north central modern Hubei 湖北 Province, belonged to a Chu ally, Lord Yi of Zeng 曾侯乙.[68] The tomb is multi-chambered, with rooms around a large central chamber equipped for lavish musical performances and great feasts with musical instruments, lacquer tables and dishes, and an enormous and elaborately inlaid set of bronzes for cooking, storing, and serving food and drink. Most astounding are the sixty-four bronze chime bells in several scaled sets originally hung along a huge wooden stand with cast bronze decorative ends. To the east is Lord Yi's personal chamber, where his bedroom contained a double coffin protected by lacquer paintings of snakes and beast-guardians as well as windows and doors. Eight young women were buried in this chamber as well. To the north of the central chamber is an armory stocked with 4,500 items of weaponry, shields and armor, horse and chariot fittings, possibly for protection. A bamboo inventory in this chamber notes the names of donors and the types of goods contributed to the tomb. To the west of the central chamber is a chamber with thirteen young women and a few of their personal possessions, such as combs. These women may have been the servants who cooked and served while the eight women in Yi's private chambers entertained him. The Lord of Zeng's elaborate display included nine Chu-style, high-footed, flat-bottomed *ding*—the number that would be accorded kings in later ritual texts—along with eight lidded *gui* incorporating Western Zhou style décor. Large and highly decorated vessel sets for liquids, such as a *pan* basin with a *zun* vase inside and *jian* basin with a *fou* inside, were decorated with densely packed three-dimensional *panchi* style reliefs that reveal the evolution of new casting technology using lost wax. The Zeng tomb included only relatively short inscriptions, for example, marking ownership or indicating bell pitch-names (allowing for the reconstruction of early Chinese music).[69] Yet its bamboo tomb-inventory list of donations of mortuary gifts is the earliest bamboo text found so far.

By contrast, a fourth century B.C.E. tomb of a rich Chu noble in Baoshan 包山, Hubei Province, was filled with grave goods (and lengthy bamboo texts), but the bronzes, though plentiful, were not inscribed and rather plain and eclectic. The tomb consisted of four small chambers around four sides of the main coffin chamber—a pattern identified as classical in

---

[68] *Zeng hou Yi mu*; for an analysis of the art, see Thote, "The Double Coffin of Leigudun Tomb No. 1."

[69] See Falkenhausen, *Suspended Music*, 5–14, 244–55; Bagley, "The Prehistory of Chinese Music."

Chu. According to the bamboo inventory, the "dining room" (facing east in most Chu tombs) also functioned as the ritual repository for "metal vessels" where most, but not all, of the bronze vessels were found. The ritual display included eighteen high-footed cauldrons of various styles, with four hooks for lifting the cauldrons out of the hot coals; a steamer vessel; two square and two spherical lidded grain vessels (*fu* and *dui*); six *hu* and two *fou* style storage vessels; a variety of large shallow *pan*-style basins; as well as musical instruments, wooden tables, and lacquer food and drinking service sets—all featuring sculptural animal motifs.[70] In this and other tombs in the area, the Chu preference for depicting naturalistic animals is expressed in the lacquerware. It was on a piece of lacquerware that China's first realistic narrative painting is found, testifying to the shift in focus from bronze to lacquer for artistic expression.[71] The emphasis on fine food is evident from the menu preserved on the bamboo inventory text; the dishes included chicken, pork, water buffalo, and fish seasoned with honey, ginger, scallions, fruits, nuts, and peppers.

A Late Warring States Mausoleum in Northern China

Another rich tomb was found in a regional outpost north of the Yellow River in modern Hebei. The tiny, almost unknown, state of Zhongshan 中山 commemorated its brief moment in history with a glorious display not only of grave goods but also of an architectural plan for a walled mausoleum.[72] This map was preserved on a bronze plate and buried with the second king of Zhongshan, King Cuo (d. 313 B.C.E.). At the center of the design was Cuo's tomb, accompanied by the four tombs of his queens and concubines. The mausoleum was to be enclosed by two layers of walls, with four additional ceremonial palaces between them. Zhao destroyed the state within thirteen years of Cuo's death, so the extensive mausoleum plan was never executed. Cuo's burial mound originally had a three-storeyed sacrificial hall built on top. The burial pit was cruciform (a traditional northern style for royal burials for this region that can be traced back to the Shang

---

[70] *Baoshan Chumu*; see also discussion in Cook, *Death in Ancient China*, 55–58.

[71] Earlier in the lower Yangzi River valley there had been a tradition of pictorial bronzes showing scenes of ritual feast preparations and the playing of bell and stone chimes; see discussion by Wu, in Loewe and Shaughnessy, *The Cambridge History of Ancient China*, 700–5. See also, Cook, *Death in Ancient China*, 119–28.

[72] See *Cuo mu*.

royal burials). Although the tomb had been looted, the eastern and western compartments of its chamber yielded a large number of burial goods, including finely crafted bronze vessels.

Sacrificial bronzes were displayed in the western compartment, and bronzes for daily living were found in the eastern compartment, in complete opposition to the Chu regional style. The ritual display included a set of ten *ding*, seven *hu*, four each of *li*, *fu*, and *dou*, as well as a set of fourteen bronze bells, showing a continued emphasis on the musical feast. The bronze vessel display not only included *mingqi*, but the only significant decoration consisted of three inscriptions incised into the surfaces of a *ding* and *hu* belonging to King Cuo and a *hu* donated by his son (see no. 78), the former two representing the longest Warring States inscriptions in existence. The finest bronze craftsmanship was reserved for a table made of interlocking gold and silver inlaid pieces in a popular dragon-and-phoenix motif attached to a round base elevated by two pairs of male and female deer. In addition, inlaid bronze screen stands, some consisting of gold and silver-inlaid sculptural beasts with serpent heads, feline bodies, and wings (and others depicting tigers devouring deer), reflect cultural influences from Inner Asia.

Late Warring States Bronze Rhetoric

Inscriptional rhetoric devolved to the utilitarian and functional. As we see in the Chu Wang Yin Han *ding* 楚王酓悍鼎 (no. 81), scribes emphasized function and craftsmanship. The lid inscription is the primary inscription, unlike times in the past when the inside of the vessel—the surface in contact with the sacrificial offering—or the face of a bell, including the striking surfaces, were primary. The lid and vessel inscriptions were both exposed for easy reference from the outside of the vessel, suggesting the secularization or, at least, the bureaucratization of the sacrificial service. However, the inscription still begins with a document of the King's merit and its relationship to the casting of the vessel. The lid inscription notes: "King Han of Chu captured weapons, and on an auspicious day of the first month brought them to be cast as the lid of a high-footed cauldron to be used to present the annual tasting sacrifice. Smelting Master Officer Qin and Assistant Ke Ci made it. (For use by the) Chief Cook" 楚王悍戰獲兵銅，正月吉日，至鑄鐈鼎之蓋，以供歲嘗冶師吏秦、差(佐)苛蠜為之。集脰(廚). The vessel inscription simply details a different set of metallurgists, the number of the vessel, and the political identity of the sponsor. This attests to the mass production of vessels and lids by traveling metallurgists. The vessel inscription notes: "Smelting Master *Pan* Ye and Assistant Qin Xia made it. (Number) three, Chu" 冶師盤野、差(佐)秦丕為之。三，楚.

This type of inscription contrasted greatly with the lengthy testimonies by the King of Zhongshan in the northeast. The overlap with the explosion of bamboo manuscript writing during this time period is seen somewhat in the Zhongshan vessel inscriptions (no. 80), but especially in Han dynasty inscriptions (no. 82). Manuscripts on bamboo and silk formed the foundations of all Chinese classics, and text production had long taken on an identity separate from bronze production; the peak period when bronze might have been considered equal in value to the bamboo text was probably during the late Western Zhou period. After that, the two veered into separate traditions.

Conclusion

The society of Bronze-Age China arose out of the complex late Neolithic culture of the middle Yellow River valley. By the time of its demise, bronze manufacture had spread beyond both the Yellow and Yangzi River systems deep into regions barely touched by the Shang or Zhou cultural traditions and perhaps in contact with early Southeast Asian metallurgy traditions. These included the Sanxingdui culture (identified by Chinese archaeologists as belonging to a precursor of the Ba 巴 and Shu 蜀 cultures) in the Sichuan Basin during the late Shang period,[73] and the Dian 滇 people in Yunnan 雲南 during the Warring States period. These more sculptural bronzes reflected local religious traditions unlike the ancestral cults of the Yellow River valley. In neither case was text added. This distinction can be made to a lesser extent for the Yangzi River cultures as well, which did not seem to share the imperative to trace lineage narratives. On the other hand, the southern elite were clearly literate, valued inscriptions, and respected Zhou tradition even as they adapted it to their own ways of feasting and aesthetics.

While bronze was used to cast weapons, horse and chariot ornaments, helmets and other accessories over the millennia, generally it was reserved for the production of ritual sets for sacrifices to the ancestral spirits. It is

---

[73] See, e.g., Flad and Chen, *Ancient Central China*, 71–107.

through the analysis of subtle changes in the ritual assemblages that we can detect changes in the sacrificial display. We see a shift from an emphasis on alcohol consumption to food in order to satisfy Zhou spirits, but then another shift to an emphasis upon music, particularly bell music, to communicate with the dead. Then, as Chu culture rose in influence, we see a shift back to drinking, but now also including musical performances. The expansion of vessel types reflects changes in the sacrificial service over time, suggesting the introduction of new preparation methods, recipes and food types. Changes in décor suggest changes in the religious function of the vessels as well as displays of technical knowledge and the political power to control this knowledge. The persistent use of animal imagery—both mythical and natural—confirms the basic idea that the vessels functioned as symbolic sacrificial offerings and conduits to the supernatural. Inscriptions were documents added to the sacrificial vessels and bells, not only for the eyes of the ancestors, but also to impress the living. Bronze was, for the Zhou elite, a medium of permanence. Inscriptions, while caught up with religious practice, also reflected the secular world and as such are valuable historical documents. Eventually, however, bronze became too cumbersome and expensive in the face of a growing literate public, as did the casting of bronze ritual assemblages. Even so, we must recognize that the use of bronze ritual sets and of bronze inscriptions was a signature of Zhou civilization, the single most formative influence in early China.

CAC
YS

Ceremony and the Creation of the Text

Beginning in the Shang, bronze vessels of various shapes and sizes were used for food and beverage offerings to royal and aristocratic ancestors. Bronze ritual vessels had existed for several centuries when, around 1250 B.C.E., they began to be cast with inscriptions. During the late Shang and the early Western Zhou periods, ending with King Zhao's 昭王 reign (995–977 B.C.E.), almost all of these inscriptions contained between one and ten characters, usually mentioning the sponsor of the vessel (often represented by a clan sign) and sometimes its purpose for the ancestral sacrifice.[74] Longer inscriptions only gradually emerged in early Western Zhou times and became increasingly frequent over the middle and later periods of the dynasty. In addition, their placement in the bronze vessels changed over time: initially hidden deep inside the vessel and hence barely visible for the human eye, the texts became not only longer over time but also more prominently placed.[75] Only in the latter part of the mid-Western Zhou period did broad-surfaced vessel shapes (such as *gui* 簋 and *xu* 盨 tureens, or shallow tripods) emerge that lent themselves to the conspicuous display of long texts. Likewise, sets of large *yongzhong* 甬鐘 musical bells that are inscribed on their outside became common only from the ninth century onward.[76] These texts were meant to be seen; they show the vessels and bells not merely as ritual objects to feast and delight the ancestors but also as representations of memory, cast in the most durable material available.

As first discovered by Jessica Rawson and later significantly elaborated upon by Lothar von Falkenhausen, the ninth century B.C.E. saw the implementation of far-reaching ritual and administrative reforms.[77] With respect to the ancestral sacrifice and its bronze paraphernalia, a number of

---

[74] Feng Yicheng, "Shang Zhou qingtongqi mingwen weizhi yanbian chutan."

[75] Venture, "Visibilité et lisibilité dans les inscriptions sur bronze de la Chine archaïque."

[76] Falkenhausen, *Suspended Music*, 158–62; for the placement of text on *yongzhong* bells, see also Feng Yicheng, "Shang Zhou qingtongqi mingwen weizhi yanbian chutan."

[77] Rawson, "Statesmen or Barbarians?"; idem, *Western Zhou Ritual Bronzes from the Arthur M. Sackler Collections*, II, 93–111; idem, "Western Zhou Archaeology," 433–48; Luo Tai, "Youguan Xi Zhou wanqi lizhi gaige ji Zhuangbai qingtongqi niandai de xin jiashuo"; Falkenhausen, *Chinese Society in the Age of Confucius*, chapter 2.

important changes can be observed: most vessels for alcoholic beverages were abandoned, with only large flasks remaining; instead, food vessels grew larger in both form and number, becoming arranged in extended sets that signified the increased importance of sumptuary rules; bronze bells were now introduced to the ensemble of ritual artifacts, adding the element of music to the ceremonies; minute detail in ornament was replaced by larger patterns that often included bold, even coarse, wave bands; and when sets of vessels and bells were inscribed, they all carried identical inscriptions. The increased size of bronze paraphernalia, together with their larger ornament and arrangement in sets, suggest a shift from a more intimate ritual of the ancestral sacrifice to one with many participants perhaps standing at some distance.

The mid- and late Western Zhou vessels and bells displayed in their design a sense of standardization, repetition, and restriction that matched the ideology of the ancestral sacrifice. The restrained patterns were in themselves emblems of the very rhythmic continuity that characterized the sum total of the ancestral sacrifice both within a single performance and as a tradition. By late Western Zhou times, the overall sense of control and continuity— from the vessel shapes and ornament to the content and calligraphy of the inscriptions—[78] had resulted in an archaizing, reiterative style that evoked the remote past in both material décor and textual references to the dynastic founders. The evidence from both tombs and hoards shows that late Western Zhou owners of bronze vessels indeed kept their older, inherited vessels alongside their own new, archaizing ones. Thus, late Western Zhou ritual ideology of memory implied the commemoration of the dynastic founding together with the self-conscious gesture of commemoration, expressed in strictly controlled fashion.[79]

There is thus no question that Western Zhou bronze inscriptions contained strong elements of historical memory. This impulse of commemoration, however, was not in the service of writing history; instead, it had

---

[78] Shaughnessy, *Sources of Western Zhou History*, 121–26; Falkenhausen, "Late Western Zhou Taste." As Rawson has noted for the late Western Zhou, "so regular is some of the calligraphy of this time that it suggests a reform of the script used for bronze inscriptions. Although such inscriptions appear precise and circumstantial, they in fact repeat common formulae, altered slightly to fit each occasion" (*Western Zhou Ritual Bronzes from the Arthur M. Sackler Collections*, 93).

[79] On late Western Zhou archaism, see esp. Falkenhausen, "Late Western Zhou Taste," 168-74; also Kern, "Bronze Inscriptions, the *Shangshu*, and the *Shijing*," I, 188–96.

its place in the ancestral sacrifice and was shaped by its religious purpose. Considerable circumstantial evidence points to brush-written archival records on perishable materials both at the royal court and in aristocratic lineages. These records underlay the longer bronze inscriptions, but they were not identical to them. The inscriptions were highly selective in content, unabashedly propagandistic in style, and, by being cast into a vessel or bell that was to be used in the ancestral sacrifice, placed in a religious context.

As the form and design of bronze vessels signified, first and foremost, their very nature as precious ritual objects together with the status of their owners, their irreducible core was the reference to their owner. In general, a bronze inscription represented the recognition of one's accomplishments that was then to be presented to one's ancestors. This becomes particularly clear from the dozens of mid- and late Western Zhou appointment inscriptions.[80] There, after reporting his achievements to the Zhou king, the appointee received a new royal command in a ceremony held in the courtyard of the royal ancestral temple. He was handed the royal charge written on bamboo and, finally, was granted the right to have a ritual vessel cast, probably in the royal workshop. After receiving the vessel, he was entitled to use it in his own ancestral sacrifices.

Within the sacrifice, the inscribed text spoke both to the ancestral spirits and to the assembled family and dignitaries, reporting the vessel owner's merits together with their recognition by the Zhou king. To serve this purpose vis-à-vis the spirits, the vessel text included the self-referential statements of dedication and prayer, through which the patron identified himself and at the same time acknowledged his ancestors, whose own virtuous deeds were now successfully continued, and who in return were asked to send down their blessings. Therefore, the inscriptions routinely referred to their bronze carriers as "precious" (*bao* 寶) or "revered" (*zun* 尊) and exhorted future generations "forever to treasure and use" 永寶用 the vessel in their sacrifices to the current patron and future ancestor.[81] They created idealized (and highly selective) accounts of the past while also, perhaps even more importantly, projecting a prospective future memory of the present. Especially in the late Western Zhou period—that is, when the dynasty was gradually declining in stability—the aristocratic inscriptions seem to reflect an intense desire for continuity and tradition.

---

[80] See especially the Shanfu Shan *ding* and the Qiu (Lai) *pan* inscriptions (nos. 56 and 63).
[81] For an extensive discussion, see Xu Zhongshu, "Jinwen guci shili."

To fulfill these functions, an inscription could be as short as noting its owner and his dedication, or it could continue with a statement on the ritual use and purpose of the vessel and a prayer for blessings ("I have made this vessel to pray ..."). Further extended, it could provide an account of the appointee's (and possibly his ancestors') merits that were based either on his earlier report to the king or on the king's appointment charge in response.[82] A small number of inscriptions furnish extensive accounts of the appointment ceremony itself, with the Qiu *pan* 逑盤 and Qiu *ding* 逑鼎 inscriptions from 786 and 785 B.C.E.—found in 2003 in Yangjiacun (Meixian, Shaanxi Province)—being the most comprehensive examples to date.

Because of their purpose, the inscriptions were both more and less than their underlying archival records. They were less because they represented radically abbreviated, selective, and idealized accounts of the past; moreover, most of them lacked information that would have been crucial for an archival document, for example, a date notation. At the same time, they were more by integrating the archival record into the framework of the sacrifice and the prayer for blessings. The final standardized formula of the vast majority of bronze inscriptions—"may sons of sons, grandsons of grandsons forever treasure and use [this vessel]" (*zizi sunsun yong baoyong* 子子孫孫永寶用) makes it clear that the durability of bronze was celebrated more for embodying the continuity of the ancestral sacrifice than for preserving a particular record over time.

The bronze inscriptions of mid- and late Western Zhou times show conscious efforts toward poetic form. Especially in the wake of the ritual reforms, a larger number of inscriptions were guided by the same principles of rhyme and meter familiar from the *Shijing*. The great majority of Western Zhou inscriptions include just a few graphs, but the two longest known bronze texts so far come close to five hundred characters, and numerous others contain from several dozen to two or three hundred. While rhyme and tetrasyllabic meter occurred already among the earliest Western Zhou inscriptions,[83] these features became increasingly regular and generic

---

[82] This tripartite structure has been reconstructed by Falkenhausen, "Issues in Western Zhou Studies," 152–56. Recently, Falkenhausen has expanded and modified his scheme to argue that the statement of dedication reflects a separate ceremony; see Luo Tai, "Xi-Zhou tongqi mingwen de xingzhi."

[83] See Behr, *Reimende Bronzeinschriften und die Entstehung der chinesischen Endreimdichtung*.

from the late tenth century B.C.E. onward. The linguistic regularity never reached that of the "Major court hymns" (*Daya* 大雅) of the *Shijing*, but the overall tendency toward an increased aesthetic control and more rigidly standardized, and hence narrowed, expression is unquestionable and continued through the inscriptions of Eastern Zhou times. It is not inconceivable that the euphonic features of inscribed texts were brought to life through recitation.[84]

A few Western Zhou bronze inscriptions indicate that they were cast not for the ancestral sacrifice but for use in banquets, yet it would be simplistic to call these contexts entirely secular. The court banquet was an extension of the ancestral sacrifice and indeed was often performed in conjunction with it: while in the sacrifice, the host feasted his ancestors; in the following banquet, he feasted his guests. Ample evidence from the *Shijing* hymns points to the convergence of the two ritual occasions, with banquet hymns including references to the sacrifice and vice versa. Moreover, later sources on Zhou ritual—especially the three ritual classics, *Zhouli* 周禮 (*Rites of Zhou*), *Yili* 儀禮 (*Ceremonies and Rites*), and *Liji* 禮記 (*Ritual Records*)— indicate that the various forms of court ritual were interconnected through their common musical performances.[85] Similarly, inscriptions that record land transactions and other legal affairs[86] were not just legal or administrative documents but, instead, based on such primary documents; the very fact that they were cast into bronze vessels brought them under the purview of the ancestral spirits.

Over time, bronze inscriptions changed together with their ritual contexts, which in turn reflected the political, social, and intellectual developments from the Western Zhou realm to the multi-state world of the Springs and Autumns and Warring States periods. Compared to their Western Zhou predecessors, most Eastern Zhou inscriptions provided less historical detail and became even more formulaic in their diction; meanwhile, the remaining longer inscriptions tended toward a mode that Gilbert

---

[84] The oral performance of inscribed texts is not unusual elsewhere; for the ancient Greek example, see Thomas, *Literacy and Orality in Ancient Greece*, 62.

[85] Kern, "Bronze Inscriptions, the *Shangshu*, and the *Shijing*," I, 164–82.

[86] Lau, *Quellenstudien zur Landvergabe und Bodenübertragung in der westlichen Zhou-Dynastie*; Schunk, "Dokumente zur Rechtsgeschichte des alten China"; Skosey, "The Legal System and Legal Tradition of the Western Zhou."

L. Mattos has aptly styled "self-panegyrical."[87] Eastern Zhou inscriptions evolved into a diction that was decidedly less concerned about the ancestors and more invested in claims for political authority, probably reflecting new and different uses of the ritual vessels beyond the ancestral sacrifice.

MKe

---

[87] Mattos, "Eastern Zhou Bronze Inscriptions," 88. Mattos's article provides a very useful survey of Eastern Zhou inscriptions. For more extensive accounts of Eastern Zhou religion and ritual practices, see Falkenhausen, *Chinese Society in the Age of Confucius*; and Cook, "Ancestor Worship during the Eastern Zhou."

The Legacy of Bronzes and Bronze Inscriptions in Early Chinese Literature

References to bronze inscriptions in received literature are surprisingly rare. By far the lengthiest appears in an undated ritual text, "Protocols of Sacrifice" ("Jitong" 祭統), currently found in the compendium *Liji*:

夫鼎有銘，銘者，自名也。自名以稱揚其先祖之美，而明著之後世者也。為先祖者，莫不有美焉，莫不有惡焉，銘之義，稱美而不稱惡，此孝子孝孫之心也。唯賢者能之。

銘者，論譔其先祖之有德善，功烈勳勞慶賞聲名列於天下，而酌之祭器；自成其名焉，以祀其先祖者也。顯揚先祖，所以崇孝也。身比焉，順也。明示後世，教也。

夫銘者，壹稱而上下皆得焉耳矣。是故君子之觀於銘也，既美其所稱，又美其所為。為之者，明足以見之，仁足以與之，知足以利之，可謂賢矣。賢而勿伐，可謂恭矣。

With regard to cauldrons with inscriptions: in the "inscription" (*ming* 銘), one "names" (*ming* 名) oneself. One names oneself in order to cite and extol what is beautiful in one's ancestors, and clearly exhibit it for later generations. Among one's ancestors, there is none without something beautiful and none without something ugly. The principle of a bronze inscription is to cite what is beautiful and not what is ugly. This is the heart of filial sons and grandsons; only a worthy can do it.

An inscription arranges and compiles the virtue and goodness of one's ancestors, so that their merit, glory, rewards, and reputation are displayed throughout the world, and in feasting them with sacrificial vessels, one attains one's name; in this way, one enshrines one's ancestors. One does honor to filial piety by displaying and extolling one's ancestors. Placing oneself near to them is complaisance; clearly exhibiting [these things] to later generations is instruction.

In an inscription, above and below [i.e. ancestors and descendants] all attain [their place] with a single reference. Thus when a noble man inspects an inscription, having praised those who are cited in it, he also praises whoever made it. Because the maker had sufficient insight to discern their [achievements], sufficient humanity to partake of them, and sufficient wisdom to profit from them, he can be called worthy. One who is worthy without boasting can be called reverent.[88]

This text praises artful and appreciative inscriptions as expressions of filial respect, but does not advise interpreting them as the truth, the whole truth, and nothing but the truth.[89] Rather, inscriptions were regarded as works of reverent commemoration. "Protocols of Sacrifice" goes on to quote an inscription in full—and probably a genuine one—but unfortunately this does not allow us to infer much about ancient palaeographical conventions, inasmuch as the received text is surely the product of intervening centuries of redaction. One might like to know how literati from the time of "Protocols of Sacrifice" would have transcribed the archaic graphs of bronze inscriptions, but the extant recension manifestly dates to the Six Dynasties (220–589 C.E.) or later, and obscures (and possibly even corrupts) whatever notation preceded it.[90] Noel Barnard has shown that hardly any other bronze inscription quoted in received literature can be trusted.[91]

Though they are not very informative on the question of how the ancients would have read bronze inscriptions, early literary sources do present a general consensus regarding the perceived importance of bronzes themselves. Specifically, bronze vessels are depicted in early literature as emblems of ritual effectiveness and political power. This should not be surprising; the late K.C. Chang, in his masterly book, *Art, Myth, and Ritual*, showed how the two went hand in hand. Chang cited an illuminating passage from the *Zuozhuan* 左傳 (*The Zuo Commentary to the Springs and Autumns*) that bears repeating here:

楚子伐陸渾之戎，遂至於雒，觀兵于周疆。定王使王孫滿勞楚子。楚子問鼎之大小、輕重焉。對曰：「在德不在鼎。昔夏之方有德也，遠方圖物，貢金九牧，鑄鼎象物，百物而為之備，使民知神、姦。故民入川、澤、山、林，不逢不若。螭魅、罔兩[=魍魎]，莫能逢之。用能協于上下，以承天休。」

The Viscount of Chu [i.e. King Zhuang of Chu 楚莊王, r. 613–591 B.C.E.] attacked the Rong of Luhun and eventually arrived at Luo, where he displayed his troops at the border with Zhou.

---

[88] Compare the translation in Legge, *The Sacred Books of China*, IV, 251–52. [89] Cf. Shaughnessy, *Sources of Western Zhou History*, 175ff.
[90] See, e.g., Guo Moruo, *Jinwen congkao*, 84–87.
[91] "Records of Discoveries of Bronze Vessels in Literary Sources," 457ff.

INTRODUCTION   lvii

King Ding [of Zhou, r. 606–586 B.C.E.] dispatched Wangsun Man[92] with humanitarian gifts for the Viscount of Chu.

The Viscount of Chu asked about the size and weight of the cauldrons [of Zhou]. [Wangsun Man] responded: "[The matter] lies with one's *de* [i.e. power derived from Heaven's approval], not with one's cauldrons. In the past, when the region of Xia had *de*, distant regions made images of creatures, and sent the Protectors of the Nine Provinces to make offerings of metal. Cauldrons were cast with representations of the creatures, including all their varieties, so as to let the people know what is divine and what is depraved. Thus when the people entered river valleys, marshes, mountains, or forests, they did not encounter anything untoward, nor did any goblins or banshees meet with them. By this means, they were able to forge cooperation between above and below, thereby securing Heaven-sent blessings."[93]

Chang himself presented this passage as evidence of a shamanic dimension of early Chinese ritual practice[94]—an argument that remains controversial.[95] But the harangue attributed to Wangsun Man is valuable for another reason as well: it is, I believe, the oldest document in which the characteristic theriomorphic ornamentation on bronzes is given a Chinese name. Today, this design is widely, but anachronistically, called *taotie* 饕餮.[96] In this text, however, the images are identified as *wu* 物, "creatures," and their function, though not explained in detail, seems to be both monitory and apotropaic: teaching the people how to avoid "untoward things" (*buruo* 不若) and keeping away goblins and banshees. Naturally, this says nothing about how the ornamentation would have been understood in Shang and

---

[92] Strictly speaking, this should be "Royal Grandson Man" (Wangsun is not a surname), but he is conventionally called Wangsun Man.

[93] Compare the translation in Legge, *The Chinese Classics*, V, 293. As my colleague Adam Smith has pointed out to me, the final line (i.e. *yong neng xie yu shangxia, yi cheng tianxiu* 用能協于上下，以承天休) is jarringly archaic and seems out of place in Eastern Zhou prose. Perhaps Wangsun Man is subtly quoting a line from an inscription on the cauldrons?

[94] *Art, Myth, and Ritual*, 63ff.

[95] For a very different view, see, e.g., Keightley, "The Shang," 262.

[96] Cf. Wang, "A Textual Investigation of the taotie."

Zhou times, when such vessels were cast,[97] but it confirms that, by the fourth century B.C.E. at the latest, the so-called "creature" images were thought to have a crucial religious purpose.[98]

Wangsun Man's speech does not end here, for he apperceives the Chu ruler's inquiries about the cauldrons as an intimation of that lord's imperial ambitions—which he regards as impertinent, since the Mandate of Heaven still resides with Zhou. (Imagine Khrushchev asking an American ambassador how much gold is in Fort Knox.) Wangsun Man continues:

桀有昏德，鼎遷于商，載祀六百。商紂暴虐，鼎遷于周。德之休明，雖小，重也。其姦回昏亂，雖大，輕也。天祚明德，有所底止。成王定鼎于郟鄏，卜世三十，卜年七百，天所命也。周德雖衰，天命未改。鼎之輕重，未可問也。

[King] Jie's *de* dimmed, and the cauldrons were moved to Shang, [where they remained] for six hundred years. [King] Zhòu of Shang [r. 1075–1046 B.C.E.?] was cruel and tyrannical, and the cauldrons were moved to Zhou. When one's *de* is blessed and brilliant, [one's cauldrons] will be heavy even if they are small. When one is depraved, refractory, dim, and disorderly, they will be light even if they are large. When Heaven favors one of brilliant *de*, there must be a basis on which it rests. King Cheng [of Zhou, r. 1042–1021 B.C.E.?] settled the cauldrons in Jiaru, and divined that for thirty generations, for seven hundred years, [his dynasty] would be mandated by Heaven. Although the *de* of Zhou has declined, Heaven's Mandate has not yet changed. It is too soon to ask about the weight of the cauldrons.

For Wangsun Man—and, implicitly, the author or authors of the *Zuozhuan* as well—the cauldrons of Zhou serve as the material embodiment of the dynasty's celestial sanction, which was itself earned, generations ago, by virtuous conduct of the Zhou founders. Centuries later, King Ding's possession of the ritual implements necessary for the regular consecration and confirmation of this relationship with Heaven signifies his enduring supremacy in the terrestrial realm as well. If King Zhuang of Chu really

---

[97] The relevant bibliography is too vast to cite in a single footnote. For a representative Chinese view, see Duan Yong, *Shang Zhou qingtongqi huanxiang dongwu yanjiu*.

[98] That is to say, the agnostic position staked out by Robert W. Bagley for earlier periods (in his "Meaning and Explanation") would not be valid for the fourth century.

wants to seize the cauldrons—that is, by synecdoche, the status of Son of Heaven—he should, instead of making inquiries about their physical characteristics, devote himself to leading a virtuous life that might attract Heaven's approval; indeed, to take a Mencian sort of interpretation,[99] in this manner the cauldrons might be vouchsafed to him without his even having to fight for them.

Later sources used the Zhou cauldrons (which were thought to number nine) as a transparent symbol of political power,[100] and it should come as no surprise that the First Emperor of Qin 秦始皇帝 (r. 221–210 B.C.E.) is depicted as having tried—in vain, of course—to fish them out of the River Si 泗水, where one (or all of them?)[101] had sunk for unknown reasons. Even with a thousand divers, the project was unsuccessful. There is a stone carving from the Wu Family Shrines illustrating the grand unconsummated affair, displaying all the confident mockery of an artist living some four centuries later.[102] It was a common theme in Eastern Han art.

Another illustrative example comes from the *Shangshu dazhuan* 尚書大傳 (*Great Commentary to the Exalted Documents*) by Fu Sheng 伏勝 (fl. late 3rd-early 2nd century B.C.E.):

武丁祭成湯，有雉飛升鼎耳而雊。武丁問諸祖己，祖己曰：「雉者、野鳥，不當升鼎。今升鼎者，欲為用也。無則遠方將有來朝者乎？」故武丁內反諸己，以思先王之道。三年，編髮重譯來朝者六國。

孔子曰：「吾於《高宗肜日》見德之有報之疾也。」[103]

When [King] Wu Ding [of Shang, r. 1250?–1192? B.C.E.] was sacrificing to Tang the Successful [i.e. the founder of the Shang dynasty], a pheasant flew by and landed on top of the handle of a cauldron, where it crowed. Wu Ding asked Zu Ji about

---

[99] E.g., *Mengzi* 1A.5–7; see the general discussion in Goldin, *Confucianism*, 64ff.

[100] K.O. Thompson (private communication) has suggested a comparison with the Sword in the Stone of Arthurian legend. Perhaps it is significant that in the Chinese tradition, the material embodiment of a ruler's legitimacy is a set of ritual vessels, whereas in the Medieval European one, it is an implement of war.

[101] The sources are not in agreement. The most famous ancient discussion of the discrepancies in the various accounts of the Nine Cauldrons is by Wang Chong 王充 (A.D. 27-ca. 100); see Huang Hui, *Lunheng jiaoshi*, 8.375–80 ("Ruzeng" 儒增).

[102] See Wu, *The Wu Liang Shrine*, 95ff.

[103] The source text is Li Fang, et al., *Taiping yulan*, 917.5b.

this; Zu Ji said: "The pheasant is a wild bird; it should not land on top of a cauldron. Now the fact that it has landed on top of the cauldron means that it wishes to be employed. Does it not follow that [people from] distant regions will come to court?" Thus Wu Ding reflected on this, and pondered the Way of the Former Kings. Within three years, [envoys] with braided hair and relay interpreters[104] had come to court from six states. Confucius said: "From *The Day of Gaozong*'s rong *Sacrifice*,[105] we see how swiftly *de* is recompensed."[106]

One of the reasons for the preservation of this vignette—from a work that survives only in fragments—must be its affinity with other examples of augury, in which the observed movements of animals, especially birds, are imbued with prognosticative significance. In the symbolic vocabulary of the time, a pheasant alighting on a bronze vessel is taken as a metaphor for the arrival of wild tribes at the king's civilized court.

The *Shijing* exemplifies another aspect of what may be regarded as the legacy of bronze inscriptions: the use of onomatopoetic phrases conveying a specific sound imbued with meaning. The most famous example is probably the opening line of the *Shijing*, "Guanguan—the ospreys" 關關雎鳩,[107] where *guan* (Old Chinese *kˤror) represents both the sound of the ospreys' call[108] and a meaning in the semantic domain of "to join"—as is only fitting for an epithalamium. Such onomatopoetic reduplicatives can be deployed powerfully in the poetics of the *Shijing*, especially the section called "Airs of the States" ("Guofeng" 國風). For example, in the first line of "The Yellow Birds" ("Huangniao" 黃鳥, Mao 131), "*Jiaojiao*—the yellow birds" 交交黃鳥,[109] the word *jiao* (*kˤraw) packs at least three layers of meaning: first,

---

[104] The term "relay interpreters" (*chongyi* 重譯) refers to teams of translators who would be employed for languages so remote that no Chinese speaker was familiar with them. The king would address the first interpreter, who would then use some common language to convey the message to the second interpreter, who could speak to the barbarians directly.

[105] Gaozong is the temple name of Wu Ding. *The Day of Gaozong's rong Sacrifice* is usually understood as the title of a text, and the received *Shangshu* contains a chapter by this name, which relates this episode with important differences.

[106] Compare the translation in Legge, *The Chinese Classics*, III, 265.

[107] Legge, *The Chinese Classics*, IV, 1.

[108] If indeed they are ospreys—we know next to nothing about the Bronze-Age meanings of zoological terms.

[109] Legge, *The Chinese Classics*, IV, 198.

it represents the call of the yellow birds (perhaps orioles); second, it means, straightforwardly, "they copulate"; and third, it evokes the crisscross flight pattern of mating birds. All these allusions to copulation present an ironic contrast with the fate of the three noble brothers in this poem, who are dissevered from their wives and forced to follow their deceased lord in death. As in the passage from the *Shangshu dazhuan*, alighting birds take on all the significance of omens, for the name of the tree on which the birds land rhymes in each stanza with the name of the brother to be executed next.[110]

In "The Guaning Ospreys" and "The Yellow Birds," the onomatopoetic reduplicatives are placed in the mouths of birds, but in the oldest poems they tend to be associated with musical instruments, especially bells.[111] Edward L. Shaughnessy has argued that the use of this device derives from bell inscriptions, which record the sounds of the very bells that they have been cast into.[112] It seems significant that, even in the earliest bell inscriptions, onomatopoetic reduplicatives convey not only the sound of the bell, but also a corresponding meaning. Take, for example, the end of the inscription from the first group of Xing bells (Xing *zhong* 瘋鐘, no. 33, below), dated to the early ninth century B.C.E.:

> 敢作文人大寶協龢鐘，用追孝，享祀照格，樂大神。大神其陟降嚴祐僕，綏厚多福。其豐豐懌懌授余屯魯、通祿、永命、眉壽靈終。瘋其萬年永寶日鼓。

> I venture to craft for my cultured [ancestors] a great treasure of harmoniously tuned bells, so as to pursue filial piety, to make sacrificial offerings to those who splendidly arrive [i.e. the ancestors], and to please the great spirits. May the great spirits, ascending and descending, solemnly bless and assist us, assuage us and grant us manifold fortune. May they—*fengfeng yiyi*—bestow on us hoards of boon, enveloping wealth, enduring life, outstanding longevity, and a numinous end. May I, Xing, treasure and peal [these bells] every day for ten thousand years.

The phrase *fengfeng yiyi* (*p*ʰoŋ-pʰoŋ lak-lak) reproduces the sound of Xing's bells as they are struck during the ceremony (perhaps accompanied

---

[110] Cf. Goldin, *The Culture of Sex in Ancient China*, 39ff.
[111] E.g., "Tingliao" 庭燎 (*Mao* 182), "Guzhong" 鼓鍾 (*Mao* 208), "Zhijing" 執競 (*Mao* 274), "You gu" 有瞽 (*Mao* 280).
[112] *Before Confucius*, 181ff. See also Kern, "Bronze Inscriptions, the *Shijing* and the *Shangshu*," 167ff.

by other instruments—*lak-lak sounds more like a clapper than a bell), but it has a definite meaning as well: "fecund and soothing." As Xing invokes his ancestors and beseeches them to rain down peace and prosperity, the bells themselves call out "Fecund and soothing! Fecund and soothing!"—echoing his prayer in their own brazen language.

Associating this kind of rhetoric in bronze inscriptions with onomatopoeia in the *Shijing* seems compelling because in each context, the onomatopoetic phrases capture both an appropriate sound and an appropriate meaning. Moreover, this poetic device could hardly have developed before bell inscriptions became commonplace in the mid-tenth century B.C.E., because other types of bronze vessels could not produce a musical tone. No one ever wrote "Clang, clang—the platter" or "Thud, thud—the cauldron." As onomatopoeia would go on to be prolific in Chinese poetry, this debt to bell inscriptions must be reckoned as a substantial one.

Antecedents of another characteristic feature of later Chinese literature, namely parallel prose, can be found in bronze inscriptions as well. The connection is more tenuous than with onomatopoeia, but there is one distinctive feature of bronze inscriptions that merits consideration in this regard: the formula *duiyang* 對揚, "to extol in response," which appears so frequently in appointment inscriptions.[113] After the King has recounted the various precedents justifying the award (acts of merit, ancestral service, etc.), and then announces the charge, the recipient will typically extol in response (*duiyang*) with gratitude and praise. Significantly, the King always speaks first; the awardee "responds" only after the King has set the terms of the occasion.

Long after bronze inscriptions had fallen out of cultural favor, compositions presenting a suitable "response" to a predetermined theme—usually set by a superior—became a common genre in Chinese literature. As Wilt Idema and Lloyd Haft explain:

> In later centuries a prominent feature of traditional Chinese education was training in the construction of pairs of parallel lines. The teacher would begin by naming any one-syllable word, whereupon the pupil was expected to produce a contrasting word of the same semantic category. For example, if the

---

[113] For a recent discussion of the phrase, with references to previous scholarship, see Wang Jing, "'Duiyang' zai shi." One leading account is Shen Wenzhuo, *Zong-Zhou liyue wenming kaolun*, 529–51.

teacher said "heaven," the pupil might answer "earth." Once the student had grasped the basic principle, he would be confronted with combinations of two characters, such as "blue heaven" or "setting sun," to which he might answer "yellow earth" or "rising moon." The number of syllables assigned was gradually increased until the student had no trouble coming up with parallel lines of three, four, six, or more syllables (as usual in prose), or with couplets of five- or seven-syllable lines as used in poetry. The couplet (*dui* or *duilian* [對聯]) itself became a modest literary genre and was a frequent choice for inscriptions and the like.[114]

A well-known example of this sort of exercise is the contest in Chapter 50 of *The Story of the Stone* 石頭記, where the denizens of the poetry garden are asked to craft lines in response to a specific theme—a passage that is particularly memorable because the elegant but unaffected vernacular of the narrator contrasts with the formal diction and syntax of the contestants' verses.

One might initially discount as farfetched any connection between this much later practice and the formulaic duiyang of bronze inscriptions were it not for the fact that the same word, *dui* 對, is used to refer to both. *Dui* can also denote a minister's response to specific queries from a sovereign. In his biography of Dong Zhongshu 董仲舒 (fl. 152–119 B.C.E.), for example, the historian Ban Gu 班固 (A.D. 32–92) chose to include, as most representative of Dong's work, his so-called *duice* 對策, "policies [formulated] in response," which were extended replies to the Emperor's questions on statecraft.[115] Han emperors used this tactic to help them discover the most talented ministers in the realm.[116] The famed statesman Gongsun Hong 公孫弘 (200–121 B.C.E.) was a humble pig farmer who attained

---

[114] Idema and Haft, *A Guide to Chinese Literature*, 108.

[115] *Hanshu* 56.2495–2524. In *Wenxin diaolong* 文心雕龍, Liu Xie 劉勰 (ca. 465–522 C.E.) defined duice as "policies deployed in response to an imperial summons" 應詔而陳政; text in Yang Mingzhao, *Zengding Wenxin diaolong jiaozhu*, 5.24.333 ("Yidui" 議對). It should be emphasized that *dui* need not have this connotation in every context; sometimes, *dui* refers merely to a conversation between two people, without any explicit distinction between superior and inferior. Moreover, *dui* can be performed by kings as well. In the Ke he 克盉 and Ke lei 克罍 inscriptions (no. 7, below), for example, the King "responds" to the offerings of the Grand Protector (*taibao* 太保).

[116] Cf. Elman, *A Cultural History of Civil Examinations in Late Imperial China*, 6.

instant renown when the Emperor was impressed by his *duice*:

太常令所徵儒士各對策，百餘人，弘第居下。策奏，天子擢弘對為第一。召入見，狀貌甚麗，拜為博士。[117]

> The Chamberlain of Ceremonies ordered each of the classically-trained scholars who had been recruited—over one hundred men—to compose a *duice*, and [Gongsun] Hong was ranked toward the bottom. But when the *ce* were submitted to the throne, the Son of Heaven selected Hong's *dui* as the best. He was summoned to an imperial audience, and, with his extremely handsome appearance, was honored as an Erudite.

What all these uses of *dui* have in common is that the display of talent comes in response to a theme or question set by someone authorized to speak first. The talented do not set the theme themselves; rather, the talented respond with words that are worth hearing, but consonant with the theme established by the superior. It may be given to you to speak, but it is not given to you to speak first. A contrast can be drawn with ancient Rome, where emperors were expected to make artful speeches before the public even after their unquestioned authority had been established.[118] In China, it was the ministers, not the sovereign, who were expected to produce artful speeches. Whereas talented Americans tend to associate success with getting ahead in society, in traditional China, talented minds regarded success as the thoughtful and constructive performance of the roles that fate had allotted them.

PRG

---

[117] *Shiji* 112.2949.
[118] See Yakobson, "Political Rhetoric in China and in Imperial Rome."

GUIDES

Chronology

Precise dates are not always ascertainable (as in the case of the Shang and Zhou kings), and there is not always a consensus regarding the beginning and ending years of conventionally named historical periods (such as Warring States). The dates of the Zhou kings in the chart below are taken from the Xia Shang Zhou Chronology Project (*Xia Shang Zhou duandai gongcheng* 夏商周斷代工程) of the People's Republic of China. The names of Kings Yì 懿 and Yí 夷 are distinguished in Modern Mandarin by tone. The import of the name Gong He 共和 is disputed, but it probably refers to Gong Hefu 共穌父 (i.e. Hefu of Gong), who assumed control of the government in the mid-ninth century B.C.E.

Shang dynasty 商			?-1046 B.C.E.
Zhou dynasty 周			1046-256 B.C.E.
	Western Zhou 西周		1046-771 B.C.E.
		King Wu 武王	r. 1046-1043 B.C.E.
		King Cheng 成王	r. 1042-1021 B.C.E.
		King Kang 康王	r. 1020-996 B.C.E.
		King Zhao 昭王	r. 995-977 B.C.E.
		King Mu 穆王	r. 976-923 B.C.E.
		King Gong 共王	r. 922-900 B.C.E.
		King Yì 懿王	r. 899-893 B.C.E.
		King Xiao 孝王	r. 892-886 B.C.E.
		King Yí 夷王	r. 885-878 B.C.E.
		King Li 厲王	r. 877-841 B.C.E.
		Gong He 共和	r. 841-828 B.C.E.
		King Xuan 宣王	r. 827-782 B.C.E.
		King You 幽王	r. 781-771 B.C.E.
	Eastern Zhou 東周		770-256 B.C.E.
		Spring and Autumn 春秋	722-481 B.C.E.
		Warring States 戰國	453-221 B.C.E.
Qin dynasty 秦			221-207 B.C.E.
Han dynasty 漢			206 B.C.E.-220 C.E.
	Western Han 西漢		206 B.C.E.-9 C.E.
	Xin dynasty 新		9-23 C.E.
	Eastern Han 東漢		25-220 C.E.

The Sexagenary Cycle

Dates in the sixty-day cycle can easily be converted according to this chart. Sexagenary dates are made combining two sequences, the ten "Heavenly Stems" (*tiangan* 天干) and the twelve "Earthly Branches" (*dizhi* 地支). (Because not all possible permutations are used—for example, there is no *jiachou* 甲丑—the total comes to sixty rather than to 120.) The ten "Heavenly Stems" were also used to indicate dates in the ten-day ritual cycle of the Shang, and as posthumous names to indicate the day in that cycle when the ancestor would receive cult offerings.[119]

1	甲子	*jiazi*	31	甲午	*jiawu*
2	乙丑	*yichou*	32	乙未	*yiwei*
3	丙寅	*bingyin*	33	丙申	*bingshen*
4	丁卯	*dingmao*	34	丁酉	*dingyou*
5	戊辰	*wuchen*	35	戊戌	*wuxu*
6	己巳	*jisi*	36	己亥	*jihai*
7	庚午	*gengwu*	37	庚子	*gengzi*
8	辛未	*xinwei*	38	辛丑	*xinchou*
9	壬申	*renshen*	39	壬寅	*renyin*
10	癸酉	*guiyou*	40	癸卯	*guimao*
11	甲戌	*jiaxu*	41	甲辰	*jiachen*
12	乙亥	*yihai*	42	乙巳	*yisi*
13	丙子	*bingzi*	43	丙午	*bingwu*
14	丁丑	*dingchou*	44	丁未	*dingwei*
15	戊寅	*wuyin*	45	戊申	*wushen*
16	己卯	*jimao*	46	己酉	*jiyou*
17	庚辰	*gengchen*	47	庚戌	*gengxu*
18	辛巳	*xinsi*	48	辛亥	*xinhai*
19	壬午	*renwu*	49	壬子	*renzi*
20	癸未	*guiwei*	50	癸丑	*guichou*
21	甲申	*jiashen*	51	甲寅	*jiayin*
22	乙酉	*yiyou*	52	乙卯	*yimao*
23	丙戌	*bingxu*	53	丙辰	*bingchen*
24	丁亥	*dinghai*	54	丁巳	*dingsi*
25	戊子	*wuzi*	55	戊午	*wuwu*
26	己丑	*jichou*	56	己未	*jiwei*
27	庚寅	*gengyin*	57	庚申	*gengshen*
28	辛卯	*xinmao*	58	辛酉	*xinyou*
29	壬辰	*renchen*	59	壬戌	*renxu*
30	癸巳	*guisi*	60	癸亥	*guihai*

[119] See also Smith, "The Chinese Sexagenary Cycle and the Ritual Foundations of the Calendar." [MP].

Conventions and Abbreviations

I. References in the footnotes are abbreviated; full information for all cited works can be found in the bibliography. All entries use the following bibliographical abbreviations for three standard collections:

Jicheng (for *Yin Zhou jinwen jicheng*)

Kimbun tsūshaku (for Shirakawa Shizuka, *Kimbun tsūshaku*)

Mingwen xuan (for Ma Chengyuan *et al.*, *Shang Zhou qingtong qi mingwen xuan*)

These are cited in full in the Bibliography. All inscriptions are also available online in "Yin Zhou jinwen ji qingtongqi ziliaoku" 殷周金文暨青銅器資料庫.

II. The transcriptions in this volume aim to associate each archaic graph with a modern character in *kaishu* 楷書 form. The translators have included modernized forms of archaic graphs in cases where the interpretation may still be open to debate, the form of the graph is relevant to the discussion, or when the graph represents a proper name. Scholarly readers can check these transcriptions against rubbings of the original texts in sources such as *Jicheng*, and may find that the contributors to this volume sometimes offer different interpretations of the same graph. Such is the nature of palaeographical research, and the editors prefer not to gloss over the open questions in this field by imposing specious uniformity.

III. Certain ancient technical terms, such as those used in dates, are routinely left untranslated, as their meaning remains uncertain. See the corresponding entries in the Glossary.

IV. In the translations, English words necessary for the understanding of the text, but not present in the original inscription, are inserted in brackets.

V. Old Chinese reconstructions follow the system laid out in Baxter and Sagart, *Old Chinese*. It should be borne in mind that these inscriptions contain many uncertain graphs, and the reconstructions of their underlying words are accordingly uncertain as well.

VI. Contributors are cited at the end of each section by their initials.

INSCRIPTIONS
Numbers 1-82

1. Ersi Bi Qi you 二祀邲其卣

This late Shang you wine vessel was discovered in 1940 at Anyang 安陽, Henan 河南 Province. Anyang is the location of Yinxu 殷墟, the Zhou name for the last Shang dynastic capital known as Da Yi Shang 大邑商, or "Great city of Shang." The wine vessel belongs to a series of three companion vessels cast for the same king at two-year intervals, in the second, fourth, and sixth years. The fourth-year Bi Qi *you* (*Jicheng* 5413) records sacrifices to the reigning king's father, Wen Wu Di Yi 文武帝乙, the penultimate King of Shang, so it is clear that all three date to the early years of the last Shang King, Di Xin 帝辛 (c. 1085–1046 B.C.E.), who was overthrown by the Zhou in 1046. Inscriptions were cast in three places on the vessel. Identical lineage emblems made up of four characters (Ya Mo Fu Ding 亞獏父丁) appear on the inner surface of both the lid and the belly of the vessel, while a longer inscription of thirty-seven characters appears on the outside bottom.

After discovery, the authenticity of the vessel was challenged, not least on the basis of the inscription's uniqueness and placement, but since then, scientific analysis has confirmed its genuineness. The second-year Bi Qi *you* (or, Ersi Bi Qi *you*) refers to *di* 帝 who ascend and descend. There is no discernible difference in the way the posthumous word *di* is written here and in the name of King Wen Wu Di Yi in the fourth-year inscription, so it may refer to Di Yi. The inscription records a *rong* 肜 libation, one of the five sacrifices in the regular cycle of Shang ancestral rites, here in honor of Ancestress Bing on her name day, *bingchen* (*ganzhi* no. 53 in the sixty-day cycle). Rites for her spouse, Tai Yi, who is also named in the inscription, would have been conducted on day fifty-two, and as we saw the king's father is referred to as Di Yi.

Transcription

丙辰，王令邲其兄（貺）𩛥于夆田，渴¹賓貝五朋。在正月遘于妣丙彡（肜）日大乙奭，唯王二祀，既裸于上下帝。

 Emblem: 獏 inside 亞, 父丁

---

¹ The interpretation of this graph and sentence is still subject of debate. Qiu Xigui punctuates "王令邲其兄（貺）𩛥于夆田渴，賓貝五朋", considering 田 to be writing *sheng* 甸, a title

Translation

On *bingchen* day, the King commanded Bi to grant X fields at Feng. Y presented Bi five strings of cowries. It was in the first month, on the day of the *rong* libation to Ancestress Bing, wife of Tai Yi. It was in the King's second year, after completing the libation to the *di* above and below.
[Emblem]

Further Reading

Jicheng 5412.

Mingwen xuan, no. 12.

Bagley, *Shang Ritual Bronzes in the Arthur M. Sackler Collections*, 526–28 and 535nn. 28–31. (Bagley refers to the vessels as Zuoce Zhi zi you 作冊隻子卣.)

Ding Meng and Jian Min, "Bi Qi you de X shexian jiance fenxi."

Du Naisong, "Bi Qi san you mingwen kao ji xiangguan wenti de yanjiu."

Jinwen jinyi leijian, 580–81.

Li Xueqin, "Bi Qi san you yu youguan wenti."

Qiu Xigui, *Gudai wenxue yanjiu xintan*.

Xia Shang Zhou duandai gongcheng 1996–2000 nian jieduan chengguo baogao: Jianben, 58.

Xie Mingwen, *Shangdai jinwen de zhengli yu yanjiu*.

Zhang Zhenglang, "Bi Qi you de zhenwei wenti."

DWP

---

designating someone in charge of agricultural matters. 渴 would be the name of such officer. See Qiu Xigui, *Gudai wenxue yanjiu xintan*, p. 347. Xie Mingwen has noted that bronze inscriptions describing bestowals almost always follow the structure of "賜 [something] 于 [someone]," supporting Qiu's interpretation. Accordingly, the sentence would read "the king commanded Bi to bestow [something] to Y, the officer for agriculture of Feng, and presented five strings of cowries." See Xie Mingwen, *Shangdai jinwen de zhengli yu yanjiu*, 288–89 [MP]."

2. Zi Huang zun 子黃尊

This round rather plain vessel with clumsy writing is also called the Yimao zun 乙卯尊 and was discovered in Dayuancun 大原村, Fengxi 灃西, near Xi'an 西安, Shaanxi 陝西 Province, in 1965. It is presently stored in the Xi'an City Cultural Preservation Archaeology Institute 西安市文物保護考古所. The vessel, curiously called a water basin (*pan* 盤) by the ancient scribe, was a vase-like vessel designed to hold alcoholic beverages. It has a trumpet-shaped mouth and a belt around the middle decorated with fanged "monster" (the so-called *taotie*) décor. Archaeologists date the vessel to the transition period at the end of the Shang and beginning of the Zhou period, around the early eleventh century B.C.E. The inscription was cast into the inside bottom of the vessel, where it is difficult to see but would come into contact with the sacral ale. The casting style is rather crude, leaving a number of graphs not firmly imprinted or partially rubbed off. Although this bronze vessel was discovered near an early Zhou capital, the person referred to as Zi 子 ("Child") is believed to be a member of the Shang royal lineage according to *Shiji* 史記 (*Records of the Historian*).[1] The lineage emblem at the end of the inscription supports a Shang origin. It depicts a child being offered up on a table of some sort, and is found on hundreds of vessels distributed all over the Yellow River Valley, with even a few examples found south in the Yangzi River valley region. Their manufacturing origin is understood to be someplace near Anyang, Henan, on the eastern end of the middle Yellow River Valley. The custom of casting lineage emblems is understood as a signature of the late Shang elite. How and why this bronze vessel was transported to the Zhou area remains a mystery.

The inscription records an award ceremony that took place on *yimao* day (*ganzhi* no. 52 in the sixty-day cycle), when Zi presented offerings at the Great Hall (or Chamber of Heaven), which is mentioned in Shang oracle-bone inscriptions as a place where one would report to the ancestors. Zi presented a tribute of valuables including jade and sacrificial animals. In exchange, the King (probably the Shang King) rewarded him with a jade tube used for pouring fine sacrificial ales, the kind that would be stored in this vessel, and a hundred strings of cowries, a valuable imported good used

---

[1] *Shiji* 3.91 [PRG].

in exchange. The cowry strings probably supplied the means for Zi's family to have the vessel cast.

The identity of Zi in this inscription is unknown. Some scholars believe the word "yellow" (*huang* 黃) is part of his name, and others that it modifies the jade gift. In the final sentence of the inscription, Zi rededicates part of the gift to a woman of the Si 姒 lineage, who, some scholars suggest, might have been his wife. She is named after a *ding* day (*ganzhi* no. 4) in the sacrificial calendar whereas the ancestor to whom she in turn dedicated the vessels was of a *ji* day (*ganzhi* no. 6). Since lineage emblems on vessels were mostly linked to ancestor dedications, the lineage association of the ancestor was Zi. Si Ding, to whom Zi dedicated this vessel, would use it to worship a *ji*-day ancestor in the Zi shrine (or perhaps all *ji*-day ancestors?). Although the emblem on this inscription is common it is partially obscured. A clearer version is found on *Jicheng* 6000:

(see also the Xing bells, no. 33, below).

Transcription

乙卯子見（覲）在大（太）室。白［□］一、珥琅九、牲（牲）百。用王商（賞）子黃瓚一貝百朋。子光（貺）商（賞）姒丁用作己寶［□］（盤?）。

Emblem (unclear): 廾子片共

Translation

On *yimao* day, Zi had an audience in the Grand Hall, where he presented one white [jade?], nine ear jades and a hundred sacrificial animal offerings. On this occasion, the King awarded Zi one yellow jade tube and a hundred strings of cowries. Zi awarded them to the Ding-day Si-lineage woman, who took this opportunity to make a precious vessel for the Ji-day ancestor.

[Emblem]

Further Reading

Jicheng 6000.

Allan, *The Shape of the Turtle.*
Itō and Takashima, *Studies in Early Chinese Civilization.*
Wang Hui, *Shang Zhou jinwen,* 25–28.
Wang Shenxing and Wang Hanzhen, "Yimao zun mingwen tongshi lun."

CAC

3. Wo FANGDING 我方鼎

A large square cauldron, also referred to as Wo *yan* 我甗, Yu *ding* 禦鼎, or Yu *gui* 禦簋, is believed to have originated in Luoyang 洛陽, Henan. The vessel is now found in the National Palace Museum in Taipei, but the lid is in the Institute of History and Philology, Academia Sinica, Taipei 台北中央研究院歷史語言研究所. It has matching inscriptions inside the lid and inside the vessel bottom. Scholars date it stylistically to either the late Shang or early Western Zhou period.

The inscription records the performance of an exorcism ritual and sacrifices to two sets of male and female ancestors. Since female ancestors and the more recently deceased were often implicated in illness, Wo may have been appealing a perceived curse. Of particular power were the two deceased women who required extra services. The rituals began on the twenty-fourth day of the sixty-day ritual calendar, a day that in later times would become the most auspicious day for recording ceremonies and bronze-casting events. Wo dedicated the vessel to his Father Ji (no. 6 in the ten-day cycle). Wo and his ancestor Father Ji both probably belonged to the Ruo 若 lineage, a name found in the emblem inside of a Ya-sign 亞.

Transcription

唯十月又一月丁亥我作禦祟（恤？）¹祖乙妣乙、祖己妣癸，祉（延）袷繫（祟？）二母。咸。與遣（追）祼二，🈳（來？）貝五朋，用作父己寶尊彝。

Emblem: 若 placed inside a 亞 cartouche.

Translation

It was the eleventh month, *dinghai* day (*ganzhi* no. 24), when Wo began with the exorcism ritual and sacrifice for Ancestor Yi and Ancestress Yi, Ancestor Ji and Ancestress Gui, and then continued with a *yue* sacrifice and fire ritual (?) for the two mothers.

---

¹ Zhao Ping'an explains that this graph indicates a sacrifice involving the lifting of sacrificial vessels, but cannot be interpreted as *ji* 祭 because *ji* indicates a sacrifice involving the presentation of meat; *Jinwen shidu yu wenming tansuo*, 1–5.

When that was complete, he additionally presented two libations and with five strings of cowries from Lai (?). He took this opportunity to make a precious sacrificial vessel for expressing reverence.

[Emblem: Ruo of Ya rank?]

Further Reading

Jicheng 2763.
Mingwen xuan, no. 125.
Jinwen jinyi leijian, 389–90.

Allan, *The Shape of the Turtle*, 74–111.
Cao Zhaolan, *Jinwen yu Yin Zhou nüxing wenhuai*, 52–53.
Wang Hui, *Shang Zhou jinwen*, 29–31.

CAC

4. Li gui 利簋

The Li *gui* caused a sensation when it was unearthed in 1976 in Lintong 臨潼, Shaanxi (near Xi'an), and it remains the earliest Western Zhou inscribed bronze discovered to date. Its 33-character inscription was composed immediately after the Zhou conquest of Shang in 1046, recording in bold calligraphy the dedication of the vessel by a Zhou court official named Li. True to form, the inscription records the significant event that occasioned the award to Li of the bronze used to cast the piece. In this case, however, the historical event was nothing less than King Wu's (1049–1044 B.C.E.) overthrow of the Shang dynasty, in which Li evidently played a role. The inscription only provides two day-dates, so that, other than functioning as a "standard vessel" for reconstructing the Western Zhou dates, its usefulness in dating is limited. Its chief historical significance lies in providing unimpeachable contemporaneous evidence of the epoch-making event—King Wu of Zhou's overthrow of the Shang dynasty by force, the climactic battle taking place at dawn on day *jiazi* 甲子, as traditional accounts have said all along.

For the most part, the interpretation of the inscription is straightforward. But the reading of the second sentence continues to be debated. Several of the selected references below bear specifically on the interpretation of the problematical passage. The crux of the difficulty has been the interpretation of the two characters *sui ding* 歲鼎. Numerous prominent authorities now concur in reading *sui* as "Jupiter"[1] and *ding* 鼎 (*zhen* 貞 / *zheng* 正 / *ding* 定) as "correct/confirm/determine". Strong evidence has accumulated in support of an astrological interpretation of the phrase, not least among which the recently discovered Qinghua manuscript *Qi Ye* 耆夜, which refers to Jupiter's role.[2] Li's official title, scribe of the right (*youshi* 右史), and his reward for some signal service both suggest that Li held an important post similar to the *taishi* 太史 or "Grand Scribe-Astrologer" of later Zhou. In a mere fourteen characters, Scribe Li records four salient facts—the main actors, the precise timing, the astrological circumstances, and the outcome.

---

[1] On the significance of Jupiter's position for prognostication, see Pankenier, Astrology and Cosmology in Early China, 197ff. and 265–95.

[2] Li Feng, "Qinghua jian 'Qi ye' che du ji qi xiangguan wenti."

Transcription

武王征商，惟甲子朝。歲鼎。克聞夙（巩）又（有）商。辛未，王在闌（?）師，賜又（右）史利金，用作覃公寶尊彝。

Translation

When King Wu rectified [= defeated] Shang, it was on *jiazi* day (*ganzhi* no. 1) at dawn. Jupiter was correctly in a favorable position. Accordingly, we were able to learn of the securing of Shang. On *xinwei* day (*ganzhi* no. 8), the King was at Jian (?) garrison; he bestowed on me, Li, Scribe of the Right, bronze used to cast for my honored forebear Tan this precious ritual vessel.

Further Reading

Jicheng 3.4131: 32–13–2.
Mingwen xuan, no. 22.

Behr, *Reimende Bronzeinschriften und die Entstehung der chinesischen Endreimdichtung*, 145–46.
Chen changyuan, "Cong 'Li gui' tan youguan Wu Wang fa Zhou de jige wenti."
Cui Hengsheng, "'Sui ding ke hun su you Shang' kaoshi."
Jinwen jinyi leijian, 61–62.
Li Feng, "Qinghua jian 'Qi ye' chudu."
Li Xueqin, *Xia Shang Zhou niandaixue zhaji*, 204–5.
Li Ziyao, "Shaanxi Lintong faxian de Wu Wang zheng shang gui mingwen kao shi."
Lintongxian Wenhuaguan, "Shaanxi Lintong faxian Wu Wang zheng Shang gui."
Liu Zhao, "Li gui mingwen xin jie."
Pankenier, "New Light on the Li *gui* Inscription."
Shang Chengzuo, "Guanyu Li gui mingwen de shidu—Yu tang Lan, Yu Xingwu tongzhi shangque."
Shaughnessy, *Sources of Western Zhou History*, 86–105.
Takashima, "Settling the Cauldron in the Right Place."
Tang Lan, *Tang Lan xiansheng jinwen lunji*, 205–8.

Tang Lan, "Xi Zhou shijian zuizao de yi jian tongqi Li gui mingwen jieshi."

Wang Hui, *Shang Zhou jinwen*, 31–34.

Wang Rencong, "Jizai Wu Wang fa shang shishi de Zhou chu zhongqi—Li gui." *Xia Shang Zhou duandai gongcheng 1996–2000 nian jieduan chengguo baogao: Jianben*, 44.

Xu Zhongshu, "Xi Zhou Li gui mingwen jianshi."

Yan Yiping, "Cong Li gui ming kan fa Zhou nian."

Yu Xingwu, "'Guanyu Li gui mingwen de shidu' yi wen de jidian yijian."

Yu Xingwu, "Li gui mingwen kaoshi."

Zhang Yongshan, "Li gui 'sui ding ke wen' buzheng."

Zhang Zhenglang, "Li gui shiwen."

Zhong Fengnian, *et al.*, "Guanyu Li gui mingwen kaoshi de taolun."

Zhou Yan, "Li gui mingwen 'sui ding' bu shi."

DWP

5. Tian Wang gui 天亡簋

The Tian Wang *gui*, also known as the Da Feng *gui* 大豐簋, was discovered at Qishan 岐山, Shaanxi, in the Zhou ancestral homeland, during the Daoguang 道光 reign period (1821–1855). The scholarly consensus is that the vessel dates from the very end of King Wu's reign, after the Zhou conquest. This *gui* and its remarkable 77-character inscription have been thoroughly studied, and it now serves as a "standard vessel" for evaluating early Western Zhou bronze typology. In addition to providing an important account of a three-day series of the highest state sacrifices, the Tian Wang *gui* inscription is also the earliest to make systematic use of rhyme, displaying careful attention to composition and prosody. (End rhymes in lines of either 9 or 10 characters are shown in bold. Numerous internal rhymes also occur.) The translation below is arranged to highlight the prosodic composition, rather than reproducing the eight lines of the original layout.

The grammar and syntax are opaque in parts, and after more than a century some characters still defy clear interpretations. Fortunately, the most important content is accessible. The inscription concerns a series of largescale state rites conducted by the king, beginning with the Great *feng* 大豐 sacrifice in the Chamber of Heaven *tianshi* 天室 on the first day (also encountered later in the He *zun* and Mai *fangzun*, nos. 6 and 14, below), followed the next day by an elaborate *yi*-sacrifice 衣祀) to *shangdi*, the Deity Above, together with King Wu's deceased father, King Wen. (A sacrificial rite by the same name figures prominently in the Shang royal cult.) This is followed on the third day by a grand feast hosted by the king, featuring the sacrificial meats and liquors. Comparison with the more detailed account of the feng sacrifice in the Mai *fangzun* indicates that the Hall of Heaven formed part of the *mingtang* 明堂, or "Hall of Light" ritual complex, with its circular Moat, and spirit terrace, where the most important sacrifices to *shangdi* (or *tian* 天) and the ancestors were conducted. The sponsor of this vessel, Tian Wang 天亡, plays a central role in the sacrifices and is richly rewarded, so that it is clear he must have been very prominent and close to the king. It may even be that this is the famous Taigong Wang Lü Shang 太公望呂尚 (also known as Tai Wang 太望 and Lü Wang 呂望) himself, the high-ranking vassal of the Shang who went over to the Zhou cause, contributed vital tactical and political counsel to King Wu during the conquest campaign, and was rewarded, according to *Shiji*,[1] with his own appanage, what would become the state of Qi 齊 in Shandong 山東.

Certain sentences in the inscription parse only with some difficulty. To illustrate: one question is whether *jiang* "descend; send down; bestow" in the second line punctuates the ritual activity by reporting the King's "descending" from performing the sacrifices, or whether "send down aid to X" (*jiang* X *you* 降 X 佑) should be read as the ancestors sending down divine aid as occurs in the earlier Shang oracle bone inscriptions. Equally plausible is to punctuate after *jiang*, and run "Tian Wang aided" together with "the King in offering the *yi*-panoply of sacrifices …" But this yields an uncomfortably long sentence for such an early inscription. Some of the characters being undecipherable, what was actually granted to Tian Wang in line eight remains a matter of speculation. The last line clearly records Tian Wang's own words of gratitude for the king's munificence, a performative declaration immortalized in bronze.

Transcription

[乙]亥王又（有）大豊。王凡（般）三（四?）方。

王祀于天室，**降**。天亡右（佑）王衣（殷）祀于王丕顯考文**王**，事喜（饎）上帝，文王德在上。丕顯王作省（德），丕肆王作相。

丕克乞衣（殷）王祀。

丁丑，王鄉（饗）大宜，王**降**。亡勛爵退囊。

唯朕又（有）蔑（慶?），每（敏）揚王休于尊簋。

Translation

On [*yi*]*hai* day (*ganzhi* no. 12), King [Wu] performed the great *feng* rites, offering to the three directions.

The King sacrificed in the Chamber of Heaven, then came down. Tian Wang assisted the King in performing the *yi*-panoply of sacrifices to his illustrious father King Wen, offering millet ale to the Deity Above and King Wen, attending on high.

"Our greatly illustrious King [Wen] established *de*; our great succeeding King [Wu] carried on, bringing an end to the Yin kings' sacrificial rounds."

[1] *Shiji*, 32.1477–1481.

INSCRIPTIONS

On *dingchou* day (*ganzhi* no. 14), the King served a feast of the sacrificial viands; the King descended to award Wang ... [gifts, titles].

"Receiving these rewards, I hasten to extol the King's grace on this precious tureen."

Further Reading

Jicheng 4261.
Kimbun tsūshaku, 1.1–38.
Mingwen xuan, no. 23.
Behr, *Reimende Bronzeinschriften und die Entstehung der chinesischen Endreimdichtung*, 481–503.
Cen Zhongmian, "Tian Wang gui quan shi."
Chen Mengjia, *Xi Zhou tongqi duandai*, I, 3–6.
Guo Moruo, *Liang Zhou jinwen ci daxi tulu kaoshi*, 3.1a–2b.
Hong Jiayi, "Guanyu 'Tian Wang gui' suo ji shishi de xingzhi."
Hsu and Linduff, *Western Zhou Civilization*, 99–100.
Huang Shengzhang, "Da Feng gui zhizuo de niandai didian yu shishi."
Jinwen jinyi leijian, 167–69.
Li pingxin, "Zhou dai Shang Tang xinzheng (yi) —'Da Feng pian ming' zhong Zhou fa shang tang de quezheng."
Li Xueqin, "'Tian Wang gui' shishi ji youguan tuice."
Liu Xiaodong, "Tian Wang gui yu Wu Wang dongtu duyi."
Lin Yun, *Lin Yun xueshu wenji*, 167–73.
Qian Boquan, "'Shuo Tian Wan gui wei Wu Wang mei Shang yiqian tongqi' yi wen de jidian shangque."
Shirakawa Shizuka, *Jinwen tongshi xuanshi*, 1–26.
Sun Changxu, "'Tian Wang gui' wen zi yi nian."
Sun Zhichu, "Tian Wang gui mingwen huishi."
Sun Zuoyun, "Shuo 'Tian Wang gui' wei Wuwang mie Shang yiqian tongqi."
Sun Zuoyun, "Zai lun 'Tian Wang gui' er san shi.
Tang Lan, *Xi Zhou qingtongqi mingwen fendai shi zheng*.
Wang Hui, *Shang Zhou jinwen*, 34–38.
Yin Difei, "Shilun Da Feng gui de niandai."
Yu Xingwu, "Guanyu tian wang gui mingwen de jidian lunzheng."
Zhou Xifu, "Tian Wang gui ying wei Kang Wang shi qi."

DWP

6. He zun 何尊

The He *zun* was cast during the reign of King Cheng 成王, making it one of the earliest inscribed bronzes from the very beginning of Western Zhou. This spectacular *zun* beaker was first unearthed near Baoji 寶雞, Shaanxi, in 1965, but its important inscription was not discovered until the vessel was cleaned and corrosion removed in 1975. In short order, China's most eminent historians and paleographers published studies analyzing the 122-character inscription and discussing its historical significance. The He *zun* commemorates a ritual feast following a solemn *feng* sacrifice to the King's ancestors. The inscription records King Cheng's hortatory declaration to He, the maker of the vessel and a member of the royal lineage present at the feast, calling on him to emulate his father by supporting the King. He then records the King's bestowal on him of thirty strings of cowries with which he financed the casting of this prized ritual vessel.

Apart from the baroque magnificence of the vessel itself, the He *zun*'s great historical importance lies in the inscription's corroboration of accounts in such early texts as the "Shaogao" 召誥 ("Declaration of the Duke of Shao") chapter in the *Shangshu* 尚書 (*Canon of Documents*), "Duoyi jie" 度邑解 ("Laying out the city") chapter in *Yi Zhoushu* 逸周書 (*Lost Shangshu of Zhou*), and elsewhere, concerning the founding of the city of Luoyi 洛邑 on the north bank of the Luo River not long after the overthrow of the Shang dynasty in 1046. First, the inscription marks one of the earliest references to the receipt of Heaven's Mandate by the dynastic founder, King Wen, and focuses on the rituals in the Chamber of Heaven temple complex; second, the He *zun* confirms that the building of an administrative center in the heart of the former Shang domain was the expressed intention of King Cheng's father, King Wu, who died only two years after conquering Shang; third, it confirms that it was during the fifth year of King Cheng's reign (1038) that construction of the new capital was begun, here for the first time named Chengzhou 成周, "Accomplished Zhou."

Besides the three characters either missing or partially obscured due to corrosion (e.g., *da ling* 大令, "Great command," in the second line, whose presence is confirmed by eminent paleographers who examined the vessel), the inscription presents few intractable problems of interpretation. An important historical question does concern how to reconcile the dating of the founding of Chengzhou in the fifth year of King Cheng's reign with the account in the *Shangshu*, "Luogao" 洛誥 ("Declaration at Luo"), of the seven-year regency of the Duke of Zhou during King Cheng's minority.[1] A year-by-year account in *Shangshu dazhuan* 尚書大傳 (*The Great Commentary to the Book of Documents*) of the Duke of Zhou's regency also dates the laying out (*ying* 營) of the new capital to the fifth year.[2] Since the *Shangshu dazhuan* account has the Duke of Zhou suppressing the rebellion of Shang loyalists in the second year, the count certainly began after the death of King Wu. The founding of Luo in the king's fifth year is now confirmed by the He *zun*, so that the *Shangshu dazhuan* account of King Cheng's "creating rituals and music" in the sixth year, and ruling in his own right in the seventh year, is entirely plausible. Thus the ordinal sequence refers to the early years of King Cheng's reign, which coincide with the Duke of Zhou's regency. The king's exhortation to He to support him, shortly after the suppression of a rebellion and just as King Cheng reaches majority and assumes the full power of the kingship, fits the historical context.

Transcription

唯王初壅（營）宅于成周。復偁武王豐福自天。在四月丙戌，王誥宗小子于京室，曰：昔在爾考公氏克逑文王，肆文王受茲［大令］。唯武王既克大邑商，則廷告于天，曰：余其宅茲中或（域），[3]自茲辥（乂）民。嗚呼！爾有唯（雖）小子亡（無）識，視于公氏，有爵於天，徹令敬享哉！叀（唯？）王恭德谷（裕）天，順（訓）我不每（敏）。王咸誥。何賜貝卅朋，用作［□］公寶尊彝。唯王五祀。

Translation

> It was when the King initially laid out his royal seat at Chengzhou. The King returned from extolling King Wu in the *feng* sacrifice, with sacrificial meat from the [Hall of] Heaven. In the fourth month, on *bingxu* day (*ganzhi* no. 23), in the ancestral temple, the King exhorted the junior princes of the royal lineage, saying: "In the past, your fathers were able to aid King Wen, whereupon King

---

[1] Legge, *The Chinese Classics*, III, 452 [PRG].

[2] The source text is Liu Shu, *Zizhi tongjian waiji*, 3.13b [PRG]. *Shangshu dazhuan* is ascribed to the early Han period, but later reconstructed from fragments.

[3] Many scholars eager to see the first evidence for a state of China read this as *zhongguo* 中國; see Glossary.

Wen received this [Great Mandate]. When King Wu conquered the great state of Shang, he reverently announced to Heaven: 'Let me dwell in this central territory and from here govern the people.' Hark! While you are still minors lacking in understanding, look to your fathers' scrupulous respect for Heaven. Comprehend my commands and respectfully follow orders! Your sovereign's reverential virtue finds favor with Heaven, which guides me in my dullness." The King's exhortation having finished, He was presented with the thirty strings of cowries used to make this treasured sacrificial vessel for (his father), Lord [X]. It was the King's fifth year.

Further Reading

Jicheng 4261.

Kimbun tsūshaku, 1.1–38.

Mingwen xuan, no. 23.

Behr, *Reimende Bronzeinschriften und die Entstehung der chinesischen Endreimdichtung*, 481–503.

Chen Gongrou, "Xi Zhou jinwen zhong de 'Xinyi,' 'Chengzhou' yu 'wangcheng.'"

He Youqi, "'Hezun' de niandai wenti."

Hsu and Linduff, *Western Zhou Civilization*, 96–99.

Khayutina, "The Story of the He zun: From Political Intermediary to National Treasure."

Itō Michiharu, "Shū Buō to rakuyū—Kason mei to Itsu Shūsho doyū."

Ma Chengyuan, "He zun mingwen chushi."

Ma Chengyuan, "He zun mingwen he Zhou chu shishi."

Tang Lan, *Tang Lan xiansheng jinwen lunji*, 187–93.

Wang Hui, *Shang Zhou jinwen*, 40–44.

Xu Xichen, "'He zun' ming zhong de 'wang' dang zhi Zhou Gong shuo."

Yan Yiping, "He zun yu Zhou chu de niandai."

Yang Kuan, "Shi He zun mingwen jianlun Zhou kaiguo niandai."

Zhang Zhenglang, "He zun mingwen jieshi buyi."

Zhu Fenghan, "'Shao gao,' 'Luo gao,' He zun yu Chengzhou."

DWP

7. KE HE 克盉 AND KE LEI 克罍

The Ke *he* and Ke *lei* were excavated in 1986 from tomb no. 1193 at Huangtupo cemetery 黃土坡, Liulihe 琉璃河, southwest of Beijing 北京. The cemetery and the nearby remains of an ancient city both belong to the polity of Yan 匽 (normally written 燕 in received orthography). Tomb no. 1193 and seven other burials that are identified as the burial of the lords of Yan and their consorts all are located in a cluster of twenty-six at the southern section of the cemetery. Though severely looted, the remaining two hundred artifacts in tomb no. 1193, particularly the inscribed bronze *he* and *lei*, provide invaluable information on the establishment of Yan by a Zhou king in the early Western Zhou period who most scholars assume was King Cheng. The two vessels are now in the collection of the capital Museum in Beijing. The inscription, 43 characters in total, appears on the interior wall of the lid and is repeated on the inside of the collared neck of both vessels. The vessels were probably commissioned by Ke, the Lord of Yan and the owner of tomb no. 1193.

Ke *he* and *lei* are among a few bronzes, such as Mai *fangzun* (no. 14, below), Yi Hou Ze *gui* (no. 9), and Da Yu *ding* (no. 11), whose inscriptions have documented the verbal commission, or *ceming* 冊命 (see glossary), that occurred upon the establishment of regional states by Zhou kings in the early Western Zhou. The investiture ceremonies of the lord and the founding of local states have long been of scholarly interest in the study of Western Zhou history. Passages in ancient texts, including *Zuozhuan* 左傳 (*Zuo Commentary to the Springs and Autumns*)[1] and the songs "Songgao" 嵩高 and "Hanyi" 韓奕 in the *Shijing* 詩經 (*Book of Odes*),[2] record the process of the founding of new states and the king's bestowing land and population to the lord. The investiture ceremony and verbal commission recorded in the inscription on Ke *he* and Ke *lei* are consistent with those historical texts. Further, historical texts, including *Shiji*, help compensate for the scarcity of data regarding the founding of Yan.

The inscription starts with the reciting of the King's verbal commission, "the King said ...," and emphasizes the key contents of the charge that bestows land and population. The land of Yan, along with six groups of people, was given to Ke 克. The inscription documents three important rites performed during the investiture ceremony: ancestral sacrifices to King Wu; the

---

[1] Legge, *The Chinese Classics*, V, 754ff. (Lord Ding, fourth year) [PRG].

[2] *Ibid.*, IV, 535–40 and 546–51, respectively [PRG].

issuing of the charge by the King; and the bestowal of colored soil, which symbolically indicated the giving of the land to the lord. Those rituals are also mentioned in other inscriptions that record the founding of a new state. Unlike later investiture inscriptions on bronze vessels, the inscripion on Ke *he* and Ke *lei* does not mention when and where the ceremony took place.

The inscription reveals the important fact, unrecorded in the historical texts, that Shao Gong 召公, the Grand Protector, to whom Yan was first bestowed, was not able to fulfill his post as the first Lord of Yan because of his vital role at the Zhou court. Instead, Ke, understood by some scholars to be Shao Gong's eldest son, went to Yan to complete the task. The situation is the same as happened in the state of Lu 魯, as recorded in a Lu song in the *Shijing* that mentions that Zhou Gong 周公, although awarded Lu by King Wu, remained at the court to assist the young King Chen. Instead, Boqin 伯禽, the eldest son of Zhou Gong, was sent to Lu.

Transcription

王曰：太保，唯乃明乃鬯，享余乃辟。余大對乃享，令克侯于匽。旃、羌、馬、叡、雩、馭、光（微）。克🔲（來?）匽，入土眔（及）厥有嗣（司）。用作寶尊彝。

Translation

King [Cheng] said: "Grand protector, you performed the *meng* ceremony, dedicating fragrant wine, and made sacrifice to your ruler. I am grateful for your dedication and blissfully respond, and command Ke to be the Lord of Yan, in charge of Qiang, Ma, Cuo, Yu, Yu, and Wei." Ke went to Yan, accepted the land and officials, and therefore made this precious sacrificial vessel.

Further Reading

Barnard, *Inscriptions*, v. 2, 1331–1403.
"Beijing Liulihe 1193 hao damu fajue jianbao."
Chen Ping, "Ke lei, Ke he mingwen jiqi youguan wenti."
Jinwen jinyi leijian, 544–45.
Li Feng, "Ancient Reproduction and Calligraphic Variations."
Wang Hui, *Shang Zhou jinwen*, 47–50.
Yin Weizhang, "Xin chutu de taibao tongqi jiqi xiangguan wenti."
Zhou Baohong, *Jinchu Xi Zhou jinwen jishi*, 1–104.

YS

8. Yan Hou Zhi *ding* 匽侯旨鼎

This bronze *ding*, commissioned by Lord Zhi of Yan 匽侯旨,[1] is now in the Sumitomo Collection 泉屋博古館, Kyoto. Though the vessel can be firmly dated to the early Western Zhou, its shape and ornamentation follow the late Shang style. Its round body is trisected into lobes at the bottom and fully covered with animal-face motifs against square spirals. The inscription of twenty-one characters appears in four columns inside the wall below the rim of the *ding*. Another bronze vessel commissioned by Zhi is a round *ding* bearing the inscription "Yan Hou Zhi cast this sacrificial vessel for his deceased father, Xin" 匽侯旨作父辛尊 (*Jicheng* 2269).

The Yan Hou Zhi *ding* inscription documents an important political practice during Zhou times: the Zhou king's reconfirmation of the lord of a state as the successor to his father and grandfather. In this case, Zhi inherited the position of Lord of Yan. A ceremonial court visit was necessary to reconfirm the passage of authority. Such ritual and political practices are seen in songs such as "Hanyi" and "Jianghan" 江漢 in the *Shijing*.[2] "Jianghan" records the King's *ceming* or verbal commission to Shao Hu 召虎, a descendant of the Duke of Shao, because of his merits in the campaign in the Han 漢 River valley. Shao Hu was awarded jade tokens, gifts, and land, which were "given accordingly as your ancestor received this." In "Hanyi," the Lord of Han was commanded to take over all the wild tribes (of the quarter), just as his ancestor had originally been charged. In addition, two additional tribes and the states of the north were granted to Lord Han. In those ceremonies, land and/or population granted to the ancestors of Shao Hu and Lord Han were reissued to them by the King. Thus, the ritual of the court visit was intended to reconfirm the subordinate roles and reassure the local lords' loyalty to the Zhou king. The same ceremonial commission was probably issued to Zhi of Yan, although it is not recorded in this *ding* inscription.

In the inauguration ceremony, the king often rewarded local lords with gifts symbolizing status and rank such as clothing, chariots, horses, flags, and bows and arrows. In limited cases, the gifts also included land, servants, slaves, and jade pieces. Token gifts, such as the twenty strands of cowry shells mentioned in the inscription of the Yan Hou Zhi *ding*, were also

---

[1] Also written as 燕侯旨, *yan* 燕 being the writing almost universally used in received literature for 匽.

[2] Legge, The Chinese Classics, IV, 546–51 and 551–55, respectively [PRG].

given. Thus, gift giving was a ceremonial gesture in which the king both displayed his generosity and strengthened personal ties to subordinates.

Transcription

匽侯旨初見事于宗周，王賞旨貝二十朋，用作姒寶尊彝。

Translation

> Lord Zhi of Yan paid his first court visit to Ancestral Zhou; the Zhou king bestowed upon Zhi twenty strands of cowry shells. Zhi cast this precious vessel for Si.

Further Reading

Jicheng 4261.

Mingwen xuan, no. 23.

Barnard, *Inscriptions*, v. 3, 1287–1295.
Cao Zhaolan, *Jinwen yu Yin Zhou nüxing wenhua*, 85.
Hamada and Umehara, *Santei Sen'oku seishō*, no. 2.
Jinwen jinyi leijian, 306–7.

YS

9. Yi Hou Ze *gui* 宜侯夨簋

This early Western Zhou inscription appears on a tureen currently in the collection of the National Museum of China 中國國家博物館 in Beijing. Measuring approximately 16 centimeters in height and 23 centimeters in diameter at the mouth, the vessel is of a type thought to have been used to hold sacrificial offerings of grain. The round vessel is supplied with four handles that extend from the sides at evenly-spaced intervals and a high, ring foot with prominent flanges in line with each handle. The decor consists of horned animal heads atop each handle, with interspaced roundel and dragon motifs around the vessel body and foot. The inscription was cast into the inside surface of the vessel floor in twelve columns of irregularly sized and spaced graphs, 126 in total. The shape and decor of the vessel and the calligraphic style of the inscription correspond to the early Western Zhou period, ca. mid-eleventh to mid-tenth century B.C.E.

The vessel was discovered in a cache of eleven bronze vessels excavated in 1954 at Yandunshan 煙墩山, Dantu 丹徒, Jiangsu 江蘇 Province, on the southern bank of the Yangzi River, near the modern city of Nanjing 南京. The inscription records the dedication of the vessel to an ancestor by the sponsor, Ze 夨, in commemoration of a royal decree that he serve as Lord of Yi. Based on the assumption that the location of the vessel's discovery can be indentified with the geographic location Yi 宜 mentioned in the inscription, the vessel's provenance has been used as evidence to suggest that the Western Zhou kings exercised substantial control over territory as far south as the lower Yangzi River Valley, over one thousand kilometers from the Western Zhou capital in the Wei River 渭河 valley.[1] However, the circumstances of the discovery at Dantu show that the vessel's provenance cannot be correlated with the inscriptional text so simplistically. The cache contained vessels of disparate origins dating to as late as the Spring and Autumn period. The complicated process by which the Yi Hou Ze *gui* came to be buried in the cache at Dantu must have stretched over several centuries, and is particularly instructive as a reminder that although the archaeological provenance of an inscribed bronze may tell an interesting story, it is not always directly relevant to the inscriptional text.

---

[1] For a summary of this debate and a study of the geographic extent of the Western Zhou state, see Shaughnessy, "Historical Geography and the Extent of the Earliest chinese Kingdoms," 13–19; also Li, *Landscape and Power in Early China*, 322–24.

Regardless of the dubious relevance of the archaeological provenance, the inscriptional text is significant in its own right as one of a handful of inscriptions commemorating the installation of a regional lord.² The ceremony described in the inscription seems to have taken place in the aftermath of the Zhou conquest of the Shang, sometime after the deaths of King Wu and King Cheng, prior kings mentioned specifically in the inscription. The unnamed reigning king, presumably Cheng's successor, King Kang, is said to have consulted maps of the Zhou attacks on the Shang and the regional states of the east to determine a suitable location for the territory to be granted to Ze. The ceremony itself took place at the chosen site, at the altar of the soil (*she* 社). The command to Ze indicates a reassignment from the territory of Yu 虞, where Ze had apparently succeeded his father as lord, to the territory of Yi. It was through aristocratic lords such as Ze that the Zhou king exercised authority in newly conquered territories in the east. The inscription implies that such polities were created on a strategic basis, though it does not make clear the particular circumstances that governed the replacement of Ze in Yi. The status of Yi before Ze's installation is not clear either. The inscription clearly implies the preexistence of a settlement at Yi, including an altar of the soil, but the ceremony may well have resulted in the creation of a new political entity, the regional polity of Yi under the hereditary leadership of Ze and the patriline that would descended from him in future generations.

The creation of such a state involved not only a grant of land, but also ritual objects and groups of people. The objects probably acted as tokens of the status conferred on Ze by the Zhou king and included ritual paraphernalia related to ancestral sacrifice and the military, indicating the importance of these two institutions for the identity of aristocratic lineages and their relationship to the Zhou royal lineage.³ The list of people assigned to the new polity clearly implies a variety of "degrees of dependency and privilege" within Zhou society.⁴ The list seems to include both local people as well as those relocated from other parts of the Zhou kingdom. The ability to dispatch such people, including those of high social status—Ze himself had formerly been lord at Yu—was a key element in the Zhou

---

² For another example, see Ke *lei* inscription, no. 7, above.
³ See Kane, "Aspects of Western Zhou Appointment inscriptions."
⁴ This useful phrase is borrowed from Keightley, "The Shang: China's First Historical Dynas-

king's authority.

Although it is not listed among the royal gifts, we might also consider the lineage name (*shi* 氏) within the act of royal prestation. The formation of a new state implied the creation of a new lineage and the adoption of a lineage name by the designated ruler and his descendants. During the Western Zhou, the name of a state and its ruling aristocratic lineage were generally identical. In the inscription of the Yi Hou Ze *gui*, we see this process reflected in the name change undertaken by Ze, who is referred to as the Lord of Yu 虞侯 in the first part of the inscription but as Lord of Yi 宜侯 at the end, reflecting his new status.[5] This phenomenon is a strong indication that the aristocratic lineages so prominent in bronze inscriptions, though defined by principles of descent, were fundamentally political institutions parallel to the Zhou royal lineage rather than families or kinship groups per se.

Transcription

唯四月，辰在丁未。王省武王、成王伐商圖，征（延）省東或（國）圖。王立（位）于宜，入土（社），南卿（嚮）。王令（命）虞侯夨曰：遷侯于宜。賜鬯[6] 酉一卣、商瓚一[□]、彤弓一、彤矢百、旅（盧）弓十、旅（盧）矢千。賜土，厥川（甽）三百[□]，厥[□]百又廿，厥宅邑卅又五，厥[□]百又卌。賜在宜王人[□]又七里[7]。賜奠七伯，厥盧（虜）[□]又五十夫。賜宜庶人六百又[□]六夫。宜侯夨揚王休，作虞公父丁尊彝。

---

ty," 285–86, but such a terminological borrowing is not meant to imply any presumed continuity in the particular socio-economic constitution of Shang and Zhou society.

[5] Note that Ze's ancestor, his deceased father, is still referred to as Lord of Yu 虞公. It is not clear from this inscription whether or not a different descendant of Father Ding 父丁 may have inherited the position of Lord of Yu after Ze's transfer.

[6] The pronunciation and precise meaning of the word here is unclear; it is likely that it indicates a type of grain used to make ale. *Jicheng* suggests to read this as *qin* 㲎, a type of fermented soybean.

[7] The transcription *li* 里 follows Li Xueqin, "Yi Hou Ze gui yu Wu guo." Although transcribed by others as *xing* 生 (姓), the graph in question, which is not clear in the rubbing, seems to have a horizontal stroke at the top that is not expected in 生. Furthermore, while *xing* is used in the collective noun *bai xing* 百姓, the present usage as a counting unit for groups of people would be unprecedented in the corpus of Western Zhou inscriptions.

Translation

It was the fourth month, and the *chen*[8] was at *dingwei* (*ganzhi* no. 44). The King inspected the map of King Wu's and King Cheng's attack on the Shang and thereupon inspected the map of the eastern regions (states?). The King stationed himself in Yi, entering the altar of the soil and facing south. The King commanded Ze, Lord of Yu, saying: "Migrate and serve as lord at Yi. I award you one pitcher of fragrant ale; one Shang ladle, one red bow and one hundred red arrows, ten black bows and one thousand black arrows. I award land, with its acreage of three hundred ..., its ... one hundred and twenty, its residential settlements thirty-five, and its ... one hundred and forty.[9] I award ... -seven wards of the King's people in Yi. I award you seven relocated elders with their dependents of ... and fifty men.[10] I award commoners of Yi, six-hundred and ... -six men. Ze, Lord of Yi, extols the King's beneficence and makes for Father Ding, Lord of Yu, this sacrificial vessel."

Further Reading

Jicheng 4320.

Kimbun tsūshaku 10.529–60.

Mingwen xuan, no. 57.

Barnard, "A recently Excavated inscribed Bronze of Western Zhou Date."

Huang Shengzhang, "Tongqi mingwen Yi Yu Ze de diwang jiqi yu Wuguo de guanxi."

"Jiangsu Dantu xian Yandunshan chutu de gudai qingtongqi."

Lau, *Quellenstudien zur Landvergabe und Bodenübertragung in der westlichen Zhou-Dynastie*, 97–104.

Li Xueqin, "Yi Hou Ze gui de ren yu di."

Li Xueqin, "Yi Hou Ze gui yu Wuguo."

---

[8] See Glossary.

[9] A rather large portion of the inscription is damaged, thus many graphs are unreadable, as indicated by ellipses.

[10] Whereas most other commentators read the graph 奠 as a loan for Zheng 鄭, the reading here follows Qiu Xigui 裘錫圭, who takes it as *dian* 奠, "to settle". See Qiu Xigui, "shuo 'Puyong'"; see also Qiu Xigui, "Shuo Yinxu buci de 'dian.'"

Shaughnessy, "Historical Geography and the Extent of the Earliest Chinese Kingdoms," 13–19.

Tang Lan, "Yi Hou Ze kaoshi."

Wang Hui, *Shang Zhou jinwen*, 55–59.

Wang Wenxuan, "Yi Hou Ze gui ji qi xiangguan wenti yanjiu zongshu."

Zhou Baohong, *Xi Zhou qingtong zhong qi mingwen jishi*.

DMS

10. Jing Hou gui 井侯簋

Most likely discovered circa 1921 near Luoyang and transported to Europe by a private collector, this vessel is currently held in the British Museum, London. Its title may also be read Xing Hou gui 邢侯簋, and it has been frequently published by other names, such as Zhou Gong gui 周公簋 and rong gui 榮簋.

The Jing Hou gui is most commonly dated to the reign of King Kang or late in the reign of King Cheng. The vessel was cast for the newly installed Marquis of Jing, a region in contemporary Hebei province that is regularly rendered as Xing 邢 in transmitted texts, and associated with the modern region of Xingtai 邢台, about 100 km north of the last Shang capital. The rulers of Jing belonged to a branch of the lineage of Zhou Gong, as indicated by the vessel dedication. This inscription appears to record the transfer of the lineage's governing authority to a new region, a phenomenon that was very common during the Western Zhou era.[1]

The inscription includes a number of disputed readings. Perhaps the most significant concerns the phrase *shangxia di* 上下帝, inscribed as a single graph unit, rendered below as "the deities above and below," in which sense it would denote the world of spirits imagined as a physical or functional hierarchy. Some commentators would break the sentence before the term *di* in order to stress that it is Heaven alone who determines the length of the Zhou mandate to rule.

Transcription

唯三月，王令榮眔內史曰：薑井侯服。賜臣三品：州人、重人、庸（鄘）人。拜稽首魯天子，受厥瀕福；克奔走上下帝無終令（命）于有周。追考（孝），對不敢墬（墜），邵（紹）朕福盟，朕（畯）臣天子。用典王令，作周公彝。

---

[1] A list of such instances is discussed in Hsu and Linduff, *Western Chou Civilization*, 158–63, who, like many others, infer that the original location of Jing was in the Wei River valley capital area, and a Jing in that region is mentioned in other inscriptions (e.g., no. 60, below). A contemporary vessel, the Zuoce Mai *fangzun* (no. 14, below), inscribed by a subordinate of the Jing Hou, narrates in interesting detail the ceremony of appointment at the capital and the ritual and social interactions between the King and the marquis upon that occasion. There are, however, scholars who hold that the inscription implies no transfer of territorial authority, but rather an initial grant of land in the modern Xingtai region.

Translation

In the third month, the King ordered Rong and the Inner Scribe, saying, "Allot to Xing Hou robes of office. Give him ministers of three categories: men of Zhou, men of Zhong, and men of Yong."

Bowing prostrate before the gracious Son of Heaven, I received his great gift. May I serve well the deities above and below, eternally under the mandate of the Zhou. In pursuance of filiality, in response [to the command] I dare not fail, continuing our blessed sacrifices, ministering steadfastly to the Son of Heaven. To record the orders of the King, I cast this vessel for Zhou Gong.

Further Reading

Jicheng 4241.
Kimbun tsūshaku 11.591–607.
Mingwen xuan, no. 66.

Wang Hui, *Shang Zhou jinwen*, 59–63.
Yang Wenshan, "Xi Zhou qingtongqi Xing Hou gui tongshi."
Yu Xingwu, "Jing Hou gui kaoshi."

RE

11. Da Yu ding 大盂鼎

According to Qing-dynasty records, the large three-legged round-bellied Cauldron of Yu (called Da Yu *ding*, or the Greater Cauldron of Yu, so as to distinguish it from a smaller one by the same sponsor) was discovered in a mud bank in Licun 禮村, Meixian 眉縣, near Qi Mountain in Shaanxi Province, possibly as early as 1821. Through a process of appropriation and barter it went therough the hands of various collectors locally and in Beijing. During the 1880s, two other cauldrons originating from the same or a nearby site, a smaller one belonging to Yu (called Xiao Yu *ding* 小盂鼎), and the other, the Da Ke *ding* (no. 46, below), joined the Da Yu *ding* in a collection in Xi'an. The Pan 潘 family (originally from Suzhou 蘇州 but living in Beijing) acquired the two "greater" cauldrons: the Greater cauldron of Yu by 1874 and the Greater cauldron of Ke by 1890. The Pan family kept the two vessels, by then considered valuable national treasures, hidden in suzhou after the fall of the Qing in 1911. Although the Pan ancestral home was repeatedly plundered, the two cauldrons survived the war buried in their ancestral shrine in a secret niche called "The Three Heads." in 1951, the Pan family handed them over to the Shanghai 上海 government, which put them in the Shanghai Museum before their eventual removal to what is now the national Museum of China in Beijing. Rubbings of both the Da Yu *ding* and Xiao Yu *ding* inscriptions have been preserved, but the latter, while the longer of the two, is only partially decipherable. It was also written in a much thinner script. A rubbing of the Da Yu *ding* was already circulating by the mid-1870s.

The site of this vessel's origin, Meixian, has produced numerous caches of inscribed and large bronze vessels of later dates, all associated with families living in the Zhou heartland, such as the Yu *ding* 旟鼎 (no. 16, below), Li 盨 vessels (no. 26), and the Shan family Qiu 逑 vessels (no. 63). Scholars date the Greater and Lesser Yu vessels to the early Western Zhou period, probably to the King Kang reign towards the beginning of the tenth century B.C.E. The Greater Yu inscription (on the Da Yu *ding*), cast in the twenty-third year of King Kang, documents the King's charge that Yu ascend to his ancestor's position. The Lesser Yu inscription, cast two years later, documents the military ritual performed after a huge and successful military campaign by Yu and Rong (also mentioned in the Greater Yu inscription). The ritual involved alcohol, animal and human sacrifices, a parade of captives, guests, officers and military personnel, as well as awards of weapons for Yu.

The award ceremony in the Greater Yu inscription begins with a typical testimony of the Zhou king to uphold the Mandate of Heaven inherited from the Zhou founders, Kings Wen and Wu; this was a lineage narrative that recorded as well in transmitted texts, such as the *Shangshu*. Other key aspects of Zhou lineage narrative alluded to in this inscription include the "creation of the state" (*zuobang* 作邦) by King Wen after the Shang lost Heaven's approval through excessive drinking. Heaven protected "the boy" (*zi* 子, a reference to King Wu of Zhou when he was young), and King Wen when he conquered the Shang, thereby "spreading [the mandate, that is, the 'law of Unifying Power (*de* 德)'] to the Four Regions." The present king may also have been alluding to his own protection and duties as king to maintain the Zhou state. Both the tales of the Yin loss due to excessive drinking and the protection of a future Zhou leader by Heaven are found in later texts, such as the *Shangshu* and the *Shijing*.

The inscription proceeds to document the king's award to Yu, who was an elder and possibly his teacher, for his loyalty as well as his military and ritual aid in the role of Grand subduer (*dafu* 大服).[1] The specific occasion for the award was the date when Yu ascended to the position of his ancestor, Patriarch Nan 南公. This position came with a particular flag, ritual costume, special alcoholic brews, and vessels, as well as a chariot with one or more horses. Numerous peoples and their lands also came under his jurisdiction. Many historians take this as evidence for an early Zhou-period state made up of land grants awarded to relatives and situated around Zongzhou 宗周 "Ancestral Zhou" as a protective "fence," as described in the *Zuozhuan* and *Shiji*. This assumption has led many scholars to read the ancestor's name Nan as a mistake for Dan, i.e. named Dan Ji 聃季, mentioned in the later accounts as a son of King Wen.

The lines include a fair amount of direct and indirect rhyming, suggesting that perhaps music was a part of the ceremony involved in the creation of many parts of this inscription. Especially obvious are the words with velar nasal finals, *-ŋ .

---

[1] It is possible to read this as simply his "great service" and not as a title. However, it appears in the sense of a prestigious title with military associations in another early inscription, the Ban gui (*Jicheng* 4341, no. 21, below).

Transcription

唯九月，王在宗周令盂。王若（諾）曰：盂，丕顯玟王（文王），受天有大令。在珷（武）王嗣玟（文）作邦，闢厥匿（慝），匍（敷）有四方，畯正厥民。在于御事，䖒，酉（酒）無敢酖，有髭（祡）蒸祀無敢醻。古（故）天異（翼）臨子，灋保先王，[敷]有四方。我聞殷述（墜）令，唯殷邊侯田（甸）雩（越）² 殷正百辟，率肄（肆）于酉（酒），古（故）喪師。巳，汝妹（昧）辰（晨）又（有）大服。余唯即朕小學，汝勿逸余乃辟一人。

今我唯即井（型）㐭（稟）于玟王正德，若玟王令二、三正（征）。今余唯令汝盂召（詔）榮敬雝德巠（經），敏朝夕入讕（諫），享奔走，畏天畏（威）。

王曰：雩？，令汝盂井（型）乃嗣祖南公。

王曰：盂，迺召（詔）夾死（尸）司戎，敏勅（諫？）罰訟，夙夕召我一人烝四方，雩（越）我其遹省先王受民受疆土。賜汝鬯一卣、冂衣、市舄、車馬。賜乃祖南公旂，用狩。賜汝邦司四白（伯），人鬲自馭至于庶人六百又五十又九夫。賜尸（夷）司王臣十又三白（伯），人鬲千又五十夫，亟（極？）䍩（䍰？遷？）自厥土。

王曰：盂，若敬乃正，勿灋（廢）朕令。

盂用對王休，用作祖南公寶鼎。唯王廿又三祀。

Translation

It was the ninth month, when the King was in Zongzhou (Ancestral Zhou), that he commanded Yu.

The King, agreeing [to Yu's promotion],³ spoke: "Yu, the Greatly Manifest King Wen received Heaven's Aid and the Great Mandate. When King Wu succeeded King Wen and created the state, he cleared the land of those noxious presences and spread [the mandate] throughout the Four Regions, correcting their peo-

---

² *Yu* 雩 is read as either locative *yu* 于 (*ɢʷa) or *yue* 越 (*ɢʷat), "and then," when it appears at the beginning of a phrase.

³ See Glossary. Following Lothar von Falkenhausen in the sense of "to agree" (*nuo* 諾), the King agrees to some aspect of the larger ceremony (outside the purview of the individual

ples. Among those in his militia vanguard,[4] when presenting the alcoholic brews [to the spirits], no one dared get drunk; and, when presenting the burnt and grain offerings in sacrifice [to Kings Wen and Wu], no one dared to offer toasts. For this reason, Heaven sheltered and watched over the boy (King Wu) and provided a model of behavior and protection for the Former King so that he could spread the mandate throughout the Four Regions. I have heard that when Yin let the Mandate fall, it was a case of losing the army because Yin's border lords and Yin's correctors, amounting to one hundred leaders, followed each other in line up to the alcohol!

"Ah! You are active in the position of Grand subduer all day.

"As for me, when it was the case of my being a young acolyte, you would not cut me—your only ruler—down. Now I[5] have already reached the stage when I have modeled myself upon and stored up the corrective *de* of King Wen. And, just like King Wen, I am commanding second and third military attacks.

"Now I command you, Yu, to join Zhao and Rong in respectfully enacting [the Zhou law of] unifying *de*: energetically enter the court to advise me at any point in the day, when presenting the memorial feasts, scurry around to express fear of Heaven's awesomeness."

The King said: "So I charge you, Yu, to model yourself upon your ancestor patriarch nan whom you have succeeded."

The King said: "Yu! When it comes to guiding and aiding me, take over the supervision[6] of warfare and energetically recom-

---

inscribed document). See Falkenhausen, "The Inscribed Bronzes from Yangjiacun" and "Royal Audience and its Reflections."

[4] Literally, "the service for driving (out the enemy)." For an investigation into the Shang phrase *yu fang* 御方 with the meaning of attacking outlying peoples, see Xia Hanyi, "Shi 'yu fang.'"

[5] I take the shift between the two first-person pronouns, *wo* 我 and *yu* 余, to indicate a shift between the King's identity as a representative of the royal lineage versus a reference to himself as a person.

[6] *Si* 死: death; used as a loanword in certain word combinations. The word represented by the graph *si* 死 *sij?* in the verb *sisi* 死司 *sij?* s-lǝj or noun *sishi* 死事 *sij?* m-s-rǝ? in middle and late Western Zhou appointment inscriptions seems to function like *shi* 尸 *lǝj, found in similar combinations, with the meaning of "to take on responsibilities" or "the responsibilities taken on."

mend punishments and forward pleas [for justice]; from dawn to dusk, help me, the One Man, present grain sacrifices to the Four Direcions so that I can make an inspection trip of the peoples and lands bequeathed by the Former Kings.

"I award you with a vessel of sacrificial millet ale, a head-cloth and a cloak, knee-covers[7] and slippers, and a chariot with horses.

"I award you the flag of your Ancestor Patriarch Nan to use in hunting.

"I award you the elders of four states as supervisors and six hundred and fifty-nine slaves ranging from charioteers to common men.

"I award you the management of thirteen royal servants, a thousand and fifty slaves moved (?) from their land."[8]

The King said: "Yu! You should act respectfully in your corrective military campaigns and not discard my charge!"

Yu took this opportunity to respond to the King's gifts and used [the opportunity] to make a treasured cauldron for Ancestor Nan Gong.

It was the time of the twenty-third annual sacrifice performed by the King.

Further Reading

Jicheng 4241.

Mingwen xuan, no. 66.

Behr, *Reimende Bronzeinschriften und die Entstehung der chinesischen Endreimdichtung,* 152–61.

Jinwen jinyi leijian, 458–62.

Li, *Bureaucracy and the State in Early China,* 104–5.

Li, *Landscape and Power in Early China,* 127–28.

Li Pingxin, "'Da Yu ding ming' 'nü me chen you da fu' jie."

Li Xueqin, "Da Yu ding xinlun."

Liu Xiang, et al., *Shang Zhou guwenzi duben,* 77–85.

---

[7] A kind of apron that protected the knees when kneeling, see Serruys, "Fang Yen IV, 5 and 31. Knee Covers."

[8] Or possibly Yu is to fortify their old lands for his own use.

Wang Hui, *Shang Zhou jinwen*, 63–71.

Zhang Changshou and Wen Guang, "Wen You xiansheng Luozhaotang cang Da Yu ding moben ba."

Zhou Baohong, *Xi Zhou qingtong zhong qi mingwen jishi*, 203–350.

CAC

12. Shenzi Ta guigai 沈子它簋蓋

A round vessel for food service dated to the early Western Zhou period, possibly from the Luoyang area in Henan, was acquired first by Liu Tizhi 劉體智 (1879–1962), who published a rubbing in 1936, and then by the Royal Museum of Art in Belgium. It is presently stored in the Academica Sinica Fu Sinian Library in Taiwan. Only the inscribed lid survives.

The inscription documents a speech by a man named Ta 它 (often read as Tuo 佗)[1] to his ancestors. Ta was the heir of a place called Shen[2], which was connected to the main lineage shrine for Zhou Gong, a position held by the uncle of King Cheng, the most famous Zhou Gong. Ta clearly belonged to a lineage of the Zhou royal family. It was Ta's duty to perform the annual ancestral sacrifices (called *di* 禘 in later texts) to the ancestors. By the Han period, this ceremony involved moving the ancestors' tablets in the shrine to reflect the changed ranks of the spirits in Heaven after mourning for the newly deceased was complete—a process that took about twenty-seven months.[3] The newly deceased in this case was Ta's father, the former patriarch, whose position Ta was inheriting and who, as a new ancestor, was a particularly dangerous spirit. Therefore Ta needed not only to perform a variety of food and alcohol services for all the ancestors going back to the founder, but also to plead for good will from his deceased father. Another occasion for such sacrifices would be after a new king took up the throne, prompting a renewal of the ranks and offices initiated by former kings.

Not much is known about the three interconnected sacrifices mentioned in this inscription: the *wan* 綩, *yin* 殷, and *zai* 載. The *wan* sacrifice is mentioned on inscriptions dating from the late Shang through early Western Zhou periods and was clearly a grand lineage feast, one in which this tureen would have been used and which involved religious instructions for the lineage youth of a certain rank. The *yin* sacrifice may have involved

---

[1] Tang Lan, *Xi Zhou qingtongqi mingwen fendai shi zheng*, 325–26, read it as Ye 也, noting that the name was unusual and the inscription seemed to include dialect words.

[2] According to Dong Shan, "Shi Xi Zhou jinwen de 'chenzi' he *Yi Zhou shu Huang men* de 'chenren,'" the phrase *shenzi* 沈子 does not refer to Shen, but should be construed as *chenzi* 訦子, i.e. "sincere son," a humble term of self-reference [PRG].

[3] For a discussion of the *di* ritual variations, see Cook, "Ancestor Worship during the Eastern Zhou," 250, 262–71.

traveling or circumambulation, or perhaps the word read as *yin* simply meant "great." The *zai* sacrifice may have been a portion of the ancestor worship ritual that incorporated cooked food.

Transcription

它曰：拜稽首，敢握卲（昭）告，朕吾考（胡耇？）令乃䲹（嬗）沈子作絤于周公宗，陟二公，不敢不絤。休同公，克成妥吾考以于顯顯受（授）令。

烏虖，唯考肇念自先王先公，迺妹克衣（殷）告烈成工（功）。

嘖，吾考克淵（蘊）⁴克，乃沈子其顧懷多公能福。

烏虖，乃沈子妹克蔑見猒（厭）于公休。

沈子肇畢狃賈嗇。作茲簋，用載饗己公，用格多公，其乳（賜）褱乃沈子它惟福，用永靈令，用妥公惟壽，它用懷鼇我多弟子、我孫，克又（有）井（型）學懿父迺是子。

Translation

> Ta said: "Bowing and knocking my head, holding up my palms, I dare to summon and announce: 'My Aged one (i.e., founder ancestor) commands that I, your replacement, Shenzi, perform a *wan* sacrificial feast at the Patriarch of Zhou main ancestral shrine to promote the Two Patriarchs. I do not dare not to present the *wan* feast.' Presenting gifts to Patriarch Tong, I am able to pacify the Aged One so that he becomes manifest and, being manifest, gives out the command.

---

⁴ The graph *yuan* 淵 (*ʔʷˤin) appears only in one other Western Zhou period inscription, the Shi Qiang *pan* (see below no.28, where it can be translated in the sense of "deep" or "profound"). Ma Chengyuan *et al.*, *Shang Zhou qingtong qi mingwen xuan*, Vol. 3, 58, n.7, suggest it is a loan for *wen* 溫 (*ʔˤun), meaning *wenke* 溫克, an expression found in the *Shijing* (Legge, The *Chinese Classics*, IV, 334) referring to "mild and restrained" behavior after drinking (obviously contrasting the Zhou with the raucous Shang). Although a sacrificial context would certainly make sense, there is no specific mention of alcohol in this inscription, so I have tentatively read it as a loan for *yun* 蘊 (*ʔun?) "reeds, gathered together" [CAC]. Both *yun* and *yuan* shared the meaning of "to gather" (e.g., reeds or fish in a deep pond). *Yuan* is found in this sense in the version of the conquest tale preserved in the "Wu cheng" chapter of the *Shangshu*: Legge, *The Chinese Classics*, III, 313 [PRG].

"Ah! It was my Deceased Father who initially held [the ancestors] in his thoughts, beginning with the Former Kings and the Former patriarchs, and so at dusk was able to perform the Yin sacrifice and announced the blazing accomplished deed.

"Oh! Aged One, you were able to gather for the conquest so that I, your Shenzi, would look back upon and hold dear the Many Patriarchs who brought good fortune.

"Ah! I, your Shenzi, at dusk give out awards, hold audience, and fill the requirements for the Patriarch's grace.

"I, Shenzi, have from early on stored up a wealth of grain and small animals. I make this tureen in order to present the *zai* sacrificial feast to patriarch Ji and to promote the Many Patriarchs [in their ranks in Heaven] so that they will award me, your Shenzi Ta, by cloaking me with good fortune. I will thereby gain eternal and numinous long-life, and, pacifying the spirit of the patriarch, will be long-lived. I, Ta, shall use [this vessel] to receive their gifts and so give our many younger brothers and sons and our grandsons the opportunity to be able to model themselves upon and learn from the refined fathers, and thus behave as proper sons."

Further Reading

Jicheng 4330.

Mingwen xuan, no. 81.

Jinwen jinyi leijian, 244–46.

Dong Shan, "Shi Xi Zhou jinwen de 'chenzi' he *Yi Zhou shu Huang men* de 'chenren.'"

Liu Yu, *Jinwen lunji*, 116, 440–44.

Tang Lan, *Xi Zhou qingtongqi mingwen fendai shi zheng*, 320–26.

CAC

13. GENG YING *YOU* 庚嬴卣 AND GENG YING *DING* 庚嬴鼎

Geng Ying commissioned a wine flask decorated with bird ornaments on its body and lid (presently in the Harvard University Art Museum, formerly the Grenville L. Winthrop collection) and a now-lost cauldron for serving sacrificial meat. In the name Geng Ying, Ying represents a surname, whereas Geng may correspond to this person's place of origin. Only names of women include surnames. The dedication to a female ancestor in the flask's inscription supports the inference that Geng Ying was female. On the basis of the date recorded on the cauldron and of the appearance of the flask,[1] the two vessels can be dated to the reign of King Mu.

Geng Ying's inscriptions attest to a unique case in which a female recipient was twice granted a royal ritual of "praising merit" (*mieli* 蔑曆) and an award of sacrificial utensils and cowries. Moreover, they reflect the bilateral exchange of visits between a member of an aristocratic lineage and the Zhou king. Both indicate that Geng Ying enjoyed an especially privileged relationship with the Zhou king. According to later texts, the Ying 嬴 clan of Qin 秦 were named after an ancient residence of Qin's. According to traditional texts, Qin rose to power during the reign of King Ping of Zhou, who raised its leader to the status of regional lord (*zhuhou* 諸侯) and appointed him to rule over the former royal metropolitan area, in present-day Shaanxi Province. Five centuries later, Qin founded the first Chinese empire (221 B.C.E.). With regard to the earlier history of the Ying clan, literary sources are terse, stating only that it already existed before the beginning of the Western Zhou period.[2] Geng Ying's inscriptions demonstrate that the Ying clan was already prominent in the tenth century B.C.E.

Geng appears in one of the inscriptions commissioned by King Zhao's warlord Nangong Zhong 南宮中.[3] Possibly, Geng was his place of residence. Here, the King "inspected the lineage of the Duke," i.e. of Nangong, and "formed a brigade," possibly in order to join the King's southern campaign. Several bronzes commissioned by Nangong Zhong and discovered in 1118 near Anzhou 安州, in present-day Hubei 湖北 province, suggest

---

[1] Such bird ornaments became popular during the second half of the tenth century B.C.E. (cf. Rawson, *Western Zhou Ritual Bronzes from the Arthur M. Sackler Collections*, II, 428–29).

[2] For example, *Shiji* 5.173.

[3] Zhong *zhi* 中觶 (*Jicheng* 6514). For another inscription by Nangong Zhong, see the Zhong *xian* 中甗 (no. 18, below).

that he never returned. To judge from the relative chronology of the inscriptions, Geng Ying could be Nangong's widow or daughter. By performing the *mieli* ritual, the King may have praised not only her personal merits, but also those of her husband or father.

Transcription (Geng Ying you)

唯王十月，既望，辰在己丑，王格于庚嬴宮。王蔑庚嬴曆。賜貝十朋又丹一柹。

庚嬴對揚王休。用乍厥文姑寶尊彝。其子子孫孫。萬年永寶用。

Translation

It was in the tenth month of the King, *jiwang*; the *chen* was in *yichou* day (*ganzhi* no. 26). The King entered the palace of Lady Ying of Geng. The King praised the merits of Lady Ying of Geng. He offered ten bundles of cowries and one receptacle of cinnabar.[4]

Lady Ying of Geng extolled in response the King's beneficence. She used this occasion to make the treasured venerated offering vessel for her cultivated aunt. May her sons and grandsons eternally use it as a treasure for ten thousand years.

Transcription (Geng Ying ding)

唯廿又二年，四月既壐望己酉，王客琱（？）宮，衣（卒）事。

丁巳，王蔑庚嬴曆，賜祼、璋、貝十朋。對王休，用乍寶貞（鼎）。

Translation

It was the twenty-second year, the fourth month, *jiwang*, on *jiyou* day (*ganzhi* no. 46). The King visited the Zhou (?) palace; he finished the service.

On *dingsi* day (*ganzhi* no. 54), the King praised the merits of Lady Ying of Geng. He offered a libation vessel or ladle, a jade

---

[4] Various authors suggest different modern equivalents of the character designating the receptacle for cinnabar sand, but none of these suggestions is fully convincing. Possibly, this was a tube made of bamboo (cf. *Mingwen xuan*, p. 37).

scepter, and ten bundles of cowry-shells. Lady Ying responded to the King's beneficence. She used this occasion to make this treasured tripod.

Further Reading

Jicheng 4330.

Mingwen xuan, no. 81.

Cao Zhaolan, *Jinwen yu Yin Zhou nüxing wenhua*, 78–82.

Li, *Landscape and Power*, 328–29.

Rawson, *Western Zhou Ritual Bronzes from the Arthur M. Sackler Collections*, II, 428–29, fig. 53.7.

Wang Hui, *Shang Zhou Jinwen*, 71–73.

MKh

14. Zuoce Mai *fangzun* 作冊麥方尊

The Zuoce Mai *fangzun* (a square alcohol container) first made its appearance in a catalogue of the Qing imperial collections compiled in 1755. There it is cited as Xing Hou *zun* 邢侯尊 because the maker, Mai, served the ruler of the state of Xing as Court Recorder (*zuoce* 作冊, lit. "maker of documents"). The wine beaker belongs to a group of four different companion pieces that Mai cast in the same year. The others found their way into a private collection in Japan, but the Mai *zun* disappeared, and all that survives is a Qing dynasty rubbing of the 153-character inscription. Internal evidence suggests that the vessel was cast in the early Western Zhou, either late in the reign of King Cheng or early in the reign of King Kang 康王. In 1978, a hoard of bronzes of similar date cast by the Lord of Xing 邢侯 was unearthed near Xingtai in southern Hebei 河北 province, long thought to be the location of the ancient state of Xing. This places the vassal state of Xing about midway between the Zhou secondary capital at Chengzhou (Luoyang) and the far northeastern state of Yan.

The Mai *fangzun* is historically important for two reasons. First, it supplies crucial details concerning the *da feng* or Great Feng sacrifice (already mentioned in the Tian Wang *gui* and He *zun*, nos. 5 & 6, above) that corroborate later textual traditions; and second, it offers an insight into the formal conduct of political and ritual affairs involving the royal center and the vassal states. It was evidently a principal purpose of the Great *Feng* rite to reinforce or reconfirm the bonds of fealty between the Zhou king and the vassal states, many of which were the domains of royal relatives. In this instance, we have a record of the investiture by King Cheng of one of the Duke of Zhou's six sons in the territory of Xing.[1] In addition to reporting the investiture and the extraordinarily prestigious gifts and privileges bestowed on the new Lord of Xing (including the use of the King's own chariot), the inscription mentions the ritual activities which the Great *Feng* ceremony comprised. These include boating on the royal barge in the circular lake called *biyong* 璧雍, sacrificial rites, and ritualized archery practice in which the King felled a wild goose, after which the new lord was invited into the King's personal quarters, a signal honor. All of this occurred at a place called Pangjing 蒡京, the location of the ritual complex where

---

[1] See *Zuozhuan*, Lord Xi 24th year (Legge, *The Chinese Classics*, V, 192), for the states apportioned to the royal relatives.

the most important state rites were conducted, possibly situated somewhere between the pre-dynastic capitals of Feng and Hao in the Wei River valley and Chengzhou in the east. At the center of the complex, within the *biyong*, was the Chamber of Heaven (*tianshi* 天室), already encountered in the Tian Wang *gui* and He *zun* (nos. 5 & 6), where sacrifices dedicated to the royal ancestors in company with *shangdi* (or *tian*) were held, and which also contained the "numinous terrace" (*lingtai* 靈台) for watching the skies. These sacred precincts display all the attributes of the Zhou "Hall of Light" (*mingtang* 明堂) described in classical sources and match closely the layout of the one *mingtang* so far discovered, built near Chang'an 長安 at the command of Wang Mang 王莽 (45 B.C.E.-23 C.E.).[2]

Transcription

王令辟（君）井（邢）侯出坯侯于井（邢）。雩若二月侯見于宗周，亡尤。會王客（格）蓉京彤祀。雩若翌日在璧灘，王乘于舟，為大豐。王射大鴻，擒。侯乘于赤旂舟，從。死（尸）咸。之日，王以侯內（入）于寢，侯賜玄琱戈。雩王在岸，已夕，侯賜諸?祼臣二百家。劑（齎）用王乘車馬、金勒、冕（?）、衣、巿、舄。

唯歸，揚天子休，告亡尤，用龔（恭）義（儀）寧侯，顯孝于井（邢）侯。

作冊麥易金于辟（君）侯，麥揚，用作寶尊彝，用作贊侯逆受揚明令。

唯天子休于麥辟侯之年鑄，孫孫子子其永亡終終用受德，綏多友，享旋徒（走）令。

Translation

The King commanded my ruler, the Lord of Xing, to depart from Pi to serve as Lord of Xing. Coming to the second month, the Lord of Xing was received by the King in Zongzhou, without mishap. In company with the King he went to Pangjing to perform a *yong*-libation. The next day, on the *biyong* lake, the King boarded the royal barge and performed the Great *Feng* rite. The

[2] Pankenier, *Astrology and Cosmology in Early China*, 343ff.

King shot at a big wild goose, felling it. The Lord rode in a barge with red banners following the King. With that, [the ceremony] was completed. That day, the King took the Lord into his private quarters and bestowed on the Lord a dagger-axe with carved black shaft. When the King was on the shore [of the *biyong*] following the evening audience, he presented the Lord with two hundred households of (vanguard? libationers?) as servitors. The King granted him the use of the royal chariot and horses, metal bridles, [ceremonial] cap, jacket, kneepads, and shoes.

Upon returning, the Lord extolled the munificence of the Son of Heaven, reporting to his ancestors that the visit concluded without mishap, and that by showing a respectful demeanor, he appeased the Lord(s?) and showed deference to the Lord of Xing.

I, Court Recorder Mai, was awarded bronze by my ruler, the Lord, whom I extol by using it to make this precious sacrificial vessel, and use to assist in the Lord's receiving and bestowing, so as to exalt his brilliant commands.

It was in the year when the Son of Heaven's munificence was bestowed upon Mai's ruler, my Lord, that this vessel was cast. May my sons and grandsons forever use it to receive the virtuous, give comfort to many friends, and present offerings, while busily carrying out their lord's orders.

Further Reading

Jicheng 6015.

Kimbun tsūshaku, 11.628–46.

Mingwen xuan, no. 67.

Guo Moruo, *Liang Zhou jinwen ci daxi tulu kaoshi*, 3.40a–42a.

Lau, *Quellenstudien zur Landvergabe und Bodenübertragung in der westlichen Zhou-Dynastie*, 105–19.

Li, *Bureaucracy and the State in Early China*.

Shaughnessy, "Historical Geography and the Extent of the Earliest Chinese Kingdoms."

Wang Hui, *Shang Zhou jinwen*, 73–78.

Yang Wenshan, "Qingtongqi 'Mai zun' yu Xingguo shifeng."

DWP

15. Zuoce Ling fangyi 作冊令方彞

This early Western Zhou inscription appears on a square wine-casket currently in the collection of the Freer Gallery of Art, Smithsonian Institution, in Washington, D.C. The angular vessel with its accompanying cover measures approximately 34 centimeters in height and 18 centimeters in width, ornamented with prominent flanges along the corners and bisecting each face of the vessel. Symmetrical decor of facing birds, dragons, and mask motifs are oriented along the axes formed by the flange on each face of the cover and body. Identical inscriptional texts of 185 graphs were cast into the interior surfaces of the cover and the floor of the body. The calligraphy and decor of the vessel correspond to the early Western Zhou period, ca. mid-eleventh to mid-tenth century B.C.E.

The vessel was discovered in 1929 in the vicinity of modern Luoyang, Henan province, but was not excavated by archaeologists under controlled conditions. Several early discussions of the inscription mention that it was discovered together with a number of other vessels sponsored by the same individual, but the exact situation of the discovery is uncertain.[1] Shortly after its discovery, the vessel was sold on the antiquities market and eventually acquired by the Freer Gallery in 1930.

The inscribed vessel was commissioned by a figure named Ling 令 in dedication to his deceased father.[2] The occasion for the vessel's creation was an award from a Duke Ming to Ling in connection with the latter's role in carrying out a command issued by the Zhou king to Duke Ming 明公. The relationship between Ling and Duke Ming is indicative of the way

---

[1] The earliest published record of the Zuoce Ling *fangyi* occurs in Luo Zhenyu, "Ze yi kaoshi," which does not, however, mention the vessel's provenance in Luoyang. More details are provided in later publications by Luo and repeated—sometimes with additional elaboration—by other scholars. For a thorough account of these records, see Barnard, "The Nieh Ling Yi." other vessels sponsored by Ling that were allegedly part of the same discovery include a pair tureens (Ling *gui* 令簋, *Jicheng* 4300–1) and a wine pot (Zuoce Ling *zun* 作冊令尊, *Jicheng* 6016), which contains an inscriptional text that is nearly identical to that of the Zuoce Ling *fangyi*. In addition to the vessels sponsored by Ling, accounts of the discovery generally include three cauldrons cast by Ling's ancestor Da (Zuoce Da *fangding* 作冊大方鼎, *Jicheng* 2760–61).

[2] Note that the vessel sponsor is referred to by three different appellations within the inscription: Ze 夨, Ling 令, and Zuoce Ling 作冊令. Were it not for the combined use of these different elements in the single appellation Zuoce Ze Ling 作冊夨令 in the inscription of the Ling *gui* mentioned above, the confusing array of names in the present inscription would have been difficult to interpret correctly. The use of multiple appellations for a single individual is common in Western Zhou inscriptions.

in which the prestige of a royal command was replicated from superior to subordinate and ultimately related to practices of ancestor worship and their associated texts.

This close connection between rituals of ancestor worship and political authority is clearly demonstrated in the implementation of the King's decree that is recounted in the inscriptional text. The process as it is narrated in the inscription is punctuated by ritual activity at key junctures. In undertaking the command from the Zhou king, the Duke's first act is to announce the royal command at the temple of his ancestors, the hall of Zhou Gong.[3] The execution of the decree is then followed by sacrificial offerings at three different sites in or around Chengzhou. From the sponsor's point of view, the command culminates with a ceremony in which Duke Ming bestows on him materials to be used in ritual sacrifice, an honor which is then conveyed to Ling's own ancestor, Father Ding 父丁.

The inscription is also important for the information it contains regarding the structure and implementation of Western Zhou government. The royal decree instructs Duke Ming to assume responsibilities at the pinnacle of the Zhou governmental administration.[4] Duke Ming's authority seems to span both the royal administration (the so-called "three affairs," which probably refer to the Supervisor of Works, Supervisor of Horses, and Supervisor of Lands) as well as the regional aristocratic states (of the four quarters). These two spheres of the Zhou kingdom came together in the city of Chengzhou, the eastern capital founded in the aftermath of a major rebellion of eastern states following the Shang conquest and the death of the dynastic founder, King Wu. Duke Ming's implementation of the royal decree takes place in Chengzhou, where the King's orders are disseminated to a range of officials and regional aristocratic lords.

Transcription

唯八月，辰在甲申。王令（命）周公子明保尹三事四方，受卿事寮。丁亥，令夨告于周公宮。公令𠉢（出）同卿事寮。唯十月月吉癸未，明公朝至于成周，𠉢（出）令，舍三事令。眔卿事寮，眔者（諸）尹，眔里君，眔百工，眔（者）諸侯：侯、田（甸）、男，

---

[3] Note that Zhou Gong in this inscription does not necessarily refer to the well-known historical figure Dan 旦, Duke of Zhou, the younger brother of King Wu. See Glossary.

[4] See Li, "'Offices' in Bronze inscriptions and Western Zhou Government Administration," 39–41.

舍四方令。既咸令，甲申明公用牲于京宮，乙酉用牲于康宮。咸既，用牲于王。明公歸自王。明公賜亢師鬯、金、小牛。曰：用禧（祓）。賜令鬯、金、小牛。曰：用禧（祓）。廼令曰：今我唯令女（汝）二人亢眔矢奭肩（左）右于乃寮以乃友事。

作冊令敢揚明公尹厥宮，用作父丁寶尊彝，敢追明公賞于父丁，用光父丁。

 Emblem：鼄冊

Translation

It was the eighth month, and the *chen* was at *jiashen* day (*ganzhi* no. 21). The King commanded the Duke of Zhou's son, Ming Bao, to manage the three affairs and the four quarters and to take charge of the corps of high officers.[5] On *dinghai* day (*ganzhi* no. 24), he commanded Ze to make an announcement at the hall of the Duke of Zhou. The Duke [i.e. Ming Bao] commanded him to go forth and assemble the high officers. In the tenth month, during lunar auspiciousness, on *guiwei* day (*ganzhi* no. 20), Duke Ming arrived in the morning at Chengzhou, displayed the command and disseminated the orders regarding the three affairs. To the high officers, the various administrators, the ward heads, the hundred artisans, and the various lords—archer-lords, fieldsman, and sires—he disseminated the orders regarding the four quarters. Having completed the orders, on *jiashen* day (*ganzhi* no. 21) he conducted sacrificial offerings at the Jing Hall, and on *yiyou* day (*ganzhi* no. 22) he conducted sacrificial offerings at the Kang Hall. Having completed this, he conducted sacrificial offerings at Wang. Duke Ming then returned from Wang. Duke Ming awarded the Kang Captain fragrant wine, metal, and a small ox, saying, "Use them to make ritual offerings." Duke Ming awarded Ling

---

[5] The *qingshiliao* 卿事寮 is one of the major divisions of the Western Zhou court. The term "three affairs" is likely a reference to the *san yousi* 参有司, the top three positions in the *qingshiliao*, consisting of the Supervisor of Works, Supervisor of Horses, and Supervisor of Lands (*ibid.*).

fragrant wine, metal, and a small ox, saying, "Use them to make ritual offerings." He thereupon issued a command, saying, "Now I order you two men, Kang and Ze, to flank me on the left and right in your offices by means of your congenial service."

Recorder Ling dares to extol Administrator Duke Ming's beneficence, herewith making for Father Ding this treasured sacrificial vessel. Ling dares to recount for Father Ding Duke Ming's gift in order to bring glory to Father Ding.

[Emblem].

Further Reading

Jicheng 9901.

Kimbun tsūshaku, 6.276–316.

Mingwen xuan, no. 95

Barnard, "The Nieh Ling Yi."

Chen Mengjia, *Xi Zhou tongqi duandai*, I, 35–40.

A Descriptive and Illustrative Catalogue of Chinese Bronzes, Acquired during the Administration of John Ellerton Lodge, 42–49.

Dobson, *Early Archaic Chinese*, 195–200.

The Freer Chinese Bronzes, 219–20.

Li Xueqin, "Ling fangyi, fangzun xin shi."

Shaughnessy, *Sources of Western Zhou History*, 193–216.

Tang Lan, *Tang Lan xiansheng jinwen lunji*, 6–14.

Wang Hui, *Shang Zhou jinwen*, 78–84.

DMS

INSCRIPTIONS

16. Yu ding 旟鼎

This large round three-legged cauldron was discovered in Yangjiacun 楊家村, Meixian, Shaanxi Province, in 1972. It is presently stored in Shaanxi provincial Museum. From the vessel's shape and decor, scholars date it to around the same time period as the Da Yu *ding* (inscription no. 11, above), i.e. during the late early Western Zhou period, possibly around King Zhao's time. This inscription is one of a handful of bronze inscriptions that feature elite Zhou women in active roles (other than simply as recipients of dowry vessels or sacrifices).

The primary wives for the Zhou kings were routinely chosen from the Jiang lineage. The lineage name of the female progenitor of the Zhou people in the *Shijing* was also Jiang. In a number of inscriptions that record Wang Jiang (the Royal Jiang Lady) either commanding or gift-giving, the King's location is mentioned first. He might be occupied performing rituals in the "Great Hall" or elsewhere in Ancestral Zhou (Zongzhou) or even off on a military expedition, as recorded on a pair of tureens (*gui*) made by Zuoce Ze Ling (discovered in Luoyang in 1929 and now in Paris, *Jicheng* 4300–1). See also Zuoce Huan *you* (no. 17, below).

Transcription

唯八月初吉，王姜賜旟田三于待劕（甸?）。師櫨（櫨）酤（酨?）兄（貺）。用對王休。子子孫其永寶。

Translation

> It was the eighth month, *chuji*, when Wang Jiang awarded Yu three cultivated fields in Dai suburb.[1] Master Lu[2] presented the toast (?) and grant. I, Yu, took this opportunity [to eulogize] the King's grace. May I have sons of sons and grandsons forever to treasure it.

---

[1] Many ancient words with the phonetic *tian* 田 (*l̥ˤiŋ) were associated with hunting. The word *dian* 甸 was cognate to these words. From the "bamboo" and "mat" significs above the field, I suspect the archaic graph actually represented the loanword "mat" *dian* 簟 (*l̥ˤim?).

[2] Read as *kai* 楷 by some.

Further Reading
Jicheng 2704.

Cao Zhaolan, *Jinwen yu Yin Zhou nüxing wenhua*, 70.
Cook, "Wealth and the Western Zhou," 262–63.
Guo Moruo, "Guanyu Meixian dading mingci kaoshi."
Shaughnessy, *Sources of Western Zhou History*, 208–9
Shi Yan, "Meixian Yangjiacun dading."
Wang Hui, *Shang Zhou jinwen*, 84–85.

CAC

17. Zuoce Huan *you* 作冊睘卣

This *you* (pouring vessel for alcohol) is now lost, but rubbings from inside the vessel and lid have survived in catalogues dating from the late Qing dynasty. It may have been in the collection of Wu Shifen 吳式芬 (1796–1856) as early as 1837 before being acquired by Pan Zuyin 潘祖蔭 (1830–1890) of Suzhou. Scholars believe the vessel was made during the time of King Zhao.

For the figure of Wang Jiang, the Zhou queen, see the Yu *ding* inscription (no. 16, above). Scholars believe that King Zhao was on a southern expedition during his nineteenth year, others that the place was located in the Wei River valley. The figure of Yi Bo (Elder of the Yi people) is a reference to a chief of a local tribe of non-Zhou origin. Generally, the Yi people were located along the eastern coastal region, but these Yi seem to be much further inland. Perhaps they were one of the many groups of Yi people who were eventually assimilated into the Zhou culture. This inscription records the subjugation of this Yi tribe by a man whose title was "document maker" (or "recorder") and who was probably a literate officer of the Zhou court. This inscription shows that elite men who were literate were also expected to participate in Zhou military campaigns. The fact that his father's post-humous name was one of the names for the ten Shang suns (Gui, *ganzhi* no. 10) suggests that Huan's patriline may have been connected to the earlier Shang political network, although some scholars believe that some early Zhou aristocrats adopted the Shang religious designations for their own ancestors.

Transcription

唯十又九年王在序（岸?）。王姜令作冊睘安尸（夷）伯。尸（夷）伯賓睘貝、布。揚王姜休，用作文考癸寶尊器。

Translation

It was the nineteenth year of the King's reign, when he was at An (?). Wang Jiang, ordered Document-Maker Huan to quell the Yi Elder. The Yi Elder visited Huan, bringing cowry shells and cloth. Huan extolled Wang Jiang's grace and took this opportunity to make for his Accomplished Deceased-father Gui a precious vessel for expressing reverence.

Further Reading

Jicheng 5407.

Cao Zhaolan, *Jinwen yu Yin Zhou nüxing wenhua*, 68.

Jinwen jinyi leijian, 576–77.

Lu Liancheng, "An di yu Zhao Wang shijiu nian nanzheng."

Wang Hui, *Shang Zhou jinwen*, 88–91.

CAC

18. Zhong xian 中甗

A steamer vessel (*yan*), also called the Fu Yi 父乙 steamer, was discovered in 1118 in Xiaoganxian 孝感縣, Hubei, along with a number of other vessels of various number. Although some records claim that there were originally nine vessels, the present set consists of six: three square *ding*, two round *ding*, and the steamer. This set came to be known as the "six Vessels of Anzhou" 安州六器. The only record of this inscription is a Song handcopy written by brush. It is obvious that the original inscription had many unclear graphs and that the copyist made the best sense he could at the time, but that errors were introduced. Much of it is hard to interpret. Even so, the inscription is important, as it documents the Zhou's southern expansion into the Han River region during King Zhao's time. The cauldron and drinking vessel inscriptions mention other southern locales and the tributes gained. Legends regarding King Zhao's expeditions to the south are recorded in later Eastern Zhou and Han texts. They mention a number of victories but ultimately defeat. The square cauldron inscriptions (two of which were identical) record that Zhong was sent south on an extended scouting journey while the king was occupied with quelling the rebellious Hu 虎 ("tiger") peoples, an ancient people mentioned also in the Shang oracle bones and possibly located to the southeast (where tiger decorated bronzes have been found).

The vessels were probably from a tomb located northwest of modern Wuhan, closer to the ancient region of E in the middle Yangzi River valley. If the tomb was Zhong's, then we might see him as an early colonizer of the south. The fact that the posthumous title for Zhong's father is in the Shang style suggests that Zhong's patriline may have originally been linked to part of the Shang network then allied with the Zhou.

Transcription

王令（命）中先省南或（域）貫行。執（設）应（居）在曾。史兒至以王令（命）曰：令汝史（使）小大邦厥又舍（捨）汝芻量，至于汝虞，小（少）多勿［孚？］。[1]

---

[1] Generally in the bronze inscriptions, the word that follows "many" (*duo* 多) is either a group of people with a particular status, such as captives, elite men, fathers, or patriarchs, or else a word like blessings or gifts that had been given in multitude.

中省自方；登（鄧）受（授）𢔽（？）邦；在鄂師次。伯買父迺以
厥人戍漢中州，曰叚，曰旟。厥人鬲（？）廿（二十）夫，厥貯
舛（？）言（音？）曰貯𤔔（？）貝。
中（？）對（？）揚（？）王[顯?]休，肆肩又（有）羞（？）。余
[□]承（？），用作父乙寶彝。

Translation

The King commanded Zhong to lead an inspection tour of the southern territory's route and set up a station in Zeng. Archivist Er arrived with the King's command and said: "You are ordered to make the small and large states which have holdings relinquish to you fodder and grain supplies, and bring to your X^2 a few of [their] many captives (?)."

Zhong went on an inspection tour from Fang; Deng gave him X^3 state; at E the army lined up by rank. The Elder, Father Mai, then took his men to defend the Middle Han river lands, calling them Jia and Ke. Of their men, there were twenty of *li* status, and, of their stores of X (Linyin?) goods, there were cowries of X cowries.

Zhong in response extolled the King's manifest grace. Displaying the offerings (?), I present them (?) and take this opportunity to make for Father Yi a precious sacrificial vessel.

Further Reading

Jicheng 949.

Mingwen xuan, no. 108.

Song Huanwen, "Anzhou liu qi bianzheng."

Tang Lan, *Xi Zhou qingtongqi mingwen fendai shi zheng*, 285–88.

Wang Hui, *Shang Zhou jinwen*, 91–93.

CAC

[2] The graph might be understood as standing for the word "change" in the sense of the sematic *geng* 更, reinforced by the phonetic *fan* 凡 *brom (somewhat close in pronunciation to "change" *bian* 變 *pron-s). What sort of place the loanword represented is unclear.

[3] The name of a place possibly near a small river. The graph seems to have the water semantic.

19. JING GUI 靜簋

A number of vessels belonging to a man named Jing 靜 ("Pacifier"), who lived during early Western Zhou, may have once been in the Qing imperial collection but are now dispersed around the world. The tureen (*gui*), with typical décor of curly dragons on the vessel body and sculptured animal heads on the handles and upper body register, dates either to the end of the King Zhao period, just before King Zhao died on one of his many campaigns to the south, or to the early King Mu period as a memorial to the earlier campaigns. We know from the inscription on the *ding* belonging to Jing 靜鼎 [1] that he was active in those campaigns. The tureen, after going through the hands of private collectors, is now located in the Arthur sackler Collection in Washington D.C., and the square four-legged *ding* is in the idemitsu Museum of Arts in Japan. The you that was part of the original set is located in the palace Museum in Taipei, Taiwan.

The archery ceremony at the Grand pool, also known as *biyong* (see also the Zuoce Mai *fangzun*, no. 14, above), was part of a harvest (or sweet ale) festival and involved shooting birds and fish. According to a much later text, *Zhouli* 周禮 (*Rituals of Zhou*), a school was located near the pool.

Transcription

唯六月初吉，王在莽京，丁卯，王令靜司射學宮，小子眔服眔小臣眔尸（夷）僕學射。雩（越）八月初吉庚寅，王以吳裘（？）、呂犅卿（合/會）䠷蓋師、邦周射于大池，靜學（教?）無尤。王賜靜鞞繠。

靜敢拜稽首，對揚天子丕顯休，用作文母外姞尊簋，子子孫孫其萬年用。

Translation

It was in the sixth month, *chuji*, when the King was located at pang capital, on *dingmao* day (*ganzhi* no. 4), that the King commanded Jing to supervise the Hall for Archery and Learning, along with the youth and their orderlies, the pageboys and their Yi servants to study archery. In the eighth month, *chuji*, on geng-

---

[1] Zhong Bosheng 鍾柏生 et al., eds., *Xinshou Yin-Zhou qingtongqi mingwen ji qiying huibian*, 1795; Zhang Maorong, "Jing fangdiao xiaokao."

yin day (*ganzhi* no. 27), the King took Wu Qiu (?) and Lü Gang to meet Master Ying of Bin and the Bang Zhou (a local ruler) to shoot at the Grand pool, where Jing instructed them without fault. The King awarded Jing a sheath with hanging decorations (pieces of jade or tassels).

Jing dared in response to clap his hands together, knock his head against the ground, and extol the Son of Heaven's greatly manifest grace. He took the opportunity to make for his Accomplished Mother, a Ji-lineage woman of Wai, a tureen for expressing reverence. May he have sons of sons and grandsons of grandsons to use it for ten thousand years.

Further Reading

Jicheng 4273.

Kimbun tsūshaku, 16.123.

Mingwen xuan, no. 170.

Jinwen jinyi leijian, 182–83.

Li, *Bureaucracy and the State in Early China*, 152–53.

Tang Lan, *Xi Zhou qingtongqi mingwen fendai shi zheng*, 361–62.

Wang Hui, *Shang Zhou jinwen*, 94–99.

Wang Zhankui, "Guanyu Jing fangding de jidian kanfa."

Xu Tianjin, "Riben chuguang Meishuguan shoucang de Jing fangding."

Zhang Maorong, "Jing fangding xiaokao."

Zhong Bosheng et al., eds., *Xinshou Yin-Zhou qingtongqi mingwen ji qiying huibian*.

CAC

20. Shi Qi ding 師旂鼎

The date of excavation and provenance of this vessel, which is also called Shi Lü *ding* 師旅鼎, are unknown. The earliest records of the Shi Qi *ding* are from the late Qing dynasty, and we know that the vessel was in the possession of several modern scholars (such as Rong Geng 容庚 [1894–1983] and Yu Xingwu 于省吾 [1896–1984]) before ultimately being placed in the palace Museum in Beijing, where it resides today.

The vessel displays fairly standard art historical characteristics of early Western Zhou *ding* (such as the general contours of the body, and the motif of long-tailed birds), and may possibly date to the tenth century, during the reign of either King Zhao or King Mu. At that time, the stability of the dynasty was in question. King Zhao died while on a military campaign to extend the borders of the Zhou state farther south, and his troops suffered overwhelming defeat, events that must surely have shaken the confidence of the Zhou ruling house. However, King Zhao's son, King Mu, was ultimately successful in reasserting Zhou authority as evidenced in part by his unusually lengthy reign. The contents of this inscription are suggestive of a time before King Mu's reconsolidation of the Zhou state.

The Shi Qi *ding* is the earliest example of a legal case from the Western Zhou inscriptional corpus. Moreover, it constitutes the only inscriptional record of mutiny. In many respects it does not read like a typical bronze inscription. For example, there is no ancestor dedication at the end of the vessel, and what is recorded by the sponsor (Captain Qi 師旂) is not an act that is incontestably worthy of recognition, even though the outcome of the trial is to his advantage. Additionally, like most inscriptions dealing with legal matters (cf. nos. 35, 36, 37, 43, and 48, below), the Shi Qi *ding* inscription is complicated by the presence of a few terms for which there are few if any comparable usages found in other bronze inscriptions, excavated texts, or received texts. Legal texts moreover tend to mention several persons whose roles relative to the sponsor of the vessel (usually the complaining party), or the defendant, are unclear.

As best as can be determined, the events described in the Shi Qi *ding* are as follows: The *pu* 僕-troops of Captain Qi refused to follow their king on campaign. After the incident, Captain Qi sent his associate, Yin 引, to report the matter to Bo Mao Fu 伯懋父. Bo Mao Fu fined Captain Qi 300 *lüe* 寽 of metal, probably to be presented to the state. However, because the captain was unable to pay such a hefty fine, Bo Mao Fu pronounced that, rather than exile the troops as he "should" (*yi* 宜), the troops were required to give to Captain Qi the amount due. In turn, Captain Qi presumably was to remit the fine to the state. Yin reported the decision to the Central Scribe, who wrote it down. Qi also made a record of the sentence in the *ding*-cauldron. The inscription ends with the explicit statement that Captain Qi commissioned the vessel in order "to mirror his verdict."

In other inscriptions, Bo Mao Fu figures as a high-ranking military and political figure with close affiliations to the royal house, who led the Yin Eight Armies 殷八師 in quelling rebellions of the Eastern and Southern Huai Yi 淮夷. Bo Mao Fu's position in the Zhou state is of interest, as he is the person who decides this case: it seems that his duties included judging cases of a military nature, or, deciding cases in which military personnel were involved.

From the initial verdict by Bo Mao Fu, we learn that, while the mutinying troops were to have been banished (a severe punishment, perhaps second only to death), Zhou captains also bore heavy legal responsibility for their troops' insubordination, much in the manner that vicarious liability operates in Western common law under the doctrine of agency known as *respondeat superior* (see also nos. 35 and 43, below). Additionally, while there seem to have been fixed sentences, arbiters also possessed discretionary authority.

This brings us to another point of interest: the implications of the economic situation at the time of the events described. Bo Mao Fu's revised verdict suggests that the state was in great need of metal, perhaps to make weapons. (Compare the fate of the Hu *ding*, no. 35, below.) We know that at the beginning of the Western Zhou, Zhou military leaders incorporated military personnel of the newly conquered shang into their own armed forces. It is likely that the *pu*-troops of Captain Qi were of Shang or eastern descent, and that the Zhou military may have been in such need of troops that they were willing to take their chances on those who had already demonstrated gross insubordination. The decision to grant a reduction of punishment, though not a pardon, to all offending parties may also have transcended purely fiscal interests: a more lenient verdict would have cast the administration in a more compassionate light.

Transcription

唯三月丁卯。師旂眾僕不從王征于方䍙。使厥友引以告于伯懋父在葊。伯懋父廼罰得忞（獻）由（鋚）三百孚。今弗克厥罰。

懋父令（命）曰：義（宜）播䜴（殂）厥不從厥右征。今毋播。其又（有）內（納）于師旂。

引以告中史書。旂對厥䇂于尊彝。

Translation

> It was the third month, *dingmao* (*ganzhi* no. 4). Captain Qi's many *pu*-troops did not follow the King on campaign to Fanglei. Captain Qi sent his *you*-associate, Yin, to take this matter and report to Bo Mao Fu at Ren. Bo Mao Fu thereupon fined captain Qi three hundred *lüe* of *you*-metal. Now, Captain Qi was unable to pay his fine.
>
> Mao Fu commanded saying, "[I] ought to banish them for this, their not following their *you*-commanding officer on campaign. Now, [I] do not banish them. They shall pay captain Qi."
>
> Yin therewith reported to the Central Scribe. [The central scribe] wrote [the results down]. Qi mirrored the verdict in [this] sacral vessel.

Further Reading

Jicheng 2809.

Lau, *Quellenstudien zur Landvergabe und Bodenübertragung in der westlichen Zhou-Dynastie*, 146–58.

Li Feng,, "Literacy and The Social Contexts", 286–87.

Skosey, "The Legal system and Legal tradition of the Western Zhou (ca. 1045–771 B.C.E.)."

Tang Lan, *Xi Zhou qingtongqi mingwen fendai shi zheng*, 313–16.

LAS

21. Ban gui 班簋

A rubbing of the Ban *gui*, also known as the Mao Bo *gui* 毛伯簋 (among other names), first appeared in the 1749 catalogue of the Qing Emperor Qianlong's collection. But at some point the vessel was lost. In 1972, a vessel that did not exactly match the description of the earlier vessel, but with the same inscription, was recovered from a metal recycling station in Beijing. After restoration, this tureen was stored in the Beijing Capital Museum. Both vessels are considered to have been made at the same time and date to the late tenth century B.C.E., early in the reign of King Mu.

Ban is the first name of a Mao 毛 lineage descendant of a union between the Zhou founder, King Wen, and a Si-lineage woman. There is a fair amount of controversy about the identity of the various characters mentioned in the inscription and how to read the inscription. Many early scholars claimed that Mao Gong, the Patriarch of Mao, must have been the same person as Ban, who is also mentioned in the inscription and who commissioned the inscription. This original judgment was based on the later tale of a Patriarch of Mao named Ban who aided King Mu.[1] This Mao Ban was a descendant of Mao Shu Zheng 毛叔鄭, who fought with King Wu to extinguish the Shang rule and is mentioned also in the *Shiji*.[2]

Later, scholars such as Huang Shengzhang explained that while Ban mentioned in the inscription may have indeed been the famed Mao Ban, the Mao Gong in this inscription was clearly his father and that military events associated with Mao Gong must have occurred before the King Mu period. Only later, after Ban was sent to war as one of his father's bodyguards, does he become a Mao Gong. In Huang's view, the success of the father's military exploits is the topic of the eulogy in the second half of the inscripton.

According to Li Xueqin, Ban was promoted from Elder of Mao (Mao *bo* 毛伯) to Patriarch of Mao (Mao *gong* 毛公) after he took charge of Guo 虢, an important defense position for the Zhou homeland, from its deceased leader. He notes that, since Ban's father, the first Mao Gong, was called Father Mao by the king, the father was probably of the same generation as the king's father, King Zhao. Father Mao's military campaign included eastern leaders from the states of Wu and Lü. Wars to the south and east were common during the Zhao and Mu reigns.

---

[1] The source is *Mu tianzi zhuan* 穆天子傳 4.4a [PRG].
[2] *Shiji* 4.125 [PRG].

Ban was promoted to the rank of Grand subduer, a title for a master of military arts who frequently went on campaigns. Since Ban is now taking up this position, his father's title then became commander-in-chief (*dazheng* 大政). In an attempt to sort through the various narrative voices, the Chinese text is sectioned by speakers rather than lumped into large paragraphs as is more typical.

Transcription

唯八月初吉在宗周甲戌，王令毛伯更虢城公服，粵王立（位），作四方極，秉緐、蜀、巢，令賜鈴、勒，咸。

王令毛公以邦冢君、土（徒）馭（御）、或³人伐東或（域）瘠（瘸?窟?）⁴戎，咸。

王令吳伯曰：以乃師左比毛父。

王令呂伯曰：以乃師右比毛父。遣令曰：以乃族從父征，出城，衛父身，三年靜東或（域），亡不成冘（尤?）天畏，否畀屯⁵陟。

公告厥事于上：唯民亡出才彝昧天令，故亡允才顯，唯敬德亡迺違。

班拜稽首曰：烏虖，丕丕玑（揚）皇公受京宗懿釐，毓文王、王姒聖孫，登于大服，廣成厥工，文王孫亡弗懷井（型），亡克競厥烈，班非敢覓，唯作邵考爽，益（謚）曰大政。

子子孫多世其永寶。

---

³ The interpretations of this graph is still a subject of debate. I suspect that the phonetic is *cheng* 呈 and the graph was a loan for *cheng* 城, a "city" or place name.

⁴ The phonetic for the original graph *gu* 骨, *kᶜut, was quite close to the word for "cave" (*ku* 窟, *khᶜut). Otherwise the term might simply be a pejorative reference to the "sickly" Rong peoples.

⁵ I read the word represented by the graph *tun* 屯 in its original sense of "to accumulate" (see Glossary) rather than *zhun* 純, "purity" or perhaps "integrity" (see inscription nos. 42, 44, and 62, below). Since the reading of "purity" is based on later transmitted texts and we do not know what the notion of "purity" might have entailed in the pre-Confucian worldview, I suspect that the meaning in the bronze inscriptions was the more concrete idea of accumulated material goods (as in agricultural stores or other awarded wealth) or of accumulated merit (as in the case of *de* 德).

Translation

It was in the eighth month, *chuji*, on *jiaxu* day (*ganzhi* no. 11) at Ancestral Zhou that the King commanded Elder Mao to renew the submission of Patriarch cheng of Guo so that [Guo] would act as a protective barrier for the King's position—the pivot for the Four regions—and to handle the Fan, Shu, and Chao. The King ordered that Elder Mao be awarded bridle bells and a bridle. And that [ritual phase] was completed.

The King commanded Patriarch Mao to attack the Cave-Rong in the Eastern territories with the High lords of the states, foot soldiers and charioteers, armed with spears and daggers. And that [ritual phase] was completed.

The King commanded Elder Wu, saying: "With your army, aid and accompany Father Mao's left flank."

The King commanded Elder Lü, saying: "With your army, aid and accompany Father Mao's right flank."

Then sending off his command, the King said: "With your lineage fighters, follow Father into battle, exit the city, and guard Father's person. If, after three years spent pacifying the eastern territories, you have lost and are unsuccessful, then you will have harmed Heaven's awesome [*de*] and negated your chance to be given wealth and promotion."

The Patriarch announced his affairs to those [spirits] above: "If it be that the people are lost and split off, thus darkening Heaven's Mandate, then let there be manifest such reverent power that they do not go against it for long."

Ban clapped his hands together and knocked his head on the floor and said: "Ah! How I extol the fine gifts the Brilliant Patriarch received in the capital's main shrine and, as progeny of the sage Descendant of the royal Si-lineage woman of King Wen, I climb to position of Grand Subduer, widening the scope and the achievements of his merits! As a descendant of King Wen, I cannot but take his model to heart. Incapable of competing with his glory, I, Ban, am not one who dares to gaze upon him, but create a vessel for my Deceased-father Zhao's bright spirit, and call him [posthumously] by the title 'commander-in-chief.'"

May continuous progeny forever treasure this vessel and the

ancestor it is dedicated to for numerous generations.

Further Reading

Jicheng 4341.

Mingwen xuan, no. 168.

Behr, *Reimende Bronzeinschriften und die Entstehung der chinesischen Endreimdichtung*, 180–85.

Dobson, *Early Archaic Chinese*, 179–84.

Guo Moruo, "'Ban gui' de zai faxian."

Huang Shengzhang, "Ban gui de niandai, dili, yu lishi wenti."

Jinwen jinyi leijian, 253–88.

Li, *Landscape and Power in Early China*, 128, 228–31, 250–53.

Li Xueqin, "Ban gui xukao."

Li Xueqin, ed., *Shang Zhou guwenzi duben*, 91–97.

Shaughnessy, *Sources of Western Zhou History*, 251–53.

Sun Zhichu, "Ban gui mingwen shidu de yixie wenti."

Tang Lan, *Xi Zhou qingtongqi mingwen fendai shi zheng*, 346–55.

Wang Hui, *Shang Zhou jinwen*, 100–6.

CAC

22. Dong *gui* 彧簋 and Lu Bo Dong *gui* 彔伯彧簋

In 1975, traces of a tomb with bronze vessels, cowries, shells, wood coffin traces, and cinnabar were discovered in Zhuangbai 莊白 village, Fufeng 扶風 County, Shaanxi province. Originally the tomb had been placed on an embankment, but dirt removed by peasants over time leveled the tomb, so that only the bottom level remained. Eighteen bronze vessels had been set up in the tomb, including large and small vessels for food and drink. One of the cauldrons still held the remains of a sheep. Other tombs in the area, including one belonging to a Ji 姬 lineage woman of Feng 豐, suggest that the deceased in this cemetery intermarried with the Zhou. Eleven out of the eighteen vessels in this tomb were inscribed. The longest inscriptions belonged to a man named Dong 彧, who may have been the original tomb occupant. Ancestral or tribute vessels were commonly dedicated to fathers or other patrilineal spirits, but Dong's own vessels were dedicated to his mother's spirit, attributing his safe return from battle to his mother's supernatural protection. The lidded round tureen, the Dong *gui*, is an especially fine vessel, decorated with classic Zhou-era curly-tailed birds on the vessel and lid, and sculptured bird handles that help date it to the King Mu period. The tureen inscription is the longest of the group found in the tomb and documents Dong's success in battle, measured by the number of ears cut off, prisoners taken, and booty accumulated.

The next-longest inscription is found on a squat four-legged lidded square cauldron, which was plain except for a band of decor with pairs of *kui*-dragons near the upper rim of the vessel (Dong *fangding* 彧方鼎, *Jicheng* 2824). This inscription records Dong's response to an award ceremony after his battles against eastern non-Zhou peoples of the Huai river region. It also makes an oblique reference to Dong taking over as a local ruler from his father, who, in the Lu Bo Dong *gui* inscription, was posthumously titled King Li:

彧曰：烏虖（乎），王唯念彧辟烈考甲公，王用肇事（使）乃子彧率虎臣御（禦）淮戎 。

彧曰：烏虖（乎），朕文考甲公、文母日庚，弋（式）休則尚，安永宕乃子彧心，安永襲彧身，厥復享于天子，唯厥事（使）乃子彧萬年辟事天子，母（毋）又（有）尤于厥身。

彧拜稽首，對揚王令，用作文母日庚寶尊鬻彝，用穆穆夙夜尊享孝綏福，其子子孫孫永寶茲烈。

Dong said: "Ah! The King is remembering Dong's sovereign, the blazing deceased-father Patriarch Jia. The King employed your son initially to lead the tiger corps to expel the Huai and the Rong (non-Zhou peoples of the southeast and northern border regions)."

Dong said: "Ah! My Accomplished Deceased-father Patriarch Jia (*ganzhi* no. 1) and Accomplished Mother Geng (*ganzhi* no. 7) took the King's grace as pattern and his honor as rule; you eternally open the heart of your son, Dong and you eternally cover his body. So he doubles his mortuary offerings to the Son of Heaven. You make your son, Dong, a local sovereign and serve the Son of Heaven for ten thousand years with no personal harm."

Dong clapped his hands together and knocked his head against the floor and in response eulogized the King's command. Taking this opportunity, I make for my Accomplished Mother Geng a treasured sacrificial meat vessel for expressing reverence to use—gravely, oh so gravely—and express reverence from dawn to dusk with mortuary and filial offerings to pacify the spirits and bring good fortune. May I have sons of sons and grandsons of grandsons eternally to treasure this blazing [bright vessel].

Another square cauldron in the set (Dong *fangding* 彧方鼎, *Jicheng* 2789) includes an inscription which documents the king's rewarding Dong during a sliced-meat sacrifice to the mythical mother of the Zhou people, Jiang Yuan (see "Shengmin" 生民, *Mao* 245 in the *Shijing*). The text on the other square cauldron, translated above, was probably Dong's eulogistic response of gratitude for the award. The inscription is as follows:

唯九月既望乙丑，在是師。王俎姜，事（使）內史友員賜彧玄衣朱襮襟。彧拜稽首，對揚王俎姜休，用作寶鬻尊鼎，其用夙夜享孝于厥文祖乙公，于文妣日戊，其子子孫孫永寶。

It was the ninth month, *jiwang*, on *yichou* day (*ganzhi* no. 2), at X Encampment, when the King presented a sliced-meat sacrifice to Jiang and commissioned the Inner Scribe, Colleague Yuan, to award Dong with a dark-colored cloak with crimson collar and lapel. Dong clapped his hands together and knocked his head on the ground and in response eulogized the King's grace during the sliced-meat sacrifice to Jiang. [Dong] took this opportunity to make a treasured cauldron for meat sacrifice and for expressing reverence, so that he might use it from dawn to dusk to present mortuary and filial offerings to his Accomplished Ancestor patriarch Yi (*ganzhi* no. 2 in the ten-day cycle) and to his Accomplished Ancestress Wu (*ganzhi* no. 5 in the ten-day cycle). May [he have] sons of sons and grandsons and grandsons eternally to treasure [it].

Other inscribed vessels, perhaps by the same person but not found in this tomb, included a tureen (Dong Zu Geng *gui* 夷祖庚簋, *Jicheng* 3865) presently located in the Shanghai Museum. Its short inscription is as follows:

夷作祖庚尊簋，子子孫孫，其萬年永寶用。

I, Dong, make for Ancestor Geng a tureen for expressing reverence. May sons of sons and grandsons of grandsons for ten thousand years eternally treasure and use [it].

[Emblem]

The above inscription is followed by an undecipherable sign (something like a thick comma under a four-pointed star) that may represent an emblem used by his lineage mortuary group. Modern scholars link such signs or emblems to people originally associated with the Shang network of allied peoples. This is also the case for people whose ancestors were named according to ten suns or days in the ritual calendar, like Dong's. It is possible that Dong's father was a member of the Shang lineage network but that his mother was a Zhou woman, although it is unclear whether or not the early Zhou had adopted this Shang custom.

Another tureen by an Elder Dong (Bo Dong *gui* 伯夷簋, *Jicheng* 4115), once in the collection of Chen Banghuai 陳邦懷 (1897–1986), confirms other inscriptions found in the tomb at Zhuangbai that show that Dong eventually obtained the rank of Elder. Only a rough hand-copy of the inscription survives. The rhetoric is slightly unusual but not inconsistent with abbreviations and usages found in the other Dong inscriptions.

> 伯威肇其作西宮寶。唯用綏神懷嘑（效？）前文人，秉德共（恭）屯。唯匄萬年，子子孫孫永寶。
>
> It was Elder Dong who first made a treasure for the Western Hall. It was for use in assuaging the spirits and embracing and calling on (imitating?) the Former Accomplished ones in order to grasp *de* and pay his respects and accumulate wealth. It was to pray for ten thousand years and for sons of sons and grandsons of grandsons eternally to treasure it.

Elder Dong is also mentioned on a pair of drinking vessels discovered in the tomb. These bizarrely shaped cups look like a combination of *zhi* cups and *hu* storage vessels, and have large elephant trunk handles to be grasped with both hands. The inscription slightly varies on the two vessels: one calls itself a "drinking *hu*" (*Jicheng* 6454) and the other a "traveling[1] sacrificial vessel" (*Jicheng* 6455). Otherwise, the inscriptions consist of simple statement of manufacture or ownership:

> 伯威作畲（飲）壺。
>
> Elder Dong made a drinking *hu*.
>
> 伯威作旅彝。
>
> Elder Dong made a traveling sacrificial vessel.

Many scholars believe that Dong was the same person as Lu Bo Dong 彔伯威, Dong, Elder of Lu; but other scholars question this association. A number of vessels commissioned by Lu Bo Dong are recorded in the catalogues of early collectors, the most famous of which is the Lu Bo Dong *gui* (translated below). The history and present whereabouts of this vessel are unknown. The rubbing was first published in 1895 by the scholar Wu Shifen. It documents the king's award to Lu Bo Dong. The idea that Lu Bo Dong's lineage was non-Zhou is confirmed by the dedication of the vessel to his father, whom he names as King Li 釐王. Leaders of some non-Zhou states were also titled as "kings" (*wang*). The Lu state seems to have been

---

[1] The word *lü* 旅 might also have referred to being lined up for display as in a sacrificial tableau, although presumably this might have been true for all sacrificial vessels.

a nearby polity that intermarried with the Zhou and was part of the Zhou economic and ritual network.

Other vessels commissioned by Lu Dong include two Lu Dong alcohol storage vessels, one *you* style, presently in the sackler Collection at Princeton University, and one *zun*, presently in the palace Museum in Taipei; and a Lu tureen (*gui*). These record gift-giving in the King's name but without his presence. Instead of the King, a general named Elder Yongfu 伯雍父 officiated. The fact that a *pan* vessel (*Jicheng* 10074) originally owned by Elder Yongfu was buried in Dong's tomb suggests that he and Dong were related. Other inscriptions connect Yongfu with military action against a group called Hu 胡 and refer to him as a Master (*shi* 師) (for example, *Jicheng* 2721).

The *you* and *zun* inscriptions (*Jicheng* 5419–20) are identical and as follows:

王令彔曰：戲，淮尸（夷）敢伐內國，汝其以成周師氏戍于
𦵖𠂤（師）²。伯雍父蔑彔歷，賜貝十朋。彔拜稽首，對揚伯
休，用作文考乙公寶尊彝。

The King ordered Dong, saying: "So! The Yi of the Huai river region dare to attack our sovereign territory! With the chief masters of Chengzhou, you shall take up guard at the Gu (or Hu?) Encampment." Elder Yong Fu praised Lu's record of merit and awarded him ten strings of cowries.

I, Lu, clapped my hands together and knocked my head against the ground and in response extolled the Elder's grace. I took this opportunity to make for Accomplished Deceased-father Yi patriarch a treasured sacrificial vessel for expressing reverence.

The tureen inscription (*Jicheng* 4122) is also a simple award record cast around the same time but for a different set of ancestors. This vessel, presently in Kyoto, Japan, is red in color:

伯雍父來自胡，蔑彔歷，賜赤金，對揚伯休，用作文祖辛公
寶簋，其子子孫孫永寶。

---

² The graph 𠂤 is generally read as a simplified version of *shi* 師 (*srij), with the special meaning of a military encampment. In most inscriptions the two words are not graphically distinct. In this inscription the earlier graph for "army, master" is differentiated with the extra sematic element on the right. Some read 𠂤 as *ci* 次 (*s-ŋij-s), "lodge". The ancient pronunciations for *shi* and *ci* were quite close.

Elder Yong Fu came from Hu and praised Lu's record of merit, awarding him crimson-colored metal.

In response, I extolled the Elder's grace and took this opportunity to make for my Accomplished Ancestor Xin patriarch a treasured meat-serving tureen. May I have sons of sons and grandsons and grandsons to treasure it forever.

Transcription (*Dong* gui)

唯六月初吉乙酉在䍙自（師）戎伐䚄。䚄率有司師氏奔追禦戎于棫林，博（搏）戎胡。朕文母競敏啟行，休宕厥心，永襲厥身，俾克厥敵，獲聝百，執訊二夫，俘戎兵、盾矛、戈弓、備矢、裨胄，凡百又卅又五款，孚戎俘人百又十又四人。衣（卒）博（搏），無尤于䚄身。乃子䚄拜稽首對揚文母福烈，用作文母日庚寶尊簋，俾乃子䚄萬年用夙夜尊享孝于厥文母，其子子孫孫用寶。

Translation

It was the sixth month, *chuji*, on *yiyou* day (*ganzhi* no. 22), at the X Encampment, when the Rong attacked X. Dong led the Master chiefs in pursuit of the Rong to expel them from Yu forest, giving the Rong and the Hu a beating. My Accomplished Mother aggressively and persistently cleared the way, gracing his heart with openness, so that she would eternally cover his body and thus enabled him to meet the enemy and capture one hundred ears, two bound prisoners [of higher status], 135 military items, including shields and spears, dagger-axes and bows, quivers and arrows, and armor and helmets, and 114 Rong captives [of lower status]. At the completion of the beating, no harm had come to Dong's body. Your son, Dong, claps his hands and knocks his head on the ground in gratitude and in response extols the Accomplished Mother's Auspicious Blazing presence and takes this opportunity to make a precious tureen for expressing reverence to Accomplished Mother Day Geng (*ganzhi* no. 7) so that you can cause your son, Dong, to live ten thousand years and use this vessel to express reverence by presenting mortuary and sacrificial offerings from dawn to dusk to his Accomplished Mother. May his sons of sons and grandsons of grandsons use and treasure it.

Transcription (*Lu Bo Dong* gui)

唯王正月辰在庚寅，王若（諾）曰：彔伯威，繇（由）自乃祖考又（有）爵于周邦右（佑）闢四方叀（惠）³弘天令。汝肇不墜。余賜汝秬鬯一卣、金車雕疇（幬）較、雕軹朱虢（鞹）靳、虎幎朱裡、金甬（童）畫昏、金軛畫轉、馬四匹、鋚勒。

彔伯威敢拜手稽首對揚天子丕顯休，用作朕皇考釐王寶尊簋。余其永萬年寶用，子子孫孫其帥帥井（型）受茲休。

Translation

It was in the first month of the King's reign, when the *chen* was in *gengyin* day (*ganzhi* no. 27), when the King, agreeing [to Dong's award], said: "Dong, Elder of Lu, beginning since the time of your ancestors up to and including your deceased-father, your family has held rank in the Zhou state for helping to open the Four regions and spreading the Heavenly Mandate. From the start, you have not let it fall. I award you a storage vessel of yellow and black millet ale, a metal decorated chariot with patterned curtained side railings, patterned girth straps and crimson leather chest covers, a tiger-skin covering with a pale red lining, a metal decorated shaft with decorated axle supports, a metal decorated yoke harness with decorated bindings, four pairs of horses, and bits and bridles."

I, Dong, Elder of Lu, dared to clap my hands together and knock my head against the ground and in response extolled the Son of Heaven's greatly manifest grace. I took the opportunity to make for my Brilliant Deceased-father King Li a treasured tureen for expressing reverence. May I eternally, for ten thousand years, treasure and use it, and have sons of sons and grandsons of grandsons who shall follow, one after another, the model of their ancestors, to receive such grace as this.

Further Reading

Jicheng 4322 (Dong *gui*), 4302 (Lu Bo Dong *gui*).

Kimbun tsūshaku, 17.209.

Mingwen xuan, nos. 174–81.

---

³ The graph 叀 is often read for the near-homonyms, *hui* 惠, *wei* 唯, or *wei* 惟.

Behr, *Reimende Bronzeinschriften und die Entstehung der chinesischen Endreimdichtung*, 188–91.

Cao Zhaolan, *Jinwen yu Yin Zhou nüxing wenhua*, 107–10, 204–5.

Cook, "Wealth and the Western Zhou," 276–79.

Huang Ranwei, *Yin Zhou qingtongqi shangci mingwen yanjiu*.

Huang Shengzhang, "Fufeng Qiangjiacun xin chu Xi Zhou tongqiqun yu xiangguan shishi zhi yanjiu."

Huang Shengzhang, "Lu Bo Dong tongqi ji qi xiangguan wenti."

Jinwen jinyi leijian, 208–9, 226–28.

Li, *Bureaucracy and the State in Early China*, 312–13.

Li, *Landscape and Power in Early China*, 96–97.

Ren Zhoufang, *Guobao jishi*, 57–64.

"Shaanxi Fufeng chutu Xi Zhou Bo Dong zhuqi."

Shaughnessy, *Sources of Western Zhou History*, 177–81.

Tang Lan, *Xi Zhou tongqi mingwen fendai shi zheng*, 395–98, 406–11.

Wang Hui, *Shang Zhou jinwen*, 109–17.

Wang Zhongwen, "'Bo dong' yu 'Lu,' 'Lu Bo Dong' zhuqi xilian wenti zhi jiantao."

CAC

23. QI GUI 趞簋

This vessel, sometimes referred to as a cauldron (*ding* 鼎), was first recorded as belonging to the late nineteenth-century collection of Li Shannong 李山農. The tureen is presently in the Calligraphy Museum 書道博物館 in Tokyo. The vessel is round, with plain décor except for a band of two *kui* dragons facing each other, and the handles are composed of tiger heads protruding from the rim design, with birds' bodies descending from their mouths. The vessel is believed to belong to the King Mu reign period. Qi dedicated the vessel to a Jiang woman who was probably his mother, making him a possible in-law of the Zhou house.

Transcription

唯三月王在宗周，戊寅王格于大朝（廟）。密叔又（佑）趞即位，內史即命。

王若（諾）曰：趞！命女（汝）作䢼師冢嗣（司）馬，啻（適）官：僕、射、士，訊小大又（友）鄰，取徵五鍰。賜汝赤市幽亢（衡）、鑾旂，用事。

趞拜稽首，對揚王休，用作季姜尊彝，其子子孫孫邁（萬）年寶用。

Translation

    It was the third month when the King was at Zongzhou, on *wuyin* day (*ganzhi* no. 15), that he arrived at the Grand Shrine. Once Mi Shu guided Qi in from the right to take his position (in the center courtyard facing north and the King), the Inner Archivist gave the command [to present the award].

    The King, agreeing [to the award], said: "Qi, I command you to act as Supreme Supervisor of Horses at Bin Encampment and [supervise] the officers matched by rank, including servants, archers, and elite youths. [I command you] to inquire about small and large [matters] and of colleagues and neighbors, collect five measures of metal as pay. I award you crimson kneepads with a dark-colored belt and a pennant fringed with small bells for use in [military and ritual] service."

I, Qi, clapped my hands together and knocked my head against the ground and in response extolled the King's grace. I took the opportunity to make for Ji Jiang (Jiang lineage woman of the third birth rank) a sacrificial vessel for expressing reverence. May [I have] sons of sons and grandsons of grandsons to treasure and use [it] for ten thousand years.

Further Reading
Jicheng 4266.
Kimbun tsūshaku, 16.114.

Jinwen jinyi leijian, 172–73.
Li, *Landscape and Power in Early China*, 51.
Tang Lan, *Xi Zhou tongqi mingwen fendai shi zheng*, 306–7.
Wang Hui, *Shang Zhou jinwen*, 118–22.

CAC

24. Hu guigai 虎簋蓋

In 1996, the inscribed lid of a tureen vessel was discovered in Danfeng County 丹鳳縣, Shaanxi. It is presently stored in the Danfeng County cultural Bureau. The lid was broken into four pieces and bears an inscription that is identical to that on another lid by the same man, named Hu 虎, currently in a private collection in Taipei. It seems that the latter lid was at one point used as a top for a square vessel in the same private collection, and it has an inscription done for a man named Lao 老 (stating that Lao was awarded by the King for fishing near the capital). Since the patina and styles of the lid and vessel match, scholars suggest that perhaps the two originally had some now unknown sort of relationship. Because the figure Mi Shu mentioned in the Hu inscription also appears in the Qi *gui* inscription (no. 23, above), this vessel is considered to be from the reign of King Mu.

The inscription on the lids documents a formal court proceeding in which the king promotes and awards Hu as an honor to the legacy of Hu's ancestors who had also served the Zhou royal house. Hu's ancestors were members of the Tiger Guard, a set of militiamen related to the royal house who protected the king. They supervised certain personnel who worked in the military horse camps, the men who ran along with the chariots and the chariot drivers. They and Hu served under a Master Xi, who was in charge of the army that protected the king in the royal network of the Five Cities.[1]

Hu himself later became a master, although he still worked with Xi, but then in southern Fanjing 繁荊 region (later recognized as a gold-producing area under Chu 楚 state control). The evidence for this is found in the Shi Hu *gui* 師虎簋 inscription (*Jicheng* 4316), a ribbed middle Western Zhou style tureen with no lid, and now preserved in the Shanghai Museum. This inscription is dated to the first year of the following king's reign. It is written in an almost identical appointment inscription style, the work of a scribe Wu 吳. The new king awards Hu a pair of crimson slippers while renewing Hu's command in honor of the king's own royal father's legacy as well as that of Hu's ancestors. In the Shi Hu inscription, the king visits a different shrine, and it is Elder Xing 邢伯 who guides him into the ceremonial chamber instead of Mi Shu, as in the present inscription. Hu had dedicated this vessel and the earlier vessels to his deceased father Day Geng (named for day no. 7 in the ritual calendar).

[1] See Li, *Bureaucracy and the State in Early China*, 196.

Transcription

唯卅（三十）年四月初吉甲戌，王在周新宮，格于大（太）室。密叔內（入）右虎即位。王呼入（內）史曰：冊令（命）虎。

曰：胾（載>哉）乃祖考史（事）先王，嗣（司）虎臣。今令（命）汝曰：更厥祖考疋（胥）師戲嗣（司）走馬馭人，眔五邑走馬馭（馭）人。汝毋敢不善于乃政。賜汝赤市、幽黃（衡）、玄衣、紃屯（純）[2]、鑾旂五日，用事。

虎敢拜稽首，對揚天子丕杯（丕丕）魯休。虎曰：丕顯朕烈祖考粦明，克史（事）先王。肆天子弗望（忘）厥孚孫子，付厥尚官。天子其萬年䣱（申）茲命。

虎用作文考日庚尊簋。子子孫孫其永寶用，夙夕享于宗。

Translation

It was in the thirtieth year, fourth month, *chuji*, on *jiaxu* day (*ganzhi* no. 11), when the King resided at the New Hall of Zhou, that he arrived at the Grand Room. Mi Shu entered and guided Hu in from the right to take his position. The King called for the inner Archivist, saying: "Record my command to Hu."

The King's command said: "So! Your ancestor and deceased-father served the former king supervising the Tiger Servants. Now I command you, saying: I renew your ancestor's and deceased father's position to aid Master Xi in supervising the horse-runners and chariot-drivers of mine and of the Five Cities. You shall not dare to be unskilled in your governance. I award you orange leather kneepads with a deep-colored belt, a dark cloak with an embroidered hem, a pennant fringed with small bells and marked with five suns, for use in military and ritual service."

I, Hu, dared to clap my hands together and knock my head against the ground and in response extolled the Son of Heaven's great magnificent abundant grace.

I, Hu, said: "Greatly manifest is my blazing ancestor's and de-

---

[2] The graph 屯, read in this case as *chun* 純, was quite close in archaic pronunciation with the word *xun* 紃, a kind of cord. The two words together sounded something like *s-dun-dᶜun, and most likely referred to tassels of some sort.

ceased-father's glimmering luminosity; they were able to serve the Former King and subsequently the Son of Heaven does not forget their descendants, so awards them higher offices. May the Son of Heaven thereby extend his honorable mandate for ten thousand years."

I, Hu, make for my Accomplished Deceased-father Geng a tureen for expressing my reverence. May I have sons of sons grandsons of grandsons to eternally treasure and use it from dawn to dusk to present mortuary offerings at the main ancestral shrine.

Further Reading

Jinwen jinyi leijian, 214–16, 250–52.

Li, *Bureaucracy and the State in Early China,* 79, 133, 166–67, 194–97, 334.

Peng Yushang, "Yelun xinchu Hu gui gai de niandai."

Wang Hui, *Shang Zhou jinwen,* 122–26.

Zhang Guangyu, "Hu gui jia, yi gai ming."

Zhang Wenyu, "Hu guigai ming jianshi."

CAC

25. Shi Wang ding 師望鼎

This large, round, three-footed cauldron, decorated with a broad band of curly-tailed dragons around the body and a smaller band of abstract *kui*-dragons closer to the lip, is now in the collection of the Art Institute of Chicago after passing through the hands of four or five collectors. The first was a Qing minister, Zuo Zongtang 左宗棠 (1812–1885), who led his army into Xinjiang around 1880 and came back with this vessel. The inscription on a now-lost tureen (*gui* 簋, *Jicheng* 4272), also by a Wang, was preserved in 1842 in a hand copy. Both vessels are believed to have been cast during the reign of King Gong of Zhou. The two inscriptions may have been connected to a single reward ceremony for the same man.

The tureen inscription is as follows:

唯王十又三年六月初吉戊戌，王在周康宮新宮，旦，王各（格）大室，即位，宰倗父右（佑）望入門，立中廷，北嚮，王呼史年冊令（命）望：死嗣（司）畢王家，賜汝赤呂巿、鑾，用事。

望拜稽首，對揚天子丕顯休，用作朕皇祖伯甲（?）父寶簋，其邁（萬）年子子孫孫永寶用。

It was in the King's thirteenth year, in the sixth month, *chuji*, on *wuxu* day (*ganzhi* no. 35), when the King resided at Kang Hall and new Hall of Zhou, when at dawn the King arrived at the Grand Room. Once the King had taken his position, chief Domestic Officer Peng Fu guided Wang in from the right, who then entered the gate and took his position in the center of the court facing northward towards the King. The King called Archivist Nian to record the command to Wang on a bamboo ledger: "Take on the responsibility of supervising the King of Bi's family. I award you crimson-circlet-patterned kneepads and a pennant fringed with bells to use in military and ritual service."

I, Wang, clapped my hands together and knocked my head on the ground, and in response extolled the son of Heaven's manifest grace. I, Wang, take this opportunity to make for my Brilliant Ancestor Elder Jia? Fu a treasured tureen. May I for ten thousand years have sons of sons and grandsons of grandsons to eternally treasure and use it.

If we assume that the Wang is the same man in both inscriptions, then we can view the Shi Wang *ding* inscription as the response narrative to the award ceremony described above on the tureen. In the tureen inscription, Wang, a man with no title yet, is recorded as receiving his first formal charge, a job that may have included functions equivalent of a house caretaker, guard, and instructor for an elite household. In the cauldron inscription, Wang immediately identifies himself using two titles, one is Grand Master (*dashi* 大師), suggesting that he was a leader among other "Master" ranked members of his generation, and the other is Little One or Youth (*xiaozi* 小子), suggesting that he was still finishing mourning for his father. The cauldron inscription was dedicated to his deceased father, but the tureen inscription was dedicated to a "Brilliant Ancestor" (*huangzu* 皇祖), a reference to any ancestor from the founding ancestor of his lineage to his grandfather. Rituals celebrating the movement of a "youth" into the position of his father probably took place during the annual rituals (*di* 禘) to all ancestors, including the founder ancestor, in the main shrine. Wang may have been a descendant of a branch lineage going back to King Kang of Zhou.

Transcription

大師小子師望曰：丕顯皇考寞（究）公，穆穆克盟（明）厥心哲（慎）厥德，用辟于先王，得屯亡敃（愍）。

望肇帥井（型）皇考，虔夙夜出內（入）王命，不敢不遂不盡。王用弗忘聖人之後，多蔑曆賜休。

望敢對揚天子丕顯魯休，用作朕皇考寞（究）公尊鼎。師望其萬年子子孫孫永寶用。

Translation

Grand Master and Youth Master Wang said:

"Greatly Manifest and Brilliant, my Deceased-father Patriarch Jiu, gravely, so gravely, was able to make his heart luminous and to carefully attend to his *de* in order to aid the Former King, and [thus] achieve wealth without being harmed.

I, Wang, from the first followed and modeled myself upon my Brilliant Deceased Father [and likewise], respectfully from morning to night, carried the King's charge in and out [of the court], not daring to forgo pursuing [enemies] to the end. The King takes this opportunity not to forget the descendant of the sage Man, increasing his record of accumulated merit and awarding gifts.

I, Wang, dare in response to extol the Son of Heaven and his greatly manifest and abundant grace, and take this opportunity to make for my Brilliant Deceased Father, patriarch Jiu, a cauldron for expressing reverence. May I, Master Wang, for ten thousand years [have] sons of sons and grandsons of grandsons to forever treasure and use it."

Further Reading

Jicheng 2812.

Mingwen xuan, no. 213.

Jinwen jinyi leijian, 425–26.

Tang Lan, *Xi Zhou qingtongqi mingwen fendai shi zheng*, 425.

CAC

26. Li FANGZUN 盠方尊 AND Li JUZUN 盠駒尊

The inscription of the Li *fangzun* was cast into the interior surface of a bronze beaker thought to have been used to contain sacrificial ale. Approximately 17 centimeters in height, the angular vessel is ornamented with large arms that curl in the shape of elephant trunks and are elaborately decorated with symmetrical dragons in a style that corresponds to the earlier part of the middle Western Zhou period. The body of the vessel bears a circular emblem that appears on several other vessels sponsored by Li 盠 and discovered together in the same cache (see below), including a pair of square wine caskets with nearly identical decor and bearing a nearly identical inscriptional text, as well as a vessel cast in the shape of a horse. The Li *juzun*, approximately 32 centimeters in height and bearing an entirely different inscription, is remarkable for its equine shape, clearly related to the content of the inscription that was cast into the exterior surface of the horse's chest and on the interior surface of the vessel cover. Both vessels are currently in the collection of the Shaanxi Museum of History 陝西歷史博物館 in Xi'an.

The Li vessels were all discovered in Lijiacun 李家村, Meixian, Shaanxi province in 1955–57. Li, the sponsor of these vessels, was a member of the prominent Shan 單 lineage, though it is not possible to discern this from any of the inscriptions sponsored by Li himself. Li's identification with the Shan lineage is documented only in the inscription of the Qiu *pan* 逑盤 (no. 63, below), a vessel commissioned at least four generations after Li by a Shan lineage descendant and discovered in the same area in 2003. The multiple caches discovered over several decades in the Meixian area are a good illustration of the way in which information from several inscriptions can be integrated to provide a fuller historical picture.

In the inscription of the Qiu *pan*, Li is included within a long list of Shan ancestors and said to have faithfully served the Zhou kings Zhao and Mu, but only the vessels sponsored by Li himself provide any significant details of that service. Based on Li's status in the *fangzun* inscription, there is good reason to assume that the events recorded may have come later in Li's career, during the reign of King Mu. The inscription of the horse-shaped *juzun* commemorates an award to Li of two colts personally selected by the king. In his response, Li highlights the relationship between the king and the numerous aristocratic lineages. The inscription on the Li *fangzun* portrays Li as one endowed with great authority within the Zhou military, with duties in the two major divisions—the Six Armies associated with the Zhou homeland in the Wei River 渭河 valley and the Eight Armies of the eastern capital, Chengzhou.¹

Transcription (*Li* fangzun)

唯八月初吉，王各（格）于周廟。穆公又（右）盠，立于中廷，北卿（嚮）。王冊令（命）尹，賜盠赤市、幽亢、攸（鋚）勒。曰：用嗣（司）六師、王行、參有嗣（司）：嗣（司）土、嗣（司）馬、嗣（司）工。

王令（命）盠曰：䯅嗣（司）六師眔八師䢒（藝）。盠拜稽首，敢對揚王休。用作朕文祖益公寶尊彝。

盠曰：天子不叚（遐）不其（期）。萬年保我萬邦。盠敢拜稽首。曰：剌剌（烈烈）朕身。更朕先寶事。

Translation

It was in the eighth month, *chuji*. The King went to the Zhou Temple. Duke Mu, to the right of Li, stood in the center of the court, facing north. The King issued a command by writ to the Chief to award Li red kneepads, a black girdle-pendant, and bridle, saying: "Use them to supervise the royal legions and the Three supervisors of the six Armies: the Supervisor of Lands, Supervisor of the Horses, and Supervisor of Works."

The King commanded Li, saying: "Concurrently supervise the establishments of the Six Armies and the Eight Armies."²

Li bowed and touched his head to the ground, daring in response to extol the King's beneficence, herewith making for my cultured ancestor Duke Yi this treasured offertory vessel.

Li says: "The Son of Heaven is without flaw and without limit. For ten-thousand years [may] he protect our ten-thousand states."

---

¹ See Li, *Landscape and Power in Early China*, 103.

² Li Feng suggests that *yi* 藝 here refers to the establishment of camps or other structures, an extension of its basic meaning, "to plant". The parsing of this and the preceding sentence follows Li's interpretation that both the royal legions and the three supervisors designate institutions within the Six Armies (Li, "'Offices' in Bronze inscriptions and Western Zhou Government Administration," 35 n.102).

Li dares to bow and touch his head to the ground, saying: "I make myself valorous [so that I may] succeed my ancestors' treasured service."

Transcription (*Li* juzun)

唯王十又二月，辰在甲申。王初執駒于昏。王乎（呼）師豦召盠。王親旨（指）盠駒賜兩。

拜稽首，曰：王弗瞾（忘）厥舊宗小子，螽皇盠身。

盠曰：王佣（朋）下不其（期），則邁（萬）年保我邁（萬）宗。

盠曰：余其敢對揚天子之休。余用作朕文考大仲寶尊彝。

盠曰：其邁（萬）年世子子孫孫永寶之。

Translation

It was in the twelfth month, and the *chen* was at *jiashen* day (*ganzhi* no. 21). The King selected colts at An for the first time. The King called out to captain Qu to summon Li. The King personally selected colts for Li and bestowed two on him.

[Li] saluted and touched his head to the ground, saying: "The King has not forgotten the young son of the old lineage and has ... Li's person."[3]

Li said "The King befriends those below without limit, and so for ten-thousand years protects our ten-thousand lineages."

Li said "May I dare to extol the Son of Heaven's beneficence. I herewith make for my cultured father, Da Zhong, this treasured sacrificial vessel."

Li said "For ten thousand years may there be generations of sons and grandsons to treasure it forever."

Transcription (*Li* juzun cover)

王拘駒▨。賜盠駒。▨雷駱子。

---

[3] The meaning of the graph 螽 and the following expression (... *huang Li shen* 螽皇盠身) are not clear.

Translation

The King selected colts at X and bestowed colts upon Li. X Lei Luo zi.[4]

Further Reading

Jicheng 6013 (*fangzun*), 6011–12 (*juzun*).
Kimbun tsūshaku, 19.312–38.
Mingwen xuan, nos. 313–14 (*fangzun*) and 262–63 (*juzun*).

Falkenhausen, "The Inscribed Bronzes from Yangjiacun," 282–83.
Li Changqing and Tian Ye, "Zuguo lishi wenwu de you yici zhongyao faxian."
Li Xueqin, "Meixian Lijiacun tongqi kao."
Tang Lan, *Xi Zhou qingtongqi mingwen fendai shi zheng*, 483–84.
Wang Hui, *Shang Zhou jinwen*, 129–33.

DMS

---

[4] The meaning of this last phrase is uncertain, as is the proper transcription of the graphs.

27. Qiu Wei *he* 裘衛盉, Wusi Wei *ding* 五祀衛鼎, and Jiunian Wei *ding* 九年衛鼎

The Qiu Wei *he* was excavated in 1975 in Dongjiacun 董家村, Qishan 岐山 County, Shaanxi; it is currently held by the Qishan County Museum. It was part of a large cache of thirty-seven vessels, which included several by the same sponsor, Qiu Wei, who lived during the middle reigns of the Western Zhou. One of the most striking aspects of these finds is the wide selection of Western Zhou aristocratic lineages that seem to have been concentrated in a small area in the western Wei river valley, in modern Fufeng and Qishan counties. Consisting of architectural structures, tombs, and pits containing a wide array of materials, from animal bones to caches of bronze ritual vessels, the remains of these lineages are sprinkled throughout the area and often self-identified in the inscriptional texts carried on the bronzes. Such bronzes are typically found in caches, shallow pits containing anywhere from a single to over one hundred pieces. The prevailing explanation for such caches is that they were deposited by fleeing Zhou aristocrats as they prepared to evacuate the Zhou plain in advance of the Xianyun 獫狁 invasion of 771 B.C.E.[1] (For more on the enemy group known as Xianyun, see the Duo You *ding*, Xi Jia *pan*, Guo Ji Zibai *pan*, and Lai *pan* inscriptions, nos. 41, 48, 49, and 63, below.)

The Dongjiacun cache contained two distinct groups of inscribed vessels. The first group consists of four vessels sponsored by Qiu Wei. The appellation Qiu, meaning "fur," may indicate that Qiu Wei or his family was involved with the production of furs and hides, which are mentioned as a commodity in two of the inscriptions that he commissioned. The earliest of the four inscriptions sponsored by Qiu Wei dates to 930 B.C.E. and commemorates a royal award, while the other three inscriptions commemorate legal decisions in land dispute cases involving Qiu Wei. The second group discovered in the cache includes over a dozen inscribed vessels sponsored by members of the Lü 旅 lineage. The style of these bronzes marks them as late Western Zhou pieces, created several generations after those sponsored by Qiu Wei. There is currently no inscriptional evidence by which to explain how Qiu Wei might relate to the sponsors of the other vessels in the cache or to the Lü lineage in general.

[1] E.g., Rawson, "Western Zhou Archaeology," 371–75. It may well be the case that some caches were buried well before 771 B.C.E. As more caches are discovered, the situation may prove to be too complex to be explained by any single historical event.

The precise dating of the Qiu Wei vessels continues to be controversial.[2] They are unusually significant because they record land transactions that throw light on the degree to which land may have become a freely alienable commodity during the mid-Western Zhou.[3] Established doctrine in Chinese tradition held that until late in the pre-Qin era, all land was understood to belong to the Zhou king alone, with other individuals having only highly restricted rights of usage of various kinds.[4] Western Zhou inscriptions regularly record the King and other nobles with hereditary land rights as bestowing control of lands on subordinates, but instances of horizontal transactions involving land, particularly cases where land or rights to land were exchanged for other material goods, without entailments of service associated with personal allegiance, suggest practices consistent with an emerging concept of ownership that approaches freeholding.

The Qiu Wei *he* records such a transaction. Its events are located in the Wei river valley capital region, where one Ju Bo 矩伯 (the Earl or Elder of Ju) receives jade goods from Qiu Wei and assigns certain lands to him. The goods are assessed at a cash value in terms of cowrie shells, and an appropriate exchange value in terms of fields is specified. While this may at first appear very close to a private sale of land ownership, there are several features that complicate the picture. Although the value of the land does not appear to have been particularly high, judging from the items exchanged for it, the complex process of "notarization," requiring the witness of five prominent members of the nobility, suggests a strong proprietary involvement on the part of political actors as well as a legal structure.

Two other inscriptions associated with Qiu Wei provide additional evidence. The Wusi Wei *ding* inscription also records a land transfer concerning Qiu Wei, one that involved a dispute adjudicated by some of the same men seen in the Qiu Wei *he*. In the Jiunian Wei *ding* inscription, similarly, the transfer of land takes place within the explicit context of a court ceremony presided over by the King, suggesting that if the full cir-

---

[2] Because the Qiu Wei inscriptions refer to an unusually large number of individuals whose names appear on other inscriptions, they have become particularly central to sorting the dates of vessels.

[3] For other inscriptions mentioning the transfer of land, see the entries for Shi Yong *yu*, Hu *ding*, and Sanshi *pan* (inscription nos. 30, 35, and 45).

[4] The *locus classicus* associated with this notion is *Shijing*, "Beishan" 北山 (*Mao* 205): "Beneath all the vast heavens, no land is not the king's; to the edges of the earth, no men are not his subjects."

cumstances of the Qiu Wei inscriptions were completely understood, they might illustrate a complex interplay between ideals of royal and individual possession.[5] Moreover, the assessed value of the land as noted in the Qiu Wei *he* and Wusi Wei *ding* may be described in words pointing towards the tax income that fields would be expected to generate, and this might suggest that what was transferred to Qiu Wei was not anything approaching "ownership," but rather something closer to rights to revenue.

The Wusi Wei *ding* is currently in the collection of the Baoji Museum of Bronze Vessels 寶鷄青銅器博物館. Measuring approximately 37 centimeters in height and 34 centimeters in diameter, the tripod is decorated with a single band of interlocking S-shaped ribbons under the lip. The inscription is cast into the inside wall of the vessel in nineteen columns of uniformly sized graphs, 207 in total. The shape and decor, as well as the calligraphy, correspond to the middle Western Zhou period.

The Wusi Wei *ding* is important historiographically because it bears one of only two fully dated inscriptions—i.e., containing a year, month, moon phase, and day—that also mention a reigning king by name, circumstances which allow one to determine a precise date for the inscription within the Zhou chronology: the fifth year of King Gong (913 B.C.E.). Such fixed dates can act as "anchor points" in periodization schemes that establish a relative chronology for bronze vessels and inscriptions based on other textual, calendrical, or visual characteristics.[6] The Wusi Wei *ding* inscription is especially useful in this regard because it contains a large number of proper names that are also mentioned in other inscriptions, which can be assigned a rough periodization on the assumption that two inscriptions mentioning a common individual must date to within one generation of each other.[7]

The Wusi Wei *ding* inscription is also significant for the light that it sheds on the adjudication of land disputes and the legal system of the

---

[5] The exceptional nature of these multiple inscriptions suggest that Qiu Wei was distinctive in his entrepreneurial approach to land acquisition. The inscription that most closely parallels the Qiu Wei *he* in its description of land transaction is the Peng Sheng *gui* 倗生簋 (*Jicheng* 4262–4265; see below, the Sanshi *pan*, no. 45, note 1).

[6] For a discussion of the Wei *ding*'s date and historiographic significance, see Shaughnessy, *Sources of Western Zhou History*, 152–55.

[7] This is not always as straightforward as it would seem, because it is essential to differentiate generic appellations that could have been used by multiple persons from appellations related to a specific individual. For an application of this methodology to the officials mentioned in the Wusi Wei *ding*, see Shaughnessy, *Sources of Western Zhou History*, 116–20. For an interpre-

Western Zhou. According to the inscriptional text, the sponsor of the vessel initiated a suit against states Lord Li, who is accused of failing to relinquish land sold to the sponsor. Adjudication of the case falls to a coterie of officials known from other inscriptions to have occupied the upper echelon of Zhou elite. Why such prominent individuals would have been called on to pass judgment in what appears to be a private land dispute is unclear. However, the increasing frequency with which land issues appear in the inscriptional record from the middle Western Zhou on may be an indication of increasing pressure on the supply of land within the Wei River valley. In carrying out the judgment, the land in question is precisely demarcated, and the local leader, *bangjun* Li, is forced to evacuate. The settlement culminates in a feast joined by representatives of both sides of the suit, and finally with the creation of the bronze ritual vessel commemorating the successful suit and dedicated to Qiu Wei's deceased father.

The Jiunian Wu *ding* is identical in style to the Wusi Wei *ding* and is dated by archaeologists to 910 B.C.E. The inscription refers to an occasion when a non-Zhou chief titled *mei'ao* 眉敖 sent an envoy to visit the Zhou king. The title is no doubt related to the later title *mo'ao* 莫敖, used by certain members of the elite in the southern state of Chu. When an envoy representing another state came to court, he would bring tribute; in exchange, the King provided gifts. This inscription documents one way in which wealth was managed in the middle tenth century B.C.E. A Zhou official, Ju, "removes" items of value presumably from a Zhou repository. As a result or in concert with this exchange of goods, other exchanges among Zhou elite take place. This particular inscription documents those exchanges that benefit or increase the wealth of the Wei family, particularly Qiu Wei, who, as a furrier or official in charge of the woods and all associated hunting products, would probably have been involved in any gift of furs.

When land was exchanged or awarded, its borders were carefully defined in a process called *feng* 封, and when land was delineated, particularly when divided among heirs, the mortuary rituals of a particular family and the relations of these rituals to the Zhou rites would be considered. This connection between the mortuary system and the granting of lands is evident in the history of the term *feng*, which by the end of the Warring States

---

tation of the names in the Wusi Wei *ding*, see Li, "'Offices' in Bronze inscriptions and Western Zhou Government Administration," 41.

period could refer to a burial mound or to a land grant (granted, no doubt, so that the elite member and his family had a proper burial ground).

In Western Zhou bronze inscriptions (as in Sanshi *pan*, no. 45, below), the word *feng* refers to the use of earthworks or trees to outline land. The land given to the Yan family was divided into four secured or closed-off areas (another meaning of *feng*). The meaning of four *feng* could refer to the four borders of one land area shared by the Yan heirs or to the division of the land into four separate areas for each of four sons. Whether this land was for purposes of cultivation or burial is unclear. Land for cultivation was called *tian* 田 (as in the Qiu Wei he and the Wusi Wei *ding*), rather than *feng* as in the Jiunian Wei *ding*.

Transcription (*Qiu Wei* he)

唯三年三月既生霸壬寅，王爯旂于豐。矩伯庶人取堇（瑾）章（璋）于裘衛，才（財）八十朋。厥賈⁸其舍（捨）田十田。矩或（又）取赤虎（琥）兩、麀韐兩、賁韐一，才（財）廿朋。其舍（捨）田三田。裘衛迺龏（矢）告于伯邑父、榮伯、定伯、京伯、單伯。伯邑父、榮伯、定伯、京伯、單伯迺令參（三）有司，司土微邑、司馬單輿、司工邑人服眔受（授）田燹遹。衛小子㻫逆者（諸）其卿（饗）。衛用作朕文考叀（惠）孟寶盤。衛其萬年永寶用。

Translation

It was in the third year, in the third month, *jishengpo*, on the day *renyin*, at the time of the King's ceremonial review of the banner troops at Feng. The subordinates of Ju Bo took possession of royal audience jades from Qiu Wei, worth eighty strings of cowries, in appropriately assessed return for which Ju Bo relinquished to Qiu Wei ten fields. Ju also received two vermillion tiger-shaped jade pendants, two deerskin aprons, and a decorated apron, in total

---

⁸ The term *jia* 賈, rendered here as "appropriately assessed return," may involve a root meaning of "store" and be a metaphor of value based on retained tax revenue. Depending on the degree to which this transaction is viewed as straightforwardly commercial, the translation may be rendered simply as "sale price," correlated with the term *cai* 財, "value." Interpreters have also read the graph as *zhu* 貯 ("store"; "storehouse") and as *mai* 賣 ("to sell"), see Li Fan, "X wei jia zheng."

worth twenty strings of cowries, in return for which Ju Bo relinquished to Qiu Wei three fields. Qiu Wei reported this transaction through an oath taken before Bo Yifu, Rong Bo, Ding Bo, Jing Bo, and Shan [Bo]. Bo Yifu, Rong Bo, Ding Bo, Jing Bo, and shan Bo then issued the appropriate orders to the regional Ministers of the Three Affairs: Minister of Lands Wei Yi, Minister of War shan Yu, and Minister of Works Fu of Yi, and to those managing the transfer of lands, Xian and Bu. Wei's retainer X then arranged a feast for all involved. Wherefore I, Wei, have cast a precious basin for my accomplished father Huimeng. May I treasure and use it forever.

Transcription (*Wusi Wei* ding)

唯正月初吉庚戌。衛以邦君厲告于井伯、伯邑父、定伯、𤼈伯、伯俗父，曰：厲曰余執龏（恭）王卹（溫）工于邵大室東逆、榮二川。曰余舍汝田五田。正（政）廼訊厲曰：汝貯田不（否）？厲廼許曰：余審貯田五田。井伯、伯邑父、定伯、𤼈伯、伯俗父廼顜，事（使）厲誓。廼令參有嗣（司）：嗣（司）土邑人趞、嗣（司）馬頌人邦、嗣（司）工陶矩、內史友寺芻帥（率）履裘衛厲田四田，廼舍寓（宇）于厥邑。厥逆（朔）疆眾厲田。厥東疆眾散田。厥南疆眾散田，眾政父田。厥西疆眾厲田。邦君厲眾付裘衛田，厲叔子夙、厲有嗣（司）䚄（申）季、慶癸、燹褮、荊人敢、井人喝屖、衛小子逆其卿（饗）觴（賸）。衛用作朕文考寶鼎。衛其萬年永寶用。唯王五祀。

Translation

It was the first month, *chuji*, on *gengxu* day (*ganzhi* no. 47). Wei made a petition regarding the affairs of the Lord Li to Jing Bo, Bo Yifu, Ding Bo, Liang Bo, and Bo Sufu, saying, "Li said, 'I have taken charge of King Gong's irrigation projects at the Ni and Rong Rivers to the east of the Shao Grand Chamber.' Li said, 'I relinquish to you five fields.'"

Officials then interrogated Li, asking, "Did you sell the fields or not?"

Li then admitted this, saying "I sold all five fields." Jing Bo, Bo

Yifu, Ding Bo, Liang Bo, and Bo Sufu then reached a verdict and made Li swear an oath. They thereupon ordered the Three supervisors—Supervisor of Lands Pu, native of Yi; Supervisor of Horses Bang, native of Qi; and Supervisor of Works Taoju—and the Interior Scribe's associate Si Zou paced off Qiu Wei's four fields of Li and then relinquished the residence at his settlement. Their northern boundary reached to Li's fields. Their eastern border reached to San's fields. Their southern border reached San's fields and Zhengfu's fields. Their western border reached Li's fields. When states Lord Li gave his fields to Qiu Wei, Li's youngest son, Su; the Li Supervisor Shen Ji; Qing Gui; Bin Biao; Gan, native of Jing; and Chang Yi, native of Jing; were received by Wei's young son, who feasted and presented gifts. Wei herewith makes for my cultured father this precious cauldron. May I, Wei, for ten thousand years forever treasure and use it. It was during the King's fifth ritual cycle.

Transcription (*Jiunian Wei* ding)

唯九年正月既死霸庚辰，王在周駒宮，格廟。眉敖者膚卓吏（使）見于王，王大黹（致），矩取眚（省）車較幩、弘（靱）虎幎、希幃（貊幃）、畫縛、鞭革、鞣帛彎乘、金甐（鐮）錽；舍矩姜帛三兩，迺舍裘衛林蓍里。

嘑，厥隹（唯）顏林，我舍顏陳大馬兩，舍顏始（姒）虞（滕？）各，舍顏有嗣（司）壽商貂裘、盠（豫）幎。

矩迺眔濂鄰令壽商眔音曰：顳履付裘衛林希里，則乃成夆（封）四夆（封），顏小子具（俱）叀（惟）夆（涌封）；壽商曧（戲），舍盠冒梯㺯皮二、巽（選）皮二、業舄皮二、肫帛、金一反（鈑），厥吳喜（聲）皮二，舍濂虐幎，爰幩䡅靱，東臣羔裘，顏下（猳）皮二。

眔受。衛小子授逆者（諸），其賸衛臣䩋（號？）肫。衛用作朕文考寶鼎，衛其萬年永寶用。

Translation

It was in the ninth year, first month, *jisipo*, on *gengchen* day (*gan-*

zhi no. 17), when the King was at the Hall of Ju in Zhou that he arrived at the shrine. One of the *mei'ao* (southern chiefs), Fuzhuo, sent an envoy to see the King, and the King grandly provided for him. Ju selected as a gift an inspection chariot with patterned side railings, wide girth-straps, tiger canopy, animal-hair decorated bag, painted yoke bindings, leather whip and cloth ties with fringes of small bells for the horse team, bronze bridle and bit pieces. He gave in exchange three bolts of cloth to Ju's wife of the Jiang lineage and then gave the woodlands and village of X to Qiu Wei.

Ah! since they were Yan's woodlands, we gave a pair of large horses to Yan Chen, ties of a green color (?) to Yan's wife of the Si lineage, and a mink cloak and boar-skin canopy (hood?) to Yan's supervisor, Shou Shang.

Ju then, going to Zhai's neighborhood, charged Shou Shang and Di, saying: "After clarifying and surveying, hand over the woods and X village to Qiu Wei, and accordingly set up four outlined lands, so that each child of Yan can create an outlined land. Shou Shang, slaughter the animals and give Li two ram hides for making hats, two *nao* skins for large slippers, and two zebu hides; give Fei cloth and one *fan*-measure of metal; give to Que Wu two rhinoceros hides; and give Zhai a X-animal canopy, monkey-skin wrap for the chariot seat with straps; give Dongchen a lamb skin, and Yan two boar skins."

They all received them. The Little One (heir) of Wei gave a feast in return to the many involved and they sent the gifts to Guofei, servant of Wei. I, Wei, used it to make a treasured cauldron for my Accomplished Deceased-father. May I, Wei, for ten thousand years eternally treasure and use it.

Further Reading

Jicheng 9456 (Qiu Wei *he*), 2832 (Wusi Wei *ding*), 2831 (Jiunian Wei *ding*).

Kimbun tsūshaku, 49.256–94.

Mingwen xuan, no. 193 (Qiu Wei *he*), no. 198 (Wusi Wei *ding*), no. 203 (Jiunian Wei *ding*).

Cao Zhaolan, *Jinwen yu Yin Zhou nüxing wenhua*, 93–95.

Cook, "Ancestor Worship during the Eastern Zhou," 241–50.

Cook, "Ritual, Politics, and the Issue of *feng*," 215–16.

Cook, "Wealth and the Western Zhou," 269–73.

He Youqi, "Xi Zhou tongqi niandai juli."

Hsu and Linduff, *Western Chou Civilization*, 275–78.

Jinwen jinyi leijian, 447–53.

Lau, *Quellenstudien zur Landvergabe und Bodenübertragung in der westlichen Zhou-Dynastie*, 301–21, 353–61.

Li, *Landscape and Power in Early China*, 122–26.

Li, "'Offices' in Bronze inscriptions and Western Zhou Government" Administration," 11, 41.

Li Fan, "X wei *jia* zheng."

Li Ling, "Xi Zhou jinwen zhong de tudi zhidu."

Li Xueqin, "Xi Zhou zhongqi qingtongqi de zhongyao biaozhi."

Li Xueqin, *Xinchu qingtongqi yanjiu*, 98–109.

Lin Ganquan, "Dui Xi Zhou tudi guanxi de jidian xin renshi."

Matsui Yoshinori, "Seshū tochi ijō kinbun no ichi kōsatsu."

Pang Huaijing, *et al.*, "shaanxi sheng Qishan xian Dongjiacun Xi Zhou tongqi jiaoxue fajue jianbao"

Shaughnessy, "Western Zhou Bronze inscriptions," 79–81.

Shaughnessy, "Western Zhou History," 327–28.

Skosey, "The Legal system and Legal tradition of the Western Zhou," 107–9, 323–31.

Tang Lan, *Tang Lan xiansheng jinwen lunji*, 494–505.

Wang Hui, *Shang Zhou jinwen*, 134–43.

Xu Tianjin, *et al.*, *Jijin zhuguo shi*, 245–53.

Zhou Yuan, "Ju Bo, Qiu Wei liangjiazu de xiaochang yu Zhouli de benghuai."

RE (*Qiu Wei* he)
DMS (*Wusi Wei* ding)
CAC (*Jiunian Wei* ding)

28. Shi Qiang pan 史墻盤

After a dry spell in 1976, farmers in Zhuangbai village, Fufeng County, Shaanxi province, discovered a cache of 103 bronze vessels, 74 of them inscribed (see also no. 33). The hoard included vessels made by at least eight different people, with dates all through the Western Zhou period. In 1996, the vessel with the longest inscription, a broad flat basin (*pan*) 46 centimeters in width at the mouth and inscribed with 284 characters, was declared a national treasure. Not only does this vessel represent a set of bronzes collected in antiquity during the entire span of the Western Zhou period, but its text also eulogized that history, naming one king after another up to the King Gong period, when the vessel was made by a man named Archivist Qiang 史墻.[1] It is usually stored in the Zhouyuan Museum in Baoji.

The basin sits on a round base. The sides of the basin and the base are decorated with curly birds with long crests and *kui*-dragon-like coiled "lightning" decor. On the base the design is more abstract and the curly animal bodies have no features such as eyes or feathers.

The text of the inscription was cast into the bottom of the vessel so that it could be read through the liquid, presumably water or alcohol-infused waters for ablution. Physically it was applied to the surface in two halves, with ten lines in one half and nine lines in the second half. Every line has fifteen characters, each one aligned with the corresponding character in the adjoining lines, except for the last line, which has twenty characters crammed into the same space. Evidently, a line with more characters than average was preferable to a hanging last line of five graphs. A rubbing of the text might to us resemble a photocopy of two pages of a book with the binding in the center, although in fact its main text was no doubt first written out on bamboo strips. The last line consists of a formulaic prayer, possibly part of a longer blessing and prayer text chanted during the ceremonial process of producing the inscription. Since there are places where two different characters are used to represent the same word, or loan graphs were used for homonyms, it seems that much of the text was orally dictated, or perhaps rhetorical formulas were copied from different texts.

The subject of the text is a lineage narrative divided into two basic eulogies: one about the Zhou kings and one about Qiang's own lineage

---

[1] For a discussion on the dating of Shi Qiang's vessel and this hoard of bronzes, see Falkenhausen, *Chinese Society*, 56–64.

and the history of his ancestor's service to the Zhou kings. The first eulogy includes Zhou kings Wen, Wu, Cheng, Zhao, and Mu. The living king, cited only as the Son of Heaven, must have been King Gong, who is praised for following the way of the ancestral kings. The first eulogy ends with a tribute to the gods of Heaven and Earth, the ultimate progenitors who not only provided supernatural protection for the kings but also made sure that non-Zhou peoples (the Man of the south, in this case) submitted to the Zhou.

The second eulogy is to the vessel-maker's ancestors, beginning with the first who served a Zhou king.[2] This founder was a Shang archivist or historian who was settled by King Wu of Zhou in a place called Wei 微 near the ancestral capital of Zhou. The incorporation of the Shang official into the Zhou household also involved intermarriage. The earliest vessel set (a *zun* and *you* for storing ritual alcohol) in the hoard was a set made for a man simply called Shang after being awarded a Ji-lineage woman (i.e. a Zhou woman) along with other gifts. Qiang, mentioning only his male ancestors, sings about four more generations of ancestors, all named in Shang style according to one of the ten suns (names of the earthly stems in the Shang ritual calendar). After listing all his forebears, including his own father, his eulogy shifts tone as it comes down to himself, the living descendant. Just as was done for the living king in the first section, Qiang testifies that he dutifully followed the path of his ancestors and served the Zhou king. This second eulogy ends with a typical dedication of the vessel (to his father's spirit) and prayer.

Qiang's ancestral duty was as Archivist (*shi* 史), a position that included divinatory arts and star-reading, the recording of lineage narratives and songs, as well as being transmitter of the kings' commands (see Shi You *gui*, no. 31, below). The inscriptions on the bells that belonged to Qiang's descendant, Xing, tell us that the Wei lineage founder brought "eulogies" (*song* 頌) with him to Zhou (see no. 33). Some scholars suggest these were odes associated with divination. Others suggest that the word *song* should be read as *rong* 容, which as a noun could have had one of two meanings, one is to represent a container, such as ritual vessel (although there seem to be no other Western Zhou or Spring and Autumn examples of this usage), and the second is a reference to one's complexion as in one's glow-

---

[2] See discussion of the lineage in Falkenhausen, *Chinese Society*, 64–73.

ing appearance after the successful performance of ritual music and the display of one's "Awesome Decorum" (see the Xing bells, no. 33, and the Cai Hou Shen *pan* and *zun*, no. 74, below). In either case, the ritual vessel or the body "contained" the substance offered or received from the spirits. While it will remain a mystery what exactly the Wei family brought from the Shang court to the Zhou court, we know that the preserver of royal and lineage songs would also have been the archivist of memory and the preserver (and creator) of history. This highly literate Shang lineage was clearly very useful to the Zhou and held an extremely high position in the Zhou court. Moreover, even with their intermarriage with Zhou, they never lost certain aspects of Shang identity.

The eulogy listing the glorious deeds of the Zhou kings, most of which typically involved military campaigns to spread the Zhou mandate to the Four Regions (all surrounding non-Zhou regions), refers only to the suppression of the eastern native peoples called the "Yi underlings" (*Yi tong* 夷童) and only to "reaching the Yin (i.e., Shang) farmers and peoples." Another version of this line has been preserved in the "Gu ming" chapter of the *Shangshu*: "Taking the opportunity to be able to reach the Yin to complete the great mandate" 用克達殷集大命. Qiang's version of this tale clearly continues an earlier version that we see in the Da Yu *ding* (no. 11, above), which also refers to "their peoples" and to the opening up of land for the establishment of the Zhou state. In either inscription, the Yin people were the objects of "control," "correction" or "cutting up." One major difference between the two versions is that the Shi Qiang *pan* never refers to the Shang officials in a demeaning manner, whereas the Da Yu *ding* claims that the reason the Shang lost the Mandate was that its officials were besotted with alcohol (a tale also mentioned in the "Admonitions about Ale", the "Jiugao" 酒誥, preserved in the *Shangshu*).[3] Interestingly, Qiang's inscription refers directly to the earth god and Zhou progenitor, Houji 后稷, who, according to a legend preserved in the *Shijing* "Birth of the people" ("Shengmin," no. 245), was sheltered as an infant by Shangdi, the Deity Above. In the Da Yu *ding* (no. 11), the tale of Heaven sheltering a youth referred to the king as a boy rather than to Houji (as in the "Birth of the people" ode in the *Shijing*); if the legend is as old as scholars claim, perhaps one might take the analogy as an oblique reference.

---

[3] Legge, *The Chinese Classics*, III, 401 [PRG].

The reading and interpretation of many unusual words in this inscription are still debated. The language of the text is rhythmical and contains rhyming and near-rhyming within and at the ends of the lines. This suggests that the lineage tale was at one time spoken, chanted, or sung.

Transcription

曰古文王初敿[4]龢于政，上帝降懿德大甹（屏），匍（敷）有上下，合受萬邦。

訊圉武王，遹征四方，達殷畯民，永不恐狄虘[5]，長（懲）[6] 伐尸（夷）童。

憲聖成王，左右綬毅（會?）剛鯀（御），用肇徹周邦。

淵悊康王，遂尹億彊。

宏魯（旅）昭王，廣笞楚荊，唯貫南行。

祇覯（景）[7] 穆王，井（型）帥宇（訏）誨（謀）。

齺（申）寧天子，天子貎（紹）饡（纘）文武長烈，天子眉無匃（害）夒（睿?）祁（祇?）上下，亟（極>緝）獄（熙）宜慕（謨），昊照亡敿，上帝司（后）𥘅（稷）[8] 尤保受（授）天子綰令：厚福豐年，方蠻亡不䢅（迅）見。

[4] The expression 敿/𥁕龢于政 recurs frequently in bronze inscriptions. 敿/𥁕 has been conventionally read as li 戾 following the *Shuowen jiezi* 說文解字. Hou Zhiyi reads 𥁕 as xie 協 "to unite"; see *Xi Zhou jinwen xuanbian*, 126. Recent arguments support the idea that the phonetic in 敿 is nie 苹; see Pham, "You cong 'nie' zhu zi lun jinwen 'li' yu chujian X zi" [MP].

[5] The Dizu people may be the same as the 翟柤 mentioned in *Guoyu* 7.266 [PRG]; see Xu Zhongshu, "Xi Zhou Qiang pan mingwen jianyi."

[6] Some read the graph as Wei 岂 (微), which is possible, except that where the name Wei is mentioned later in this same inscription, the graph is clearly distinguished with an additional hand semantic [CAC]. Chen Shihui transcribes as 影, writing the name of a city established at the end of the Shang dynasty, and punctuates 永不恐狄，虘影戈尸（夷）童, "never feeling fearful of the Di, went to Shan (?) to punish the Yi underlings", reading 虘 as cu 徂 "to go." Others read it as name of a people, punctuating 永不恐狄虘影, "never feeling fearful of the Di, the Zu, and the Shan (?)." See Chen Sipeng *Xi Zhou Shi Qiang pan xin shi* [MP].

[7] This graph is read either as *jing* 景 (*C.qraŋ?) or as *xian* 顯 (*qʰˤenʔ); the latter reading is strengthened somewhat by the switch of the phonetic 見 (*N-kˤen-s, closer in pronunciation to *xian*) for the element 頁, also seen in *xian* 覯 (see inscription no. 67). The problem is that these graphs occur in inscriptions where the more conventional forms of *xian* also appear, as in the expression *pixian* 丕顯. I suspect that the graphs in question represent an alternative pronunctiaion of *xian* (and a meaning closer to *jing*?) used in certain ritual expressions.

[8] See Qiu Xigui, "Shi Qiang pan ming jieshi"; some read this graph as *xia* 夏 or *you* 憂.

青（靜）幽高祖，在微靈處，雩（越）武王既戈（裁）殷，微史烈祖乃來見武王，武王則令周公舍寓（于）周俾處。

甬（通）更（惠）乙祖，述（仇）⁹ 匹厥辟，遠猷腹心。

子厴 ¹⁰ 粦 ¹¹ 明，亞祖祖辛，毓（亞）¹² 毓子孫，繁䄑（髮＞祓）¹³ 多釐（釐），櫅角龔（熾）光，義（宜）其禋祀。

害（獻＞胡?嘏?）犀（遲?夷?）¹⁴ 文考，乙公瀺（遽 ¹⁵）爽，得屯無諫（諫），農嗇（穡）歲替（稼）。

唯辟孝友，史墻夙夜不墜，其日蔑曆，牆弗敢取（沮），對揚天子丕顯休令，用作寶尊彞，烈祖文考弋（式）寵（寶）¹⁶，受（授）牆爾䰜（祉）¹⁷ 福，懷髮（祓）彔（祿），黃耈彌生，龕（堪）事厥辟。

其萬年永寶用。

---

⁹ See Chen Jian, *Jiaguwen kaoshi lunji*, 20–38, esp. 21, 25; Sena, "Arraying the Ancestors," 69 [MP].

¹⁰ Some consider the graph 子 to be a loan for *zi* 孜 or *zi* 茲. The second graph is made up of three parts, the roof section 冂 with a possible version of *shou* 受 and a *ru* 入 underneath, so some read the graph as an unusually complex version of *na* 納. Instead of the bottom hand semantic in shou, some read a 子 with a 糸 between that and the top hand. I suspect the combination had something to do with fecundity and producing a lot of descendants.

¹¹ See Smith, "Rejoinder," 431–33 [MP].

¹² This graph is distinct from the graph read as *yin* 禋 (found in this same section) in only one detail, the right-hand semantic is 攴 instead of 礻. The original phonetic 亞 may have meant "swollen" in the sense of something dammed up or intentially blocked. Some read it as *zhen* 甄 in the later sense of "to transform." In the ode describing the birth of Houji (*Mao* 245), his mother performed the *yin* sacrifice and experienced *zhen* 震, a divine "movement" as symbolic of pregnancy before giving birth. The problem with this as a reading is that the ancient pronunciation does not seem to be close (*zhen* 亞, *qin, versus *chen* 辰, *dər).

¹³ Note that the word *fa* or *fei* 祓 seems to have had different pronunciations in archaic chinese as well (represented by the graphs for 髮 or 祓), depending on the phrase in which it was used. This evidence strengthens the idea that sections of the inscriptions were originally spoken.

¹⁴ The words represented by the graphs in the paraenthesis are close in pronunciation to the original graphs. The same combination appears in the mid spring and Autumn period Wangzi Wu *ding* (no. 73). Some suggest that the word written *hai* 害 should be read *shu* 舒, but the two words were not close in pronunciation.

¹⁵ Some read *ju* 遽 as "to strive" (*jing* 競) based on later commentaries on similar word combinations. The two words were not close in pronunciation.

¹⁶ Some read *zhu* 貯, "stored goods". See also the abbreviated version of this graph in a similar phrase in Zuoce Ling *fangyi* (no. 15).

¹⁷ The right half of the archaic graph is taken as the phonetic, *chu* 處, *t.qʰaʔ. From the context, a reading of "blessing" *zhi* 祉, *tʰrəʔ, seems likely.

Translation

It is said that in antiquity, when King Wen first took control and brought harmony to governing the people, the Deity Above sent down refined *de* and grand protection, which King Wen spread out to all the spirits above and below, and thus united and received tribute from the ten thousand states.

Sincere and forceful, King Wu went out on a corrective mission to the Four regions, reaching as far as Yin's farmers, and, never feeling fearful of the Zu branch of the Di (northern peoples), he punished the Yi underlings (eastern peoples).

Exemplary and sage, King cheng, together with those on his left and right, formed a solid driving force to open up and clear the land for a Zhou state.

Profound and wise, King Kang thereupon had governors settle the borderlands.

Vastly arrayed with armies, King Zhao broadly beat the chu-Jing peoples, thus connecting the southern passage.

Prayerful and illuminated, King Mu took [the former kings] as models and followed the great plan.

Continuing the pacification (of non-Zhou peoples), the Son of Heaven respectfully maintains the longstanding glory of Kings Wen and Wu. The Son of Heaven, extending their glory without harm, loyally prays to those spirits above and below; broadening the far-reaching strategy, he shines bright like the sky without tiring. The Deity Above and Hou Ji provided special protection, giving the Son of Heaven extended long life, large fortunes, and abundant harvests. The Man peoples (southern peoples) of the outer regions have all hastened to visit.

Tranquil and somber, the High Ancestor located Wei in a numinous place and, once King Wu had cut up the Yin, my glorious ancestor Archivist Wei went to visit King Wu, who then commanded Zhou Gong to lodge him in Zhou and give him a place to stay.

All-encompassing and kind, Ancestor Yi assisted and acted as a counterpart for his ruler and took on the ruler's distant plans as if they were as close as his own abdomen and heart.

Fecund and numinously bright, Ya-ranked [lineage branch

founder] Ancestor Xin abundantly produced sons and grandsons, purging them all of noxious influences and providing numerous gifts. With animals of equal-sized horns, blazing and radiant, he made them suitable for the annual purification ritual [to the former kings].

Great and far-reaching, my Accomplished Deceased-father, Patriarch Yi, energetic and bright, piled up goods without debt. With the planted grains harvested and annual sowing [performed], he acted as a leader, both filial to his parents and friendly to his brothers and cousins.

Both filial [to those above him in lineage rank] and comradely [with those equal in lineage rank], I, Archivist Qiang, from dawn to dusk do not fail to accumulate merit awards daily. I, Qiang, dare not obstruct [the flow of merit] and so respond to the King's gift and extol the Son of Heaven's greatly manifest gift and command. With this, I make a precious sacrificial vessel, an adorned treasure, for expressing reverence to my glorious ancestor, my Accomplished Deceased-father, who in turn gives to me, Qiang, blessings and good fortune; and I embracing his spirit, exorcise evil, and gain prosperity to live a long life to a hoary old age, in service to his highness.

May I have ten thousand years to treasure and use [this vessel] forever.

Further Reading

Jicheng 10175.

Mingwen xuan, no. 225.

Chen Jian, *Jiaguwen kaoshi lunji*, 20–38.

Chen Shihui, "Qiang pan mingwen jieshuo."

Chen Sipeng "Xi Zhou Shi Qiang pan xin shi."

Falkenhausen, *Chinese Society in the Age of Confucius*, 55–73.

Hou Zhiyi, *Xi Zhou jinwen xuanbian*.

Jinwen jinyi leijian, 685–90.

Lau, *Quellenstudien zur Landvergabe und Bodenübertragung in der westlichen Zhou-Dynastie*, 184–204.

Li Xueqin, "Lun Shi Qiang pan jiqi yiyi."

Li Xueqin, *Xinchu qingtongqi yanjiu*, 73–82.

Li Zhongcao, "Shi Qiang pan mingwen shishi."

Lian Shaoming, "Shi Qiang pan mingwen yanjiu."

Lian Shaoming, "Shi Qiang pan mingwen yu Xi Zhou shidai de zhengtong shiguan."

Liu Shi'e, "Qiang pan, Lai pan zhi duibi yanjiu."

Liu Xiang, "'Yi wushi song chu' jieshi—Du jinwen zhaji."

Pham Lee-Moi, "You cong 'nie' zhu zi lun jinwen 'li' yu chujian X zi".

Qiu Xigui, *Guwenzi lunji*, 282–83.

Qiu Xigui, "Shi Qiang pan ming jieshi."

Ren Zhoufang, *Guobao jishi*, 77–83.

Sena, "Reproducing Society," 108–10.

Sena, "Arraying the Ancestors in Ancient China: Narratives of Lineage History in the 'Scribe Qiang' and 'Qiu' Bronzes."

"Shaanxi Fufeng Zhuangbai yihao Xi Zhou qingtongqi jiaocang fajue jianbao."

Shan Zhouyao, "Qiang pan X-zi shishi."

Shaughnessy, *Sources of Western Zhou History*, 183–92.

Smith, "Rejoinder to Jonathan Smith, Research Note on Shun 舜."

Sun Zhichu, "Qiang pan mingwen jinshi."

Tang Lan, *Tang Lan xiansheng jinwen lunji*, 209–23.

Wang Hui, *Shang Zhou jinwen*, 143–56.

Yin Shengping, et al., eds., *Xi Zhou Wei shi jiazu qingtongqi yanjiu*.

Yu Haoliang, "Qiang pan mingwen kaoshi."

Yu Xingwu, "Qiang pan mingwen shier jie."

Xu Zhongshu, "Xi Zhou Qiang pan mingwen jianyi."

Zhao Cheng, "Qiang pan mingwen bushi."

29. Shi Zai ding 師𩛥鼎

Discovered in a cache of bronze vessels in 1974 in Qiangjiacun 強家村, Fufeng County, Shaanxi Province, this cauldron is presently stored in the Shaanxi Provincial Museum. It is a large, 85 cm-high, round-bellied cauldron with three legs completely free of decoration except for series of simple bands around the upper edge. Archaeologists date it to the eighth year of King Gong's reign (910 B.C.E.). The inscription commemorates an award by King Gong to the vessel-maker, Master Zai (read as 載), for his loyal service to the king's father, King Mu, and for his taking charge of the present king's education when he was a boy, thus enabling him to "become skilled at the Former King's *de*."

Master Zai was promoted to his father's position of Grand Master, a high-level bodyguard and tutor of the King. This inscription makes it clear that Zai's accumulated merit or "inner charismatic power" (*de* 德) descended from his ancestor, who had also worked for a Zhou king, and that the King's *de* had descended from the founding Zhou kings. In Zai's and the King's cases, they both had to earn the right to their fathers' positions by building up enough *de*.

The celebration of Zai's promotion and display of *de* was probably performed on the occasion of an annual *di* 禘 ritual, which, according to later accounts, was when the ancestral tablets in the main ancestral shrine were moved up in rank. Zai's father's spirit had moved into the rank of "sage ancestor" (*shengzukao* 聖祖考), a process that may have taken up to twenty-seven months of mourning and mortuary rituals on the part of his son. During the period of mourning for the father, the son remained in the status of "youth" or "Little One" (*xiaozi* 小子). From Master Zai's father's name, we know that he belonged to a branch of the Guo family. The Ancient First Ancestor (*guxianzu* 古先祖) was the Guo lineage founder.

It is significant that the word for "year" used in this inscription was not the by then typical word *nian* 年, signifying the Zhou agricultural year, but the word *si* 祀, signifying the ritual year made up of six cycles of the shang sixty day calendar. This archaic usage signified the fact that the award ceremony took place during the grand ceremony to all the Guo ancestors, including the most distant founder. The founder's name, Gu 蠱, is an odd one, as the word from Shang times onward referred to a illness inflicted by females upon males or by a spiritual curse. For this reason, many scholars attempt to explain it as a loanword, none satisfactorily. In the inscription,

Gu is written with *tu* 土.

There are many archaic graphs in this inscription for which only partial modern equivalents can be found. For example, the original graph for the name of the vessel-sponsor, Zai, was written with the phonetic *cai* 才, as is commonly found in the archaic form of *zai* 載. However, in the archaic writing of the name of the sponsor, the "chariot" 車 element is replaced with a "food" 食 element. The right hand part of the graph, now rendered as the "dagger-axe" 戈, was originally written as "two bound hands" 廾.

The importance of oral speech or song in the performance of the rituals, part of which is preserved in the inscriptions, is supported by the rhythmic repitition of the word *de* 德 (see also the Bin Gong *xu*, no. 53) and the rhymes (such as *de* and *bi* 辟, *tˁək and *bek) and near-rhymes within and at the end of lines in the testimonies of the King and Zai.

Transcription

唯王八祀正月辰在丁卯 。

王曰：師翻（載），汝克盡（盡）乃身，臣朕皇考穆王；用乃孔德璱（遜>遁？）屯（遜？）¹，乃用心引正乃辟安德，叀（惟）余小子肇淑先王德。

賜汝玄袞䋣屯（純）、赤巿、朱衡、鑾旂、大師金雁（膺）、攸（鋚）勒，用井（型）乃聖祖考，粦明命辟前王事余一人。

翻（載）襟²（拜）稽首休伯大師尸任載臣皇辟。天子亦弗忘公上父胡德。

翻（載）蔑曆伯大師不自作，小子夙夕尃（敷）古先祖烈德，用臣皇辟，伯亦克崇古先祖蠱（蠱），孫子一𠦪（任？）³皇辟懿

---

¹ The graph with the phonetic *sun* 孫 (*sˁun) is generally read as *xun* 遜 "modest, yielding," which would work with the Confucian idea of "purity" (*chun* 純), as is often the interpretation here. The word *xun* also meant "to present offerings" and "to withdraw (quickly)" (*dun* 遁, *lˁun) which makes it closer to 遜. The word was also close to the archaic pronunciation of *tun* 屯 *dˁun. I suspect the two words functioned here as a binome, something like *lˁun-dˁun, with the sense of offering (documents, advice, tribute) to the king or spirits and quickly withdrawing. In this sense, the expression is similar to other expressions for performing the business of the court, such as "coming in and going out" (*churu* 出入).

² The archaic graph 襟, here written with a 示 semantic, was usually written with a 手 semantic

德，用保王身。

甗（載）敢肇王，卑天子萬年，▨（裘>求?）▨（裘?）⁴伯大師武臣保天子，用厥烈祖介德。

甗（載）敢對王休，用妥作公上父尊于朕考號季易父報宗。

Translation

> It was the [time of the] King's eighth annual ancestral rite, the first month; the *chen* was in *dingmao* (*ganzhi* no. 4).
> The King said: "Shi Zai, you have exhausted yourself in the service of my Brilliant Deceased Father, King Mu, using your resounding *de* to present offerings and withdraw, loyally guiding and correcting your ruler's latent *de*, so that I, the Little One, became skilled in the Former King's *de* from the beginning.
> "I award you a dark cloak with embroidered trim, a crimson skirt, a vermilion belt, a pennant fringed in bells and silk threads, a 'Grand Master' metal-decorated horse girth strap and reins with a metal head ornament to use when you model yourself upon your Sage-ancestor and Deceased-father who made the mandate numinous and bright for (their) rulers, the Former Kings, and [in the same way, you] serve me, the one Man."
> I, Zai, clapping my hands together and knocking my head against the ground, [extol the King's] gift [regarding the fact that] the Elder Master passed on to Zai the responsibility of serving the Brilliant ruler. The Son of Heaven, at the same time, did not forget the extensive accumulated merit of the patriarch, my Father Above.
> I, Zai, extol the merit of the Elder Grand Master and, not

---

when transcribed in this common phrase as *bai* 拜 . With the 示 semantic it is elsewhere a loan for the archaic homonym *fei* 袚, see the Zuoce Ling *fangyi*, no. 15, above.

³ The archaic graph, composed of two elements, 甚 (*t.ɢəm?) and 冊 (*tsʰrek), with the first clearly a phonetic, is read by some to be a phonetic loan for 任 (*nəm-s) in the sense of "to protect, be responsible for."

⁴ There is no agreement on how to interpret these two obviously related graphs. I suspect that they are elaborate forms of *qiu* 裘 with the second graph emphasizing the leather aspect of the cloth; the semantic 韋 is a common loan for 革.

acting on my own, I, the Little One, from dawn to dusk spread the blazing *de* of the Ancient First Ancestor and use it to serve the Brilliant ruler, just as my Elder was able to perform the fire sacrifice for the Ancient First Ancestor Gu, so [his] descendents could all be entrusted with the refined *de* of the Brilliant ruler and use it to protect the King's person.

I, Zai, dare to be awarded by the King—may the Son of Heaven have ten thousand years! I pray to Elder Grand Master Qiu to martially serve and protect the Son of Heaven using his blazing ancestor's Great *de*.

I, Zai, dare to respond to the King's gift and use it to pacify and make for the patriarch Father Above a vessel for expressing reverence to my deceased father Guo Li Yi Fu and to perform the sacrificial reporting ritual at the [main] ancestral shrine.

Further Reading

Jicheng 2830.

Kimbun tsūshaku, 6.237, 607.

Mingwen xuan, no. 202.

Cook, "Auspicious Metals and southern spirits," 220–23.

Li Xueqin, *Xin chutu qingtongqi yanjiu*, 94–97.

Sena, "Reproducing society," 161–63.

Tang Lan, *Xi Zhou qingtongqi mingwen fendai shi zheng*, 492.

Wang Hui, *Shang Zhou jinwen*, 156–61.

Wu Zhenfeng and Luo Zhongru, "Shaanxisheng Fufengxian Qiangjiacun chutu de Xi Zhou tongqi."

Yu Haoliang, *Yu Haoliang xueshu wencun*, 7–24.

Yu Xingwu, *Jiagu wenzi Shilin*.

CAC

30. Shi Yong *yu* 師永盂

This middle Western Zhou inscription appears on a bronze bowl discovered in 1969 at Hubin 湖濱, Lantian 藍田, Shaanxi Province, in the valley of the Ba River 灞河, a small tributary that flows northward into the Wei River 渭河 at a point about 30 kilometers east of the Western Zhou capitals at Feng 豐 and Hao 鎬. Measuring approximately 47 centimeters in height and 58 centimeters in diameter, the vessel is currently in the collection of the Xi'an Museum 西安博物館, Shaanxi Province. The surface of the vessel is decorated with bands of dismembered mask patterns under the flared lip and on the ring foot, with a band of triangular pendants occupying the central part of the vessel body. Two upturned U-shaped handles and two animal heads with upturned trunks are positioned around the mouth of the vessel at regular, ninety-degree intervals. The decor and calligraphy of the vessel suggest a middle Western Zhou date, ca. mid-tenth to mid-ninth century B.C.E.

The Shi Yong *yu* was sponsored by Captain Yong 師永 in dedication to his ancestor in order to commemorate a land grant from the Zhou king. While we know very little about the sponsor,[1] other individuals mentioned in the inscription appear frequently in the corpus of Western Zhou bronze inscriptions, making the Shi Yong *yu* a crucial inscription for establishing the rough contemporaneity of a large network of individuals, who were active during the middle Western Zhou.[2] One member of this network is Duke Yi 益公, a figure who seems to have enjoyed eminent status in the Zhou court around the time of King Gong. In the inscription of the Shi Yong *yu*, Duke Yi presides over a coterie of officials responsible for implementing the King's command to grant lands to Captain Yong. Interestingly, this group is nearly identical to that which adjudicated a land dispute in the Wusi Wei *ding* 五祀衛鼎 (see no. 27, above), making it very likely that the Shi Yong *yu* dates to the same reign, only seven years later, in 906 B.C.E.

Although it is not clear whether the panel headed by Duke Yi represented any formal or standing authority in the Western Zhou government or just an ad hoc assembly of the Zhou elite, land transfers were evidently

---

[1] For the title Captain (*shi* 師), see Glossary.

[2] The key figure in this network is Jing Bo 井伯, who is mentioned in both the Shi Yong *yu* and the Wusi Wei *ding* 五祀衛鼎 (no. 27, above). For a study of this network and the associated methodology, see Shaughnessy, *Sources of Western Zhou History*, 116–20.

seen as matters of great importance to the state. Unlike the lawsuit described in the inscription of the Wusi Wei *ding*, the land granted to Yu comes as a result of a gift from the Zhou king. A number of people, perhaps local officials, are then ordered by Duke Yi to transfer to Captain Yong the lands in question, consisting of fields on either side of the Luo River 洛河, probably a reference to the tributary flowing southeast into the Wei River near its conjunction with the Yellow River.[3] The granting of land to officials was probably an important economic link between the Zhou court and the aristocratic families that staffed the royal administration with their sons. Such land, offered in exchange for service and loyalty, would have been an important source of wealth for the many aristocratic lineages that inhabited the Wei River valley. The inscription concludes with a proclamation of homage to the Zhou king and dedication of the ritual vessel to Captain Yong's deceased father and ancestor, Elder Yi 乙伯.

Transcription

唯十又二年初吉丁卯。益公內（入）即命于天子。公廼出厥命，賜畀師永，厥田淪（陰）易（陽）洛，疆眔師俗父田。厥眔公出厥命：井伯、榮伯、尹氏師俗父、遣仲。公廼命酉（鄭）嗣（司）徒圅父、周人嗣（司）工眉、𢦏史、師氏邑人奎父、畢人師同付永厥田。厥逨（率）塄（履?），厥疆宋句。永拜稽首，對揚天子休命。永用作朕文考乙伯尊盂。永其邁（萬）年孫孫子子，永其逨（率）寶用。

Translation

It was the twelfth year, *chuji*, on *dingmao* day (*ganzhi* no. 4). Duke Yi entered and accepted the command from the Son of Heaven. The Duke then brought out his command and bestowed a gift on Captain Yong.[4] The fields were to the north and south of the Luo

---

[3] Note that this location is at a considerable distance from the locus of the vessel's discovery, on the other side of the Wei River (Li Feng, *Landscape and Power in Early China*, 172 no.80).

[4] Tang Lan argues that the graph transcribed as 畀 depicts a crossbow bolt but is here used as a loan graph for the word *bi* 畀 (to give). The word evidently had a specialized usage concerning awards or transfers of land titles. This is also the way the word is employed in the Zhong *fangding* 中方鼎 (*Jicheng* 2785) and the Guo Cong *xu* 虢从盨 (*Jicheng* 4466). See Tang Lan, "Yong yu mingwen jieshi" and "Yong yu mingwen jieshi de yixie buchong."

River, bordering the fields of Captain Sufu. Those who brought out the command together with the Duke were Jing Bo, Rong Bo, Captain Sufu of the Yin clan, and Qian Zhong. The Duke then commanded Hanfu, Supervisor of Lands at Zheng; Dui, Supervisor of Works of the Zhou people; the Ya Scribe and Marshal, Kuifu, native of Yi; and Captain Tong, native of Bi, to relinquish these fields to Yong. They paced off the boundaries and made the border at Songju. Yong saluted with his hands and touched his head to the ground, daring in response to extol the Son of Heaven's beneficent command. Yong herewith makes for my cultured father, Elder Yi, this sacrificial *yu*-vessel. May Yong for ten-thousand years have sons and grandsons, whom Yong may lead to treasure and use [it].

Further Reading

Jicheng 10322.

Kimbun tsūshaku, 48: 191–200.

Mingwen xuan, no. 207.

Chen Banghuai, "Yong yu kaolue."

Jinwen jinyi leijian, 677–79.

Lau, *Quellenstudien zur Landvergabe und Bodenübertragung in der westlichen Zhou-Dynastie*, 222–27.

Qi Guiyan, "Yong yu ming canzi kaoshi."

Skosey, "The Legal System and Legal Tradition of the Western Zhou," 337–39.

Tang Lan, *Tang Lan xiansheng jinwen lunji*, 168–81.

Wang Hui, *Shang Zhou jinwen*, 161–63.

DMS

31. Xun GUI 詢簋 and Shi You GUI 師酉簋

These two inscriptions are important documents reflecting the organization of the Western Zhou defense and the relations of the Zhou with non-Zhou neighbors during the middle and late Western Zhou periods. The Xun *gui* was discovered in 1959 in Sipocun 寺坡村, Lantian County, Shaanxi Province, on the southern periphery of the Western Zhou metropolitan area. The tureen, with small zoomorphic handles attached to the body below the rim and pierced with large rings, is modestly decorated with rows of concave horizontal ribs, like comparable vessels from the middle Western Zhou period.

Xun, having a position of Captain (*shi* 師, cf. inscription no. 32 below), was a subordinate of Duke Yi (Yi Gong 益公), a military commander and influential courtier during King Gong's reign (for Yi Gong's war against Guai Kingdom, see the Guai Bo *gui* inscription, see no. 42, below). Xun was appointed as a general coordinator of activities of various military divisions, including the royal guard ("tiger-warriors," *huchen* 虎臣), foot soldiers, border watches, and many groups of non-Zhou peoples called Yi 夷, who performed services for the Zhou. The area under Xun's control stretched from central Shaanxi to the eastern royal residence, Chengzhou, in central Henan—a distance of about 400 kilometers.

After the discovery of the Xun *gui*, scholarly attention turned to the Shi You *gui* in the collection of the National Palace Museum in Taipei. Its inscription informs us that Captain You was charged by the King to assume general control over the "tiger-warriors of the City" and several groups of aliens. Hence, Captains Xun and You performed similar services in overlapping areas, although You controlled a smaller territory and a smaller number of subordinates. Xun dedicated his tureen to his ancestor, referred to by his temple name Yi Bo, and his wife of Ji 姬 surname, whereas You dedicated his vessel to "his deceased father Yi Bo" and his mother Jiu Ji 兂姬, i.e. a woman surnamed Ji. (Jiu 兂 was probably her temple name.) Some scholars have therefore suggested that Yi Bo referred to in inscriptions of both Xun and You was the same person and, consequently, that You was Xun's father. This is unlikely, considering shape and décor on the Shi You *gui*.

The Shi You *gui*, in contrast to the Xun *gui*, bears many late Western Zhou features: massive vertical loop handles decorated with three-dimensional dragon heads, and three small feet attached to a stand and decorated with high-relief feline heads, and with ornamental belts of horizontal scale and ring shapes on the stand, as well as on the rims of its body and lid. Nevertheless, Shi You and Xun could have belonged to the same family, one that practiced the Shang custom of giving temple names to ancestors according to the Heavenly Stems of the Chinese calendar. By chance, two ancestors belonging to different generations were named after the Yi stem.

Other sponsors of bronze objects can be identified as Xun's relatives with more confidence. The Xun *gui* was found in a hoard together with fifteen other bronzes, many of them identified with Mi Shu 弭叔 and Mi Shu Captain Cha 弭叔師察. In 1963, a bronze tureen commissioned by Mi Bo Captain Ji 弭伯師籍 was found in the nearby Wangchuan 輞川 commune. These finds indicate that, in Western Zhou times, this locality was called Mi 弭, and that it was a residence of the lineage to which all these persons, including Captains Xun and You, belonged. Possibly, Mi represented one of the Captains' Lineages (*shi shi* 師氏) residing in strategically important places and constituting the base of the Zhou military forces—the so-called "eight western and six eastern Captaincies" (*shi* 師, often translated into English as "garrisons" or "armies"). Ancient Mi was located in the valley of Zi 滋 River (presently known as the Ba 灞 River). Flowing down from the northern slopes of the Qinling Mountains towards present-day Xi'an, it offered a channel for movement into the Dan 丹 and Han 漢 River valleys that served as conduits between the Zhou and non-Zhou polities of the south. This also explains why so many aliens were under Captain Xun's command and why his subordinates included border watches.

Transcription (*Xun* gui)

王若曰：旬！不顯文、武受令（命），則乃祖奠周邦。今余令（命）汝嗇官、嗣（司）邑人，先虎臣後庸：西門夷、秦夷、京夷、彙夷、師笒側（鍘）薪、[趡]華夷、弁豸夷、廚人；成周走亞、戍：秦人、降人、服夷！易女玄衣黹屯（純）、載市、絅、黃（衡）、戈琱戟、厚必（柲）、彤沙、鑾旂、攸（鋚）勒用事！

旬稽首、對揚天子休令（命）。用乍文祖乙伯同姬尊簋。旬萬年！子子孫孫永寶用！

唯王十又七祀，王才射日宮。旦，王各，益公入右旬。

Translation

The King spoke as follows (*wang ruo yue*):[1] "Xun! Illustrious Kings Wen and Wu received the Mandate, whereas your ancestors established the state of Zhou on their orders. Now I command you to assume the office of *chiguan*.[2] Administer the people of the City, first taking care of the tiger-warriors, then ordinary men: aliens from Ximen, aliens from Qin, aliens from Jing, aliens from Chuo, wood-cutters of Captain Ling, aliens from X-Hua, aliens from Bianzhi, and men of Yu; in Chengzhou, administer the foot soldiers and frontier guards: men of Qin, men of Jiang, and aliens who perform services for Zhou! I bestow upon you a dark robe with embroidered border, leather kneepads, a light robe, a jade pendant, a halberd with a carved handle, a weapon with a handle wound with rope, cinnabar sand, a flag with tinkling bells, and a horse harness. Use them for service!"

Xun bowed his head, extolling in response the beneficent command of the Son of Heaven. He used this occasion to make this sacrificial tureen for his cultivated ancestor Yi-bo and his spouse of Ji surname. May Xun last for ten thousand years. May his sons and grandsons eternally use this vessel as a treasure.

This was the seventeenth sacrificial year of the King. The King was in the Shooting-Sun Palace (?). At dawn, the King entered. Duke Yi entered, accompanying Xun on his right-hand side.

Transcription (*Shi You* gui)

隹王元年正月，王才吳，各吳大廟。公族鳴（？）鼇入右師酉，立中廷。王呼史䚡（禀）冊命師酉：嗣乃祖。啻官邑人：虎臣、西門夷、䝞夷、秦夷、京夷、弁豸夷。新賜汝赤巿、朱黃（衡）、中絅、攸（鉴）勒。敬夙夜！勿灋（廢）朕令（命）！

師酉拜稽首。對揚天子不顯休命。用乍朕文考乙白寏（宛）姬尊簋。酉其萬年！子子孫孫永寶用！

---

[1] See Glossary.
[2] A title whose meaning is disputed; see Li, *Bureaucracy and the State in Early China*, 192 no. 5.

Translation

In the first year of the King, in the first month. The King was in Wu. [He] entered the Great Temple of Wu. Hong (?) Li of the Duke's lineage entered, [accompanying] Captain You on his right-hand side. [They] took their positions in the Middle Yard. The King ordered Secretary Lin to read aloud the command to Captain You. "Succeed your ancestors! Be the *chiguan* for the men of the City: the tiger-warriors, aliens of Ximen, aliens of Chuo, aliens of Qin, aliens of Jing, aliens of Bianzhi. I bestow anew upon you red kneepads with a scarlet pendant, light inner clothing, and a horse harness. Be respectful morning and night! Do not neglect my command!"

Captain You bowed, touching his head to the ground. [He] extolled in response the illustrious beneficent command of the Son of Heaven. [He] used [this occasion] to make [this] sacrificial tureen for his deceased father Yi Bo [and his mother] of Jiu Ji. May You [last] for ten thousand years! May [his] sons and grandsons eternally use [this vessel] as a treasure!

Further Reading

Jicheng 4321 (Xun gui), 4288 (Shi You *gui*).

Mingwen xuan, nos. 220 (Xun *gui*) and 192 (Shi You *gui*).

Chen Shihui, "Xun gui yu Mishu gui xiaoji."

Gu Jiguang, "Xun gui kaoshi zhi yi."

Guo Moruo, "Mishu gui ji Hong gui kao shi."

Huang Shengzhang, "Guanyu Xun gui de zhizuo niandai yu Hu Chen de shenfen wenti."

Li, "Succession and Promotion."

Li Fuquan, "Xun gui mingwen de zonghe yanjiu."

Rong Geng, "Mishu gui yu Xun gui kaoshi de shangjue."

Tang Lan, *Xi Zhou qingtongqi mingwen fendai shi zheng*, 425–28.

Xia Hanyi, "Fu bu fu, zi bu zi."

Wang Hui, *Shang Zhou jinwen*, 164–67.

MKh

32. Shi Xun *gui* 師詢簋

After the discovery of the Xun *gui* (no. 31, above) in 1959, scholars began to reevaluate a brush-written copy of an inscription on a vessel called Shi Xun *gui*, preserved only in a catalogue from 1144. The style of the two Xun inscriptions is very similar, although the military duties that are mentioned differ. Particularly notable is that both inscriptions include the date and other data descriptive of the award or appointment ceremony at the end of the inscription instead of at the beginning. The Xun *gui* was dated to the seventeenth year of a king's reign, probably King Gong, and the Shi Xun *gui* to the first year of a king, presumably the following king, King Yì.

As a child, King Yì had been protected by Xun, who was in charge of the palace guards, the Tiger Corps. Then the King found himself on the throne in the position of renewing Xun's charge while still in mourning (as a Little One or "youth") and still not finished with his education in the ancestral rites. The disasters that the King mentions here may have been the death of his father or perhaps an eclipse recorded for 899 B.C.E. This inscription also belongs to a group of contemporary inscriptions which feature the counselor Elder Rong 榮伯. Elder Rong may have been quite old by this time, as he was also the escort for Xun's father, Tong, during the previous reign (*Jicheng* 4270–71). Tong and his father had both married Zhou-lineage women, so Xun's role in the palace, like those of his forefathers, was as a trusted member of the extended family.

Transcription

王若（諾）曰：師訇，丕顯文武，膺受天令，亦則於（唯）[1] 汝乃聖祖考克尃（傅）右先王，作厥肱股用夾召厥辟奠大令（命），盭龢雩（于）政，肆皇帝亡昊（斁），臨保我又（有）周，雩（越）四方民亡不康靜。

王曰：師訇，哀才（哉）！今日[2]（昊？）天疾畏降喪，首（慎？）[3] 德不克畫，古（故）亡丞于先王，鄉（嚮）汝汲純卹周邦綏位余小子載乃事，唯王身厚福，今余惟纛（申）就乃令，令汝更

---

[1] The graph depicted in the hand-copy is *yu* 於 but is most likely a mistake for *wei* 唯.

[2] I suspect the graph 日 is a partial writing of the word *hao* 昊 which is a more common adjective for Heaven.

[3] The graph 首 is likely also a mistranscription. I suspect a version of the word *shen* 慎, "to care

INSCRIPTIONS   113

（惠）䧻我邦小大猷，邦佑漢辪（乂），敬明乃心，率以乃友干吾王身，欲汝弗以乃辟陷于難。賜汝秬鬯一卣、圭瓚、尸（夷）狁三百人。

訇稽首，敢對揚天子休，用作朕烈祖乙伯同益姬寶簋，訇其萬囟（斯）年子子孫孫永寶，用作州宮寶。

唯元年二月既望庚寅，王格于大室，榮內右訇。

Translation

> The King, agreeing [to Xun's promotion], said: "Master Xun! Just as the greatly manifest Kings Wen and Wu took on Heaven's command, you take as standard your Sage Ancestor Deceased Father. He capably tutored and aided the Former Kings, working for them as if he were their arms and legs and he helped promote as law the Great Mandate bringing peace and harmony to government. This brought the Brilliant Deity's unwearying gaze down upon us, and so protected our possession[4] of Zhou and eliminated any unhappiness or disquiet among the peoples of the Four Regions."
>
> The King said: "Xun, how sad! Now Bright Heaven, upset and fearsome, sends down destruction; as for taking care of the *de*, I am not able to delineate [its pattern], so that I have lost the legacy of the Former Kings. I face you, who have urgently and sincerely worried about the Zhou state and calmed the throne; I, the Little One, am the one to record your service, and personally reward you richly. Now I am renewing your command, and command you to enact with benevolence and in a unifying manner the major and minor plans of our state, giving nationwide aid and maintaining vast control; pay your respects and illuminate your heart [with *de*]; and to lead your allies to guard my person. I hope that you will not mire your ruler in difficulties. I award you one container of fragrant black millet ale, a jade handled ladle, and three hundred

---

for, be attentive to," was meant. The expression *shen de* 慎德, "being attentive to your *de*," was extremely common in Western Zhou period inscriptions and in transmitted texts (see n. 25 above, and nos. 46, 62, and 63 below). It was likely a form of self-cultivation.

[4] In other words, having the divine right to rule.

Yi and Yun captives."

I, Xun, knocked my head to the floor and dared to eulogize the Son of Heaven's gift. I take this opportunity to make a precious tureen for my Blazing Ancestor Yi Elder Tong and Yi Ji [of the Zhou lineage]. May, I, Xun, have for ten thousand years sons of sons and grandsons of grandsons to treasure [it] forever. I have made it for use in the hall of Zhou.

It is the first reign year, second month, *jiwang*, on *gengyin* day (*ganzhi* no. 27), when the King arrived at the Grand Chamber and Rong escorted Xun in from the right.

Further Reading

Jicheng 4342.

Kimbun tsūshaku, 31.185.

Mingwen xuan, no. 245.

Jinwen jinyi leijian, 256–58.

Li, *Bureaucracy*, 101, 125–26, 131.

Li Xueqin, "Shi Xun gui yu 'Zhai gong.'"

Shaughnessy, *Sources of Western Zhou History*, 117, 255–57, 269.

Wang Hui, *Shang Zhou jinwen*, 181–85.

CAC

33. Xing zhong 㝬鐘 and related inscriptions

Of the 103 bronze vessels and bells found in the Zhuangbai hoard in Fufeng, Shaanxi Province, in 1976, the majority belonged to a man named Xing 㝬. Forty-three bronzes were clearly marked with his name and a few others belonged to the same era—Kings Yi through Xiao—and were probably part of his collection. His personal ritual display included: one round and one square cauldron (*ding*), five inscribed identical hollow-legged cauldrons (*li*), and two other non-matching *li*, two inscribed *xu*-style tureens, one inscribed high-legged eating dish (*dou*), two inscribed *fu*-style serving vessels, two inscribed spatulas, two inscribed *hu*-style alcoholic beverage storage vessels, four ladles of different sizes, two inscribed archaic *jue*-style drinking beakers, seven small *ling*-bells, and one of the earliest sets of tuned bells in the world: four inscribed Style IV chime bells (Group A), six inscribed Style V bells (Group B), three inscribed Style VI bells (Group C), one inscribed Style VII bell (Group D).

The number of bronzes, particularly the extensive bell set with four styles of bells (each representing a separate casting event), show that Xing (Archivist Qiang's son, see no. 28, above), was the wealthiest member of the Wei family. But by the time the Zhuangbai cache was buried, it no longer belonged to him. Instead, the owner may have been the unnamed husband of a woman named Da 大 who had ten identical inscribed *li* vessels in the hoard, which were awarded to her by a man named Elder Former Father (Bo Xian Fu 伯先父) (*Jicheng* 649–658). Since this may have been Da's father, it is possible that the vessels were part of her dowry. The occasion was probably her marriage to a Wei descendant and for use in the Wei shrine. The inscriptions on her vessels are typical of hundreds of similar dedications from men to women during the second half of the Western Zhou period.

伯先父作妖尊鬲。其子子孫孫永寶用。

> Elder Former Father made *li*-vessels for Da to express reverence. May she have sons of sons and grandsons of grandsons eternally to treasure and use it.

Of Xing's own vessels, the earliest were the two *hu*-vase-style alcohol storage vessels (*Jicheng* 9726–9728):

唯三年九月丁巳，王在鄭饗醴，呼虢叔召瘨賜羔俎。

己丑，王在句陵饗逆酒，呼師壽召瘨賜豝俎。

拜稽首敢對揚天子休。用作皇祖文考尊壺。瘨其萬年永寶。

It was in the third year of the King's reign, ninth month, on *dingsi* day (*ganzhi* no. 54), when the King was in Zheng at a feast celebrating the sweet-wine ritual; he called Guo Shu to summon Xing and award him an altar table of lamb meat.

On *jichou* day (*ganzhi* no. 26), when the King was at Gouling feasting and celebrating a gift of ale, he called Shi Shou to summon Xing and award him an altar table of boar's meat.

Xing clapped his hands together and touched his head to the ground and dared in response extol the Son of Heaven's grace. He took the opportunity to make for his Brilliant Ancestor and Accomplished Deceased-father *hu*-vessels for expressing reverence.

May I, Xing, have ten thousand years eternally to treasure them.

In the following year, Xing cast two *xu*-tureens (*Jicheng* 4462–4463):

唯四年二月既生霸戊戌，王在周師錄宮格大室即位。司馬共佑瘨。王呼史年冊賜：幣、靳鞃、巿、鋚勒。

敢對揚天子休。用作文考寶簋。瘨其萬年子子孫孫永寶。

 Emblem： 木羊冊

It was in the fourth year of the King's reign, second month, *jishengba*, on *wuxu* day (*ganzhi* no. 35), when the King arrived at the Hall of Zhou Master Lu. Once he had ascended to the Grand Chamber and taken his seat, Sima Gong guided in Xing from the right. The King called Archivist Nian to make a record and award Xing a leather belt, reins with embroidery, kneepads, and a bit and bridle.

Xing dared in response to extol the Son of Heaven's grace and took this opportunity to make for his Accomplished Deceased-father treasured *gui*-tureen. May I, Xing, have ten thousand years and sons and grandsons eternally to treasure them. [Emblem]

This inscription ends with a lineage emblem depicting a "goat" 羊 under a "tree" 木 in between two graphs depicting "bamboo-strip texts" 冊. It is unusual to find such an emblem so late in the Western Zhou era. In Xing's case, it can be traced back to the branch lineage founder (called Yazu Zu Xin 亞祖祖辛 in the Shi Qiang *pan*, no. 28, above), who is considered the owner of the King Zhao-period Qi 㫃 group of inscribed vessels also found in the hoard. These vessels bear the same emblem. The emblem was carried on by his son, Feng 豐 (presumed to be Qiang's father, Yi Gong 乙公), and, although it does not appear on the Shi Qiang *pan* (or the one other vessel with Qiang's name, a *jue* drinking vessel), Qiang must have also used it. The Wei family cache also included another emblem found on a matching pair of *zun* and *you* vessels in the collection that date back to the late Shang or early Zhou period (*Jicheng* 5404–5405). This one, ▮ , consisting of a "son" 子 held up by two hands forming a graph meaning "to offer up, pay respects" 共, and placed between one or two back-to-back "pallet" 爿片 graphs, is considered a typical Shang emblem produced at Anyang and perhaps symbolic of the Shang house itself, which, according to later texts, had the lineage name of *zi* 子 (see the Zi Huang *zun*, no. 2, above). The Shang bronze found in the Wei-family cache records an award to a Zhou-lineage woman (Ji) by a ruler called by the singular epithet of *di si* 帝司, which some read as "deceased King's heir" (*disi* 帝嗣). Others suggest it could be read as "deceased King's wife, the queen" (*di hou* 帝后).

Other bronze inscriptions document queens' granting of awards to elite women, in this case to a Zhou woman of the Ji 姬 lineage (compare the early Spring and Autumn period Jin Jiang *ding*, no. 68, below). Besides precious cowries, the queen awarded her arrows measured by the metal's weight. Because the arrows were of the type with strings attached, normally associated with hunting, perhaps she or her guard used them in rituals.

This inscription suggests to us that part of setting up the Wei family within the Zhou-controlled region involved intermarriage. It also suggests that the Wei family may have been originally related to the Shang court before Shi Qiang's and Xing's ancestor broke off, establishing their own branch lineage and separate emblem.

唯五月，辰在丁亥，帝司（后？）賞庚姬貝卅朋，䙷（弋）

絲廿孚（鋝）。

商用作文辟日丁寶彝。

It was in the fifth month, when the chen was in *dinghai*, that the Queen awarded Geng Ji thirty cowries and 20 *lüe* worth of arrows with silk tassels.

Shang took this opportunity to make a precious sacrificial vessel for Ruler Wen, Day Ding.

Nine years after Xing had cast the two *hu* mentioned above, the King once again rewarded Xing, causing him to cast another pair of *hu* (*Jicheng* 9723–24). The ceremonial document is very formal, if short. In the shrine, palace, or office (*gong* 宮)[1] near Chengzhou, the centrally located Zhou administrative city, Xing was guided in by a Father Xi. A very similar document found in a bronze cache in Chang'an District features a Patriarch Xi guiding in a Master for awards during the first year of what was perhaps the next king after Xing's.[2] The award list on the two new *hu*-vessels belonging to Xing notes only a gift of ritual or prestige clothing:

唯十又三年九月初吉戊寅，王在成周司土淲宮格大室即位。徲（犀）父佑瘨。

王呼作冊尹冊賜畫袞牙襮赤舄。

瘨拜稽首對揚王休。瘨其萬年永寶。

It was in the thirteenth year, ninth month, *chuji*, on *wuyin* day (*ganzhi* no. 15), when the King was at the Hall of Situ Hu in Chengzhou, arrived at the Grand Chamber and took his seat. Xi Fu guided in Xing from the right.

The King called Record-maker Yin to award Xing a patterned cloak with tooth-patterned trim and a pair of crimson slippers.

I, Xing, clapped my hands together and bowed my head to the floor and in response extolled the King's grace. May I, Xing, have ten thousand years to eternally treasure them.

Archaeologists found eight identical *gui*-style tureens belonging to Xing

---

[1] See Li Feng's discussion in *Bureaucracy and the State*, 114–17, 142.
[2] For Xi Gong 遲公, see the four tureens, the Yuannian Shi Li *gui* 元年師旋簋 (*Jicheng* 4279–82).

of the Wei family in the cache discovered in 1976 in Zhuangbai, Fufeng, Shaanxi (*Jicheng* 4170–77). They are round vessels with horned animals on the handles and attached to square stands with open holes so that they could be used for cooking. The decor consists of panels of vertical ribs and two registers of large fish-scales running around the lip of the vessels on the main body and lid. The lids have flat round rings on the top that serve as handles and stands for serving. The inscription is similar to that found on the bells, although much simplified. In this version, his ancestors were praised for "supervising" (*si* 司) the performance of Awesome Decorum (*weiyi* 威儀), a musical performance signaling achievement in the military and ritual arts, thus confirming their roles as ritual masters (see Shi Qiang *pan*, no. 28). Interestingly, the graph writing "supervise, manage" was originally the same graph used for "inherit, succeed into the position of" (*si* 嗣). It suggests that this type of official duty may have been inherited within a family. The Wei family role as historians involved training elite sons, including their own, in the proper performance of their lineage narratives.

痶曰：顯皇祖考嗣（司）威義（儀），用辟先王。不敢弗帥用夙夕，王對痶楙（懋）賜佩，作祖考簋。其醇（享）祀大神。大神綏多福，痶萬年寶。

Xing said: "My manifest Brilliant Ancestors and Deceased-father supervised the performance of Awesome Decorum in order to serve the Former Kings. Because I would not dare not to follow their model and used it (in serving the ancestors and king) from dawn to dusk, the King responded to (this legacy inherited by Xing) and decorated me, Xing, with dangling jade ornaments. I took this opportunity to make tureens for my ancestors and deceased-father. May the tureens be used to present mortuary offerings in the annual sacrifice to the Great Spirits so that they, once calmed, may multiply my good fortune and cause me, Xing, to have ten thousand years in which to treasure the tureens."

Except for the inscriptions on the eight *gui*-tureens, discussed above, and the bells (discussed below), the remaining inscriptions on vessels dated to

---

[3] An unprovenanced *ding* vessel documented a gift of the vessel to a Wei Bo and Yuan Shi, probably his wife (see the Hui *ding*, *Jicheng* 2490). It has the same emblem as on the two *xu*-tureen vessels made by Xing, as mentioned above.

Xing's generation are simple statements of manufacture. Five high-footed *li*-style cauldrons and two engraved ladles belonged to an Elder of Wei 微伯, a relative in the same sub-branch as Xing (*Jicheng* 516–20, 972–73).³ Xing honored his father, Qiang (see no. 28, above), with a set of three vessels in the old-fashioned *jue*-style—drinking vessels once popular in the Shang. He referred to Qiang as Father Ding, confirming the adherence of the Wei people to the sixty-day ritual calendar.

The *gui*-tureen discussed above and bell inscriptions are different from the other inscriptions because they are not records of reward ceremonies or simple statements of manufacture. Instead, like the Shi Qiang *pan*, they record a song by the gift recipient or vessel sponsor and are marked with the oral cue *yue* 曰, "to speak." In Qiang's case and in one group of Xing's bells the words were marked not as his but as those anciently handed down through time. In either case, the inscriptions might be understood as part of the "response" (*dui* 對) or the text of the eulogy sung when the awardee "extols" (*yang* 揚) the gift-giver (such as the king).⁴ None of these texts is marked with family emblems. In both the Shi Qiang *pan* and the bells, we see a focus on memorializing the present in terms of a lineage history. These inscriptions remind us that in the bone and bronze inscriptions of Shang and Western Zhou periods, words referring to the time of the ancestors refer to either recent "remembered" past, *xi* 昔 (involving kings and individuals either present or recently deceased), or "narrated" mythical past *gu* 古 (involving the Former Kings, particularly hero-founders such as Wen and Wu). (See, for example, the He *zun*, no. 6, above, or the Da Ke *ding*, no. 46, below.) The distinction is somewhat blurred in the transmitted texts, but *gu* remains the term most closely resembling our notion of "antiquity." In transmitted texts, *gu* was the mythical time of all hero-kings (not just Wen and Wu) and a time that early Confucians promoted as a source of emulation (consider the "Yaodian" 堯典 chapter of the *Shangshu*, as well as the *Lunyu*).

In Group A, each of the four bells has the same inscription cast onto the bell in typical style: first down along the right side of the bell, continuing into the middle, and finishing down the other side. Xing first eulogizes his ancestral lineage, and their performance of "Awesome Decorum." The Wei family seemed to specialize in the ritual arts and be involved in the preservation of songs and texts. The word "eulogy," *song* 頌 (*s-[ɢ]oŋ-s), was a near-homonym for the "complexion, attitude," *rong* 容 (*[ɢ](r)oŋ),

⁴ See Glossary.

borne when one performed Awesome Decorum, possibly a dance as well as a song. The culmination of "Awesome Decorum" training is represented in the Group A inscription when the heir "grasped the luminous *de*," the *de* or merit and wealth accumulated by the lineage heads through the generations.

The inscription on the six bells of Group B is not repeated, but continuous across all the bells; it retells the tale of the founding of Zhou by Kings Wen and Wu and of the Wei founder ancestor being resettled in Zhou, earlier recorded in the Shi Qiang *pan* but with the added detail that he brought with him fifty-one songs or performance types.

The inscription on the three Group C bells is a simple statement of manufacture but with the added oath that they would be used for ten thousand years. The bell in Group D is similar in size to the group A bells but has slightly different decor and a different inscription that was cast in a grid pattern, also along the edges and in the central panel. Differences in the writing style of graphs found in both groups suggest also the hand of a different scribe or artisan. The song on this bell continues to attest to Xing's ritual performance and to praise the ancestors. Xing offered up animals with horns wrapped in foil. The fragrances of meat and alcohol offerings helped the descendants summon the spirits to descend to the festivities. Lulled with music, which could include singing, dancing, and instrumentals, the spirits handed out blessings to the sound of thunderous bell music.

The use of reduplicative binomes, such as *fengfeng yiyi* 豐豐㲋㲋 (繹繹)[5] (*$p^h(r)oŋ$-$p^h(r)oŋ$ lak-lak), represented the sound of the music, including bells (possibly represented by the velar nasal finals *-ŋ), which was particularly associated with the moment of blessings being sent down by the ancestors to their descendants. The words, like charms, also represented abundance.

---

[5] Interpreting the poetic binome behind this reduplicated archic graph depends on which element is taken as the phonetic. If we accept the upper part as *tu* 兔 (*$\mathfrak{l}^\mathfrak{s}$a-s) then the word *yi* 繹 (*lak) in the common binome *yiyi* is a candidate. If we accept that *quan* 泉 (*G^war), then the word *huan* 桓 (*$G^{wˤ}ar$) in the common binome *huanhuan* is possible. The latter binome is common in Western Zhou inscriptions but was written with the 亘 phonetic (see group D bell inscriptions, below). Some read it as *chuo* or *zhuo* 兔 (see the Xun *gui*, no. 31, above). If this was the phonetic, then we might expect something like *$t^\mathfrak{s}rawk$, still possibly transforming into the later *yiyi* if the initial instead of the final changed over time or region. For a variety of readings, see inscription nos. 44, 46, 57, 60, 62, and 63. Often 豐 in this set was written with an added 攵 signifier. Compare the interpretation in no. 62.

Transcription (Group A)

瘨曰：丕顯高祖、亞祖、文考，克明厥心，疋（胥）尹彝
（典）⁶厥 威義（儀）用辟先王。瘨不敢弗帥祖考秉明德，貊
（昭）夙夜左（佐）尹氏。

皇王對瘨身楙（懋）賜佩，敢作文人大寶協龢鐘。用追孝龏
（享）祀，邵（昭）各（恪）樂大神，大神其陟降嚴祜，業綏厚
多福，其豐豐龠龠（繹繹）授余屯魯、通祿、永令（命）、眉壽
靈終。瘨其萬年永寶日鼓。

Translation

Xing said: "Greatly Manifest High Ancestor, Ya-ranked Ancestor, and Accomplished Deceased-father, [you] were all able to make your hearts so luminous and, as governing officers, to make your [display of] Awesome Decorum so regular that [you] could use [it] to serve the Former Kings. I, Xing, do not dare not to follow [the pattern of my] ancestors and Deceased-father in grasping the luminous *de*; I glorify [them] from dawn to dusk aiding the Governor Chiefs.

The Brilliant King has in response decorated me with dangling jade jewelry; I dare to make for my Accomplished Ones a great treasure, a [set of] harmonious chime-bells in order to pursue [the spirits in memory] and present filial mortuary offerings to perform the annual sacrifice [to the former kings and ancestors]; summoning [them] and [making them] arrive, [we] entertain the Great Spirits with music and [cause] them to ascend and descend, sternly providing blessings; the stand [of bells] calms [the spirits], who then multiply the good fortune. May they—so fruitful and mighty—give me bountiful abundance, surpassing emoluments, eternal life, extended longevity, and a numinous end. May I, Xing, for ten thousand years eternally treasure and daily ring [these bells].

---

⁶ Some read the graph as *xu* 敘.

⁷ The word describing a series of bells, *lin*, was written various ways over the centuries, but basic components of the ancient graph include 亩, 林, or 秝. See, for example, the Jing Ren Ning *zhong*, no. 60. See also Glossary.

Transcription (Group B)

曰古文王，初盭龢于政，上帝降懿德大甹（屏），匍（敷）有四方，會受萬邦，雫（越）武王既弋（裁）殷，微史烈祖來見武王，武王則令周公舍寓（于）以五十頌處。

今癏𠂤夕虔敬卹厥死（尸）事，肇作龢林⁷鐘，用融（庸）綏厚多福，廣啟癏身，勴⁸于永令（命），懷受余爾齰（祉）福靈終。癏其萬年，嚌（齊）角鼗（熾）光，義（宜）文神無彊𩁧（景）福，用璃（寓）光興身，永余寶。

Translation

It is said that in antiquity King Wen first brought harmony to government so that the Deity Above sent down Refined *De* and Grand Protection encompassing the Four Regions and convening and receiving [the submission of] the ten thousand states. Ah! Once King Wu had cut the Yin to pieces, my Glorious Ancestor, Archivist Wei, came to Zhou to appear before King Wu, who then commanded the Patriarch of Zhou to settle him in a place for the Fifty Eulogy Performances.

Now I, Xing, from dawn to dusk steadfastly express my respect and devotion to take over the ancestral service, and so take the initiative to make harmonious chime bells in order to calm the spirits, along with the fragrance of cooked food, so they provide blessings and good fortune, expand and open my person, so that I can rejoice in eternal life and can embrace and receive in me

---

⁸ The phonetic of this unknown word is probably 力 (*k.rək) and a loan for 樂 (*[r]ˤawk) "to enjoy" on a number of bell and other vessel inscriptions of the middle and late Western Zhou period (*Jicheng* 64, 145–48, 188–90, 4242). It is also found in a late Western Zhou inscription, Fan Sheng *gui* 番生簋 (*Jicheng* 4326), in place of the word *deng* 登 (*k-tˤəŋ) in a phrase similar to a Ban *gui* phrase (no.21, *Jicheng* 4341). The phrase X *yu yongming* 勴于永命 appears as the desired result of prayers to the ancestral spirits, namely eternal life. Although the graph certainly does not represent the word *deng*, it would seem to share the meaning of achieving a certain status. In that sense, it is similar in function to *ge* 格 (*kˤrak) which can mean to "arrive to, step up to (a shrine)" and was pronounced similarly, so perhaps we might consider the 勴 graph to represent a dialect version. It can also be a loan for *ke* 恪 "to pay respects to." Note that this mystery graph was written differently from examples for "to celebrate" *jia* 嘉 (*kˤraj), but such examples primarily exist on the Shang oracle bones and in inscriptions after the Western Zhou, suggesting almost a complementary distribution of the Western Zhou mystery word and *jia*.

your fine good fortune and have a numinous end. May I, Xing, for ten thousand years use horned animals that glitter with light to present meat sacrifices to the Accomplished Spirits without end, and illustrate my good fortune, thereby lodging the radiance in my person so as to make eternal my treasuring of it.

Transcription (Group C)

作協鐘萬年日鼓。

Translation

I, Xing, made harmonious bells to ring daily for ten thousand years.

Transcription: (Group D)

瘋趄趄（桓桓）夙夕聖爽，追孝于高祖辛公、文祖乙公、皇考丁公。龢林鐘用邵（昭）各（格>恪）喜侃樂前文人。用祷（祓）壽匄永令（命），綽綰䚃（髮>祓）祿屯魯。弋（式）皇祖考高對爾，烈嚴在上，豐豐彙彙（繹繹），融（庸）綏厚多福，廣啟瘋身，勵（恪）于永令（命），懷受余爾髒（祉）福。

瘋其萬年，橖（齊）角䰞（熾）光，義（宜）文神無疆覿（景）福，用璃（寓）光瘋身，永余寶。

Translation

I, Xing, perform with a martial step from dawn to dusk for the Sage Lights; pursuing in memory and presenting filial offerings to High Ancestor Patriarch Xin, Accomplished Ancestor Patriarch Yi, and Brilliant Deceased-father Patriarch Gong. With harmonious chime bells, I summon their spirits and make them arrive, giving the Former Accomplished Ones pleasure and musical entertainment. I take this opportunity to exorcise bad luck for longevity and beg for eternal life, and have extended to me a purging of noxious influences and emoluments in abundance.

So, Brilliant Ancestors and Deceased-father on High, I respond to you, blazing and stern, residing above—so fruitful and mighty—calmed by the fragrance of cooked food, you provide blessings and good fortune, expand and open my person, so that I can rejoice in eternal life and can embrace and receive in me your fine good fortune.

May I, Xing, for ten thousand years perform the sacrifices of horned animals who glitter with light and present the meat sacrifices to the Accomplished Spirits without limit, and so illustrate my good fortune, taking this opportunity to lodge the radiance in my Xing's, person so make eternal my treasuring of it.

Further Reading

Jicheng 247–50 (Group A), 251–56 (Group B), 257–59 (Group C), 246 (Group D), 4170–77 (*gui*), 649–58 (Bo Xian Fu *li*), 9726–77 (Sannian Xing *hu*), 4462–63 (Xing *xu*), 9723–24 (Shisannian Xing *hu*), 516–21 (Wei Bo *li*), 7461–64 (Xing *jue*).

Kimbun tsūshaku, 50.387–93

Cao Jinyan, "Shi tu."

Falkenhausen, *Suspended Music*, 25–32.

Li Xixing, *Shaanxi qingtongqi*, 264–66.

Li Xueqin, *Wenwu zhong de guwenming*, 258–64.

Shaughnessy, *Sources of Western Zhou History*, 112–20, 255–56.

Yin Shengping, *Xi Zhou Wei shi jiazu qingtongqi qun yanjiu*.

CAC

34. Yin Ji *ding* 尹姞鼎 and Gong Ji *li* 公姞鬲

The vessels cast by a woman from the lineage of Ji 姞 (not a royal Zhou lineage) tell us that there was a tradition of gift-giving and award for women as well as men. This woman seems to have been married to a powerful Zhou man named after the shrine of Mu 穆, the Patriarch of Mu—possibly the title held by certain descendants of the earlier King Mu of Zhou.[1] His wife was quite prominent. First, she was titled *yin* 尹 (assuming that it is not a place name), suggesting that she was the wife of a ritual officer in the shrine, and then as *gong* 公, indicating that she was the wife or widow of a patriarch (whose title might have been posthumous). Her vessels all date to around King Xiao's reign and are all *li*-style cauldrons, even though the two by Yin Ji called themselves *ding*. Pictures of *li*-style cauldrons cast by Yin Ji and their rubbings were first published in Kyoto, Japan, by Umehara Sueji in 1947. A *li* vessel by Gong Ji has been in the Avery Brundage Collection of the Asian Art Museum in San Francisco since around 1936. Since they are quite close in decorative style, it is possible that these vessels originally came from the same cache or tomb. The Gong Ji inscription is not as well preserved.

In each inscription, the Zhou queen, referred to as the Heavenly Lord (*tianjun* 天君), rewarded the Ji woman for her record of merit (*mieli*). This merit might have involved ritual service. It seems likely that both inscriptions were cast for her to use in order to honor her husband's memory, and that he died while still a governor (*yin*) but was promoted to patriarch (*gong*) after the proper mortuary rituals were performed. The first ceremony took place in a shrine built for her use in a wood by her deceased husband, and she was given jade and horses. In the second inscription, the queen rewarded her during the harvest festival (*feng* 豐; see the Zuoce Mai *fangzun* and the Jing *gui*, nos. 14 and 19, above) or sweet ale feast (*xiangli* 饗醴; see the Xing inscriptions, no. 33, above), and she was awarded a large number of fish after a man named Zi Zhong 子仲, perhaps a royal son, went fishing in the sacred Great Pool.

The rank of a Gong Ji (i.e. a Ji 姞 lineage woman of gong rank) was high enough that she could command and award gifts, as seen in the Ci 次 *you* and *pan* set made around the same time (*Jicheng* 5405, 5994):

唯二月初吉丁卯，公姞令次司田人。次蔑歷、賜馬、賜裘。

---

[1] For another vessel mentioning Mu Gong, see the Yu *ding* (no. 40, below).

對揚公姞休。用作寶彝。

It was on the second month, *chuji*, on *dingmao* day (*ganzhi* no. 4), when Gong Ji ordered Ci to supervise the field workers. Ci was awarded a horse and a fur cloak for his record of merit.

[Ci] responded by praising Gong Ji's grace. He takes this opportunity to make a treasured sacrificial vessel.

Women of the Ji lineage intermarried with the royal Zhou and with rulers of nearby states who considered themselves kings; for example, Guo Wang Ji 郭王姞 was a Ji woman married to the King of Guo. (Generally, scholars consider Guo a Zhou satellite, so it would seem unusual for the local ruler to call himself King; however, other rulers in nearby states with relations to the Zhou, such as Ze 夨, also had kings.) An early Zhou *gui* by a man named Jing (see no. 19, above) was dedicated to his Accomplished Mother Outer (affinial) Ji 文母外姞 after he was awarded for his success in archery at the Great Pool. The term "outer" (*wai* 外) reflects the need to distinguish consanguineal from affinial Ji, that is those that belong to the Zhou lineage by blood versus those related by marriage and non-Zhou by origin. Later texts suggest that women bearing their natal lineage names had to worship outside the city, away from their husbands' main shrines. This fits with the idea that Yin Ji's shrine was in the woods. What is hard to understand is why her shrine was built before she was dead, unless the Ji lineage was so powerful that women had to continue certain rituals even after marriage.

Transcription (*Yin Ji* ding)

穆公作尹姞宗室于繇林。唯六月既生霸乙卯，休天君弗望（忘）穆公聖鄉² 明釱（粥）事先王，各（格）于尹姞宗室繇林。君蔑尹姞歷，賜玉五品、馬三匹。

拜稽首，對揚天君休，用作寶齋。

Translation

The Patriarch of Mu made an ancestral shrine room for Yin Ji in the Yao³ Woods. It was in the sixth month, *jishengpo*, on *yimao*

---

² See Chen Mengjia, "Xi Zhou tongqi duandai," 119. See also Smith, "Rejoinder," 431–433 [MP].

³ This character can also be pronounced *zhao*. Conventionally, the more frequent *yao* is here adopted [MP].

day (*ganzhi* no. 52), when the Heavenly Lord, giving gifts, did not forget the Patriarch of Mu, the Sage, who, luminous and bright, protected and served the Former King. The Lord arrived at the room of the main shrine of Yin Ji in the Yao Woods. The Lord praised the record of Yin Ji's accumulated merit and awarded her five pieces of jade and three horses.

Yin Ji clapped her hands together and knocked her head on the floor, and in response extolled the Heavenly Lord's gift. She took this opportunity to make a precious lidded cauldron.

Transcription (*Gong Ji* li)

唯十又二月既生霸，子仲漁[大]池，天君蔑公姞歷，吏（使）賜公姞魚三百。

拜稽首對揚天君休，用作齋鼎。

Translation

It was in the twelfth month, *jishengpo*, when Zi Zhong fished in the Great Pool, and the Heavenly Lord praised the record of Gong Ji's accumulated merit and sent Gong Ji three hundred fish as an award.

Gong Ji clapped her hands and knocked her head on the ground and in response extolled the Lord of Heaven's grace. She took this opportunity to make a lidded cauldron.

Further Reading

Jicheng 754–55 (Yin Ji *ding*), 753 (Gong Ji *li*).
Kimbun tsūshaku, 14.794–810.
Mingwen xuan, no. 316 (Yin Ji *ding*).

Cao Zhaolan, *Jinwen yu Yin Zhou nüxing wenhua*, 82–84.
Chen Mengjia, "Xi Zhou tongqi duandai."
Chen Yingjie, "Jinwen zhong 'jun' zi zhi yiyi ji qi xiangguan wenti tanxi."
Sena, "Reproducing Society," 177, 201, 224, 277n.69.
Shaughnessy, "Toward a Social Geography of the Zhouyuan during the Western Zhou Dynasty," 23.
Smith, "Rejoinder to Jonathan Smith, Research Note on Shun 舜."

CAC

35. Hu *ding* 曶鼎

The Hu *ding* (also called Yao 舀 *ding*) no longer exists; however, a forgery (possibly made during the Qing dynasty) is located in the Shanghai Museum. The original vessel is said to have been found in Chang'an in 1778, 1779, or in 1782, but was melted down during the Taiping Rebellion 太平天國 (1850–1864), the metal being used for weapons and ammunition. One Qing scholar examined and studied the vessel and its inscription in person before its destruction, and much of our information derives from these records. Fortunately, a rubbing of the inscription from the original vessel exists, and past concerns about the inscription's authenticity have been laid to rest. From the contents of the inscription we can affirm that the vessel would have been cast during the first quarter of the ninth century B.C.E., during the reign of King Yì.

A Qing description depicts the cauldron as measuring two *chi* 尺 in height, four chi in circumference, and with a belly depth of about nine *cun* 寸. Its legs were adorned with ox heads. The inscription itself refers to the vessel as a type of "ox cauldron."

The inscription is lengthy, comprising approximately 400 characters. It is also unique in that it is actually composed of three different inscriptions each of which records events that occurred at three different times during the life of a man named Hu 曶. Each section of the inscription will be discussed separately below as Hu *ding* I, II, and III.

Hu *ding* I

This inscription, the briefest of the three, is a standard record of investiture. In it, we learn that in what was possibly King Yì's first year (899/97 B.C.E.), the King, speaking through an intermediary, charged Hu with supervising divinatory affairs, thus continuing his family's traditional line of service to the royal house, at least since the days of his deceased grandfather. For his service, Hu was awarded by the King a few gifts commonly seen in investiture ceremonies and which possessed symbolic significance. In addition, Hu received red metal (possibly copper) and tri-colored jade from Xing Shu 邢叔, a man who also appears in Hu *ding* II.

The Xing lineage is known from the very early Western Zhou. Received texts record that, late in his reign, King Cheng invested one of the sons of the Duke of Zhou with lands known as Xing 邢 in order to provide the capital area with a buffer zone to fend off attacks by northern enemies.

The Mai *zun* 麥尊 inscription (see no. 14), from the reign of King Cheng, corroborates the investiture of one Xing Bo 邢伯. Xing family members appear in numerous inscriptions from that point onwards, usually in close service to the royal house, and often acting as guarantors (*youzhe* 右者) to investees. It is possible that Xing Shu is the guarantor of Hu in the present inscription. In one other inscription from the Western Zhou, the Hu *hu* 智壺 (*Jicheng* 9728), the guarantor of the person referred to as Hu is one Xing Gong 邢公, perhaps a member of the main Xing lineage (as opposed to Xing Shu, perhaps a member of a Xing cadet lineage). This would suggest that members of the Xing lineages were directly superior to members of the Hu family.[1]

It is possible that the Hu family was of eastern or Shang descent, as in the inscriptional record persons named Hu tended to serve in capacities most commonly associated with easterners, such as diviners or scribes. (Compare the scribe named Hu in the Ying *yi* inscription, no. 36, below.) Persons charged with divinatory and scribal functions would have wielded a certain amount of power, and it would have been sensible for the Zhou to have appointed high-ranking Zhou officials to supervise them.

Transcription (*Hu* ding I)

唯王元年六月既望乙亥。王在周穆王大[室]。

[王]若曰：智，令（命）汝更乃祖考嗣卜事。賜汝赤🜨[市][旂]。用事王在䜈应。

井（邢）叔賜智赤金䚡。

智受休[令（命）][于]王。智用兹金作朕文考究伯䚡牛鼎。智其[萬][年]用祀。子子孫孫其永寶。

Translation

It was the King's first year, sixth month, *jiwang*, on *yihai* day (*ganzhi* no. 12). The King was at the Grand Hall of King Mu at Zhou.

The King said thus (*wang ruo yue*):[2] "Hu, [I] command you to succeed your deceased grandfather and deceased father in su-

---

[1] Some scholars read Hu as a personal, not a family, name.
[2] See Glossary.

pervising divination affairs. I award you red kneepads, [a girdle pendant, and a pennant]. Use them to serve the King at the X Detached Palace Residence."

Xing Shu awarded Hu red metal and tri-colored jade.

Hu received the beneficent [command from] the King. Hu uses this bronze to make my cultured deceased father, Jiu Bo, X ox *ding*-tripod. May Hu [for ten thousand years] use it to perform cult. [May his] sons' sons and grandsons' grandsons eternally treasure and use it.

Hu *ding* II

Because the inscription is corrupt in numerous key places, the interpretation of events provided here represents but one possible option.

This inscription records a complex case of a private sales transaction in which it appears that the seller, Xian 限, tried to renege on the original terms of a deal, and was sued by the purchaser, Hu 曶. There are many persons who figure in the process: the plaintiff, Hu; the defendant, Xian; the arbiter, Xing Shu 邢叔 (whom we met in Hu *ding* I); Hu's proxy, Pu 儥 / 賮 (who represents Hu throughout most of the proceedings); and two persons who might be sales intermediaries or legal officials, Xiao Fu 效父 and Shi 氐 / 甕 / 晵. There is also a minor character, Lüe 孚, who is perhaps another functionary of Hu.

It is unclear just how much time elapsed between the lodging of the original complaint by Pu on behalf of Hu and the decision by Xing Shu, but it does seem that the events described in the inscription could not all have transpired at one meeting. First, Pu, not Hu, did the legwork of lodging the complaint, yet Hu was present at the end of the proceedings. Second, Shi, who testified at the outset, was not present for the rendering of the verdict.

The inscription presents us with several points of interest, for example: the number of people testifying before Xing Shu; the fact that Hu lodged the complaint before Xing Shu, who may have been Hu's guarantor at his investiture; the presentation of evidence by Pu, and the interpretation of that evidence by the arbiter as the basis for rendering his decision; the existence of what are perhaps sales intermediaries or legal officials who, before any legal maneuverings on the part of Hu, seemed to be involved in seeing that the transaction was carried out; the fact that Hu was a fairly wealthy man who owned livestock; the ruling that the men whose labor was purchased by Hu had to remain on their own settlements and tend to their fields, even as they were in service to Hu; and the lack of an ancestor dedication at the end of the inscription (cf. Shi Qi *ding*, no. 20, above). Of particular interest is the mention of wooden planchettes that were hung at the "King's third gate." We know that in the Eastern Zhou, laws were sometimes displayed in public places. The planchettes of the present inscription appear to record a stipulation about the applicability of bartering in sales transactions that involve the "King's people," indicating that not all laws were universally applicable.

Transcription (*Hu* ding II)

唯王四月既生霸。辰在丁酉。井（邢）叔在異爲[□]。

[曶]使厥小子䝼以限訟于井（邢）叔。余既買³汝五[夫。][效]父用匹馬束絲。

限許曰：氐則俾我償馬。效[父][則]俾復厥絲束。

嬰效父迺許。

䝼曰：于王參（三）門[□][□]木榜用賸（贖）⁴。誕賣茲五夫用百寽。非出五夫。[效][父]訊（詢）。迺啻又訊（詢）。眔蠯（數）金。

井（邢）叔曰：在王人迺賣用[賸]不逆付。曶母（毋）俾弐于氐。曶則拜稽首受茲五夫。曰陪曰恆曰陰曰甯曰鼕曰省。

使寽以告氐。迺俾[限]以曶酒及羊絲三寽用至（致）茲人。

曶迺誨于氐[曰：]汝其舍䝼矢五束。⁵ 曰弋（必）尚俾處厥邑。

田（佃）[厥]田。氐則俾復令。曰：諾。

---

³ The graph rendered here and below as *mai* 買, "to purchase, buy," can also be interpreted as *mai* 賣, "to sell," or *shu* 贖, "to barter, exchange, trade." Both 贖 and 買 suit the present context but differ in the information they provide about mid-Western Zhou commercial transactions. It does seem, from the stipulation on the wooden planchettes mentioned later in the inscription, that there was a distinction made between conducting transactions with currency and with goods.

⁴ I tentatively read this graph as *shu* 贖, "to barter, exchange, trade." It may also be possible to understand this as a type of currency, although this would alter our understanding of how the testimonies are interrelated.

⁵ Some scholars read the original graph as *bing* 秉, which is a measure word for "arrows." Some have suggested that the five (bundles of) arrows are symbolic of the five men.

Translation

It was the King's fourth month, *jishengpo*. The *chen* was at *dingyou* (*ganzhi* no. 34). Xing Shu was at Yi acting as (?).

Hu sent his functionary, Pu, to file suit against Xian before Xing Shu. [Pu, on behalf of Hu, said,] "I, [Hu,] have purchased the use of five [men] from you, [Xian]. [Xiao] Fu [on my behalf] used a horse and a bolt of silk [as payment]."

Xian acknowledged this and said, "Shi then caused me to make compensation for the horse,[6] and Xiao Fu then caused [me] to return Hu's silk bolt."

Shi and Xiao Fu then assented.

Pu said, "At the King's third gate (?) (?) ... wooden planchettes [state that one may] use bartering. By extension, to purchase [the use of] these five men, [Hu] used one hundred lie of goods. [Xian] did not produce the five men. [Xiao Fu] told untruths; then Shi also told untruths. They conjointly [attempted] to extract precious metal [from Hu]."

Xing Shu said, "Among the King's people, to purchase using [bartering] does not run counter to [the proper terms of] payment; Hu did not cause duplicity with regard to Shi." Hu then, clasping [his hands] and kowtowing, received these five men, who were called Pei, Heng, You, X, and Xing.

[Hu then] sent Lüe to report [the decision to] Shi. [Shi] thereupon had [Xian] use Hu's liquor, together with a sheep and three lie of silk, and therewith bring forth these men.

Hu was then instructed by Shi, [who said,] "May you relinquish to Pu arrows in the amount of five bundles." [Shi also] said, "It is necessary still to cause these men to dwell on their *yi*-settlements and tend to [their] fields." Shi then caused [Hu] to repeat the order [given to him]. [Hu] said, "So be it."

Hu *ding* III

This is the only extant case of theft in the inscriptional record. Twenty servants of Kuang 匡 (also called Kuang Ji 匡季) stole ten *zi* 秄 of grain from Hu in a year of famine. Hu lodged a complaint against Kuang before

---

[6] It seems that something happened to the horse after Hu gave it to Xian, so that Xian was unable to return it, or it had depreciated in value.

Dong Gong 東宮 (possibly a member of a collateral branch of the Zhou royal house in charge of the Eastern Palace), who found Kuang responsible for repaying the grain stolen by his subordinates. This is reminiscent of the Shi Qi *ding* (no. 20, above), in which the doctrine of *respondeat superior* operated. It also calls to mind the theory of compensatory damages, whereby the actual loss suffered is recovered. Kuang, unable to find his men, offered Hu fields and laborers, and pleaded not to suffer whippings, the apparent punishment for theft. Hu rejected this offer.

Hu then again reported Kuang to Dong Gong. The second ruling was that the original ten *zi* were to be repaid, along with what might possibly be viewed as punitive damages amounting to another ten *zi*. Furthermore, if the twenty *zi* were not paid by the following year, that amount was to be doubled, bringing the total to forty *zi*. Kuang was forced to offer Hu seven fields and five men, apparently in lieu of the original ten *zi* of grain, and Hu this time accepted. However, Kuang did not make the payment of the second ten *zi* by the following year, and so we are left with the note that Hu was still seeking the remaining thirty *zi* of grain from Kuang. Like the Hu *ding* II and Shi Qi *ding* inscriptions, this inscription does not contain an ancestral dedication, but rather seems focused on imparting or cementing information relating to a legal case.

Transcription (*Hu* ding III)

昔饉歲。匡眾厥臣廿夫寇智禾十秭。以匡季告東宮。東宮迺曰：求乃人。乃弗得。汝匡罰大。匡迺稽首于智。用五田。用眾一夫曰益。用臣曰疐[曰]朏曰奠。曰：用茲四夫。稽首曰：余無攸（所）具寇。正[□]。不[俾]鞭余。智或（又）以匡季告東宮。智曰：弋（必）唯朕[禾]償。東宮迺曰：償智禾十秭。遺十秭爲廿秭。[汝]來歲弗償則付四十秭。迺或（又）即智用田二又臣[一][夫]。凡用即智田七田。人五夫。智覓匡三十秭。

Translation

Formerly, in a year of famine, twenty *chen*-servants [from among] Kuang's multitudes stole ten *zi* of Hu's grain. [Hu] took Kuang Ji and petitioned before Dong Gong. Dong Gong then said [to Kuang Ji], "Seek your men. If [you] do not obtain them, you, Kuang, will be fined greatly." Kuang thereupon kowtowed to Hu.

[Kuang] used five fields, used one man from his multitudes called Yi, and used *chen*-servants called Zhi, Fei, and Dian, and said, "I shall use these four men." [Kuang] kowtowed, saying, "I do not have all that which was stolen. Truly ... Do not cause me to be whipped." Hu again took Kuang Ji and made a petition before Dong Gong. Hu said, "Necessarily it may only be my [grain] that is compensated." Dong Gong thereupon said, "Make compensation for Hu's grain in the amount of ten *zi* and make a gift [to him] of ten *zi*, thus making [a total of] twenty *zi* [of grain]. If, in the coming year, [you] have not compensated him, then pay forty *zi*." [Kuang] thereupon again approached Hu using two fields and one further *chen*-servant. In all, he approached Hu using seven fields and five men. Hu seeks from Kuang thirty *zi* [of grain].

Further Reading

Jicheng 2838.

Lau, *Quellenstudien zur Landvergabe und Bodenübertragung in der westlichen Zhou-Dynastie*, 368–83.

Skosey, "The Legal System and Legal Tradition of the Western Zhou."

Sun Changxu, *Sun Changxu guwen zixue lunji*, 163–261.

Wang Hui, *Shang Zhou jinwen*, 167–76.

LAS

36. Ying *yi* 儥匜 and Ying *yigai* 儥匜蓋

This *yi* vessel, an elongated pitcher (resembling a gravy boat), and its accompanying lid were found in 1975 along with three dozen other notable vessels in a cache in Dongjiacun, Qishan County, Shaanxi Province. They are currently housed in the Qishan County Museum. The vessel itself (also called Zhen 朕 *yi* and Xun 訓 *yi*) is unusual in two respects. First, it possesses a lid, rare for elongated pitchers before the Spring and Autumn. Second, rather than possessing a single inscription that is repeated in both the body and the lid, as is the case with most (though not all) inscribed lidded vessels, there is only one inscription, which begins in the belly of the *yi*-pitcher and extends into its lid.

As with the Shi Qi *ding* (no. 20, above), the date of the Ying *yi* is based in large part on art-historical criteria. The elongated pitcher (referred to in the inscription itself not as an *yi* but as a *he* 盉) arose as a vessel form sometime during the late mid-Western Zhou to the early late-Western Zhou. (The majority of *yi* date to the reign of King Li.) This coincides well with the décor: a simple ribbing prominent among late mid-Western Zhou bronzes. Scholars date this vessel to between the reigns of King Xiao and King You.

The inscription is unique in its recounting of a case of perjury. It also suggests a prior case involving the defendant. The inscription begins not with the details of the case, but immediately with the verdict rendered. The sequence of events, including both those alluded to and those included in the inscription, seems to be as follows. At some point before the present case, a man called by the title Cowherd (*muniu* 牧牛), swore to return five men to his captain, Ying 儥. This oath seems to have been ordered by a court. However, Cowherd did not return the men. Instead, he appears to have lodged a countersuit against Ying, and in so doing committed perjury by violating his previous oath. A new verdict was reached, during which the arbiter, Bo Yang Fu 伯揚父, mitigated the punishment, again evidencing the practice of (judicial) discretion (see Shi Qi *ding*, no. 20, above), and also providing some insight into gradations of punishments.

The punishments mentioned, many of which were not inflicted, are unusual in their corporal nature, and are not seen elsewhere in the inscriptional record. It is worth noting, however, that even though the most serious of corporal punishments mentioned (one thousand whippings in conjunction with inked facial cuts) was not applied, the corporal element of the final verdict—a whipping of five hundred strokes—may have been sufficient, depending on the implement used, to result in serious injury or even death, thus attesting to the severity with which perjury and/or lodging a suit against one's superior was viewed.

Transcription

唯三月既死霸甲申。王在荓[1]上宫。

伯揚父廼成詧曰：牧牛虩（徂）乃可（何）甚。汝敢以乃師訟。汝上（尚）卲（懾）先誓。今汝亦既或（有）厎（果）誓夐（敷）。格眚睦儥。宁（返）兹五夫。亦既厎（果）乃誓。汝亦既從辭從誓。弋可。

我義（宜）鞭汝千。嚴（黥）馘（劓）[2]汝。今我赦汝。宜鞭汝千。黜（劓）馘（劓）汝。今大赦汝。鞭汝五百。罰汝三百寽。

伯揚父廼或（又）事（使）牧牛誓。曰：自今余敢夒（擾）乃小大史（吏）。乃師或（又）以汝告則致乃鞭千嚴（黥）馘（劓）。

牧牛則誓。及以告吏（史）䙴吏（史）䀇于會。牧牛辭誓成罰金。

儥用作旅盉。

Translation

> It was the third month, *jisipo, jiashen* (*ganzhi* no. 21). The King was at Pang's Upper Palace.
>
> Bo Yang Fu thereupon completed a verdict: "Cowherd, this [time] you have gone too far! You dared to bring litigation against your Captain. You are still duplicitous [with regard to your] former oath. Now you must simply completely bring your oath to

---

[1] There are three main views on the identification and location of Pang, which occurs in around two dozen Western Zhou inscriptions: 1) that it is identical with Haojing 鎬京; 2) that it is Fengjing 豐京; and 3) that it is located somewhere outside the Feng and Hao area. The Zhou king was also at Pang during the events of the Sixth Year Diao Sheng *gui* (no. 37).

[2] This and the following graphs that deal with tattooing and facial scarring are not seen elsewhere in any Chinese source.

fruition and proclaim it. Arriving at Se, make peace with Ying and return those five men [of his]. [You] must simply bring your oath to fruition. You must simply follow [your] sentence and follow [your] oath. Would that be possible!

"I ought to whip you one thousand [times] and impose the punishment of inked facial cuts on you. Now, I mitigate your [punishment]. I ought to whip you one thousand [times] and impose simple facial scarring on you. Now, [I] greatly mitigate your [punishment]. [I sentence] you to be whipped five hundred [times], and fine you three hundred *lie*."

Bo Yang Fu thereupon again caused Cowherd to take an oath: "From now on, if I, [Cowherd,][3] dare trouble your lesser or greater officials, or if your Captain again takes you and petitions, then [I, Bo Yang Fu], will impose your [original punishment of] one thousand whippings and inked facial cuts."

Cowherd then swore the oath. Ji therewith reported to Scribe Xiong and Scribe Hu at Hui. Cowherd's sentence and oath completed, he was fined bronze.

Ying herewith makes this travelling *he*-pitcher.

Further Reading

Jicheng 10285.

Skosey, "The Legal System and Legal Tradition of the Western Zhou."
Tang Lan, *Xi zhou qingtongqi mingwen fendai shi zheng*, 508–13.
Wang Hui, *Shang Zhou jinwen*, 176–81.

LAS

---

[3] Soon hereafter, in this same oath, the subject turns from the first person to the second person. When bronzes were cast, it is assumed that a text of the events, or some retelling thereof, was presented to the foundry. Here it seems clear that two versions of the oath, one with direct speech and the other with a summary of its import, were conflated.

37. Fifth-Year Diao Sheng *gui* 五年琱生簋 and Sixth-Year Diao Sheng *gui* 六年琱生簋

These inscriptions constitute two related records of a single series of events which occurred over a fifteen-month period beginning in the fifth year of King Xuan (823/821 B.C.E.) and concluding in the following year (822/820 B.C.E.). The Fifth-Year Diao Sheng *gui* is housed at the Yale University Art Museum; the Sixth-Year vessel is in the National Museum of China. Although the inscriptions are relatively brief, there are difficulties in the text which have fueled an ongoing debate that questions whether the vessels were commissioned by Diao Sheng or Shao Bo Hu 召伯虎 (in which case they are referred to as Shao Bo Hu *gui* I and Shao Bo Hu *gui* II). However, the recent discovery in a cache in Fufeng of two *zun* vessels containing an identical inscription bearing on this case, the contents of which occur between the two *gui* inscriptions, lends support to reading the vessels' commissioner as Diao Sheng 琱生. The inscriptions on the *zun* date to the fifth year, ninth month.

The events described in the two *gui* inscriptions concern a dispute involving some land, servants and laborers of Diao Sheng. However, it is Shao Bo Hu, a member of Diao Sheng's ancestral house, who is credited with bringing the dispute to a resolution. As with all inscriptions bearing legal contents, some of the terms are rare and thus subject to varying interpretations.

At the time that the Fifth-Year Diao Sheng *gui* inscription begins, the lands, *pu* 仆-servants and *yong* 庸-laborers of Diao Sheng apparently had already been the subject of several legal inquiries. The inscription relates that either Diao Sheng, or Shao Bo Hu on Diao Sheng's behalf, first presented a *hu*-vessel to Fu Shi 婦氏, the female emissary of Shao Bo Hu's widowed mother and family matriarch (referred to in the Fifth-Year Diao Sheng *gui* inscription as Jun Shi 君氏, and in the Sixth-Year Diao Sheng *gui* inscription posthumously as You Jiang 幽姜). The *zun* vessels indicate that Fu Shi might have been the wife of Shao Bo Hu. Fu Shi relayed the command of the family matriarch concerning the laborers and land in question. The contents of the command are highly enigmatic, but whatever their exact meaning, it would seem that Diao Sheng was favored by the command, and so Diao Sheng, or Shao Bo Hu on Diao Sheng's behalf, gave to Fu Shi a bolt of silk and a *huang* 璜-jade, probably intended as a sign of gratitude for the matriarch's command. The inscription then records Shao Bo Hu acknowledging that he had conducted an inquiry into the matter, and that he would carry out the command pronounced by his mother and his deceased father. Diao Sheng then presented a *gui* 珪-jade tablet, probably to Shao Bo Hu. It is not clear whether Diao Sheng himself was present when the matriarch's command was relayed, or, whether Shao Bo Hu was representing him there.

The events in the Sixth Year Diao Sheng *gui* occur fifteen months later. Shao Bo Hu reports that he has been successful in implementing the command of his parents, both of whom are now deceased. He had taken cowrie shells given to him by "the duke" or "ducal house" (*gong* 公) and used them in lodging a lawsuit and an investigation. Shao Bo Hu questioned the Supervisor concerning the matter of Diao Sheng's *yi* 邑-settlements. There is mention of registers (*dian* 典) that were signed but not sealed immediately, and which probably recorded the transaction, as it were. In light of this favorable outcome, Diao Sheng extolled the beneficence of his ancestral lord or matriarch (*zongjun* 宗君), and dedicated the vessel to his ancestor, Shao Gong 召公, who was possibly the deceased father (or at least also an ancestor) of Shao Bo Hu.

There are several noteworthy features of the inscriptions. For example, from other inscriptions and received texts it is believed that both Diao Sheng and Shao Bo Hu were of royal lineage. The role of a powerful woman in the entire legal process is unusual, as is the presence of an emissary who is incontestably female. Upon the death of a father (Shao Bo Hu's father was deceased at the time of the events in the Fifth-Year Diao Sheng *gui* inscription), it seems that the mother assumed authority within the family. And although the command may first have been issued by Shao Bo Hu's father and only executed by his mother, it is possible that it is the matriarch's beneficence which Diao Sheng extols in the dedicatory portion of the Sixth-Year Diao Sheng *gui* inscription. The use of emissaries or assistants (for Diao Sheng it may have been Shao Bo Hu, and for the family matriarch, Fu Shi) when one was involved in legal cases is seen in other inscriptions as well, e.g., Hu *ding* II (no. 35, above). Several gifts— here a *hu*-vessel, silk, and various jade objects—are given by Diao Sheng to others as part of the legal process, a practice seen in other Western Zhou bronze inscriptions with legalistic contents (e.g., Hu *ding* II, where Hu is instructed to present his proxy with five bundles of arrows at the conclusion of the proceedings). The mention of registers, and at least, we assume, one copy thereof, suggest a record-keeping system in which both the state and individuals had access to proof of land rights. And finally, the length of time required for the dispute to be resolved might be considered excessive—the immediate events described in the inscriptions span a full fifteen months—suggesting that, while textual and inscriptional materials from the Western Zhou lay stress on not prolonging legal matters, the Western Zhou bureaucracy, in fact, might have faced problems expediting legal disputes.

Transcription (*Fifth-Year Diao Sheng* gui)

唯五年正月己丑。琱生又（有）事。召來合（答）事。余獻婦氏以壺。告曰：以君氏令曰：余老止。公僕庸土田多諫（諫）。弋伯氏從許。公宕其參（三）汝則宕其貳（二）。公宕其貳（二）汝則宕其一。余惠于君氏大章。報婦氏帛束璜。

召伯虎曰：余既訊。我考我母令余弗敢亂。余或（又）至（致）我考我母令。

琱生則堇（覲）圭（珪）。

Translation

It was the fifth year, first month, *jichou* (*ganzhi* no. 26). Diao Sheng had a matter of concern. Shao came to respond to the matter. I, [Diao Sheng,] made a presentation to Fu Shi using a *hu*-vessel. [Fu Shi] reported, saying, "I use Jun Shi's command, which says: 'I am growing old. The Duke's *pu*-servants, *yong*-laborers, land, and fields are much investigated. Would that Bo Shi[1] comply with and acknowledge that when the Duke expands three of them, you may expand two of them, and when the Duke expands two of them, you may expand one of them.'"[2] I, Diao Sheng, was favored by Jun Shi with great distinction and requited Fu Shi with a bolt of silk and a *huang*-jade.

Shao Bo Hu said, "I have already conducted an inquiry. I will

---

[1] Most commentators interpret *bo shi* 伯氏 as a polite form of address for Shao Bo Hu, although the context suggests it might refer to Diao Sheng.

[2] The object of the verb *dang* 宕 is unclear. "To exceed" is another possible translation of the verb.

submit to the command of my deceased father and my mother. I dare not disorder it. Moreover, I will bring about the command of my deceased father and my mother."

Diao Sheng then presented [to Shao Bo Hu] a *gui*-tablet.

Transcription (*Sixth-Year Diao Sheng* gui)

唯六年四月甲子。王在𦳝。³召伯虎告曰：余告慶。曰：公厥稟貝用獄諫（諫）。爲伯又（有）底又（有）成。亦我考幽伯幽姜令。余告慶。余以邑訊有𦳝。余典勿敢封。今余既訊有嗣。曰：宸令。余今既一名典獻伯氏。則報璧。

琱生對揚朕宗君其休。用作朕烈祖召公嘗簋。其萬年子子孫孫寶用享于宗。

Translation

It was the sixth year, fourth month, *jiazi* (*ganzhi* no. 1). The King was at Pang. Shao Bo Hu reported, saying, "I report felicitous news. The cowries supplied by the Duke were used for the lawsuit and investigation, and on behalf of Bo (the Elder), there was achievement and completion [in regard to this matter], and also [with regard to] the command of my deceased father, You Bo, and deceased mother, You Jiang. I report felicitous news. I took [the matter of the] *yi*-settlements and inquired of the Supervisor. I did not dare to seal the registers. Now, I have already inquired of the Supervisor. [The Supervisor] said, 'Submit to the command.' Now, I have already once put my name to the registers and presented them to Bo Shi (i.e. Diao Sheng).⁴ [Bo Shi] then requited me with a *bi*-jade."

[I,] Diao Sheng in response extol my ancestral lord's beneficence, and herewith make for my emblazoned ancestor, Shao Gong, this *gui*-tureen for use in *chang* sacrifices. May for ten thousand years my sons' sons and grandson's grandsons treasure and use it to offer feasts [to the ancestors] in the ancestral temple.

---

³ See note 1 to the Ying *yi* (no. 36, above).
⁴ Shaughnessy, "The Dowager v. the Royal Court," suggests that references to *bo* and *boshi* point to Diao Sheng, who he suggests is the elder in his cadet lineage.

Further Reading

Jicheng 4292 (Fifth-Year Diao Sheng *gui*), 4293 (Sixth-Year Diao Sheng *gui*).

Cao Zhaolan, *Jinwen yu Yin Zhou nüxing wenhua*, 87–88.

Shaughnessy, "The Dowager v. the Royal Court: A Ninth-Century B.C. Case of Family Law Recorded in Chinese Bronze Inscriptions."

Skosey, "The Legal System and Legal Tradition of the Western Zhou."

Wang Hui, *Shang Zhou jinwen*, 189–96.

LAS

38. Shi Mi gui 史密簋

This vessel (broken and without a base or a lid) was discovered by the local people of Ankang 安康, Shaanxi, in 1986, and finally confiscated by the police in 1988 and placed in the Ankang City Museum. The inscription inside the vessel bottom is obscured in places but still decipherable.

The content describes an uprising of Yi people in the vicinity of the nascent Qí 齊 state, which may have been at risk of joining the rebellion (see Wunian Shi Shi gui 五年師旋簋, *Jicheng* 4216–18, where the Zhou had to subdue Qí). Two important Zhou officials, Master Su and Archivist Mi, at the command of the King, attacked and turned Qí and some of the rebellious Yi into troops. Ever since the legendary conquest of the failing Shang house, the Zhou had to march east repeatedly to quell rebellions (see *Jicheng* 2739, 2741, 4029, 4239). Although later Qí inscriptions reveal long-term influence from Zhou rhetorical traditions and hence cultural exchange (see Shu Yi *zhong*, no. 69, below), the distance clearly allowed the Qí people some independence and the ability to hold onto regional traditions. According to later transmitted texts, the Qí people tended to choose their own rulers without consulting the Zhou.

The Qí army was made up of three types of soldiers: those belonging to the ruling lineage, foot soldiers, and soldiers from adjoining areas. There were many different peoples inhabiting the coastal region including those in Qí, the majority of which were classified as non-Zhou or "Yi." Many Yi had been assimilated over the years, paid tribute to the Zhou, or cooperated with the Qí lineage and likely intermarried with them as well. A number of small bronze-casting polities evolved out of assimilated Yi peoples south of the Qí polity closer to the Huai River valley, including Qǐ 杞 (not to be confused with Qí 齊) and Zhōu 舟, the latter possibly boat people—both mentioned below. It is clear that some Yi groups either were never loyal to the Zhou or vacillated in their loyalties. The meeting between some of these groups mentioned below suggests at least some level of political organization, derived from centuries of conflict with the more organized states of first the Shang and then the Zhou. After the Western Zhou period, the conflict with the Yi continued but is recorded mostly as a problem for the Chu state as it expanded eastward.

Transcription

唯十又二月，王命師俗、史密曰：東征敆（合）南夷、盧虎[1]會杞夷、舟夷，讙（讙）不折（慭>憖）；廣伐東域、齊師、族土（徒）遂人，乃執鄙寬[2]亞。

師俗率齊師遂人左，周伐長必。史密右，率族人，釐（萊）伯、僰人眉（殿），周伐長必，獲百人。

對揚天子休，用作朕文考乙伯尊簋。子子孫孫其永寶用。

Translation

It was in the twelfth month, when the King commanded Master Su and Archivist Mi, saying: "March east against the allied Southern Yi peoples; the Luhu are meeting with the Yi peoples from Qǐ and Zhōu and rabble-rousing; launch a broad attack against the eastern territory and the Qí army, with its lineage foot soldiers and followers, until you capture the border town of Guaya."

Master Su led Zhou's left flank army with the Qí army to attack Changbi; Archivist Mi led Zhou's right flank army, with the the lineage brigades of Elder Lai and the Bo people at the back, to attack Changbi. We captured one hundred people.

In response [to being rewarded], I extolled the Son of Heaven's grace and took the opportunity to make for my Accomplished deceased-father Elder Yi a tureen for expressing reverence. My I have sons of sons and grandsons of grandsons forever to treasure and use it.

Further Reading

Li, *Bureaucracy and the State in Early China*, 170–73, 264–68.

Li, *Landscape and Power in Early China*, 97–100, 300, 306–8.

Li Qiliang, "Shaanxi Ankangshi chutu Zhou Shi Mi gui."

Li Xueqin, *Xinchu qingtongqi yanjiu*, 140–41.

---

[1] Many see the Lu as separate from the Hu peoples. However, it is possible that the two words together functioned as a binome, *ra-qhˤra, and represented a non-Sinitic name for a single group.

[2] Some read this graph as *kuan* 寬.

Li Xueqin, *Zouchu yigu shidai*, 170–78.
Liu Yu and Liu Yan, *Jinchu Yin Zhou jinwen jilu*, 2.375–76.
"Shaanxi Ankangshi chutu Xi Zhou Shi Mi gui."
Shaughnessy, "Western Zhou History," 312–13, 324, 347.
Wang Hui, *Shang Zhou jinwen*, 197–202.
Zhang Maorong *et al.*, "Ankang chutu Shi Mi gui jiqi yiyi."
Zhou Baohong, *Jinchu Xi Zhou jinwen jishi*, 105–76.

CAC

39. Hu GUI 㝬簋 AND Hu ZHONG 㝬鐘

The Hu *gui* was discovered in 1978 in Qicun 齊村 in Famen, Fufeng County, Shaanxi Province, and is presently stored in the Fufeng Museum. It was designed in typical late Western Zhou fashion, with a simple décor of vertical ribbing with two ribbons of abstract curly-cloud décor around the top and base of the large round vessel (set on a square base). Also typical of contemporary fashion were the two elaborate and somewhat abstract dragon head–bird feet handles. No lid has been preserved. The inscription on the bell set (also known as Ancestral Zhou Bells 宗周鐘), on the other hand, was first recorded in the nineteenth century. It is not known how many bells composed the original set, but one is presently in the Palace Museum in Taipei. The rhetoric of the tureen, this bell set, and another bell set cast seven years earlier than the *gui*-tureen provide similar phrases and ideas among them, so much so that it is obvious that they derive from a single narrative tradition for celebrating annual sacrifices to the Former Kings and the ancestors and deceased father of Hu.

Scholars date the vessels to the King Li reign period for a number of reasons: one is based on the late Western Zhou style décor, another on the evidence that these vessels may have belonged to the Zhou king himself. The rhetoric was unusual; instead of a document of the King's promoting an official, the inscription expresses anxiety over the King's maintaining his "position" (*wei* 位)—a term that can refer to being on a throne. Finally, many scholars accept that the name 㝬, read as Hu 胡, was the personal name of King Li, as mentioned in *Shiji*.[1] If the Hu of the Hu *gui* and Hu *zhong* did represent a king's name and the inscriptions were cast by a king, that would be the only example of a king's own vessels and hence highly unusual. Even so, most scholars accept this idiosyncrasy as further proof that they belonged to King Li, because according to tales preserved in later texts, he was arrogant, violent, and constantly broke the rules for proper behavior and ritual, resulting in his being forced to flee the capital at one point. Not every scholar is

---

[1] *Shiji* 4.141 [PRG]. King Li's personal name, Hu, was not uncommon and was applied as the name for various peoples, including a Yi group. Around the time of King Li, there was also a group of elite peoples named Hu that seem to have lived in southeastern Shaanxi. They inter-married with the Rui 芮 people to their north. A later Hu state was located in Yan City district of Henan province.

convinced that the Hu bronzes are exceptions to the rule, particularly since the Hu inscriptions follow a pattern seen in other bronzes (see Shi Zai *ding*, no. 29, above) where, after a speech or appointment by a king, the subject justifies his manufacture of the bronze to commemorate the event.

King Li's inscriptions clearly document narratives drawn from the central court. The Hu *gui* commemorates the twelfth annual sacrifice to the spirits of the Former Kings. Like many other inscriptions (such as the Da Yu *ding*, no. 11, above), the inscription begins with a statement by the King regarding his own legitimacy to be promoted from the status of heir, one still in mourning, a Little One (*xiaozi*). The tureen, he claimed, was made to present the mortuary sacrifices that were necessary to advance his father's spirit into the realm of the ancestors, the Brilliant Di's court. Once fully ascended, the spirits could protect their descendants and send down good fortune. The approximately twenty-seven months (or three ritual years if later ritual texts are correct) that the King spent in mourning seemed to be the defining moment of his adulthood, involving elaborate rituals displaying his ability to follow the patterns set by the Former Kings. In the Hu *gui*, he revisits this time period during the ceremonies to the Former Kings in his twelfth year on the throne.

Earlier, in his fifth year, Hu had documented his continued mortuary sacrifices to his father's spirit on a bell. This bell was discovered in 1981 in Baijiacun 白家村, in Fufeng, Shaanxi Province (*Jicheng* 358). The content is somewhat similar to that of the later Hu tureen (in his twelfth year) and bell inscriptions (possibly of the same time period), discussed below. The fifth-year ceremony also refers to him as a *xiaozi*, when he succeeded in his own rituals to the Former Kings. The term *xiaozi* appears to be the term that an elite son used when addressing his father's spirit.

明福文乃受大命，匍（敷）右（有）四方。余小子肇嗣先王配上下，作厥王大寶，用喜侃前文人，前文人庸厚多福，用龏（申）貂（昭）先王受皇天大魯令（命），文人陟降，余黃（廣）烝受余屯魯。用雝不廷方。

㝬（胡）其萬年永畯尹四方，保大令（命），作疐（至）²

---

² Some read *zhi* as *dui* 對 because *zhi* seems to appear in place of *dui* in the common expression "extol in response" (*duiyang* 對揚) (see Li Xueqin, *Chushi Qinghua jian*, 198–201).

在下，御大福其各（格）。

唯王五祀。

Luminous, fortunate, and accomplished, you, [father and ancestral kings,] received the great mandate and spread it throughout the Four Regions. I, a Little One, from the beginning inherited it from the Former Kings. I match through ritual those spirits above and below, and so make for those kings a great treasure. This will make the Former Accomplished ones happy and content and so multiply my good fortune and it will extend and glorify the great abundant mandate, which the Former Kings received from Brilliant Heaven, and make the Accomplished Ones ascend and descend. I broadly inherited the mandate and, receiving abundant wealth, take this opportunity to unify the noncompliant regions.

May I, Hu, for ten thousand years eternally govern the Four Regions and protect the great mandate, making it come to fulfillment and reside in the one down below. I perform the ritual of driving out the enemies and evil spirits, bringing on great fortune, and so may ascend [to the position of King in the main shrine].

It was the King's fifth annual sacrifice.

Whereas the tureen celebrated the end of Hu's mourning and his advancement to his father's position, the undated bell inscriptions translated below seem to reinforce this position and his right to carry on the Zhou Mandate of Heaven. The rhetoric supports the idea that this Hu was indeed King Li. He restates his legitimacy to inherit the legacy of Heaven's Mandate to exorcise non-Zhou peoples and their spirits from the Four Regions or at least to force them to submit. He particularly noted the case of one rebel, a leader of southern and eastern Yi peoples, who, five generations earlier, during the time of King Zhao, had dared to occupy some of the southern territory. The name of this leader, called "the subject" (Fuzi 服子), was written in a curious manner: the graph for *fu* was simplified whereas the graph for *zi* was unusually complex and ornate, suggesting the *zi* was a title such

---

The reconstructed form for *zhi* 至 (*ti[t]-s) is closer to that for *zhi* 靁 (*[t-l]ri[t]-s), than *dui* (*tˤəp-s), and works better in context.

as "chief" 及夒.

It seems that King Li, who was probably having problems with the Yi people, took as his model King Zhao, an aggressive king who died attacking southern peoples. But the occasion for worship involves the three long-lived ones, Kings Wen, Wu, and Cheng, possibly represented by stars in the sky. This annual ceremony to the Former Kings must have included the most dangerous spirit for Hu, that of his father. Since Hu refers to his father as a Former King, it makes sense that he was in fact King Li.

The Hu bell inscription is unusual in another respect. It is the earliest to include such an extensive array of rhyming repetitive binomes to represent the musical sounds of descending blessings. Not until the Qin and Jin inscriptions of the early Spring and Autumn period would there be such an emphasis on recording these sounds in the inscribed testimonies of legitimation and succession. Repetitive binomes are common in the older songs and eulogies of the *Shijing*. In the Hu bell, the first set describes the sounds of the bell and the second set records the ancestors speaking through the instruments.

Transcription (*Hu* gui)

王曰：有余唯小子，余亡康晝夜，經離先王，用配皇天，廣㭊（至）朕心，墜（遂）于四方，肆余以餿士獻民，禺（稱）螜（戻）先王宗室。

猷（胡）作䵼彝寶簋，用康叀（惠）朕皇文烈祖考，其各（格>恪）前文人，其瀕在帝廷，陟降䰜（申）貂（昭）皇帝大魯令（命），用令保我家、朕立（位）、猷（胡）身，陁陁降余多福，害（憲>顯）烝，宇慕遠猷。

猷（胡）其萬年將實朕多禦，用求壽，匄永令（命），䏎（畯）在立（位），作𢕛（至）在下。

唯王十又二祀。

Translation

The King said: "When I was a Little One, I, working constantly, without a break from dawn to dusk, to act in accord with the Former Kings' [model] and thereby match Brilliant Heaven's [pattern], was able make my heart broad and reach (the point of enlightenment, i.e. 'luminous *de*'), so that I could promote the mandate in the Four Regions, and so I, with the educated youth who pour libations and the [other elite] people who present food offerings, raise the sacrifices and present them in the shrine room for the spirits of the Former Kings."

I, Hu, made sacrificial meat vessels and precious tureens in order to bring happiness and benefits to my Brilliant Accomplished Blazing Ancestor and Deceased Father so that he could be advanced to the rank of a Former Accomplished One and be aligned in order of rank in the Deity's court, where [with] the ascending and descending spirits [he] glorifies the Brilliant Deity's great and abundant charge so that I can use this mandate to protect our home, my position, and my person. The [spirits] poured much good fortune down upon me so I display the grain sacrifices for them and make great plots and distant plans (for the advancement of the Zhou mandate).

May I, Hu, for ten thousand years present meat offerings and perform multiple campaigns to drive out the enemy and evil spirits. I take this opportunity to seek longevity and pray for an eternal life to stabilize my position, thus causing the mandate to arrive to me, who resides below.

It was the King's twelfth annual sacrifice.

Transcription (*Hu* zhong)

王肇遹省文武堇（勤）疆土，南或（域）[3] 反燮（服子）敢陷處我土。王敦伐其至，撲伐厥都，反燮（服子）廼遣閒來逆昭王，南夷東夷具見，廿又六邦。

唯皇上帝百神保余小子，朕猷又（有）成亡競，我唯司配皇天。

王對作宗周寶鐘，倉倉恩恩（鏓鏓），雝雝（鎗鎗>喈喈）[4]

[3] See Glossary.

[4] The original word written as 喈 in the *Shijing* was in the bronze inscriptions usually written with a 金 semantic (but later with a 戈) element, with the phonetic in most examples clearly being 者 (although many scholars earlier transcribed this element as 先 and recently the same element on newly discovered Qin bo-bell was transcribed as 肅, showing continued disagree-

雖雖（雝雝），用昭各（格）丕顯祖考先王，先王其嚴在上，彙彙（繹繹）豐豐，降余多福，福余順孫，參壽唯利，猷（胡）其萬年，眈（畯）保四或（域）。

Translation

From the beginning, the King followed [the way of the Former Kings], and inspected the borderlands labored upon by Kings Wen and Wu. He went to the southern territory, where Fuzi dared to invade and occupy some of our land. The King furiously punished his vanguard warriors and pummeled their capital. Fuzi then sent an envoy to put a stop to it. Once the envoy came to present tribute to King Zhao, all the southern and eastern Yi peoples, totaling twenty-six states, paid a visit [to the Zhou king].

It was the Brilliant Deity Above and the One Hundred Spirits that protected me, the Little One, so that my plan would be successful and without strife, and we could take charge of the ritual of matching the pattern of Brilliant Heaven.

I, the King, in response [to the gift of this legacy] made precious chime bells for Ancestral Zhou—clanging and ringing, singing like birds in harmony! (*[s.r]ˤaŋ-[s.r]ˤaŋ tsʰˤoŋ-tsʰˤoŋ kˤrəj-kˤrəj q(r)oŋ-q(r)oŋ)—and use them to summon and promote the Greatly Manifest Ancestor Deceased Father and Former King. The Former King is stern up above, and—so mighty and fruitful! (*lak-lak pʰ(r)oŋ-pʰ(r)oŋ)—sends down to me much good fortune and blesses me with obedient progeny. By benefit of the Three Long Lived Ones, may I, Hu, for ten thousand years govern and protect the Four Territories.

Further Reading

Jicheng 4317 (Hu *gui*), 260 (Hu *zhong*).

---

ment). The elements 者 (*tA?) and 皆 (*kˤrij) and 隹 (*tur) seem to have little phonetically in common, I suspect that the use of one graph for the other was an ancient transcription error. The archaic graph for *jie* was written with one or two 虎 over a 曰, a form that had been simplified in Warring States bamboo texts but was still in use on bronze texts (see the Zhongshan inscription, *Jicheng* 240). This suggests that the "Daya" odes may have been written in archaic forms of writing not always understood by the scribes in charge of their transmission. Compare the interpretation in no. 62.

Mingwen xuan, nos. 404–5.

Behr, *Reimende Bronzeinschriften und die Entstehung der chinesischen Endreimdichtung*, 255–60.

Cook, *Death in Ancient China*.

Falkenhausen, *Suspended Music*, 44–45, 101–2.

Fang Jicheng, "Guanyu Zong Zhou zhong."

He Linyi and Huang Xiquan, "Hu gui kaoshi liu ze."

Jinwen jinyi leijian, 105–6 (Hu *gui*), 497–99 (Hu *zhong*).

Li, *Bureaucracy and the State in Early China*, 162, 295.

Li, *Landscape and Power in Early China*, 102–7, 131–34.

Li Chaoyuan, "Xi Zhou jinwen zhong de 'wang' yu 'wangqi.'"

Li Xueqin, ed., *Shang Zhou guwenzi duben*, 122–26.

Luo Xizhang, "Shaanxi Fufeng faxian Xi Zhou Liwang shi Hu gui."

Shaughnessy, *Sources of Western Zhou History*, 169–72.

Tang Lan, "Zhou wang Hu zhong kao."

Wang Hui, *Shang Zhou jinwen*, 206–10, 211–14.

Yang Shaoxuan, "Zong Zhou zhong, San Shi pan, yu Mao Gong ding suo jizai de Xi Zhou lishi."

Zhang Yachu, "Zhou Li Wang suo zuo jiqi Hu gui kao—Jian lun yu zhi xiangguan de jige wenti."

Zhang Zhenglang, "Zhou Li Wang Hu gui shiwen."

CAC

40. Yu ding 禹鼎

A version of this inscription, commonly called Mu Gong *ding* 穆公鼎, was known as early as the Song dynasty. The current and more fully legible inscription was found on a vessel excavated within a large cache in 1942 at Renjiacun 任家村 in Qishan County, Shaanxi. It is now in the collection of the National Museum of China in Beijing.

During the reign of King Li, the royal government's control over non-Zhou peoples on the eastern periphery eroded, even as the royal armies were engaged in defending of the Wei River homeland in the west from incursions by non-Zhou tribes from the northwest. In this inscription, the vessel master, Yu, celebrates his role in the defeat of an insurrection led by a former ally of the Zhou, E Hou 噩侯 (the Marquis of E, equivalent to the modern 鄂). Other extant inscriptions cast by or about this man provide additional information. E Hou, whose major settlement was probably located near the border between modern Henan and Hubei, controlled territory in the Huai River region. His sobriquet, Yufang 御方, was probably a title conferred by the Zhou: Protector of the Borderland (and thus close to the literal meaning of the Western term "marquis").[1]

The marquis had previously campaigned together with the Zhou king against Zhou enemies in the southeast, various peoples belonging to the Yi 夷, non-Zhou peoples who had long settled the regions of the lower Yangzi and Huai Rivers. In the E Hou *ding* 噩侯鼎 inscription (*Jicheng* 2810), which clearly precedes the Yu ding, E Hou pays a visit to the Zhou king after a joint military victory. In that account, the two rulers (conceivably the predecessors of the figures in the Yu *ding*) are pictured in unusual ceremonial harmony. But the Yu *ding* inscription reveals the fragility of this remote political alliance: if the narrative is to be believed, E Hou appears to have seized on the weakness of the Zhou under King Li to mobilize in revolt the very groups he was deputed to pacify. Yu, a descendant of Mu Gong, a high minister to the former King Xiao, records his service leading royal armies under the general control of court minister Wu Gong in suppressing the marquis's rebellion.

---

[1] See Xia Hanyi, "Si 'Yufang.'"

Transcription

禹曰：丕顯趠趠（桓桓）皇祖穆公，克夾召先王奠四方。肆武公亦弗叚（遐）朢（忘）朕聖祖考幽大叔、懿叔。命禹肖朕祖考，政于井（邢）邦。肆禹亦弗敢憃，賜（惕）共（恭）朕辟之命。

烏虖哀哉！用天降大喪于下或（國），亦唯噩侯馭方率南淮夷、東夷，廣伐南或（國）、東或（國），至于歷内。

王迺命西六師、殷八師，曰：撲伐噩侯馭方，勿遺壽幼。肆師彌怵匌怛，弗克伐噩。

肆武公迺遣禹率公戎車百乘、斯（厮）馭二百、徒千，曰：于匡朕肅慕。叀（唯）西六師、殷八師，伐噩侯馭方，勿遺壽幼。雩（越）禹以武公徒馭至于噩。敦伐噩。休獲厥君馭方。肆禹有成。敢對揚武公丕顯耿光。用作大寶鼎。禹其萬年，子子孫孫寶用。

Translation

Yu said, "My brilliant and august ancestor Mu Gong was able to support and assist the Former Kings to settle the four quarters. Nor did Wu Gong let recede from his memory my sage grandfather, You Dashu, and my late father, Yishu. He has ordered me, Yu, to assume the government of Xing[2] as my forbears before me. I shall not dare to be slothful and careless; I shall revere the charge of my lord!

"But alas! Heaven sent down great calamities to the lands below, and E Hou Yufang led the Southern Yi of the Huai River region and the Eastern Yi in broadly attacking the lands of the South and East, disrupting our state within.

"Thereupon the King charged the six divisions of the West and the eight divisions of Yin saying, 'Fiercely attack E Hou Yufang, and spare neither young nor old!' But the armies were filled with fear, and could not attack E.

"Thereupon Wu Gong deputed me to lead one hundred of his war chariots with two hundred charioteers and a thousand in-

---

[2] On the territory of Xing 邢 (originally written 井), see Jing Hou *gui* (no. 10, above).

fantry troops accompanying, saying, 'Lead my six divisions of the West and eight divisions of Yin to set my solemn plan aright, and attack E Hou Yufang, sparing neither young nor old!'

"Thereupon I, Yu, led the troops of Wu Gong against Yufang, reaching all the way to E. I struck boldly at E, and happily captured its lord, Yufang. Having succeeded, I dare to raise in thanks the shining brilliance of Wu Gong. Wherefore was cast this great precious cauldron; may my descendants treasure it forever."

Further Reading

Jicheng 2833.
Kimbun tsūshaku, 27.442–63.
Mingwen xuan, no. 407.

Chen Jinyi, "Yu ding kaoshi."
Chen Shihui, "Yu ding shiwen jiao."
Creel, *The Origins of Statecraft in China*, 236–38 *et passim*.
Li, *Landscape and Power in Early China*, 103–5.
Guo Moruo, *Liang Zhou jinwenci daxi tulu kaoshi*, 1.91.
Shaughnessy, "Western Zhou Bronze Inscriptions," 82–83.
Shaughnessy, "Western Zhou History," 330–31.
Xia Hanyi, "Shi 'Yufang.'"
Wang Hui, *Shang Zhou jinwen*, 214–20.
Xu Zhongshu, "Yu ding de niandai jiqi xiangguan wenti."
Zhang Xiaoheng, "Shao Yu ding kaoshi."
Zhou Xunchu and Tan Youxue, "Yu ding kaoshi."

RE

41. Duo You ding 多友鼎

The Duo You *ding* was excavated in 1980 in Xiaquancun 下泉村, Chang'an County, Shaanxi Province, and is currently held in the Shaanxi Provincial Museum. It is a lengthy account of a critical battle between Zhou forces and the strong army of the Xianyun 玁狁, an adversary from the Northwest, and an inscription of unusually rich historical value.

The Duo You *ding* is usually dated to the reign of King Li, although there are arguments for dating it several decades later, to the year 816 B.C.E., during the reign of King Xuan. The sponsor, Duo You 多友, was called upon to help repel an ongoing series of assaults that the Xianyun had launched down the river valleys of the Luo 洛 and Jing 涇 Rivers, which flow south through mountainous terrain into the Wei River valley, carving an invasion path towards the capital region of the Zhou. The Xianyun campaign was a potent threat aimed at the heart of the Zhou government, and its suppression was essential to the continued life of the dynasty—indeed, several decades later a failure to repel similar attacks from another alien group, the Rong, forced the Zhou from their homeland base and brought an end to all prospects of restoring political power to the surviving dynastic government.

The perilous state of the Zhou dynasty at this time is highlighted by considering this vessel along with the previous one. In the Yu *ding* inscription (no. 40, above), we see some actors identical with those of the Duo You *ding*, Wu Gong (Duke Wu) and Yu (referred to here as Xiangfu 向父),[1] mobilizing with some difficulty to suppress rebellion in the eastern reaches of the Zhou domain. The near simultaneous threats from the east and northwest are strong indications of the declining strength of Zhou power.

Transcription

唯十月,用玁狁放(方)瘴(興),廣伐京師,告追于王。命武公遣乃元士,羞追于京師。武公命多友率公車,羞追于京師。癸未,戎伐筍,衣(依)俘,多友西追。甲申之脣(晨),搏于郑。多友右(有)折首執訊。凡以公車折首二百又[□]又五人,執訊廿又三人,俘戎車百乘一十又七乘。衣(依)復筍人俘,或

---

[1] A different vessel, the Shu Xiangfu Yu *gui* 叔向父禹簋 (*Jicheng* 4242), establishes the strong likelihood of this identification.

（又）搏于龏。折首卅又六人，執訊二人，俘車十乘。從至，追搏于世。多友或（又）有折首執訊。乃越追至于楊冢。公車折首百又十又五人，執訊三人。唯俘車不克以，衣（依）焚，唯馬毆盡（盡），復奪京師之俘。

多友迺獻俘馘訊于公。武公迺獻于王。迺曰武公曰：汝既靜京師，賚（賷），汝賜汝土田。丁酉，武公在獻宮，迺命向父：召多友，迺徙（陟）于獻宮。公親曰多友曰：余肇事汝，休，不逆。又（有）成事，多禽（擒），汝靜京師。賜汝圭瓚一，湯鐘一鐪，鐈錼百勻（鈞）。

多友敢對揚公休，用作尊鼎。用朋用友，其子子孫永寶用。

Translation

It was in the tenth month. Because the Xianyun had arisen and launched a broad attack upon the Jing garrison, it was reported to the King that troops be put in pursuit of them. The King commanded Wu Gong, "Dispatch your finest soldiers to the Jing garrison in orderly pursuit." Wu Gong commanded Duo You to lead the Duke's chariots to the Jing garrison in orderly pursuit. On *guiwei* day (*ganzhi* no. 20) the raiders attacked at Xun and took captives. Duo You pursued them west. On the morning of *jiashen* day (*ganzhi* no. 21) we struck them at Zhu. Duo You beheaded enemies and took captives. The chariot corps altogether cut off two hundred . . . five heads and took thirty-three captives. It also seized 117 enemy chariots and rescued captives from Xun. We struck another party at Gong, beheading thirty-six and taking two captives, along with ten chariots. We further pursued raiders to Shi, where Duo You again cut off heads and took prisoners. Then we chased them [by chariot] as far as Yangzhong, where the Duke's chariot corps beheaded 115 men and took three prisoners. Their chariots could not be brought along and were accordingly burned; the horses were driven back with the troops and the remainder of the captives from the Jing garrison were recovered.

Duo You presented the loot, scalps, and captives to the Duke. Wu Gong presented them to the King, who addressed Wu Gong, saying, "You have now brought peace to the Jing garrison, and I will reward you. I present you with lands and fields."

On the day *dingyou*, Wu Gong was at the Hall of Presentation and ordered Xiangfu to summon Duo You, who came to the Hall of Presentation. The Duke himself addressed Duo You, saying, "I sent you off and your conduct was excellent and free of disobedience. You succeeded in this affair, caught many enemies, and you brought peace to the Jing garrison. I present you with one fine soup steamer, one set of bells, and one hundred measures of copper."

Duo You dared to extol the grace of the Duke, wherefore is cast this precious cauldron, wherewith to befriend companions. May my descendants treasure it forever.

Further Reading

Jicheng 2835.

Mingwen xuan, no. 408.

Huang Shengzhang, "Duo You ding de lishi yu dili wenti."

Lau, *Quellenstudien zur Landvergabe und Bodenübertragung in der westlichen Zhou-Dynastie*, 275–83.

Li, "Ta Yū tei meibun o meguru rekishi chiri teki mondai no kaiketsu."

Li Feng, *Landscape and Power in Early China*, 147–49.

Liu Huan, "Duo You ding 'jing X' diwang kaobian."

Liu Xiang, "Duo You ding ming liang yi."

Liu Yu, "Duo You ding ming de shidai yu diming kaoding."

Shaughnessy, "The Date of the Duo You ding and Its Significance."

Tian Xingnong and Luo Zhongru, "Duo You ding de faxian yu qi mingwen shishi."

Wang Hui, *Shang Zhou jinwen*, 220–26.

Zhang Yachu, "Duo You ding mingwen wenti."

RE

42. Guai Bo gui 乖伯簋

Known from the nineteenth century, this inscription has also been published as the Guifeng *dui* 歸夆敦, the Mi Bo Guiyuan *gui* 羋白歸苑簋 and as the Qiang Bo *dui* 羌伯敦. Shirakawa transcribes the name of the sponsor, Guai, with an archaic character close to Mi 羋, the surname of the kings of Chu. The vessel is now in the National Museum of China in Beijing.

The Guai Bo *gui* presents a number of puzzles. The sponsor is referred to by several different naming formulas: a conventional title, Guai Bo (Earl of Guai); Guifeng (apparently a personal name); and *mei'ao* 眉敖, which appears to be an alternative title. There is a strong textual tradition that associates the term *ao* with the titles of rulers of Chu, a polity known from Western Zhou times, but famous as the dominant southern culture of the Eastern Zhou era, principally associated with the middle Yangzi River valley. The language or languages of the larger Chu region were indeed distinct from that of the Zhou people, and some terms associated with Chu, such as *mei'ao*, appear to be phonetic representations of non-Chinese words, reflecting possible ritual leadership positions.[1] The surname of the Chu royal lineage was Mi 羋, and the decision by some interpreters to read the name of the sponsor as Mi Bo reflects their belief that we are dealing with a ruler associated with the Chu people. As a record of Zhou-Chu relations during the mid-Western Zhou, this inscription would be noteworthy for its claim that the ancestors of the Chu house, clearly acknowledged as an independent political entity, were key allies in the Zhou conquest era, as well as for depicting ongoing tensions between the two states: the vessel's main account of a comradely meeting of rulers is preceded by apparent military conflict.

However, vessels from Guai have recently been excavated in the upper Jing 涇 River valley, about 100 km northwest of the Western Zhou capital, and these include references to campaigns against the Rong peoples, from further northwest. This conflicts with the southern implications of the term *mei'ao* and an association of the inscription with the Mi lineage of Chu. The location of the state of Chu during the Western Zhou has been a matter of long debate. Good evidence suggests it may have been well to the northwest of its later Yangzi base, in the upper reaches of the Dan River, whose source is only about 70 km east of the Western Zhou capital,

---

[1] Cook and Major, eds., *Defining Chu*, 54.

but even were we to place Chu this far north, it would still not allow us to reconcile the location with the site of the recent Guai vessel finds, well above the Wei River valley.² On the other hand, early place names, including Chu, are also recorded in the Qian 汧 River valley, located close to and west of the Jing 涇,³ suggesting that perhaps the sponsor of the Guai Bo *gui* occupied a garrison colony detached from a lineage homeland in the southeast. The best choice presently seems to be to avoid a strong claim for an association of this vessel with Chu, while remaining open to some form of that claim as further evidence is explored.

Transcription

唯王九年九月甲寅，王命益公征眉敖。益公至告。二月，眉敖至見，獻帛。己未，王命中（仲）致歸（饋）乖伯貔裘。王若曰：乖伯，朕丕顯祖文王、武王，雁（膺）受大命。乃祖克奉（弼）先王，異（翼）自也（他）邦，又（有）芇于大命。我亦弗豖（曠）享邦。賜女貔裘。

乖伯拜手稽首。天子休弗望（忘）小裔邦。歸夆敢對揚天子丕杯（丕丕）魯休。用作朕皇考武乖幾王尊簋。用好（孝）宗朝（廟）享。夙夕好朋友與百者（諸）婚遘（媾）。用旂屯（純）彔（祿）永命，魯壽子孫。歸夆其邁（萬）年，日用享于宗室。

Translation

It was in the King's ninth year, in the ninth month, on *jiayin* day (*ganzhi* no. 51). The King ordered Yi Gong to campaign against the *mei'ao*. Yi Gong returned and made a report. In the second month, the *mei'ao* arrived to be seen in audience, bearing tribute gifts. On the day *jiwei*, the King ordered Zhong to present a badgerskin coat to Guai Bo. The King's words were, "Guai Bo, when

---

² See Blakeley, "In Search of Danyang," for a meticulous review of the historical geography of the earliest Chu capitals; also Falkenhausen, *Chinese Society in the Age of Confucius*, 265.

³ Chen Pan, *Chunqiu dashi biao lieguo juexing ji cunmie biao zhuanyi*, 217. A Western Zhou vessel recently recovered from this region bearing the place name Dan 丹 may provide new evidence of this association (see Zhang Enxian and Wei Xingxing, "Zhouyuan yizhi chutu Dan Shu Fan *yu*").

my grand and brilliant ancestors Kings Wen and Wu received the great mandate, your ancestors aided those Former Kings, assisting from their country in the receipt of the mandate. And indeed, not having allowed our rule of the state to lapse, I present to you this badgerskin coat."

Guai Bo bowed prostrate at the grace of the Son of Heaven, that this small and distant state has not been forgotten. I, Guifeng, dare to extol in response the splendid grace of the Son of Heaven, wherefore is cast this precious *gui* for my august late father, martial King Ji of Guai. May I use it to make filial offerings at my ancestral temple from dawn to dusk, to delight friends and my many relatives by marriage. I pray for grace and everlasting life for myself and my descendants. May I, Guifeng, live for ten thousand years, using this tomake daily offering at my ancestral shrine.

Further Reading

Jicheng 4331.

Kimbun tsūshaku, 25.282–95.

Mingwen xuan, no. 206.

Jinwen jinyi leijian, 241–43.

Li, *Landscape and Power in Early China*, 183–86.

Shaughnessy, *Sources of Western Zhou History*, 117–20, 172–73.

RE

43. Guo You Bi *Ding* 酅攸比鼎 AND Guo You Bi *Guigai* 酅攸比簋蓋

These inscriptions are identical (one on a *ding* cauldron and one on the lid of a *gui*-tureen), and it is likely that, were we to have the body of the *gui*, we would also find it repeated therein. The décor, shape, and calligraphy of the *ding* are typical of the late Western Zhou, and the lengthy reign in the date notation places the events of the inscription to 795 B.C.E., during the reign of King Xuan. The *ding* is currently housed in Kyoto, Japan, at the Kurakawa Cultural Antiquities Research Center, while the lid is located in Beijing at the National Museum of China.

The significance of this inscription, which is concerned with the misappropriation of Guo Bi's 酅比 fields, is enhanced by the inscription in the Guo Bi *xu* 酅比盨 (*Jicheng* 4466), which details a different instance of wrongful acts committed against Guo Bi's fields and *yi* 邑-settlements. The events in the *xu* inscription occurred in 801 B.C.E., six years before the *ding* and *guigai* inscriptions. While the *xu* vessel inscription presents many difficulties of interpretation, we do learn that King Xuan ordered a number of Guo Bi's fields and settlements to be returned to him by Zhang 章 and Fu 复 (whose subordinates had somehow harmed Guo Bi's fields), and also that some fields of Zhang and Fu be turned over to Guo Bi. (The operative theory of *respondeat superior* is also seen in the Shi Qi *ding* inscription [no. 20, above] and the Hu *ding* III [no. 35], and that of damages in the Hu *ding* III.)

The dedications in the *ding* and *guigai* and *xu* inscriptions yield interesting information about Guo Bi's ancestry. Both are dedicated to Guo Bi's grandfather (*huang zu* 皇祖), Ding Gong 丁公, and his father (*huang kao* 皇考), Hui Gong ఼公. In addition, both inscriptions end with an identical family emblem. Family emblems of this sort are typical of descendants of Shang and eastern lineages, and it may be that Guo Bi was descended from a mixed stock of easterners and Zhou.

When we combine the contents of the inscriptions we arrive at the following conclusions about the plaintiff. Guo Bi was a powerful landowner who had the financial wherewithal and ritual authority to commission a number of vessels. His relations with the King were intimate enough to enable him to lodge complaints directly with the sovereign. It may well be the case that Guo Bi resided in the capital area, as that is where the activities in both inscriptional groups appear to have taken place.

The inscriptions also yield interesting information about legal proceedings. First, the King would sometimes intervene in and even preside over cases, though only, it seems, if one's connections permitted. Second, when there was disagreement between the plaintiff (Guo Bi) and defendant (You Wei Mu 攸衛牧) as to the charge, rather than demonstrating partiality towards Guo Bi by immediately deciding the case in his favor, the King ordered an investigation, or perhaps an inspection (probably of the fields concerned). The scribe then informed one Guo Lü 虢旅 (no relation to Guo Bi) of the findings. Although the case had originally been brought before the King, this Guo Lü was the ultimate arbiter and ordered You Wei Mu to swear the post-decision oath. (Compare the Ying *yi* inscription, no. 36, above.) The severity of this oath, in which it seems that You Wei Mu is calling down a self-imprecation of death should he violate the terms of the court decision, is reminiscent of certain oaths seen in Eastern Zhou covenant texts. (See also the oath in the recently discovered Diao Sheng *zun* inscriptions.) Also of interest in the *ding* and *guigai* inscription is that once Guo Bi's fields in You 攸 were returned to him by You 攸 Wei Mu, his name became Guo You 攸 Bi, evidencing a practice, followed at least sometimes, of changing one's name to reflect land holdings.

Transcription

唯三十又一年三月初吉壬辰。王在周康宮夷大室。

鬲比以攸衛牧告于王曰：汝孚（捊）我田。牧弗能許鬲比。

王令（命）省。史南以即虢旅。虢旅迺使攸衛牧誓曰：敢弗具付鬲比其祖射（謝）分田邑則殺。[1] 攸衛牧則誓。

比作朕皇祖丁公皇考叀公尊鼎。鬲攸比其邁（萬）年子子孫孫永寶用。

Translation

It was the thirty-first year, third month, *renchen* (*ganzhi* no. 29). The King was in the Yi Great Chamber of the Zhou Kang Palace.

---

[1] In addition to *sha* 殺, this graph has varyingly been read as *cheng* 懲 "to punish," *zhu* 誅, "to execute," and *fang* 放, "to banish."

Guo Bi took You Wei Mu and petitioned the King, saying: "You, [You Wei Mu,] misappropriated my fields." Mu was unable to agree with Guo Bi.

The King ordered an investigation. Scribe Nan took [the results] and approached Guo Lü. [Guo Lü] thereupon caused You Wei Mu to swear an oath, saying, "[If I] dare not completely pay [to] Guo Bi those fields and yi-settlements given over to and divided by his ancestors, [may I] be killed." You Wei Mu then swore the oath.

Bi makes for his august deceased grandfather, Ding Gong, and august deceased father, Hui Gong, this sacrificial *ding*-cauldron. May Guo You Bi for ten thousand years [have] sons' sons and grandsons' grandsons eternally treasure and use it.

Further Reading

Jicheng 2818 and 4278.

Skosey, "The Legal System and Legal Tradition of the Western Zhou."

Wang Hui, *Shang Zhou jinwen*, 226–28.

LAS

44. Guo Shu Lü zhong 虢叔旅鐘

The inscriptional text of the Guo Shu Lü *zhong* was cast on a set of late Western Zhou chime-bells, five of which are extant and located in various museums in China and Japan. Though allegedly discovered together in Chang'an, the bells were quickly dispersed among private collectors. The current locations of the five extant bells are: Palace Museum, Beijing (*Jicheng* 238); Calligraphy Museum, Tokyo (*Jicheng* 239); Shanghai Museum (*Jicheng* 241); Sumitomo Collection, Kyoto (*Jicheng* 243); and the Shandong Provincial Museum (*Jicheng* 244). In addition to the five extant pieces, two other bells are known only from rubbings or handcopies of the inscriptions published in nineteenth-century catalogs. The precise date of the discovery is unknown, but the inscription was first published in 1804.[1]

Sharing a uniform decorative scheme but varying in height from 65 centimeters to 26 centimeters, the bells would have formed a chimed set to be used as part of a musical ensemble during ritual performance. On each bell the central part of striking area is decorated with a dual dragon pattern. A smaller bird pattern appears to the right, marking the strike-point for the second tone.[2] The entire inscriptional text appears on each of the four largest bells, but is split over the three smallest ones.[3]

The sponsor of these bells, Guo Shu Lü 虢叔旅, was a younger son of the Guo 虢 lineage, an aristocratic lineage descended from the younger brother of King Wen and mentioned frequently in bronze inscriptions. While Guo Shu Lü does not correspond to any figure known in transmitted texts, Guo Lü 虢旅, almost certainly the same individual, is mentioned in two other late Western Zhou inscriptions (Guo You Bi *ding* and Guo You Bi *guigai*, no. 43, above), in which he adjudicates a land dispute on behalf of the Zhou king.

The inscription records the dedication of the bell-chime to the sponsor's ancestor Hui Shu 惠叔, Guo Shu Lü's deceased father. Using poetic

---

[1] Ruan Yuan, *Jiguzhai zhongding yiqi kuanshi*, 3.11.

[2] Each bell in the set is capable of producing two tones, depending on where the bell is struck. On this important acoustic phenomenon, see Falkenhausen, *Suspended Music*, 80–84. Falkenhausen also notes (*ibid.*, 165) that the bird pattern marking the second tone is omitted from the largest bells in the set, as is typical of late Western Zhou bell chimes.

[3] The inscriptional text is not complete on the three smallest bells; it lacks the final fifteen graphs, which would have appeared on an eighth bell, which was evidently omitted from any published record. Interestingly, on the Shanghai Museum bell, the first graph of each of the first three columns is omitted.

language and formulaic expressions, the sponsor praises his father's virtue and pledges to follow his example in rendering service to the Zhou king. Unspecified awards from the Zhou king serve as the occasion for the creation of the bell-chime, used both to report the honor bestowed upon the sponsor and to make a prayer for the favor of his ancestor and the continuity of the lineage.

Transcription

虢叔旅曰：不（丕）顯皇考叀（惠）叔，穆穆秉元明德。御于厥辟，得屯（純）亡敃（愍）。旅敢肇帥井（型）皇考威義（儀），[□]御于天子。迺天子多賜旅休。旅對天子魯休揚。用作[朕]皇考叀（惠）叔大林龢鐘。皇考嚴在上，異（翼）在下。豐豐彙彙，降旅多福。旅其萬年子子孫孫永寶用享。

Translation

> Guo Shu Lü declared: "My greatly illustrious and august father, Hui Shu, solemnly held fast to primal and bright virtue. In serving his sovereign, he attained purity without defect. I, Lü, dare to undertake to follow the model of my august father's awesome propriety in ... serving the Son of Heaven." Thereupon the Son of Heaven greatly bestowed his beneficence upon Lü. In response, I, Lü, extol the Son of Heaven's generous beneficence, herewith making for my[4] august father, Hui Shu, this grand set of harmonious bells. August father, reverent above and protective below, abundantly send great fortune down upon Lü! May Lü for ten thousand years have sons and grandsons to forever treasure and use these bells in sacrifice."

Further Reading

Jicheng 238–44.

Kimbun tsūshaku, 26.368–81.

Mingwen xuan, no. 427.

Li, *Landscape and Power in Early China*, 251–58.

DMS

[4] The graph *zhen* 朕 is omitted from the version of the inscription on the largest bell (*Jicheng* 238).

45. Sanshi pan 散氏盤

Also published as the San *pan* 散盤 or Zeren *pan* 夨人盤, as well as other less frequently encountered names, this vessel is said to have been found in Shaanxi Province during the eighteenth century. It was for a time believed to have been destroyed in the 1860 burning of the Qing Summer Palace by Western forces, but comparisons with early rubbings confirm that the destroyed object was a replica. The vessel is now stored in the Palace Museum, Taipei.

The Sanshi *pan* dates from the reign of King Li, and is unique among extant Western Zhou documents. Its inscription appears to be the text of a deed to lands that were ceded to the San clan by the ruler of Ze as compensation for attacks upon the estate lands of San. We do not know what prompted Ze to agree to compensation or what third party may have adjudicated the dispute. The text records in painstaking detail the boundaries of the land transferred and the oaths sworn by officers in the service of Ze as guarantees. It closes with the certification of the recording scribe.[1]

The territories of San and Ze were located in the Wei River valley, the fertile basin extending west from the Yellow River's bend. The Zhou capital region lay towards the eastern end of the valley; San and Ze were farther west. The San lineage was associated with the Zhou, while Ze has generally been understood to be a lineage that had been part of the Shang polity; the more tenuous allegiance of the Ze to the Zhou realm is signaled by the appropriation of the term "king" (*wang* 王) by its leader in this inscription. However, evidence indicates that the rulers of Ze were members of the Zhou royal Ji lineage, and there is a variety of instances in which this term is applied to leaders other than the Zhou king without any sign of political resistance to Zhou rule (see, for example, Lu Bo Dong *gui*, no. 22, above, but also Guai Bo *gui*, no. 42, where political relations are more complex).

While there are earlier precedents for memorializing the transfer of land in bronze (for example, the vessels of Qiu Wei, no. 27, above), the intent of those inscriptions appears to be celebratory, and the vessels are

---

[1] Although this is the only such inscription extant, we have a record dating from an earlier period that suggests that this form of ceremonial/legal record was established practice. In that text, known as the Peng Sheng *gui* 倗生簋 (or Ge Bo *gui* 格伯簋) inscription (*Jicheng* 5011), after a problematic land transaction, the parties reassessed the land parcels in question: "recorded this with scribe Zhiwu and raised earthen markers to set boundaries, casting a precious vessel wherewith to register (*dian* 典) the fields of Ge Bo."

private possessions intended for normal ceremonial use. The Sanshi *pan* appears to have been cast as an imperishable record of the deed itself,[2] the recorder Zhongnong's certification at the close of the inscription providing the legal force of a notary. It is unclear, however, whether Zhongnong is the scribe of the San lineage or of the King of Ze, or perhaps of an outside adjudicating power unmentioned in the inscription, such as the Zhou itself.

Transcription

用矢撲散邑，迺即散用田。眉（堳）[3]自瀗涉，以南，至于大沽一封。以陟，二封，至于邊柳，復涉瀗，陟雩，𢾅邊陝。以西，封于播城木，封于芻逨（萊），封于芻道內，陟芻，登于厂泉，封剶岸，陝陵，剛（崗）岸，封于罟道，封于原道，封于周道。以東，封于卓東彊。右還，封于眉道。以南，封于谷逨（萊）道。以西，至于堆莫。眉（堳）井邑田自根木道，左至于井邑封道。以東，一封，還以西，一封，陟剛（崗）三封，降。以南，封于同道，陟州剛（崗），登岸，降棫，二封。

矢人有司眉（堳）田：鮮、且、微、武父、西宮襄、豆人虞、丂、彔貞、師氏右眚、小門人繇、原人虞芇、淮、司工虎李、龠豐父、唯人有司刑丂，凡十又五夫，正眉（堳），矢舍（捨）散田。

司土屰（逆）寅、司馬單昆、邦人司工京君、宰德父、散人小子眉（堳）田戎、微父、效𦈢父、𩒨之有司橐、州京、焂從𥛔，凡散有司十夫。

唯王九月辰在乙卯，矢俾鮮、且、𢾅、旅，誓曰：我既付散氏田，器有爽，實有散氏心賊，則爰千、罰千，傳棄之。鮮、且、𢾅、旅則誓。迺矢俾西宮襄、武父，誓曰：我既付散氏溼田、牆（畛）田，余有爽變，爰千、罰千。西宮襄、武父則誓。

厥為圖。矢王于豆新宮東廷。厥左執要，史正中（仲）農。

---

[2] Cf. Li Feng, "Literacy and the Social Contexts of Writing in the Western Zhou," 287–93.

[3] The character *mei* 眉 is a place name later in the inscription; however, Ma Chengyuan argues for the reading *mei* 堳 "boundary" at this point and several others (*Mingwen xuan*). Ma's reading permits a more cogent interpretation of the inscription as a whole and is adopted here. Some read it as a verb, *lü* 履, "to pace off [the boundary]." This simplifies the syntax, but accords less closely with the graph.

Translation

Because Ze attacked the estate of the San clan, the possession of certain fields is transferred to the San. The boundary of these lands, setting out from Mei, crosses the river Xian, goes south to the earthen boundary marker at Great Salt Marsh. Climbing, it follows two markers on the rising ground and then down to the Willow Fringe. It recrosses the Xian, climbs to Yu and proceeds to Tuanmei. Turning west, it goes to the marker at the trees by Bo City, the marker in Chu Meadow, and the marker within the Chu Road. Climbing up to Chu, it ascends at Han Spring, following the markers at the embankment at Zhu, Mei Ridge, and the cliff bank. It follows the marker at the Shan Road, the marker at the Yuan Road, and the marker at the Zhou Road. Turning east, it follows the marker at the eastern border of Zhuo. Turning back to the right, it follows the marker on the Mei Road. Going south, it follows the marker on Gu Meadow Road. Then turning west, it follows on to Hongmu. Further, the boundary of other transferred lands, setting out from the fields of the Jing estate, follows the Genmu Road, left to the marked road bordering the Jing estate, east to the marker, then back west to the next marker. It climbs past the three markers up the hill, descending south to the marker on the Tong Road. It climbs up Zhou Hill, ascending at the embankment and descending past the two markers at Yu.

These were the officers from Ze who demarcated the boundary: Xian, Ju, Wei, Wufu, Xiang of Xigong, Yu of Dou, Kao, Forester Zhen, Commandant Yousheng, Yao of Xiaomen, Yunai of Yuan, Huai, Officer of Works Huxiao, Yue Fengfu, Officer Jingkao of Gong. Altogether fifteen men demarcated the boundary of the lands that Ze ceded to San.

Officer of Lands Niyin, Grand Marshal Shankun, Officer of Works Jingjun of Bang, Steward Defu, Prince Rong of San clan at Meitian, Weifu, Xiao Jufu, Officers Tuo Ke, Zhoujing, and Shu Congli: altogether ten officers for San.

In the King's ninth month, on *yimao* day (*ganzhi* no. 52), Ze directed Xian, Ju, X, and Lü to pledge an oath, swearing, "We have given the clan of San these fields and their implements. If we renege on our agreement, we will have robbed the San clan of their trust and will be fined a thousand *yuan*, receive a thousand lashes, and be exiled." Xian, Ju, X, and Lü so swore. Then Xigong Xiang and Wufu were made to swear, saying, "We have given the clan of San these open fields and cultivated fields. If we renege on our agreement, we will be fined a thousand *yuan* and receive a thousand lashes." Xigong Xiang and Wufu so swore.

They made a map for the King of Ze in the east court of the New Palace at Dou.

— Keeper of the left tally, the official scribe Zhongnong.

Further Reading

Jicheng 10176.
Kimbun tsūshaku, 24.191–228.
Mingwen xuan, no. 428.

Akatsuka, *Kōkotsu kinbun kenkyū*, 603–6.
Chen Ziyi, "San Shi pan Shiguwen dili kaozheng."
Huang Baoyue, "San pan jin shi."
Itō Michiharu, *Chūgoku kodai ōcho no keisei*, 185–91.
Lau, *Quellenstudien zur Landvergabe und Bodenübertragung in der westlichen Zhou-Dynastie*, 334–45.
Li, *Landscape and Power in Early China*, 186–87.
Li Feng, "Literacy and the Social Contexts," 287–93.
Skosey, "The Legal System and Legal Tradition of the Western Zhou," 387–92.
Wang Hui, *Shang Zhou jinwen*, 228–35.
Yi Peiji, "San shi pan shiwen."
Yu Yongliang, "Ji san Shi pan."
Zhang Binglin, "Lun San Shi pan shu er zha."
Zhang Xiaoheng, "San pan kaoshi."

RE

46. DA KE *DING* 大克鼎 AND RELATED INSCRIPTIONS

In 1890, a cache of bronze vessels was unearthed in Renjiacun, Fufeng County, Shaanxi Province, including about 120 different vessels. Many seemed to belong to a prominent late Western Zhou landowner and official named Ke 克, the large cauldron called the Da Ke *ding* (or Greater Cauldron of Ke), a set of seven Xiao Ke *ding* (Lesser Cauldrons of Ke), a set of chime-bells (Ke *zhong*), a large *bo*-style bell (Ke *bo*), and a *xu*-style tureen (Ke *xu*). The bronzes were sold off separately and are now dispersed around the world. The Pan 潘 family bought the Da Ke *ding* along with the Da Yu *ding* and took them to Tianjin 天津, but around 1923, during the political disruption following the fall of the Qing dynasty, the two vessels were hidden in Suzhou. Around 1950, the family turned their collection over to the state. The Da Ke *ding* is presently part of the permanent exhibition of bronze vessels in the Shanghai Museum. It is also called the Shanfu Ke *ding* because *shanfu* 膳夫, indicating a high minister who managed governmental affairs inside and outside of the court,[1] was one of the titles held by this wealthy member of the Ke family. By Han times, the role of *shanfu* involved control over sacrificial foods and such events. In bronze inscriptions, a ritual aspect to the role is hinted at by the gift of an orchestra, because the primary use of an orchestra would be at ancestor worship events. The status of owning an orchestra was high. It implied a strong ancestor cult and good relations with the Zhou court. From other vessels, we know that Ke had graduated to the rank of Master (*shi* 師) and was once a member of the elite Tiger Guard that protected the king and eventually was sent out on military missions. This is strong evidence that Ke was a member of the extended Zhou lineage.

The Da Ke *ding* is an enormous vessel, weighing over 200 kilograms, about 93 centimeters high, with three large animal-hoof style feet (emerging from horned mask-like animal faces of earlier fashion), and a round 43-centimeter-deep belly decorated on the outside with a large register of wavy lines of abstract interlocked cicada patterns under an upper register of facing *kui*-dragons whose eyes on either side of a flange form a mask, as is typical of late Western Zhou style. The long inscription is divided into two sections of fourteen lines. The first section shows the obvious use of what scholar Noel Barnard termed "relievo guidelines"[2] marked into the

---

[1] See Glossary.

[2] E.g., Barnard and Wan, "The Casting of Inscriptions in Chinese Bronzes" [PRG]. On the

original clay mold and forming a grid for the scribe, who could then form evenly spaced lines each with ten graphs.

The text of the Da Ke *ding* inscription is most famous as evidence for the redistribution of land among the elite during the late Western Zhou period. As a reward for Ke's work as *shanfu*, the Zhou king, possibly King Xiao, essentially extended his contract or charge and awarded him ritual clothing and the cultivated fields and slaves formerly belonging to other families, such as the once prominent Jing 井 (read by many scholars as Xing 邢), possibly around the Qian River valley, which is northwest of modern Xi'an. The king also rewarded him with musical instruments for an orchestra and musicians (young slaves who had worked under an Archivist, called *shi xiaochen* 史小臣). The document listing the awards was only the second half of the inscription. The first half begins with Ke's own eulogy to his ancestors, particularly Master Huafu, possibly his grandfather, who had served King Gong. Often the eulogies by the awardee and the gift-giving or award document were cast separately onto different vessels, but here they are joined in a single document.

The Ke chime bell inscriptions and the Ke *bo* (*Jicheng* 209) inscription seem to refer to different events. The inscription is inscribed fully on the single *bo* but is broken into pairs on the chime bells, so that the first half of the inscription begins on one bell and ends on the second (*Jicheng* 204–205, 206–207, 208-second is missing). The pairs are not together in a single museum but dispersed in such places as Tianjin, Shanghai, Kyoto, and Nara (Japan). The *bo*, presently in the Tianjin Museum, is about 64 centimeters high and decorated with a large openwork flange, the type seen later on the Qin bells of the early Spring and Autumn period. The inscription on the large *bo*-style bell clearly refers to a different award event.

唯十又六年九月初吉庚寅，王在周康烈宮，王呼士曶召克，
王親令克遹涇東至于京師，賜克甸車、馬乘。

克不敢墜，專（敷）奠王令（命）。

克敢對揚天子休，用作朕皇祖考伯寶林鐘，用匄屯叚永令
（命）。

克其萬年子子孫孫永寶。

peculiarities of this inscription, see also Barnard and Cheung, *The Shan-fu Liang Ch'i Kuei and Associated Inscribed Vessels*, 261–62; Li Feng, "Xi-Zhou qingtongqi mingwen zhizuo fangfa shiyi"; Škrabal, "Writing before Inscribing," 318–26 [MP].

It was in the sixteenth year of the King's reign, ninth month, *chuji*, on *gengyin* day (*ganzhi* no. 27), when the King was at the Hall of Kang and Lie in Zhou. The King called for the Educated Youth Hu to summon Ke. The King personally charged Ke to make a survey of the territory from east of the Jing River to the capital encampment. The King awarded Ke a field wagon and a horse mount.

I, Ke, do not dare to fail to spread and make the King's command law.

I, Ke, dare in response to extol the Son of Heaven's grace and take this opportunity to make a set of treasured chime-bells for my Brilliant Ancestor and Deceased-father, the Elder, so as to pray for abundant blessings and eternal life.

May I, Ke, have ten thousand years and sons of grandsons to eternally treasure them.

The seven Xiao Ke *ding* were graduated in size, with the largest about 57 centimeters tall. Like the bells, these vessels are presently dispersed in museums in China and Japan. The décor is similar to that of the Da Ke *ding* (and one also shows use of relievo-guidelines), but the inscription, repeated on each vessel (*Jicheng* 2796–2802), has more in common rhetorically with that found on the bells. But it clearly records an event that took place at another time:

唯王廿又三年九月，王在宗周，王命善（膳）夫克舍于成周，遹正八師之年。

克作朕皇祖釐季寶宗彝。克其日用䈰，朕辟魯休，用匄康勵（樂）³，屯右（祐）眉壽，永令（命）霝（靈）終，邁（萬）年無疆。克其子子孫孫永寶用。

It was in the King's twenty-third year, the ninth month, when the King resided at Zongzhou, the year that the King commanded *shanfu* Ke to lodge at Zongzhou and perform a defensive survey and correction of the armies of the Eight Masters.

I, Ke, made for my Brilliant Ancestor Li Ji treasured sacrificial

---

³ This archaic graph may be loaned here for "enjoyment" (*le* 樂, *[r]ˤawk); see no. 33, note 8, above.

vessels for the main shrine. I, Ke, will daily use them to present sacrificial meat for my ruler's abundant grace. I use the vessels to pray for peace and joy, much divine aid, extended longevity, eternal life, a numinous end, and ten thousand years without end. May I, Ke, have sons of sons and grandsons of grandsons to eternally treasure and use [these vessels].

Of *xu*-style tureens, in this set there are three with inscriptions, two with the same one (obviously a pair), and the third on a different topic. The first two are by Master Ke 師克 (*Jicheng* 4467–68) and the third by Shanfu Ke (*Jicheng* 4465), presumably all the same man. The Master Ke inscriptions may be earlier than the Shanfu Ke inscriptions, because they memorialize Ke's taking over the ancestral role of protecting the king, a common aspect of the rank of Master. The document begins with a eulogy by the King to the Zhou founders, their receipt of the Heavenly Mandate, and Ke's ancestral link to Zhou. In the next speech, the King eulogizes Ke's father and then refers to Ke's own duties and the rewards he was presently giving him. Finally, the inscription ends with the familiar expressions of gratitude and prayers.

王若（諾）曰：師克，丕顯文武，膺受大令（命），匍（敷）有四方，則緐（由）唯乃先祖考又（有）爵于周邦，干（扞）害（憲>閑）王身，作爪牙。

王曰：克，余唯經乃先祖考克令臣先王，昔余既令（命）汝。今余唯䌛（申）就乃令（命），令（命）汝更乃祖考，䰙（兼?）[4]嗣（司）左右虎臣。賜汝秬鬯一卣、赤市、五黃（衡）、赤舄、牙（邪）僰（幅）、駒車、賁較、朱虢（鞃）、靳、虎冪、繡裏、畫轉、畫輯、金甬、朱旂、馬四匹、鋚勒、素鉞。敬夙夕勿灋（廢）朕令（命）。

---

[4] The reading possibly *jian* 兼 (*[k]ˤem) follows Wang Hui's analysis (*Shang Zhou jinwen*, 188, n. 7). It appears to be a graph with no history older than Middle Western Zhou (see also the Fan Sheng *gui*, *Jicheng* 4326) and no later than the late Spring and Autumn period inscription the Shu Yi bells from Qi's inscription. The earliest version of the graph is composed of the possible phonetic 丘 (*[k]ʷʰə) or 韭 (*s.kuʔ) with semantic elements 廾 below and 孔 on the right side (see also different variants in inscriptions, nos. 26, 46, 55, 63, 69). It occurs in combination with *si* 司 in combined phrases similar to *shesi* 攝司 (*kə.ŋep-s.lə), meaning "to handle, assist" and to *guansi* 官司 (*kʷˤan-s.lə), meaning "to manage; be a manager," see *guansi* in Glossary. A second usage for this mystery word is the sense of "to carry on (an ancestral duty)" (see the Ni bell, *Jicheng* 60–63).

克敢對揚天子丕顯魯休，用作旅盨（盨），克其萬年子子孫孫永寶用。

The King, agreeing [to Ke's promotion], said: "Master Ke, Greatly Manifest Kings Wen and Wu took on the burden of the Great Charge, and spreading it throughout the Four Regions; a long time ago it was your former ancestor and deceased father who had rank in the Zhou state and who guarded the King's body, acting as the Claw-and-Tooth warrior."

The King said: "Ke, I continued for you the charge of your former ancestor and deceased father, Ke Ling's, service to the Former King, and which I have previously charged you with. Now I am extending your charge and commanding you to replace your ancestor and deceased father supervising the Tiger Male Slaves on the Left and the Right. I award you one container of fragrant wine, crimson knee covers with five round jades, crimson slippers, an overlapping collar, a pony chariot, patterned side-railing, crimson leather broad girth straps, a tiger-skin covering with a pale red lining, decorated bindings, decorated axle supports, metal yong-bell, crimson pennant, four horses, bit and bridle, and a plain ax. Be respectful from dawn to dusk and do not waste my charge.

I, Ke, dared to extol the Son of Heaven's greatly manifest and abundant gift and took this opportunity to make a display tureen so that I, Ke, might for ten thousand years have sons of sons and grandsons of grandsons to forever treasure and use it.

The Shanfu Ke *xu* 膳夫克盨 (*Jicheng* 4465, presently located in the Art Institute of Chicago) was clearly from the same cache as the Ke cauldrons and bells, whereas the provenance of Shi Ke *xu*-tureens is not as well documented, although they were discovered around the same time in the same area. This inscription was cast during the same period of the ritual calendar and in the same shrine as the bells, but two years later. Interestingly, this inscription is on a food vessel but records bell music along with the descent of blessings from the ancestors:

唯十又八年十又二月初吉庚寅，王在周康穆宮，王令尹氏友、史趞，典善（膳）夫克田人。

克拜稽首，敢對天子丕顯魯休揚，用作旅須，唯用獻于師尹、倗（朋）友、聞（婚）遘（媾）。

克其用朝夕享于皇祖考，皇祖考其豐豐彙彙（繹繹），降克多福，眉壽永令（命），畯臣天子。克其日賜休無疆，克其萬年子子孫孫永寶用。

It was in the eighteenth year, twelfth month, *chuji*, on *gengyin* day (*ganzhi* no. 27), when the King resided in the Hall of Kang and Mu in Zhou, that the King commanded the Chief Officer and Colleague Archivist Jin to document the field workers [given to] *shanfu* Ke.

I, Ke, clapping my hands together and bowing my head to the ground, dared to respond to the Son of Heaven's greatly manifest abundant grace and to extol him. I took this opportunity to make a display *xu*-tureen, only for presenting sacrificial offerings to Master Yin, the colleagues matched in rank, and marriage relations.

May I, Ke, use it to present mortuary offerings to the Brilliant Ancestor and Deceased-father from dawn to dusk. Then may the Brilliant Ancestor and Deceased-father—so fruitful and mighty—send down to [me,] Ke, manifold good fortune, extended longevity, eternal life, for me to serve the Son of Heaven. May I, Ke, daily receive [his] grace without limit. May I, Ke, for ten thousand years have sons of sons and grandsons of grandsons to eternally treasure and use [this vessel].

There are other late Western Zhou period Ke vessels from different sites in the same area, but the relationship of the Ke mentioned in these vessels to the Ke in the vessels from the Renjiacun cache is uncertain. For example, the Elder Ke *hu*-style alcohol storage vessel 伯克壺 (*Jicheng* 9725) documented in a Song period catalogue, and which no longer seems to exist, records a gift of thirty slaves to an Elder Ke from an Elder Grand Master 伯大師. This Elder Ke extols the grace of an Elder Colleague of the king's who received Divine Grace 天右(祐)王伯友, which would make the Elder Grand Master a cousin or relative of the same generational rank as the king. Elder Ke dedicated the vessel to his deceased father's spirit, whom he refers to as "Grave Deceased-father Middle-son Hou [Descendant]" 穆考仲後. On a *gui*-style tureen, a De Ke 德克 inscribed a simple dedication and prayer to his ancestors.

Transcription

克曰:穆穆朕文祖師華父恩(聰)慶厥心,宇靜于猷,盃(淑)悊(慎)厥德,肆克恭保厥辟恭王,諫辥(乂)王家,叀(惠)于萬民,柔遠能邇,肆克智(知)于皇天,聞于上下,得屯亡敃,賜釐無疆,永念于厥孫辟天子,天子明哲,覭(顯)孝于神,經念厥聖保祖師華父,勋(恪)克王服,出內(納)王令,多賜寶休。丕顯天子,天子其萬年無疆,保辥(乂)周邦,畍(允)尹四方。

王在宗周,旦,王格穆廟,即立(位),䚽(申)季右(佑)善(膳)夫克入門,立中廷,北鄉(嚮)。王呼尹氏冊令善(膳)夫克。

王若(諾)曰:克,昔余既令汝出內(納)朕令(命),今余隹䚽(伸)就乃令,賜汝叔市參冋(絅)、苻蔥。賜汝田于野。賜汝田于渒。賜汝井寓(宇)䥫、田于峻,以厥臣妾。賜汝田于康。賜汝于田于匽。賜汝田于陴原。賜汝田于寒山。賜汝史小臣、霝(靈)龠(籥)鼓鐘。賜汝井、微、䥫人,鞀(兼?)賜汝井人奔于量。敬夙夜用事,勿灋(廢)朕令(命)。

克拜稽首,敢對揚天子丕顯魯休,用作朕文祖師華父寶䵼彝。克其萬年無疆,子子孫永寶用。

Translation

Ke said: "Grave, so grave, my Accomplished Ancestor Master Hua Fu, who made his heart full of enlightened blessings, his plans tranquil and quieting, and his *de* skillful and attentive, was able reverently to protect his ruler, King Gong, while also remonstrating and ordering the royal household. He was benevolent to the ten thousand peoples, weakening those far away and enabeling those nearby, and thus became known to Brilliant Heaven and heard among the spirits above and below, thus increasing his wealth without insulting the spirits, who thus gave him endless presents. He always thought of me, his descendant, and of his ruler, the Son of Heaven. The Son of Heaven, being enlightened and wise, made illustrious filial offerings to the spirits while continuously keeping in mind his Sage Protector, Ancestor Master Huafu. Huafu respectively acted as the King's Submitter, bringing the King's charge in and out of the King's domain. Huafu was often awarded precious gifts. Greatly Manifest Son of Heaven! May you have ten thousand years without end, and be protected in your control over the Zhou state and be entrusted to govern the Four Regions."

The King was in Ancestral Zhou. At dawn, he arrived at the shrine of Mu, and, once he had taken his place, Shen Ji escorted shanfu Ke through the gate from the right to his position in the center of the court, facing northward. The King called the Chief Officer to give the recorded charge to *shanfu* Ke.

The King, agreeing [to Ke's promotion], said: "Ke, I previously charged you to bring my commands in and out [of the court]. Now I extend your charge and award you plain knee-covers with a trifold style belt, green-onion-colored in the center. I award you fields in Ye. I award you fields in Pei. I award you Jing with a domicile in Geng (?), the fields in Jun (?), along with their male and female slaves. I award you fields in Kang. I award you fields in Yan. I award you fields in Boyuan. I award you fields in Hanshan. I award you an archivist, an acolyte, and bells and drums along with numinous wind instruments. I award you the peoples of Jing, Wei, and Geng, and in addition I award you all the Jing peoples who fled into Liang. Respectfully serve from dawn to dusk and do not cast off my charge."

I, Ke, clapped my hands together and knocked my head against the ground and dared to respond and extol the Son of Heaven's greatly manifest generous gift. He took this opportunity to make for my accomplished Ancestor Master Hua Fu a treasured sacrificial vessel for meat. May I, Ke, have ten thousand years without end and sons of sons and grandsons and grandson forever to treasure and use it.

Further Reading

Jicheng 2836.

Kimbun tsūshaku, 28.490–511.

Mingwen xuan, no. 297.

Barnard and Cheung, *The Shan-fu Liang Ch'i Kuei and Associated Inscribed Vessels*, 28–30, 45, 246, 261–67, 342, 348.

Cao Zhaolan, *Jinwen yu Yin Zhou nüxing wenhua*, 104.

Chen Banghuai, "Ke bo jianjie."

Cook, "Auspicious Metals and Southern Spirits," 233–34.

Duan Shaojia, "Dui Shi Ke xu gai he X ding mingwen jianbie de shangque."

Duan Shaojia, "Shi Ke xu gai kaoyi."

Guo Moruo, "Shi Ke xu ming kaoshi."

Jinwen jinyi leijian, 454.

Lau, *Quellenstudien zur Landvergabe und Bodenübertragung in der westlichen Zhou-Dynastie*, 233–55.

Li, *Landscape and Power in Early China*, 122–26, 131, 160, 225.

Li Feng 李峰, "Xi-Zhou qingtongqi mingwen zhizuo fangfa shiyi."

Luo Fuyi, "Ke xu."

Sena, "Reproducing Society," 209–97.

Shaughnessy, *Sources of Western Zhou History*, 111, 187.

Shaughnessy, "Toward a Social Geography of the Zhouyuan during the Western Zhou-Dynasty," 27–28.

Škrabal, "Writing before Inscribing."

Tang Lan, "Guanyu Da Ke zhong."

Yu Xingwu, "'Shi Ke xu ming kaoshi' shu hou."

CAC

47. Shi Song *gui* 史頌簋 and related inscriptions

Among the many different officials documented in Western Zhou bronze inscriptions, the "scribes" (*shi* 史) or "maker of records" (*zuoce* 作冊) are mentioned with particular frequency, being "the most powerful ritualist[s] and minister[s] in the King's service."[1] At the Late Shang royal court – and probably also throughout Zhou times–these high officials were also in charge of divination. In the Western Zhou epigraphic record, they appear as the chief functionaries for the proclamation of royal appointment charges as well as royal representatives on important military and diplomatic missions. Dozens of Western Zhou bronze inscriptions were cast in their name with their official title. Many more inscribed bronze vessels may have belonged to scribes without references to them as such. This status of scribes as high-ranking political and ritual officials is likewise reflected in the way they are mentioned in received texts, from the earliest (possibly Western Zhou) layers of the *Shijing* and *Shangshu* to the *Zhouli*, a late Warring States or early imperial text that furnishes an idealized account of Zhou administrative institutions. In the *Zhouli*, all but one of the high-level scribal offices are listed under the Ministry of Ritual (*chunguan* 春官): the scribe of the interior (*neishi* 內史), the scribe of the exterior (*waishi* 外史), the scribe in royal attendance (*yushi* 御史), the grand scribe (*taishi* 大史), and the minor scribe (*xiaoshi* 小史). "Maker of records" was essentially the same office; in some inscriptions, two terms were combined into a single designation, as in *zuoce neishi* 作冊內史. Inscriptions show that the offices of both "scribes" and "makers of records" were headed by "overseers" (*yin* 尹). From inscriptions, it appears that "maker of records" (a title known from Shang oracle bones) was more frequently used in early Western Zhou times before gradually giving way to "scribe," especially "scribe of the interior."

A large assemblage of inscribed bronze vessels was cast in the name of Scribe Song 史頌 (*Jicheng* 10220), showing him as a high court official who was granted royal permission to have his accomplishments represent-

---

[1] Cook, "Scribes, Cooks, and Artisans," 250. See also Zhang Yachu and Liu Yu, *Xi Zhou jinwen guanzhi yanjiu*, 26–36; Chen Hanping, *Xi Zhou ce ming zhidu yanjiu*, 119–29; Huang Ranwei, *Yin Zhou qingtongqi shangci jinwen yanjiu*, 128–37; Lai Changyang and Liu Xiang, "Liang Zhou shiguan kao"; Xi Hanjing, *Zhou dai shiguan yanjiu*; Shirakawa Shizuka, *Kōkotsu kimbungaku ronshū*, 1–68, 103–67.

ed in bronze. The longest known inscription contains sixty-two characters and was cast in a set of (at least) four *gui* tureens (each time with the inscription repeated in both the vessel and its lid, *Jicheng* 4229–36) and two *ding* tripods (*Jicheng* 2787–88). It is unclear when these vessels were cast; proposed dates range from the time of King Gong to that of King Xuan.

The following line-up of the different Scribe Song inscriptions does not suggest their original sequence of production but the way in which a high Western Zhou official could represent himself in longer or shorter form in his bronze vessels, from an account of a particular accomplishment to the very core of an inscription, the "statement of dedication" that indicates the ownership of the vessel. It is not certain whether the various vessels were all cast on the same occasion, but it is clear that Scribe Song's accomplishments underlay his right to have them cast. Thus, even the vessels with the shortest inscriptions point to his considerable status.

Transcription (*Shi Song* gui)

惟三年五月丁巳，王在宗周。令史頌省穌。𤔲（姻）友里君百姓，帥䚄盩于成周。休有成事，穌賓，章馬四匹，吉金。用作𩫖彝，頌其萬年無疆，日逘（揚）天子䫅（顯）令，子子孫孫永寶用。

Translation

It was [the King's] third year, the fifth month, the day *dingsi*, when the King was in Ancestral Zhou. He commanded me, Scribe Song, to inspect the area of Su. I led the [local] officers of [royal] rule, the eminent men of the village, and the noble families from Su to assemble and swear allegiance in Chengzhou. With [royal?] blessing, I accomplished the matter. [Representatives from] Su attended my audience and presented me with a jade tablet, four hourses, and auspicious metal. On account of this, I have made this meat-offering vessel. May I, Song, enjoy ten thousand years without limit, daily extolling the Son of Heaven's illustrious mandate! May sons of sons, grandsons of grandsons, forever treasure and use this vessel!

Transcription (*Shi Song* yi 史頌匜[2])

史頌作匜。其萬年，子子孫孫永寶用。

Translation

I, Scribe Song, have made this *yi* vessel. May I enjoy ten thousand years! May sons of sons, grandsons of grandsons, forever treasure and use this vessel!

Transcription (*Shi Song* fu 史頌簠)

史頌作簠，永寶。

Translation

I, Scribe Song, have made this *fu* vessel. May it forever be treasured!

Further Reading

Jicheng 2787–89 (*ding* tripods); 4229–36 (*gui* tureens); 4481 (Shi Shong *fu*); 10093 (Shi Song *pan*); 10220 (Shi Song *yi*).

Kimbun tsūshaku, 24.174–90.

Mingwen xuan, nos. 430 (Shi Song *gui*), 433 (Shi Song *yi*), 431 (Shi Song *fu*).

Cook, "Scribes, Cooks, and Artisans."

Kern, "The Performance of Writing in Western Zhou China." Li, "On the Typology of Chu Bronzes," tables 1–11.

Wang Hui, *Shang Zhou jinwen*, 236–38.

MKe

---

[2] The same text of fourteen characters, in the same arrangement, is repeated on another *pan* 盤 water basin, only with the vessel designation in the first phrase changed from *yi* to *pan* (Shi Song *pan* 史頌盤, *Jicheng* 10093).

48. Xi Jia *pan* 兮甲盤

Vessels containing copies of this inscription are located in the Calligraphy Museum in Tokyo and at the Chinese University of Hong Kong. In 2014, a privately owned vessel with the same inscription was exhibited in Wuhan. The date of the inscription is most commonly accepted as the fifth year of King Xuan (823 B.C.E.).

During the late Western Zhou, the Zhou kings were regularly troubled by incursions from outside peoples, including the Xianyun 玁狁, who are mentioned in the present inscription, and they were also ever trying to maintain their position of prominence in the Central Plains region by exacting tribute from outside peoples, such as the Southern Huai Yi 南淮夷. From the Xi Jia *pan* inscription we learn that the Huai Yi had long been paying tribute to the Zhou court in the form of silk, unspecified commercial goods, and people (or the labor thereof). Similar evidence is found in an early Eastern Zhou poem from the *Shijing*,[1] suggesting that their unequal balance of power continued into the Spring and Autumn period, even after the Zhou house had become sorely weakened. It needs to be remembered that both of these documents reflect a Zhou perspective, and that in the minds of the Huai Yi (and other peoples), the Zhou were more likely seen as extorting such "tribute."

The present inscription tells that King Xuan campaigned against the Xianyun, and it was during this military expedition that Xi Jia 兮甲 (later referred to as Xi Bo Ji Fu 兮伯吉父) earned much military merit. The bulk of the contents records the King's command to Xi Jia to tax and regulate the accumulated goods of the realm, which included those of the Many Lords and persons worthy enough to have surnames, as well as the Southern Huai Yi. It also states the consequences for those who chose not to obey the ruling on taxation and market goods, especially the Huai Yi, but also members of the Zhou state.

The importance of the Xi Jia *pan* inscription is better understood when read in concert with the inscriptions, all identical, found on the two Shi Huan *gui* 師寰簋 and one Shi Huan *guigai* 師寰簋蓋 (*Jicheng* 4313 and 4314), which also date to around the same period. In that set of inscriptions, we learn that the Huai Yi failed to abide by the King's ruling to pay

---

[1] Legge, *The Chinese Classics*, IV, 620 [PRG].

tribute.

Thus, Captain Huan was charged by the King with launching a campaign of "rectification" (*zheng* 征) against the Huai Yi. He was also to pronounce verdicts on certain specified Huai Yi leaders. The lopping off of enemy heads and capturing of enemies for interrogation, seen in the Xi Jia pan, also figure here.

Read together, these inscriptions provide evidence suggestive of an overlap between the military and legal spheres. The Zhou believed verdicts should be pronounced upon enemy leaders. The fact that the Zhou military commander who campaigned against the enemy was the party responsible for pronouncing such verdicts is reminiscent of the Shi Qi *ding* inscription (no. 20, above), in which a high-ranking military officer pronounced the verdict on Captain Qi and his troops. Finally, "arresting" (*zhi* 執) and "interrogating" (*xun* 訊) enemies is vocabulary that is also seen in more strictly legal contexts from the Western and Eastern Zhou periods.

Transcription

唯五年三月既死霸庚寅。王初格伐玁狁于䣙（彭）虞（衙）。

兮甲從王。折首執訊。休亡敃（泯）。

王賜兮甲馬四匹駒車。王令甲政（徵）䌛成周四方賨（積）至于南淮夷。淮夷舊（久）我帛晦（賄）人。毋敢不出其帛其賨（積）其進人其貯（賈）。毋敢不即餗（次）即市。敢不用令（命）則即井（刑）撲（薄）伐。其唯我諸侯百姓厥貯（賈）毋不即市。毋敢又入（納）繺（亂）宄賈。則亦井（刑）。

兮伯吉父作盤。其眉壽萬年無疆，子子孫孫永寶用。

Translation

It was in the fifth year, third month, *jisipo*, *gengyin* (*ganzhi* no. 27). The King for the first time arrived to campaign against the Xianyun at Pengya.

Xi Jia followed the King [on campaign]. Lopping off heads and arresting prisoners for interrogation, he was beneficent and without disorder.

The King bestowed upon Xi Jia four horses and a colt-drawn

chariot. The King commanded Jia: "Tax and regulate the stored [goods] of the four quarters of Chengzhou all the way to the Southern Huai Yi people. For a long time, the Huai Yi have been people who pay paid us in silk. They shall not dare not to send out their silk, their stored [goods], their proffered people,[2] or their commercial goods. They shall not dare not to approach the military outposts and the markets [with these things]. If they dare not to employ this command, then we will forthwith punish them and launch a coercive campaign. If they be our Many Lords and Hundred Surnames, the commercial goods shall not not arrive at the markets. They shall not dare, moreover, to remit disorderly or ill-gotten commercial goods; otherwise, they will also be punished."

Xi Bo Ji Fu makes this *pan*-basin. May he have long life for ten thousand years without limit, and may his sons' sons and grandsons' grandsons' eternally treasure and use it.

Further Reading

Jicheng 10174.

Mingwen xuan, no. 437.

Chen Lianqing, "Xi jia pan kaoshi."
Skosey, "The Legal System and Legal Tradition of the Western Zhou."
Wang Hui, *Shang Zhou jinwen*, 241–44.

LAS

---

[2] This may refer to their sending people to the Zhou to serve as laborers, troops, tribute bearers, or deliverers of tax payments.

49. Guo Ji Zibai pan 虢季子白盤

This late Western Zhou inscription appears on a basin that is distinctive both for its shape and for its enormous size. Measuring 87 x 137 centimeters, the vessel is thus far the only example of a rectangular *pan*, which were low, typically circular vessels used to contain water for sacrificial rituals. Each side of the Guo Ji Zibai *pan* is ornamented with a pair of ring handles held in place by animal heads modeled in high relief. The exterior surface of the vessel is decorated with a narrow band of abstracted mask patterns under the lip, above a wider band of wave décor. The inscription of 106 characters was cast into the interior surface of the vessel bottom. The spacious, grid-like layout of the calligraphy as well as the décor of the vessel is typical of the late Western Zhou, ca. mid-ninth to mid-eighth century B.C.E.

The vessel was discovered in 1840 in Baoji, Shaanxi Province, at the western end of the Wei River valley.[1] The vessel remained in private circulation until the founding of the People's Republic of China in 1949, when, like many bronzes in private collections, it was bequeathed to the state and became part of the collection of the Palace Museum, and eventually transferred to what is now the National Museum of China.

The Guo Ji Zibai *pan* is a good example of a type of inscription celebrating the military valor of its sponsor. As is typical of such inscriptions, the sponsor's military exploits are portrayed in heroic terms, with formulaic expressions that must have been highly evocative of battlefield stories that had become enshrined in historical memory and literary tradition. Success in battle is portrayed in terms of the number of enemy kills or captures; and the sponsor of Guo Ji Zibai *pan* is said to have excelled at both. The inscription then gives an account of the sponsor's appearance at the Zhou court to present trophies of enemies slain in the form of severed ears, earning him the praise of the Zhou king and an award of military paraphernalia. It is this award that occasioned the creation of the bronze vessel.

The sponsor of the vessel, referred to in another inscription as Duke Xuan of Guo 虢宣公, was the ruler of Guo, one of the regional aristocratic states vital to Zhou rule.[2] The participation in military operations

---

[1] The inscription was first published in Xu Tongbo, *Conggu tang kuanshi xue*, 10.31. Although Qing dynasty administrative records specify the location of the discovery as Guochuansi 虢川司, the precise location of this site within Baoji is difficult to determine. For a discussion of possible locations and the scholarship behind them, see Li Feng, *Landscape and Power in Early China*, 253.

against Zhou enemies, such as that described here, would have been one of the primary obligations of such regional lords. Scholarly consensus dates the inscription to the reign of King Xuan, in which case the twelfth year mentioned in the inscription would correspond to the year 816 B.C.E. Although Duke Xuan of Guo does not correspond to any historical figure known from transmitted texts, the state of Guo and its rulers would soon play a prominent role in the factional struggles behind the fall of the Western Zhou in 771 B.C.E.[3]

The inscription recounts a battle with the Xianyun that took place on the north side of the upper Luo River, in northern Shaanxi Province. Culturally distinct from the Zhou, the Xianyun occupied the highlands beyond the northern and northwestern frontier of the Zhou cultural area, in what is now Gansu, Ningxia, and northern Shaanxi Provinces.[4] Zhou–Xianyun hostilities from the middle Western Zhou period onward are documented in various inscriptions and received texts, but the situation seems to have been exacerbated during the reign of King Xuan. (Campaigns against the Xianyun are also documented by the Xi Jia *pan* [no. 48, above] and the Lai *pan* [no. 63, below] inscriptions.) Less than fifty years after Guo Ji Zibai's campaign, during the reign of King Xuan's successor, the Xianyun would launch a successful invasion resulting in the downfall of the last Western Zhou king and the permanent migration of the Zhou court out of the Wei River valley.[5]

Transcription

唯十又二年正月初吉丁亥。虢季子白作寶盤。不（丕）顯子白壯武于戎工（功）。經緵（維）四方，搏伐玁狁于洛之陽。折首五百，執訊五十，是以先行。趠趠（桓桓）子白獻馘于王。王孔加（嘉）子白義。王各（格）周廟宣廟（榭）爰卿（饗）。王曰：白父孔覯（顯）有光。王賜乘馬，是用左（佐）王。賜用弓、彤矢，

---

[2] See the Guo Xuan Gong Zibai *ding* 虢宣公子白鼎 (*Jicheng* 2637). The use of the personal name Zibai in both inscriptions is the key to this identification.

[3] For a detailed study of these events and the role of Guo, see Li Feng, *Landscape and Power*, 195, 200, 213–15.

[4] For a study of the Zhou-Xianyun war, see Li Feng, *Landscape and Power*, 141–92.

[5] In historical accounts the invaders are usually referred to as *quanrong* 犬戎. Regarding the identity of this term with Xianyun, see Li Feng, *Landscape and Power*, 343–46.

其央。賜用戉，用政(征)䋣(蠻)方。子子孫孫萬年無疆。

Translation

It was in the twelfth year, first month, *chuji*, on *dinghai* day (*ganzhi* no. 24). Guo Ji Zibai makes this precious basin. Greatly illustrious Zibai was mighty and martial in his fighting achievements. Reconnoitering and protecting the four directions, he attacked the Xianyun at the north bank of the Luo. He severed five hundred heads and arrested fifty prisoners, and in this he was first. Valiant Zibai presented the severed ears to the King. The King greatly praised Zibai's uprightness. The King went to the Grand Pavilion of the Zhou temple and then held a banquet. The King said: "Baifu (i.e. Zibai)[6] is greatly illustrious and bright." The King awarded him a set of four horses with which to assist the King. He awarded him a bow and red arrows; may they be on the mark. He awarded him an axe with which to attack the barbarian regions. For ten thousand years may there be sons and grandsons without end.

Further Reading

Jicheng 10173.

Kimbun tsūshaku, 32.800–813.

Mingwen xuan, no. 440.

Li Feng, *Landscape and Power in Early China*, 141–92, 195, 200, 213–15, 253.

Tang Lan, *Tang Lan xiansheng jinwen lunji*, 415–26.

Xu Tongbo, *Conggu tang kuanshi xue*, 10.31.

DMS

---

[6] Zibai 子白 and Baifu 白父 represent two different forms of the sponsor's personal name. Evidently the main component of that name is Bai 白, to which either a prefix *zi* 子 or suffix *fu* 父 could be appended. The latter format, used by the King when addressing the sponsor, was a standard format for style names (*zi* 字) during the Western Zhou.

50. BUQI GUIGAI 不嬰簋蓋

A lid with an inscription by a man named Buqi has been circulated among various collectors since at least the nineteenth century. In 1980, the Buqi vessel, combined with an unrelated lid, was discovered in a tomb in Shandong considered to date to the Western Zhou period. The vessel is now in the local Tengzhou City Museum 滕州市博物館, and the lid is in the National Museum of China.

This inscription documents the battles with the non-Zhou peoples who were invading Zhou from the west and north and labeled by the Zhou as the Xianyun and Rong. Scholars believe that these battles occurred during the reign of King Xuan, and the repeated incursions by the Xianyun and Rong peoples, as scholars such as Li Feng show,[1] would ultimately lead to the demise of the Zhou rule and their flight out of their ancestral home in the Wei River valley. Some scholars speculate that the Elder Chief (Bo Shi 伯氏) was the leader of the Qin 秦 people.

Buqi's mother was a member of the Zhou lineage, and Buqi himself had clearly been trained in the military arts and had some connection to the Zhou. The fact that he is referred to as "a Little One" (*xiaozi* 小子) means that at the time of this reward he had not yet finished mourning his father and hence not completed his graduation into the class of Masters (*shi* 師).

Transcription

唯九月初吉戊申，伯氏曰：不嬰馭方，玁狁廣伐西俞（隃）。王令我羞追于西。余來歸獻禽（擒）。余命汝御追于䇂。汝以我車宕伐玁狁于高陶。汝多折首執訊。戎大同，從追汝。汝伋戎大敦搏。汝休弗以我車陷于艱。汝多禽（擒），折首執訊。

伯氏曰：不嬰，汝小子，汝肇誨（敏）于戎工（功）；賜汝弓一、矢束、臣五家、田十田，用從乃事。

不嬰拜稽手休，用作朕皇祖公伯孟姬尊簋，用匄多福，眉壽無疆，永屯靈冬（終），子子孫孫其永寶用享。

[1] Li Feng, *Landscape and Power*.

Translation

It was in the ninth month, *chuji*, on *wushen* day (*ganzhi* no. 45), when the Elder Chief said: "Buqi, the Border Guard! The Xianyun have broadly attacked our western range. The King commanded us to advance and pursue them in the west. I come back to offer captives. I commanded you to drive out and pursue them in Ke. You attacked the Xianyun without restraint in Gaotao with our chariots. You chopped off heads and bound captives in great numbers. The Rong people had a great gathering and pursued you. You met the Rong and fought them with great fury, and then you rested, so that our chariots would not be mired in difficulties. You took many captives, cut off heads and bound captives."

The Elder Chief said: "Buqi, you are but a Little One, and yet you from the beginning have been diligent about your military merit. I award you one bow, a bundle of arrows, five families of servants, and ten fields to follow you in service."

I, Buqi, clapped my hands together and knocked my head against the ground in response to the gift and took this opportunity to make a tureen for expressing reverence to my Brilliant Ancestor, Patriarch Elder [father] and Elder Ji-lineage [mother], to use to pray for much good fortune and longevity without limit, eternal wealth and a numinous end. May I have sons of sons and grandsons of grandsons eternally to treasure and use it to present mortuary feasts.

Further Reading

Jicheng 4328–29.

Kimbun tsūshaku, 32.193.

Mingwen xuan, no. 441.

Lau, *Quellenstudien zur Landvergabe und Bodenübertragung in der westlichen Zhou-Dynastie*, 284–90.

Li Feng, *Landscape and Power in Early China*, 119, 124, 153–55.

Li Xueqin, *Wenwu zhong de gu wenming*, 524–27.

Wang Hui, *Shang Zhou jinwen*, 245–48.

CAC

51. Ying Hou Jiangong *zhong* 應侯見工鐘

This late mid-Western Zhou inscription was cast repeatedly into a set of bronze chime-bells. Although the inscription represents a single text, it was cast piecemeal into multiple bells that have since been dispersed. Four bells, each bearing only a portion of the text, are currently known. The earliest known piece was part of a private collection in Japan, now housed in the Calligraphy Museum in Tokyo.[1] Because this bell bore only the second half of the text, its connection was not immediately recognized when a different bell bearing the first half was discovered in 1974 at Hongxing 紅星, Lantian, Shaanxi Province. Decades later, two additional bells also bearing the first half of the inscription were acquired by the Poly Art Museum in Beijing.

The casting of an inscriptional text over a whole set of bronzes was common from the middle Western Zhou onward. When such a set included pieces of different sizes, longer inscriptional texts would be split over the smaller pieces, each piece bearing a portion. This was especially common with bronze chime-bells, which were typically created in graded sets that could produce a range of pitches when bells of different sizes were struck. The extant Ying Hou Jiangong bells, which vary in height from 26 centimeters to 36 centimeters, were thus likely to have been part of a larger set of chime-bells.[2]

The sponsor of these bells was the ruler of Ying 應, one of the regional aristocratic states installed by the Zhou kings. According to literary texts written during the Eastern Zhou period, Ying was created in the early Zhou period, when various sons of King Wu were established as aristocratic lords. The corpus of Zhou bronze inscriptions contains several dozen that mention members of the Ying lineage, ranging in date from the early to the late Western Zhou.[3] Excavations since 1979 in Pingdingshan, Henan Province, have uncovered a large cemetery associated with the Ying

---

[1] A rubbing of this inscription was first published in Nakamura Fusetsu, *Sandai Shin-Kan no ihin ni shiruseru moji* in 1934.

[2] The excavated bell and one of the bells in the Poly Museum measure 26 centimeters, while the other Poly bell measures 36 centimeters. The height of the bell in Japan is not available in the published sources. Zhu Fenghan argues that there may have been two sets of bells, since one would not expect two bells of exactly the same size in a single bell-chime; "Ying Hou Jiangong zhong," 159.

[3] Xu Shaohua, *Zhoudai nantu lishi dili yu wenhua*, 210–13.

lineage, confirming the location of the Ying state at the north end of the Nanyang 南陽 basin, roughly 125 kilometers southeast of the Zhou eastern capital at Chengzhou.[4]

The inscription records the dedication of the bell-chime to the sponsor's ancestor, Lord of Ying, on the occasion of a gift from an unnamed Zhou king.[5] The inscription implies that the king's award may have been a response to the sponsor's own gift to the Zhou king upon the king's return from Chengzhou. The king's gift, a bow, arrows, and a team of four horses, was awarded at a ceremony that took place at Zhou, in the Wei River valley, some 500 kilometers from Ying. The inscription suggests that travel over long distances by both the Zhou king and the regional lords was instrumental in maintaining ties between the court and the aristocratic lineages of the east.

Transcription

唯正二月初吉。王歸自成周。雁（應）侯見工遺（饋）王于周。辛未，王各（格）于康［宮］。榮伯內（入）右雁（應）侯見工。賜彤弓一、彤矢百、馬四匹。見工敢對揚天子休，用作朕皇祖雁（應）侯大林鐘。用賜眉壽永命。子子孫孫永寶用。

Translation

It was in the regular second month, *chuji*.[6] The King returned from Chengzhou. Jiangong, Lord of Ying, made a gift to the King at Zhou. On *xinwei* day (*ganzhi* no. 8), the King went to Kang Hall.[7] Rong Bo entered at the right side of Jiangong, Lord of Ying, who was awarded one crimson bow, a hundred crimson arrows, and four horses. Jiangong dares in response to extol the Son of Heav-

---

[4] On the strategic location of Ying and other regional states, see Li Feng, *Landscape and Power in Early China*, 70–72. For a study of several inscriptions unearthed from the cemetery at Pingdingshan, see Shaughnessy, "New Sources of Western Zhou History," 78–82.

[5] Though there is little evidence by which to precisely date this inscription, a second set of vessels sponsored by the same Lord of Ying suggests a late mid-Western Zhou date (ca. early ninth century B.C.E.) by virtue of their shape and decor. These Ying Hou Jiangong *gui* are also recent Poly Museum acquisitions; Zhu Fenghan, "Ying Hou Jiangong gui."

[6] The term "regular" (or perhaps "official") in the date notation may reflect discrepancies between the royal calendar and that of the Ying lineage. On a similar usage in an Eastern Zhou inscription, see Chen Mengjia, "Shou xian Cai hou mu tongqi."

[7] The excavated piece reads just *kang* 康 instead of *kang gong* 康宮.

en's beneficence, herewith making for my august ancestor Lord of Ying this grand set of bells. Through it may I be awarded long life and an eternal mandate.[8] May sons and grandsons forever treasure and use it.

Further Reading

Jicheng 107–8.

Kimbun tsūshaku, 48.230–36.

Mingwen xuan, no. 234.

Falkenhausen, *Suspended Music*, 58–59.

Ren Song and Fan Weiyue, "Ji Shaanxi Lantian xian xin chutu de Ying Hou zhong."

Ren Song, "Ji Shaanxi Lantian xian xin chutu de Ying Hou zhong yi wen buzheng."

Shaughnessy, "New Sources of Western Zhou History," 79.

Zhang Guangyu, "Lantian xin chutu de Ying Hou zhong yu shudao cangqi de fuhe."

Zhu Fenghan, "Ying Hou Jiangong zhong."

DMS

---

[8] The term "mandate" here refers to the individual's life-span as mandated by Heaven.

52. Ju Fu xugai 駒父盨蓋

This *xu* lid was discovered in 1974 in Sufang 蘇坊, Wugong County 武功縣, Shaanxi Province, under the fragments of a bronze bell and an earthenware jar, and next to a jade circular pendant (*bi* 璧). Possibly, these objects all came from a looted and destroyed tomb. The vessel's body was not found. Sufang is attested as a settlement of the Western Zhou period. No further excavations have been conducted. The lid is typical for the late ninth century B.C.E. Although the date reference in the inscription does not include the *ganzhi* designation, the object can be dated without doubt to the eighteenth year of King Xuan, i.e. either 810 or 808 B.C.E., depending on whether in this case the King's actual accession to the throne (827 B.C.E.) or his official enthronement after the mourning period (825 B.C.E.) was regarded as his "first year." The bronze food container is called a "travel *xu*" (*lü xu* 旅盨), indicating that its intended use was for rituals performed away from home. The *lü xu* were often commissioned by persons charged with military or civil responsibilities in distant locations.

The inscription is an important historical document reflecting communication between the Zhou and their counterparts and rivals in the south and the southeast, peoples of the Huai River Valley. Usually collectively referred to as Yi 夷, they could sometimes also be called Rong 戎 or Man 蠻, all of these terms not necessarily identifying their particular ethnic affiliation, but rather pointing to their non-Zhou identity. The Ju Fu *xu* indicates that the peoples of the Huai River were expected to submit tribute to the Zhou king. It is not unlikely that such obligations were bilateral, i.e. that the Zhou kings required the rulers of the Zhou regional states (*zhuhou* 諸侯) to maintain the reciprocity with the Huai Yi.

King Xuan's general, Nanzhong, commanded Ju Fu to set out from the metropolitan Zhou area and to proceed first to the southern *zhuhou*, possibly in order to convince them to provide some products for exchange. Ju Fu had his traveling sacrificial vessel cast in the southernmost of these states, Cai 蔡, located around present-day Shangcai 上蔡 in the south of Henan Province. From there, accompanied by another royal representative, Gao Fu, he had to go farther south in order to negotiate with rulers of the Huai countries. The language of Nanzhong's command implies that Ju Fu had to convince all sides to resume their communication by means of diplomacy. Nevertheless, as the *Shijing* reflects, a new war between the Zhou and the "Southern States" of the Huai River broke out. As the "Chang wu"

常武 ode relates,[1] they were headed by the ruler of Xu 徐, located north of presentday Anhui 安徽 Province. General Nanzhong and other warlords were able to vanquish Xu and to force its ruler to appear before the Zhou king with expressions of loyalty.

Transcription

唯王十又八年正月，南仲邦父命駒父：即南諸侯。遂（帥）高父見南淮尸（夷）、厥取厥服。堇（謹）尸（夷）俗。彖（遂）不敢不敬畏王命。逆見我、厥獻厥服。我乃至于淮小大邦。亡敢不［囗］具逆王命。

四月，還至于蔡，作旅盨。駒父其萬年永用多休。

Translation

This was in the eighteenth year of the King, the first month. Nanzhong Ban Fu commanded Ju Fu: "Attain [the cooperation of] the regional rulers of the south. Lead Gao Fu to visit the Yi-peoples of Huai River and to see what they collect, what they contribute. Be cautious with regard to the Yi people's customs. May nobody then even dare not to respect and fear the King's command. [Let the Huai Yi] welcome and visit us with their offerings and contributions. Thereupon we will attain the smaller and greater countries of Huai River valley. May nobody dare not ... and fully to welcome the King's command."

In the fourth month, [Ju Fu] returned and attended Cai. He made this sacrificial container for travels. May Ju Fu for ten thousand years eternally use it for many blessings.

Further Reading

Jicheng 4464.

Mingwen xuan, no 442.

Huang Shengzhang, "Ju Fu xu gai mingwen yanjiu."

Wang Hui, *Shang Zhou jinwen*, 252–54.

Xia Hanyi, *Wengu zhixin lu*, 160–65.

MKh

[1] Legge, *The Chinese Classics*, IV, 557 [PRG].

53. Bin Gong xu 燹(豳)公盨

The corrosion-covered tureen was purchased by representatives of the Poly Art Museum in Beijing from a Hong Kong antiquities shop in 2002. The vessel is missing a lid and is unusual in some respects. The long-tailed birds in the rib of design around the rim indicate to most scholars that it dates to the middle Western Zhou period. While cleaning the vessel, the staff of the Shanghai Museum discovered a 98-character inscription with content that generated a great deal of scholarly excitement and debate.[1] The content and wording are unusual and suggest to some scholars that the vessel, despite its archaic use of long-tailed bird décor, was in fact much later in date or that it was produced in a local foundry away from the central Zhou. "Bin" 豳 is how the paleographer Liu Yu reads the archaic graph 燹;[2] others read it as Sui 遂 instead.[3] The "fire" 火 and "mountain" 山 elements were frequently confused in the Western Zhou period. The graph appeared on other inscriptions and remained unidentified. From its occurrence in other Western Zhou inscriptions, it must have been geographically close to Zhou, despite certain aspects of the vessel itself that seem unlike any other Zhou vessel or inscription.

Unlike most Western Zhou bronze inscriptions that eulogize the Zhou founder kings and the founding of the Zhou state, this inscription begins with the creation myth linked to the Sage King Yu 禹, a figure who, according to later legends, helped shape the world, control the floods, exorcise bad spirits, and was a model of frugal living and piety.[4] He was also credited with founding the Xia 夏 dynasty. In this inscription, Yu, like King Wen in Zhou myth, received the "mandate" directly from Heaven (or the Deity Above). There is no mention of any intermediary fealty to the Zhou kings, a phenomenon that is not again attested in the bronze inscription corpus until the Spring and Autumn period, after the dissipation of Zhou hegemony.

The seeming independence of the inscription's author from Zhou au-

---

[1] As with any unprovenanced vessel there are concerns over its authenticity. Art historical analysis and reconstruction of the ancient rhyming supports the historicity of the vessel and text, see Cook, "Sage King Yu and the Bin Gong Xu."

[2] Personal communication.

[3] Xing and Li Xueqin, see Further Reading.

[4] Cf. Anne Birrell, *Chinese Mythology*, 146–59.

thority is belied by the place name Bin, which, according to later texts, was the site first settled by the Zhou ancestors, possibly in the Xunyi district of Shaanxi. Some scholars note that *bin* was also written 邠, suggesting a link to the Fen River 汾河 area in neighboring Shanxi Province, an area once home to a sophisticated Neolitic culture as well as influenced by the first bronze-making culture at Erlitou (see Introduction). Some theorize that the Zhou people originated in this region. The people of Bin seem to be firmly linked to early Zhou traditions, but ones perhaps no longer so tightly connected to the lineage branch that moved to Qishan and eventually began the state of Zhou in Zongzhou. The narration of the creation myth of Yu's people and the birth of "our king" confirms a sense of allegiance with the royal lineage on the part of the Patriarch of Bin, the narrator. This royal lineage was probably that of the ascendant Zhou, although the lack of any reference to a specific Zhou king leaves that question open.

The identification of Bin with the pre-Zhou founder-ancestors, on one hand, and the connection to the royal family, on the other, helps to explain the uncanny connection between rhetoric and vocabulary also found in transmitted texts, such as the *Shangshu*, that were perhaps recounted by peoples who traced their history to pre-Zhou ancestors, such as Yu. The ritual described after the recitation of the creation myth was no doubt associated with traditional annual sacrifices to the founder spirit and all ancestral spirits up to the present. Comparison of the language of this ritual to songs in the *Shijing* and legends about the legendary founder of Fen (Gong Liu 公劉) as preserved in the *Shiji*, as well as the music associated with him, suggests a link to harvest festivals and celebrations of Houji—the agricultural god and mythical Zhou progenitor.

While many inscriptions have rhymed sections and an internal rhythm evident in paired and repeated words, this entire inscription—except for the last line—reads like an ode. At the end of the song, the present Patriarch of Bin and lineage representative of the historical founders announced to the people and spirits, as he might after an auspicious result to a divination, the people's continued successful cultivation of *de* 德—a process that began when the founder-ancestor first "matched" Heaven's pattern. The word *de* ended almost every other line of the two main verses and was mentioned six times throughout the inscription.

Transcription[5]

天命禹尃(敷)土，隨(墮)山濬川，
迺差方設征(政)，降民監德，
迺自作配饗，民成父母，
生我王作臣，厥顯(顯)惟德，
民好明德，顨(飤)在天下。
用厥邵(昭)好，益敬懿德，
康亡不楙(懋)，孝友吁(訏)明，
經齊好祀無鬨(期)心好德，
婚媾亦惟協，天釐用考神，
復用祓祿，永御于寧。
燹公曰：民惟克用茲德亡侮。

Translation

Heaven charged Yu to spread the earth, collapsing mountains and deepening rivers,
So he distinguished the regions and set up the governing structures, descended among the people and examined their *de*.
So, based on this, Yu created the sacrificial feast matching [his sacrifices in return for Heaven's mandate],[6] and the people became parents, Giving birth to Our King and acting as his servants,
What they made manifest was *de*.
The people cared for the King's and Yu's luminous *de* and provided food for All Under Heaven.
Employing it to glorify and care for the King's and Yu's way of *de* and to pay abundant respects to their refined *de*,

---

[5] For a more detailed study of this inscription and the variety of transcriptions of the archaic graphs still debated by scholars, see Cook, "Sage King Yu and the Bin Gong *xu*"; Xing Wen, *The X gong xu*; and Chen Shu, "Collected Interpretations of the X Gong *xu*."
[6] Or performing the ritual of "matching" Heaven's pattern.

Contentedly, they all worked hard and behaved filially and collegially, enlarging and illuminating the King's and Yu's way of *de*,

Practicing purification, they took care with the annual sacrificial performance, performing it endlessly; the people held in their hearts the care of *de*.

Relations are likewise all harmonious, and Heaven's gift is used for Deceased-father spirits,

May the spirits repeatedly expel bad fortune, provide wealth, and eternally guide the people towards tranquility.

Bin Gong said: "The people have been able to employ this *de* without harm."

Further Reading

Allan, "Some Preliminary Comments on the *X Gong Xu*."

Chen, "Collected Interpretations of the *X Gong Xu*."

Chen Yingjie, "Bing Gong xu mingwen zaikao."

Cook, "Ancestor Worship during the Eastern Zhou."

Cook, "Sage King Yu and the Bin Gong *xu*."

Li Ling, "Lun X gong xu faxian de yiyi."

Li Xueqin, "Lun X gong xu jiqi zhongyao yiyi."

Qiu Xigui, "X gong xu mingwen kaoshi."

Shaughnessy, "The *Bin Gong Xu* Inscription and the Origins of the Chinese Literary Tradition."

Xing, ed., *The X gong xu*.

Zhou Baohong, *Jinchu Xi Zhou jinwen jishi*, 177–310.

Zhu Fenghan, "X gong xu mingwen chushi."

CAC

54. Wu Hu *ding* 吳虎鼎

A poorly preserved 41-centimeter high round three-legged cauldron with a simple ribbon of décor around the lip was discovered in 1992 in Xujiazhai 徐家寨, Chang'an County, Shaanxi. Because of the mention of King Li, using his posthumous title, scholars assume this vessel must have been made during the reign of his successor, King Xuan. Moreover, since the inscription has a complete dating formula, it functions as an important benchmark for dating bronze inscriptions and for Western Zhou history. It is important for a number of other reasons as well. First, the content of the inscription is similar to that of the late Western Zhou period Sanshi *pan* (no. 45, above), which had been considered a unique document outlining territorial borders and recording the exchange of lands. The Jiunian Wei *ding* inscription (no. 27, above) of the middle Western Zhou period documented an exchange of lands and goods, but did not outline the borders in deed-like fashion as do the Sanshi and Wu Hu documents. This shows the development of bureaucratic documents in the Zhou government. The fact that versions of these documents were incorporated into sacrificial bronze inscriptions shows that land holdings and the exchange of wealth were considered important to the overseeing ancestral spirits. Many scholars believe that the original documents were written on bamboo strips and stored in archives, although none survives from before the fifth century B.C.E.[1]

Officials involved in land exchange included scribes for making the records (*yin* 尹, elsewhere called *zuoceyin* 作冊尹) and archivists for preserving the records (*shoushi* 守史; see Shi Song *gui*, no. 47, above). Besides the making of documents, the land had to be surveyed and the borders agreed upon by a cast of other officials. In this case, these included the Zhou court *shanfu*, who was in charge of carrying out the king's orders, and the Supervisor of Works (*sigong* 司工), who, along with the Supervisor of Land (*situ* 司徒), functioned as chief engineers overseeing projects involving building or other land-related projects. Because boundary-making (*feng* 封) involved creating earthen walls or planting trees, these officials' approval and oversight were essential. In this case, the land was not a new

---

[1] See Škrabal, "Writing before Inscribing," for a recent discussion of manuscripts used in the inscription-making process [MP].

grant, but in fact inherited by Wu Hu from an earlier member of his family, Wu Ying, who had died during the previous king's reign.

Transcription

唯十又八年十又三月既死霸丙戌，王在周康宮徲（夷）宮，衛（導）² 入右吳虎。王令善（膳）夫豐生、司工雍毅申剌（厲）³ 王令（命），取吳蘁舊疆付吳虎。厥北疆窞⁴ 人眾疆，厥東疆官人眾疆，厥南疆畢人眾疆，厥西疆荎姜厥疆。厥蓋（俱）履封：豐生、雍毅、白（伯）衛（導）、內司土（徒）寺奉。

吳虎拜稽首天子休。賓善（膳）夫豐生章（璋）、馬匹；賓司工雍毅章（璋）、馬匹；賓內司土（徒）寺奉璧。

爰（援）⁵ 書尹友（右）守史由廼賓史奉韋（瑋）兩。

虎拜手稽首，敢對揚天子丕顯魯休，用作朕皇祖考庚孟尊鼎。其子子孫孫永寶。

Translation

It was in the eighteenth year, thirteenth month, *jisipo*, on *bingxu* day (*ganzhi* no. 23), when the King resided at the Kang Hall and Yi Hall of Zhou. Dao entered and guided Wu Hu in from the right. The King commanded *shanfu* Feng Sheng and *sigong* Yong Yi to extend King Li's command regarding taking the old borders of the Wu Ying territory and giving them to Wu Hu. These borders include land up to the Dan peoples' territory to the north, the Guan peoples' territory to the east, the Bi peoples' territory to the south, and the Pang Jiang lineage's territory to the west. Those who surveyed it all and marked its boundaries included

---

² Lack of clarity in the original inscription causes some to transcribe the graph with the element 寸 and others without, resulting in reading the graph as either 導 or 道.
³ This graph is routinely transcribed as *lie* 烈, but here is a loan for *li* 厲.
⁴ Some read *Han* 涵.
⁵ Alternatively one could read this graph as small jade disc 瑗 and as part of the gifts in the previous line. I follow Li Feng, "Literacy and the Social Contexts," 280, in understanding it in the sense of "handing over a document."

Feng Sheng, Yong Yi, Elder Dao, and Inner[6] *situ* Sihui.

Wu Hu clapped his hands and bowed his head to the ground in response to the Son of Heaven's grace. He presented a jade staff and a pair of horses to *shanfu* Feng Sheng, a jade staff and a pair of horses to *sigong* Yong Yi, a large jade disc to Inner *situ* Sihui.

Handing over the document, the scribe aided Conservation Archivist Si, who presented to Archivist Hui two fine jades.[7]

I, Hu, clapped my hands and bowed my head to the ground, daring in response to extol the Son of Heaven's greatly manifest and abundant grace. I took this opportunity to make for my Brilliant ancestor and Deceased-father Geng Meng a cauldron for expressing reverence. May I have sons of sons and grandsons of grandsons to eternally treasure it.

Further Reading

Li Feng, "Literacy and the Social Contexts," 280–82.

Li Xueqin, "Wu Hu ding kaoshi—Xia Shang Zhou duandai gongcheng kaoguxue biji."

Li Xueqin, *Xia Shang Zhou niandaixue zhaji*, 147–50.

Liu Yu and Lu Yan, *Jinchu Yin Zhou jinwen jilu*, 2.237–38.

Mu Xiaojun, "Shaanxi Chang'anxian chutu Xi Zhou Wu Hu ding."

Škrabal, "Writing before Inscribing"

Wang Hui, *Shang Zhou jinwen*, 255–58.

CAC

---

[6] There is debate as to whether Nei was the personal name of Elder Dao or if it was short for *neishi* 內史 when combined with another title, such as *situ*. Situ Hui in this inscription seems to have functioned in both types of roles. Li Feng, "Literacy and Social Contexts," 280, reads it as place name Rui 芮.

[7] Li Feng, "Literacy and the Social Contexts," 280, reads "two furs" instead of "two fine jades." Since the other gifts (besides horses) were jades, I follow the latter reading.

55. MAO GONG DING 毛公鼎

Discovered around 1850 in Qishan County, Shaanxi Province, one of the longest inscriptions known (497 graphs), on this massive cauldron, was first published in 1854. It is a bronze three-legged round cauldron, about 54 centimeters tall, and plain except for the ribbon of simple decor around the lip. It circulated among a number of collectors[1] until 1930 when Ye Gongchuo 葉恭綽 (1881–1968) of Shanghai purchased it and hid it from the Japanese. In 1941, Chen Yongren 陳詠仁 purchased it and eventually negotiated with the Nationalist government for its display in the Palace Museum. In 1948, it was taken to Taiwan and is presently located in the Palace Museum in Taipei.

Because the King referred to the Patriarch of Mao as Father Xin 父 厝 in this inscription, scholars believe that the latter belonged to a set of Zhou relatives older than the present king, who was probably King Xuan. The Mao 毛 family was an old Zhou family who seemed to reach a peak of wealth during the late Western Zhou period, as exemplified by the grand size of the vessel and its unusually long inscription.

The prose in the inscription is more sophisticated than in inscriptions from earlier periods and has more in common with texts preserved in the *Shangshu*. It also reveals a relatively more complex bureaucratic state, one in which corruption had become a problem. The inscription consists of five speeches by the King. In the first, the King eulogizes his Zhou royal ancestry and the receipt of the Mandate of Heaven by the founder kings. He does not list the intervening kings, nor does he particularly eulogize his father. Whereas most similar eulogies serve to legitimize the present king's rule, this one expresses the profound concern that the Zhou mandate is about to be lost because of the severe unrest among peoples in the surrounding regions and the obvious lack of Zhou control over them. In the second statement, the King charges Fu Xin to protect his position and help assure that the Mandate of Heaven continue through his reign. The third statement concerns the proper execution of government of outlying territories. This involved setting up administrative offices for the collection of levies on products from fields and forests as well as better oversight of younger officers. The King suggests that it was bureaucratic malfeasance that caused much of the present crisis of the Zhou state. The fourth state-

---

[1] These include a number of famous collectors, including Chen Jieqi 陳介祺 (1813–1884), who purchased it in 1852 and sold it to Duan Fang 端方 (1861–1911) in 1910.

ment warns against corruption and abuse of office by Xin.

In the fifth statement, the King adds new duties to Mao Xin's 毛厝 charge. Mao Xin was in charge of all the major state administrative and ritual offices. He also supervised the protection of the King through his management of the lineage, particularly the lineage militia called the Tiger Guards or Tiger Servants. The King then awards him with ritual alcohol, clothing, jades, and horse and chariot paraphernalia that symbolize his high rank.

Transcription

王若（諾）曰：父厝，丕顯文武，皇天引厭厥德，配我有周。雁（膺）受大命，率褱（懷）不廷方，亡不閈（觀？）于文武耿光。唯天將集厥命，亦唯先正敬[2]辥（乂）厥辟，爵堇（勤）大命，肆皇天亡斁，臨保我有周，不（丕）巩（鞏）先王配命。敃（旻）天疾畏（威），司（嗣）余小子弗彶，邦將害（曷）吉，翩翩（蠢蠢）四方，大從（縱）不靜。烏虖（呼），趲（懼）余小子，圂（溷）湛于艱，永鞏（恐）先王。

王曰：父厝，今余唯肇經王命，命汝辥（乂）我邦、我家內外，憂（擁）于小大政，粵（屏）朕立（位），虩（赫）許（戲）上下若否雩（于）四方，死（尸）母（毋）童（動）余一人在立（位），引唯乃智（知）余非，庸又聞（昏）。汝母（毋）敢妄（荒）窜（寧），虔夙夕叀（惠）我一人，雍我邦小大猷，母（毋）折緘，告余先王若德，用卬（仰）邵（昭）皇天，𦂅（紳）貂（紹）大命，康能四或（域），俗（欲）我弗作先王憂。

王曰：父厝，雩（越）之庶出入事于外，尃（敷）命尃（敷）政，埶（設）小大楚（胥）賦。無唯正聞（昏），引其唯王智，䢔唯是喪我或（域），厤（歷）自今，出入尃（敷）命于外，厥非先告父厝，父厝舍（捨）命，母（毋）有敢憂（擁）尃（敷）命于外。

---

[2] The graph read here as *jing* 敬, "respectfully," is problematic. For this reading, see a similar usage on the Shu Huan Fu *you* 叔趯父卣, *Jicheng* 5428.

王曰：厝，今余唯肅（申）先王命，命汝亟（極）一方，𤔲（弘）我邦我家，母（毋）³雖（推）于政，勿雍（壅）建庶人宁（貯?），母（毋）敢龔橐（拱苞）⁴，龔橐（拱苞）廼敄（侮）鰥寡。善效（教）乃友（有）正，母（毋）敢湎（湎）于酒，汝母（毋）敢墜在乃服，貊（昭）夙夕，敬念王畏（威）不易。汝母（毋）弗帥用先王作明井（型），俗（欲）汝弗以乃辟陷于艱。

王曰：父厝，巳（已）曰及⁵茲卿事寮、大史寮于父即尹。命汝兼（兼?）司公族，雩（越）參有司、小子、師氏、虎臣，雩（越）朕褻事，以乃族干（扞）吾（敔）王身，取徵卅爰（鋝），賜汝秬鬯一卣、祼圭瓚寶、朱市恖（蔥）黄、玉環、玉瑹（琮）、金車、賁幭較、朱鞹靷靳、虎冟熏裏、右厄（軛）、畫縛、畫𨍩、金甬（桶）、錯衡、金踵、金杫、約盛、金簟第、魚葡𥳐、馬四匹、鋚勒、金𩵂、金膺、朱旂二鈴。賜汝茲䞈，用歲用政（征）。

毛公厝對揚天子皇休，用作尊鼎，子子孫孫永寶用。

Translation

The King, agreeing [to Mao Gong Xin's promotion], said: "Fu Xin, the Greatly Manifest Wen and Wu, whom Brilliant Heaven extended and filled with its *de* and who matched Heaven's *de* with our possession of Zhou, shouldered the responsibility of receiving the Great Mandate. They led and took in those regional states that did not come to court, so that they all paid tribute to the radiant glory of Wen and Wu. Once Heaven had completed their mandate and likewise caused the Former Correctors to respectfully

---

³ Some read the graph as 女 (which would then be read as *ru* 汝 "you"). The archaic graphs for 母 and 女 were distinguished only by dots marking the breasts for the graph 母. The rubbing suggests the presence of the two dots.

⁴ These two graphs are generally read as *gongbao* 拱苞 (*k<r>oŋ pˤ<r>u) in the sense of taking bribes ("holding/giving a package in two hands"). The second graph is transcribed as 橐 with the phonetic *fou* 缶 (*puʔ), but in the original, the phonetic seems closer to *gu* 古 (*kˤaʔ) which is found in varients of graphs for different types of containers, such as *hu* 壺 (*gˤa) and *fu* 簠 (*paʔ). The archaic graph itself looks much like those for *gu* 鼓 (*kˤaʔ) "drum." See also Cook, *Ancestors, Kings, and the Dao*, 129 n. 60.

⁵ The graph is not clear. Some transcribe as 殁 (抄).

govern those [lesser] rulers who labored diligently for the Great Mandate, it was the case that Brilliant Heaven did not tire of the Zhou and, looking down from above, protected our possession of Zhou, and greatly firmed the Former King's ability to match Heaven's Mandate. Vast Heaven quickly turns terrifying, so that when I, a Little One, succeeded to the throne, the mandate became unobtainable. How will the state gain an auspicious sign? The Four Regions, rumbling with turmoil and chaos, are in great disorder and unsettled. Alas! It frightens me, the Little One, that Zhou is so mired in difficulties, that it will eternally frighten the Former Kings."

The King said; "Fu Xin, now I have from the beginning modeled myself on the Former Kings' Mandate. I command you to govern our state and our household, both inside and outside the walls and boundaries, stubborn in governmental matters both big and small, and protective of my position. Now fierce, now permissive (playful?), the spirits above and below permit and forbid (activities beneficial to Zhou) in the Four Regions. When you take on your duties do not upset me, the One Man, residing in my position, but guide me with your understanding should you hear anything of my errors. You shall not dare to disturb the peace, but, behaving respectfully from dawn to dusk, work for the benefit of us and me, the One Man, unifying the great and large plans of our state. You shall not cut the thread of communication, but report to me the manifestations of de allowed by the Former Kings so that I may look up and summon Brilliant Heaven to extend and continue the Great Mandate, bringing peace to the Four Territories and not be the cause of the Former Kings' woe."

The King said: "Fu Xin, when it comes to the matter of the many officers whose business is to bring my commands in and out of court, going abroad to spread the mandate and the Zhou government and to set up official levies [on lands and products] small and large, with no case of a Corrector (i.e. an officer) causing confusion, guide them to act according to what I, the King, understand as proper; otherwise they will cause the death of our state. Until now, those who busy themselves (running commands in and out of court), spreading the mandate abroad, have not first informed you, Fu Xin. When you, Fu Xin, give out commands, do not dare to be naive when spreading the mandate abroad."

The King said: "Fu Xin, now I am extending the Former King's command and ordering you to act as a ridgepole to unite the many regions and to enlarge our state and household. Do not promote others in the government; you should not obstruct the establishment of stored goods among the many (lower officers, or people).

Do not dare to pocket goods, as this would harm widows and widowers. Skillfully educate your peer Correctors and do not dare to let them sink into drunkenness. You shall not dare to fail in your service, but continue from dawn to dusk to glorify and think of how your King's awesome behavior and position shall remain unchanging. You shall not be someone who does not follow or make use of the luminous model created by the Former Kings, nor shall you be one who mires your ruler in difficulties."

The King said: "Fu Xin, finally, when it comes to those [higher-ranked] officers of the Prime Minister and of the Grand Archivist whom you already manage, I command that, in addition, you oversee the Three Supervisors, the children, the masters, and the Tiger Corps of the Patriarchal Lineage when managing my affairs, so that your lineage militia may guard my person. You will draw a salary of thirty units of metal. I award you one ewer of fragrant fine ale, a jade staff and inlaid ladle for libations, crimson knee covers with an onion-green belt, jade circlets, jade (treasures?), metal decorated chariot with handrail and decorated curtain, crimson suede girth straps and neck decor, tiger canopy with dark lining, yokes with painted straps, painted leather straps (connecting the carriage to the axle), metal shaft, inlaid yoke crossbar, metal fittings under the rear of the carriage crossbar and metal axle fittings with complete bindings, metal decorated woven screen, fish-skin quiver, four horses, bits and bridles, metal horse head ornaments, metal breast decor, crimson pennant with two small bells. I award you with these gifts for use in the annual sacrifices and in executing government."

I, Xin, the Patriarch of Mao, in response extolled the Son of Heaven's brilliant grace and took this opportunity to make a cauldron for expressing reverence. May I have sons of sons and grandsons of grandsons to eternally treasure and use it.

Further Reading

Jicheng 2841.
Kimbun tsūshaku, 30.637–700.
Mingwen xuan, no. 447.

Barnard, "Chou China."
Barnard, *Mao Kung Ting, a Major Western Chou Period Bronze Vessel*.
Dong Zuobin, "Mao Gong ding kao nian."
Dong Zuobin, "Mao Gong ding shiwen zhushi."
Gao Heng, "Mao gong ding ming jianzhu."
Jinwen jinyi leijian, 463–69.
Li, *Landscape and Power in Early China*, 122–23, 128.
Shaughnessy, *Sources of Western Zhou History*, 38–39, 45, 59, 75–76, 81–83.
Tang Lan, *Tang Lan xiansheng jinwen lunji*, 86–93, 466–69.
Wang Hui, *Shang Zhou jinwen*, 259–70.
Zhang Changshou and Wen Guang, "Ba Luozhaotang cang Mao gong ding taben."
Zhang Changshou and Wen Guang, "Mao Gong ding chutu nianfen de yi ze ezhuan."
Zhang Guangyuan, "Xi Zhou qi Mao gong ding: Bolun Aozhou Bana boshi wuwei zhi shuo."

CAC

56. Shanfu Shan *ding* 膳夫山鼎

The Shanfu Shan *ding* tripod was found sometime in the first half of the twentieth century in Fufeng County, Shaanxi Province. Its inscription of 121 characters contains a precise date of 789 B.C.E., placing it in the reign of King Xuan. It is one of some eighty midor late-Western Zhou appointment inscriptions where the King, or sometimes a high-level aristocrat, issues a formulaic "charge" (*ming* 命; also written *ling* 令, "order") or bestowal (*ci* 賜) with which he commands the appointee to accede to a certain position and bestows on him insignia and paraphernalia. Such inscriptions appeared in the wake of the broad ritual, administrative, and military reforms that began during the reign of King Mu, when the Zhou dynasty tried to recover from the disastrous results of King Zhao's southern military campaign, which had resulted in defeat and the death of the King. The appointment inscriptions seem to reflect a newly elaborated court ritual, performed in the royal ancestral temple, as well as a dramatically increased bureaucratic order.

The Shanfu Shan inscription records the appointment of the royal food steward (*shanfu* 膳夫), named Shan 山, whom the Zhou King addresses personally and by name. What distinguishes the Shanfu Shan *ding* inscription is the fact that, together with just a handful of other inscriptions, it furnishes an extensive account of the appointment ceremony itself. To date, only six late Western Zhou inscriptions provide such comprehensive records, namely, those of the Song *ding* 頌鼎 (ca. 825 B.C.E.?), which is repeated on at least three *ding* tripods, five *gui* tureens and their lids (no. 47, above), and two *hu* 壺 vases and their lids; the Feng *ding* 鼎 (*Jicheng* 2815, 809 B.C.E.); the Huan *pan* 寰盤 (800 B.C.E.), which is repeated on at least one *ding* (*Jicheng* 10172 and 2819); the Shanfu Shan *ding* (789 B.C.E.); and the two separate Lai *ding* (no. 63, below, dated to 786 and 785 B.C.E.), which are repeated on two and ten *ding*, respectively. Remarkably, all these inscriptions come from the reign of King Xuan, dating from nearly the beginning of his forty-six year reign to nearly its end. While the two Lai *ding* inscriptions are considerably longer, the Song, Feng, Huan, and Shanfu Shan inscriptions are largely identical in their wording. Thus they seem to reflect a new epigraphic convention that began around, or shortly after, the time of King Xuan's ascension. In addition, they testify to an institutional memory, probably located in the royal archives, that preserved and perpetuated not only historical knowledge but also the very form, down to the specific wording, in which appointments were bestowed, announced, and finally cast in bronze. The vessels of choice for these inscriptions were mostly wide and shallow tripods, tureens, and water basins that offered sufficient space on their insides not only to accommodate a long inscription but also to render it clearly visible, hence turning it into a defining part of the vessel's visual appearance. The vessels were cast under the authority and apparently also in the foundry of the Zhou royal court and then transferred to the appointee, who would then use them in his family's ancestral temple.

Elaborate appointment inscriptions such as the one on the Shanfu Shan *ding* testify vividly (if in standardized form) to the importance of both the administrative ceremony and the ancestral sacrifice, and to the close and complex relations between the two in mid- to late Western Zhou times. The highly standardized idiom of the inscription represented the nature of codified, authoritative ritual at the royal court together with the appointee's integration into the king's ritual and administrative system. Providing a formulaic narrative of the appointment ceremony, the inscriptions are fundamentally dialogical, including the speeches by (or on behalf of) the king as well as the appointee.

Transcription

唯卅有七年正月初吉庚戌，王在周，格圖室。南宮乎入右膳夫山，入門，立中庭北嚮。王呼史奉冊令山。王曰：山，令汝官司舍獻人于曩，用作憲司貯，毋敢不善。賜汝玄衣黹純赤巿（韍）朱衡（璜）鑾旂。

山拜稽首，受冊佩以出，反入堇章。山敢對揚天子休令，用作朕皇考叔碩父尊鼎，用祈匄眉壽綽綰永令靈終，子子孫孫永寶用。

Translation

It was in the thirty-seventh year, first month, *chuji*, on *gengxu* day (*ganzhi* no. 47), when the King, while in the Zhou [ancestral temple], approached the map chamber. Nangong Hu entered to the right of Food Steward Shan, who entered the gate and took his position in the middle of the hall, facing north. The King called out to Scribe Hui to announce the written command to Shan. The King said: "Shan, I command you to administer and supervise the libation presenters at Ke; use this command to serve as a model in supervising stored goods—do not dare not to be good! I bestow on you a black jacket with brocaded hem, red kneepads, a scarlet demicirclet, and a pennant with bells."

Shan bowed, touching his head to the ground. He received the bamboo slips [with the written appointment] and suspended them from his girdle before exiting; in return, he submitted the jade tablet (with his previous, now updated appointment?). I, Shan, dare in response to extol the Son of Heaven's blessed command and on account of this make for my august deceased father, Shu Suofu, this sacrificial tripod! I entreatingly pray for extended longevity and expansive continuity, and for an eternal charge until my numinous end! May sons of sons, grandsons of grandsons, forever treasure and use this tripod!

Further Reading

Jicheng 2825.

Kimbun tsūshaku, 26.357–61.

Mingwen xuan, no. 445.

Jinwen jinyi leijian, 445–46.

Kern, "Bronze Inscriptions, the *Shangshu*, and the *Shijing*," 156–64.

Kern, "The Performance of Writing in Western Zhou China."

Shaughnessy, "Western Zhou Bronze Inscriptions," 74–76.

Tang Lan, *Tang Lan xiansheng jinwen lunji*, 115–67.

MKe

57. Jin Hou Su zhong 晉侯穌(蘇)鐘

During the recent excavation of a vast Jin 晉 state burial ground in the Tianma 天馬–Qucun 曲村 area of Shanxi (located north of the middle Yellow River valley and south of a large range of mountains), archaeologists discovered a tomb with sixteen inscribed bells commissioned or collected[1] by a ruler of Jin named Su. Unfortunately, this tomb was robbed and fourteen of the bells were spirited away to Hong Kong for sale on the antiquities market, where they were purchased by the Shanghai Museum in 1992. The last two bells of the inscription are preserved in the Shanxi Archaeological Research Institute.

Inscribed vessels from other tombs provide a list of nine different rulers, but the Jin Hou Su bells have the lengthiest record. The bells consist of two sets of eight bells graduated in size and with a 355-character inscription incised across all sixteen bells. The fact that the inscription is incised into the surface of the bell after it was cast, rather than at the same time, complicates scholars' efforts to date the inscription. It is thought to come from the reign of either King Li or King Xuan, and documents the journey of the Jin ruler with the Zhou king in a battle against Yi peoples in the east. It gives precise dates, so scholars know that the journey took forty-four days during the thirty-third reign year of the king. We just do not know which king.

The inscription records that at the beginning of the king's thirty-third reign year, he departed from Zongzhou, first stopping at Chengzhou, around fourteen days later. Then, setting off from Chengzhou, he rendezvoused with the Jin ruler and his army to attack the Eastern Yi peoples. During the third month, he and the Jin ruler worked together to attack a number of cities and capture hundreds of prisoners, most of whom they beheaded. When they returned to Chengzhou, the King led an award ceremony for Jin Hou Su during the sixth month in the Grand Chamber, probably the central hall of the Zhou ancestral shrine at Chengzhou (a local Zhou hall as the main shrine would have been in Zongzhou). Less than ten days later, they went on attack again, resulting in an even bigger ceremony in the Grand Chamber and more awards. Su 穌 (穌 > 蘇) is

---

[1] Some Chinese scholars have argued that each bell in the set was originally cast elsewhere, and they were collected over time by the Lord of Jin. See, e.g., the comments by Gao Zhixi 高至喜 in "Jin Hou Su zhong bitan," 62–63; and Wang Zichu, "Jin Hou Su zhong de yinyuexue yanjiu," esp. 26ff. The editors are grateful to Wang Haicheng for these references.

another name for a Jin ruler named Ji 籍 in the genealogy of Jin rulers preserved in the *Shiji*: he was the eighth Lord of Jin, posthumously known as Xian Hou 獻侯, and came to power in the sixth year of King Xuan's reign and died in the sixteenth year of the same reign.² Since this inscription begins in the thirty-third year of the King, however, either there is an error in Sima Qian's understanding of Jin history or the identification of Jin Hou Su as Xian Hou is mistaken. Proponents of a King Li date point to the bell styles; the mention of a man named Father Yang 揚父 (Su's escort in the second ceremony), who also cast bronzes during the King Li period; transmitted historical records that seem to better fit the earlier king's reign; as well as the fact that records involving the king in an formal award ceremony begin to disappear during the late Western Zhou period. On the other hand, scholars have also brought up a number of complicating factors involving the analysis of other vessels in the same tomb and debates over the chronology of all nine lords in light of Jin history. This issue has still not been resolved. Nevertheless, all agree that the Jin burial ground has provided an immense amount of data on the society of a strong regional state that rose during the Western Zhou.

The style of the inscription is similar to that of the *Chunqiu* 春秋, which is a collation of annals and lineage narratives from various local states that are presumed to date to the eponymous Spring and Autumn period. Like most inscriptions, this one focuses on a single event (i.e., the battle agains the Eastern Yi), but the annalistic style of dating every movement of the ruler, in this case the Zhou ruler, is the same as that used for the annals of local rulers during the Spring and Autumn period. The Jin ruler preserved the part of the Zhou annals that he felt his ancestors would be interested in, namely his successful work for the king's military mission against non-Zhou peoples. Because of errors in the sequences of days recorded (55–40–39–15–24–27), it seems that the Jin copyist may not have had the original Zhou record on hand or may have simply mixed up some of the day names. Nevertheless, the sequential nature of the dating has provided historians a unique set of data for analyzing the ancient calendar system, particularly the nature of the so-called "moon phase" categories of days (e.g., *jishengpo*, *jisipo*; see Glossary).

---

² *Shiji* 14.519–21 and 39.1637 [PRG].

Transcription

唯王卅又三年,王親遹省東或(域)南或(域)。

正月既生霸戊午,王步自宗周。

二月既望癸卯,王入格成周。

二月既死霸壬寅,王償(追?)³往東。

三月方(旁)死霸,王至于蕢⁴,分行。王親令晉侯穌(蘇):率乃自(師),左洀(覆)䟓,北洀(覆)[囗],伐夙夷。晉侯穌(蘇)折首百又廿,執訊廿又三夫。王至于𩰿⁵城。王親遠省自(師)。王至晉侯穌自。王降自車立(位)南鄉(嚮),親令晉侯穌:自西北遇(隅)敦伐𩰿城。晉侯率厥亞旅小子戜人先陷入,折首百執訊十又一夫。王至,淖淖列列,夷出奔。王令晉侯穌:率大室小臣車僕從,捕逐之。晉侯折首百又十,執訊廿夫;大室小臣車僕折首百又五十,執訊六十夫。王唯反(返)歸在成周。公族整自(師)宮。

六月初吉,戊寅,旦,王格大室即立(位)。王呼善(膳)夫曰:召晉侯穌。入門立中庭。王親賜駒四匹。

穌拜稽首,受駒以出,反(返)入,拜稽首。

丁亥旦王(御)于邑,伐宮。

庚寅旦王各(格)大室,嗣(司)工揚父入右晉侯穌。王親齊晉侯穌秬鬯一卣、弓矢百、馬四匹。

穌敢揚天子丕顯魯休,用作元穌揚鐘,用邵(昭)各(格)前文人。前文人其嚴在上翼在下,豐豐褱褱(繹繹),降余多福。

穌其萬年無疆,子子孫孫永寶茲鐘。

---

³ The archic graph appears to share the phonetic 自 (*C.tˤuj) with *zhui* 追 (*truj).

⁴ I suspect that the graphic components transcribed as 尸 were abbreviated birds 隹 and that this graph represented a variant of *ji* 集.

⁵ Read by some as *xun* 勳 (see Liu Yu and Lu Yan, *Jinchu Yin Zhou jinwen jilu*, 69).

Translation

It was in the King's thirty-third year, when the King personally went on an inspection trip to the eastern and southern territories.

In the first month, *jishengpo*, on *wuwu* day (*ganzhi* no. 55), the King proceeded from Zongzhou.

In the second month, *jiwang*, on *guimao* day (*ganzhi* no. 40), the King went in through (the gate of the city) Chengzhou.

In the second month, *jisipo*, on *renyin* day (*ganzhi* no. 39), the King set off eastward in pursuit of the enemy.

In the third month, *pangsipo*,[6] the King arrived at Ji and divided the procession. The King personally ordered Jin Hou Su: "Lead your armies to the left and survey Guan,[7] go north and survey X, and then attack the Su Yi peoples." Jin Hou Su chopped off 120 heads and captured twenty-three prisoners for interrogation. The King arrived at Xun city. The King personally inspected the army from a distance. The King went to Jin Hou Su's encampment. The King descended from his chariot and took up [his] position facing southward, and personally ordered Jin Hou Su: "Pressure and attack Xun city from the northwest corner." Jin Hou led the troops of the secondary lineage group, including the [elite] youth and spearmen as the vanguard down into [the city]. They chopped off one hundred heads and captured eleven prisoners for interrogation. The King arrived and the Yi peoples fled in a confused mob. The King ordered Jin Hou Su: "Lead the acolytes of the Grand Chamber[8] and charioteers to catch and pursue them." Jin Hou chopped

---

[6] Xu Fengxian explains that of the six calendar dates given in the Jin Hou Su bell inscription, only *pangsipo* is not specified by a sexagenary day. This she finds as evidence that the term does not refer to a lunar phase ("Using Sequential Relations of Day-Dates to Determine the Temporal Scope of Western Zhou Lunar Phase Terms"). Unfortunately, there is no consensus regarding what the term probably means (see "Jin Hou Su zhong bitan").

[7] Taking *guan* 藋 as the phonetic and as the name of a place. Some interpret it as "watchtower" 觀 (Liu Yu and Lu Yan, *Jinchu Yin Zhou jinwen jilu*, 1.11–3, 65). This would be the only evidence for a watchtower in the inscriptions. The word *guan* appears as a name or extremely rarely as a verb "to observe" (see *Jicheng* 5433). In the majority of cases for the verb *sheng* ("survey, inspect") the object is territory or specific sites, although we see in this inscription the king inspected the army. There is also one case of checking out a road to a site (see *Jicheng* 2722).

[8] The *xiao chen* 小臣 is an ancient category of minor officials, that while being low level or even minors, helped professionals in ritual music and, here, obviously warfare. The fact that

off 110 head and captured twenty prisoners for interrogation. The acolytes of the Grand Chamber and charioteers chopped off 150 heads and captured sixty prisoners for interrogation. It was when the King was heading back, returning to Chengzhou, that the Patriarch's lineage [militia] prepared the encampment and hall (for the King to present awards).

In the sixth month, *chuji*, on *wuyin* day (*ganzhi* no. 15), at dawn, the King arrived and entered the Great Chamber, and, after taking up his position, the King called the *shanfu*, saying: "Summon Jin Hou Su." I entered through the gate and stood in the center of the courtyard (facing northwards and the King). The King personally awarded me four ponies.

I, Su, clapped my hands together and bowed my head to the ground and took the ponies out of the court and then returned and again clapped my hands together and bowed my head to the ground.

On *dinghai* day (*ganzhi* no. 24), at dawn, the King drove a chariot to the walled settlement and attacked its hall.

On *gengyin* day (*ganzhi* no. 27), at dawn, the King arrived and entered the Grand Chamber. The Supervisor of Artisans, Yang Fu, entered, guiding Jin Hou Su in from the right. The King personally gave Jin Hou a *you*-vessel of fragrant black millet ale, a bow with one hundred arrows, and four horses.

I, Su, dare to extol the Son of Heaven's greatly manifest and abundant grace and take this opportunity to make supremely harmonious bells for extolling his accomplishment and to summon the Accomplished Ones. May the Accomplished Ones, residing sternly up above and protecting those below—so fruitful and mighty—send down to me much good fortune.

May I, Su, have for ten thousand years without limit sons of sons and grandsons of grandsons eternally to treasure these bells.

---

they belonged originally to the Grand Chamber suggests a ritual role associated with the main lineage shrine.

Further Reading

Barnard, *Inscriptions*, v. 1, 89–196.

Falkenhausen, *Chinese Society in the Age of Confucius*, 80–91.

Jin Hou mudi chutu qingtongqi guoji xueshu yantaohui lunwenji.

"Jin Hou Su zhong bitan."

Liu Yu and Lu Yan, *Jinchu Yin Zhou jinwen jilu*, 1.11–3, 58–87.

Ma Chengyuan, "Jin Hou Su bianzhong."

Nivison and Shaughnessy, "The Jin Hou Su Bells Inscription and Its Implications for the Chronology of Early China."

Shim, "The 'Jinhou Su *bianzhong*' Inscription and Its Significance."

Song Lingping, *Jinxi muzang zhidu yanjiu.*

Wang Zichu, "Jin Hou Su zhong de yinyuexue yanjiu."

Xu, "The Cemetery of the Western Zhou Lords of Jin."

CAC

58. Kunbi Wang zhong 昆疕王鐘

Once in the collection of Luo Zhenyu 羅振玉 (1866–1940), this bell, now lost, had typical late Western Zhou style décor. The inscription consisted of a simple statement of manufacture followed by a blessing, an extremely common style of inscription found on bronze vessels and implements of all sorts during the second half of the Western Zhou period. The bell, a product of generic production as a gift or perhaps for trade with allies, was produced by the King of Kunbi, a state that considered itself equal to and separate from the Zhou lineage network. The Zhou used the term "state" (*bang* 邦) to refer both to itself and to other states outside its network. As in the Shang, when "regions" (*fang* 方) represented non-Shang networks and clans, the "states" both conflicted and traded. The title of King was used among some northwestern peoples, such as those of the state of Ze 夨 (see nos. 9 and 45, above). The leaders of Chu, located along the tributaries of the middle Yangzi River Valley—i.e., "the South"—were infamous in later literature for insisting on their right to be addressed as kings. Leaders of Zhou-network states (known as *guo* 國 by the Eastern Zhou period and maybe earlier) were addressed only as the "protector lords" (hou 侯), referring to those who had sworn to come to the defense of the Zhou state, or, in the case of lineage relatives, as "patriarchs" (*gong* 公).

Nevertheless, scholars suggest that at this time the state of Kunbi was probably located northeast of the Wei River valley, not far from the Western Zhou.[1] Whether or not relations with the Zhou were a factor in the casting of this inscribed bell is unclear. The scribe had been exposed to Zhou-trained teachers, but the script style was unusually ornate and decorative, as if written for display only. Scholars generally believe that bronze-casting implied control over a vast economic network, and access to remote mines, as well as to a local bureaucracy of scribes and artisans, and hence only the Zhou government had enough power at that time and therefore controlled casting. By the late Western Zhou period, however, Zhou control over its network weakened, and previously subdued leaders inside and outside the Zhou network became more independent. The Kunbi king does not acknowledge any patron at all, simply stating his ownership and prayer for blessings.

---

[1] See Li Feng, *Landscape and Power in Early China*, 186–87.

Transcription

昆疕王貯作龢鐘。其萬年子孫永寶。

Translation

The King of Kunbi, Zhu, cast a harmonious bell. May he for ten thousand years have sons and grandsons eternally to treasure it.

Further Reading

Jicheng 46.

Cook and Major, eds., *Defining Chu*, 1–20, 51–61.
Hsu and Linduff, *Western Zhou Civilization*, 186–226, 288–344.
Li Feng, *Landscape and Power in Early China*, 143, 186–87.

CAC

59. Chu Gong Jia zhong 楚公豪鐘

The mid-nineteenth-century collection of Chen Jieqi 陳介祺 once held a five-bell set cast by a ruler of Chu named Jia 豪. Most of the set is now the Sumitomo Collection in Kyoto. The inscriptions on the bells seem to have been written by two different hands at two different times. Group One, consisting of three bells, had cloud and bird patterns, and referred to the bells as "treasured Chime-bells"; Group Two, consisting of two bells, had dragon and thunder décor, and referred to the bells as "reddish bronze" (with the loanword *yang* 鍚 for the more common *tang* 湯). This word may have indicated an intentionally higher copper content used in casting, producing a redder bell. A dagger-axe blade belonging to Chu Gong Jia was found among a number of ancient bronzes recovered by the Hunan Provincial Museum in the 1950s. This blade, unlike northern or Yellow River Valley blades, was wide and triangular in shape, with black leopard-like spots cast in a pattern along the edge and centerline towards the hilt. The inscription reads: "The dagger-axe grasped by Chu Gong Jia" 楚公豪秉戈.

In an attempt to match Jia with the Chu royal genealogy given in *Shiji*, a number of scholars equate him with the ruler called Xiong Zhi Hong 熊摯紅, who was a contemporary of King Li of Zhou. (The identification is made on the basis of the fact that the name Jia was sometimes written with the phonetic *zhi* 至.) In Chu documents, their leaders were never referred to as *xiong*, "bear."[1] There is no bronze or excavated textual evidence for the usage, and in the transmitted textual tradition it seems to have begun with the Qin and possibly was pejorative in nature. On the other hand, the Qin pronunciation of the graph for "bear" (*C.ɢʷ(r)əm) may have been similar to the Chu pronunciation of the title *yin* 酓 (*qem?), attested on Warring States period Chu bronzes found in the lower Yangzi River valley, where Chu had been pushed by Qin.

The fact that the Chu ruler made the bells "of his own accord" (*zi* 自) symbolizes independence from the Zhou, even more so than the King of Kunbi (no. 58). This style of inscription became common by the Spring and Autumn Period and confirms the beginning of a strong rise of Chu to a position of dominance by the Warring States period.

---

[1] Recently discovered bamboo texts reveal the odd example of *xiong* used in place of *yin*, suggesting that different scribes might use either graph. See Henansheng wenwu kaogusuo, *Xincai Geling Chu mu*.

Transcription

楚公豪自作寶大林鐘，孫孫子子其永寶。

Translation

> The Patriarch of Chu made of his own accord a treasured set of chime bells. Grandsons of grandsons, sons of sons—may they eternally treasure it.

Further Reading

Jicheng 42–44.
Kimbun tsūshaku 40.530.
Mingwen xuan, no. 468.

Cook, "Auspicious Metals and Southern Spirits."
Cook, "Myth and Authenticity."
Cook, "Scribes, Cooks, and Artisans."
Cook and Major, eds., *Defining Chu*, 1–20, 51–61, 67–76.
Gao Zhixi, "Chu Gong Jia' ge."
Jinwen jinyi leijian, 477.
Li Ling, "Chuguo tongqi mingwen biannian huishi."
Liu Binhui, "Chuguo youming tongqi biannian gaishu."
Zhang Yachu, "Lun Chu Gong Jia he Chu Gong Ni bo de niandai."

CAC

60. Jing Ren Ning *zhong* 井人妄鐘

This inscription spans two bells cast as part of a set, and there are multiple versions of the set, which is cited by various names, such as Jing *bianzhong* 井編鐘 and Xing Ren Ning *zhong* 邢仁妄鐘. One set is located in the People's Republic of China, where the bell inscribed with the initial portion of the text (*Jicheng* 109) is now in the Shanghai Museum. It has been known for centuries and its provenance is unrecorded. The second bell (*Jicheng* 112) was excavated in 1966 at Qizhen 齊鎮, Fufeng County, Shaanxi Province, and is held in the Baoji Municipal Museum. Another set is located in Japan, where the initial portion of the text (*Jicheng* 110) is held in the Calligraphy Museum in Tokyo; the companion piece (*Jicheng* 111) is held in the Sumitomo Collection in Kyoto. The inscription is dedicated to Hefu 龢父, whom some commentators take to be Gong Hefu 共龢父, whose control of government during the decade before 841 B.C.E. interrupted the succession of Zhou kings (according to *Shiji*). Some have even argued that the character *jing* 井 should be read as a vaiant of *gong* 共. If the identification holds, then this inscription implies that the vessel sponsor, Ren Ning, is Gong Hefu's son or grandson, and would date the inscription to the reign of King Xuan. Other scholars, however, including both Shirakawa and Ma Chengyuan, doubt the identity with Gong Hefu, and date the vessel to the reigns of Kings Yí or Li.

Transcription

井人妄曰：顯盈（淑）文祖、皇考，克質（哲）[1]厥德，得屯（純）用魯，永終于吉。妄不敢弗帥用文祖、皇考，穆穆秉德。妄憲憲聖爽，寔處宗室。肆妄作龢父大林鐘。用追孝，侃前文人。前文人其嚴在上。豐豐彙彙[2]，降余厚多福無疆。妄其萬年，子子孫孫永寶用享。

Translation

Ren Ning of Jing said, "Bright and pure, my patterned grandfather and august father were able to make bright their virtue in full integrity and grace, and lived their full measure of years in good

---

[1] Often read as variants for *shen* 慎.

[2] These graphs are standard onomatopoeics for bell tones, appearing also in the Guo Shu Lü *zhong* and Liang Qi *zhong* inscriptions (nos. 44 and 62). Compare the interpretation of these

for ancient chinese bronze inscriptions tune. I, Ning, dare not fail to emulate the austere grasp of virtue of my patterned grandfather and august father. I ever bear in mind their sage rectitude rooted in our clan shrine. Wherefore was cast this *lin*-bell³ for Hefu, so as to pursue filial service pleasing to my patterned forebears. May my patterned forebears look down from above and shower upon me blessings without measure. May I, Ning, live forever, and may my descendants ever treasure and receive this vessel's pleasure."

Further Reading

Jicheng 109–12.

Kimbun tsūshaku, 31.776–84.

Mingwen xuan, no. 396.

Behr, *Reimende Bronzeinschriften und die Entstehung der chinesischen Endreimdichtung,* 245–49.

RE

---

graphs in nos. 33 and 62. Musicality is echoed in text by rhyme as well; the latter portion of the text is rhymed (in varied meter) on the phonetics for *shang* 上 (*daŋʔ-s), *jiang* 疆 (*kaŋ), and *xiang* 享 (*qʰaŋʔ). Compare with the interpretation in nos. 33 and 62.

³ See Glossary.

61. Ni *zhong* 逆鐘

Four bells, dated by some scholars to the reign of King Xiao and others to the late Western Zhou, were discovered in 1975 in Diantoucun 店頭村, Yongshou County 永壽縣, Shaanxi. They are stored in the Xianyang Research Institute of Cultural Artifacts and Archaeology. The twelve-line inscription is continuous across the four bells, with three lines cast into each central panel. The décor consists of simple scrolls, with the scrolls cast irregularly in the *zhenggu* 正鼓 (lower central rim) striking area.

In this inscription we see a local adaptation of the royal award ceremony. The patron is not the Zhou king but a local lord named Shu Shi 叔氏, even though from the dating formula marking "the King's first reign year," he considers himself a member of the Zhou state. His family rank, *shu*, reveals that he was a "younger" sibling or cousin of the lineage patriarch. In imitation of cereomonies involving the Zhou king, Shu Shi has an archivist assisting him and "agrees" (*ruo yue*, see Glossary) with the reward (it is not clear if he was reading from a written record).

The ceremony is held in the "main lineage shrine" (*damiao* 大廟), which given the fact that these bells were discovered in the Zhou homeland, should refer to the royal Zhou ancestral shrine, but only the King is recorded as officiating ceremonies there. On the other hand, main lineage shrines in other localities, sometimes visited by the Zhou king, were clearly distinguished (see the Shi You *gui*, no. 31). For Shu Shi to officiate, it would seem that his elder siblings were dead or deposed (hence the use of "chief" *shi* 氏 in his name). Contrary to the central court ceremony, there is no guide to usher the awardee, Ni, and no record of where Ni was positioned in relation to the patron. The inscription documents Ni's promotion to the hereditary position, held by his father and ancestors, of managing the household. Ni was probably a member of the same lineage but of lower status. To celebrate the promotion, Ni cast these bells to broadcast the news to his ancestors.

Transcription

唯王元年三月既生霸庚申，叔氏在大廟。叔氏令史甬召逆。叔氏若（諾）曰：逆，乃祖考許？（胥？）政于公室。今余賜汝毌（干/盾）五錫戈彤綏，用龏（兼？）于公室，僕庸臣妾、小子室家。毋（毋）又（有）不聞智（知）。敬乃夙夜用粵（屏）朕身，勿瀘(廢)朕命，母(毋)墜乃政。

逆敢拜手稽。

Translation

It was in the King's first year, the third month, *jishengpo*, on *gengshen* day (*ganzhi* no. 57), that Shu Shi resided in the Great Shrine. Shu Shi commanded Archivist Cha to summon Ni. Shu Shi agreed [to Ni's promotion], saying: "Ni, your ancestor and Deceased-father officiated in the governing of the Patriarch's house. Now, I award you five shields and a dagger-axe with a red tassel for use when you assume the management of the Patriarch's House, the servants and male and female slaves, the children, and the household. Do not let me learn what I should not hear about. Be respectful about your task of protecting my person from dawn to dusk and do not cast off my command; do not let your governing fail."

I, Ni, dared to clap my hands and knock my head against the ground.

Further Reading

Jicheng 60–66.

Kaogu yu wenwu 1981.1, 10 (rubbing).

Mingwen xuan, no. 274.

Barnard, *Inscriptions*, v. 1, 26–30.

Jinwen jinyi leijian, 479–81.

Wang Hui, *Shang Zhou jinwen*, 186–89.

CAC

62. Liang Qi zhong 泑(梁)其鐘

The bell set was discovered in 1940 in Renjiacun, Fufeng County, Shaanxi Province, in a hoard also containing various other vessels bearing inscriptions with the sponsor's name (Liang Qi 梁其) and title (*shanfu* 膳夫, steward). It originally included six inscribed bells, of which three are today in the posession of the Shanghai Museum, one in the Nanjing Municipal Mueseum, one in the Musée Guimet in Paris, and one in an unknown collection, purportedly in Japan. The inscription is divided into two parts spread over the central cartouche (*zheng* 鉦) and the lower right striking pane (*gu* 鼓) of two bells, comprising a total of 147 characters alltogether. Bell no. 2, held in the Shanghai museum, has a height of 55.4 cm and a width of 32.7 cm between the lateral projecting rims (*xian* 銑).

The inscription uses several expressions typical of prayers inscribed during the second half of the Western Zhou, such as *kang wu* 康娛, "peaceful bliss," *chun you* 純祐, "pure protection," and *yong lu* 甬祿, "perennial blessings," and is rich in reduplicated four-syllable phrases, iconically conveying the resonance of the bell and the munificence of the spirits invoked by it. It also refers to the notion of *de*, here translated as "charisma," which, it seems, not only was invoked by the vessel-maker in order to identify himself with ancient political and ritual role models, but also implied a claim as to his own role in the present and future employment by the Zhou king.

Although metrically not wholly regular, the inscription is rhymed throughout. In the following scheme, each line in a rhymed sequence is headed by a Roman numeral. Each syllable is then represented by a lower-case x. At the end of a line, an upper-case letter (e.g., "A") indicates a full or perfect rhyme; a lower-case letter (e.g., "a") indicates a half- or imperfect rhyme; and an upper-case X indicates an unrhymed syllable.

The different rhyming sections correspond roughly to a scheme where A = remote past, B = recent deeds of the vessel sponsor, C = the making of the bell, D = formulaic prayer formula to the spirits, E = benefit from the spirits, F = final dedication, with several intervening non-rhymed lines. The frequent usage of synonyms and phonological correspondences in this inscription shows a quite sophisticated stylistic awareness and sense of aural performativity.

	xxx				
I	xxxxx	a	XIV	xxxx	C
II	xxxx	A	XV	xxxx	C
III	xxxx	A	XVI	xxxxxxxx	X
IV	xxxx	X	XVII	xxxxxxx	X
V	xxxx	X	XVIII	xxxx	X
VI	xxxxxxxx	a	XIX	xxxxxxx	d
VII	xxx	A	XX	xxxx	D
VIII	xxx	X	XXI	xxxxxxx	D
IX	xxx	a	XXII	xxxxxx	E
X	xxxxxxxxxxx	B	XXIII	xxxx	E
XI	xxxxxxxx	b	XXIV	xxxxxx	F
XII	xxxxxxxxxx	c	XXV	xxxx	F
XIII	xxxxxxx	C	XXVI	xxxx	X

Transcription

汈（梁）其曰：

不（丕）顯皇且（祖）考$_a$，

穆穆翼翼$_A$

克恁（慎）厥德$_A$，

晨（努）臣先王，

𢗁（得）屯（純）亡啟。

汈（梁）其肇帥井（型）皇且（祖）考$_a$，

秉明德$_A$，

虔夙夕，

辟（弼）天子$_a$。天子

INSCRIPTIONS

肩事沔（梁）其身邦君大正$_B$。

用天子寵蔑沔（梁）其曆（曆$_b$），

沔（梁）其敢對天子不（丕）顯休揚$_c$，

用乍（作）朕（朕）皇且（祖）考䚄鐘$_c$，

鎗鎗（倉倉）鏓鏓（恖恖$_c$），

鉥鉥（徵徵）鏙鏙（雔雔$_c$），

用卲（召）各（格）喜伹（侃）前文人，

用 𣃔（祈）匄康䚄（娛）屯（純）右（祐），

䊆（綽）綴（綰）通（甬）彔（祿）。

皇且（祖）考其嚴才（在）上$_d$，

豐豐（磅磅）彙彙（礴礴$_D$）^{1}，

降余大魯福，亡斁$_D$，

用镾（懼）光沔（梁）其身$_E$，

勳（樂）于永令（命$_E$）。

沔（梁）其萬年無彊（疆$_F$），

龕（堪）臣皇王$_F$，

眉壽永寶！

Translation

I, Liang Qi said: "The illustrous and august deceased ancestral fathers—devoutly (*mriwk-mriwk) and warily (*ɢʷrəp-ɢʷrəp) were they able to cultivate their charisma, diligently to serve as retainers for the former kings, to acquire perfection without exhaustion. I, Liang Qi, set out to mold myself compliantly upon the august

---

^{1} Compare with the interpretation in no. 33.

deceased ancestral fathers. Abiding by their luminescent charisma, acquiescent day and night, I served the Son of Heaven. The Son of Heaven imposed upon me, Liang Qi, personally to serve as Lord of the Fief and Great Regulator. Through the grace of the Son of Heaven, what I, Liang Qi, have experienced is recognized. I, Liang Qi, dare to reciprocate the illustrious and clement commendation of the Son of Heaven, by having made a harmonious bell for my august deceased ancestral fathers, [which is] humming and resonating (*tsʰˤaŋ-tsʰˤaŋ tsʰˤoŋ-tsʰˤoŋ), glittering and glowing (*treŋ-treŋ q(r)oŋ-q(r)oŋ). Use it to summon, reach out to and exhilarate the cultivated men of yore! Use it to pray and supplicate for peaceful bliss and pure protection, for rich perennial blessings! May the august deceased ancestral fathers sternly reside on high; may they copiously (*pʰ(r)oŋ-pʰ(r)oŋ pˤak-pˤak) send down great and generous bliss to me, without flagging; may they in joyful mood glorify my, Liang Qi's, person, so that I delight in eternal life! May there be myriad years for Liang Qi, without end, so that he will be capable of serving as a retainer to the august kings! May you eternally treasure this bell in long life!"

Further Reading

Jicheng 187–88.

Mingwen xuan, no. 397.

Behr, *Reimende Bronzeinschriften und die Entstehung der chinesischen Endreimdichtung*, 249–53.

Barnard and Zhang Guangyu, *The Shan-fu Liang Ch'i Kuei and Associated Inscribed Vessels*.

Chen Peifen, "Fan you, Feng ding ji Liang Qi xu mingwen quanshi."

Guo Moruo, "Shaanxi xinchu qiming kaoshi."

Kong Decheng, "Liang Qi zhong mingwen shiwen."

WB

63. Qiu (Lai) *pan* 逑(淶)¹盤

In 2003, farmers in the village of Yangjiacun, Meixian, Shaanxi Province, discovered a hoard of twenty-seven inscribed bronze vessels once belonging to a certain Shan 單 family. The cache included twelve *ding* cauldrons, nine *li* cooking vessels, a pair of square *hu* beverage storage vessels, a *pan* basin, a *yu* basin, a *yi* pouring vessel and a *he* pouring vessel. The abstract vessel décor is typical of the late Western Zhou, with undulating wave and scale patterns, but with a few outstanding examples of naturalistic animal ornamentation. The *he* vessel, shaped like a teapot, has four bird-claw legs to go with a curly-beaked bird lid; an animal-head spout with a long neck, floppy ears, protruding eyes, and a high nose; and a dragon-headed handle linked to the lid by means of a tiger. The body is round, with concentric circles of feather and scale décor around a spiraled abstract dragon in the center. The *yu* (high-walled basin) in which the *he* was placed features a pair of elephant-trunk flanges opposite the high looped handles (somewhat similar to the handles on the Shi Qiang *pan*, no. 28, above) that suggest a means for lifting and moving this vessel after it was filled with water for bathing rituals. The *yi* vessel, shaped like a gravy boat, has bird-claw feet similar to those on the *he*, but they clearly show dragonheads consuming the birds, so that only the lower bird body and feet show. The handle of the *yi* consists of a snake-like dragon biting the lip of the vessel. The *hu* pair combines the late Western Zhou wavy patterns with intertwined snake-like dragons with sculptured heads, features continued in later vessels, particularly those in the Yangzi River region.

From the décor and names mentioned in the inscriptions, scholars have been able to link this cache of bronze treasures to other caches in the area, including bells and earlier vessels belonging to the Shan lineage (see Li *fangzun* and *juzun*, no. 26, above). The lists of Zhou kings and the specific dates provided in the cauldron inscriptions provide important dating information. As in the Shi Qiang *pan* inscription, lineage history is traced back only as far as the first ancestor to work with the Zhou, even though in both cases the lineages belonged to the late Shang network. This confirms

---

¹ While Lai 淶 follows the initial transcription in the official report, new evidence supports Qiu as the most accurate reading, see Chen Jian, *Jiaguwen kaoshi lunji*, 20–38; cf. Smith, "'What Difficulty Could There Be?'" Qiu Xigui proposed the transcription 遼, see Qiu Xigui, "X Gong Xu mingwen kaoshi," 15–16. For other interpretations, see Shaughnessy, "The Writing of a Late Western Zhou Bronze Inscription," 846 no. 2 [MP].

that lineage founders had to receive authority from the reigning king for ancestor-worship rituals that used bronze vessels. Unlike the Shi Qiang *pan* inscription, which listed each king (and the ancestor working for that particular king) separately, the Qiu inscriptions group some of the Zhou kings into pairs. Also noteworthy in this list is the use of posthumous epithets, which when translated into English reflect a hagiographic order of high-ranking ancestral spirits. The founder, the Patriarch of Shan (Shan Gong 單公), was aligned with Kings Civil (Wen 文)[2] and Martial (Wu 武); the Patriarch the Younger (Gong Shu 公叔) with King Accomplished (Cheng 成); New Chamber the Second (Xinshi Zhong 新室仲) with King Happiness (Kang 康); Father Li, Beneficence the Second (Hui Zhong Lifu 惠仲盠父), with Kings Light (Zhao 昭) and Dark (Mu 穆); Elder Ling (Ling Bo 零伯) with Kings Reverence (Gong 恭) and Fine (Yi 懿); Fine the Second (Yi Zhong 懿仲) with Kings Filial (Xiao 孝) and Peaceful (Yi 夷); Reverence the Younger (Gong Shu 龏叔) with King Danger (Li 厲);[3] and finally Lai himself with the reigning Son of Heaven 天子, which could only be King All-encompassing (Xuan 宣) (r. 827–782 B.C.E.). The content of the inscription on the *pan* basin suggests that it was cast earlier in Qiu's career than the two cauldrons, which were cast in the forty-second and forty-third years of the King's reign, around 786 and 785 B.C.E.

The ancestral epithets reveal a complex multi-trunk tree of lineage relationships, one in which the connections of the branches to the trunks is not always clear—suggesting that while the Shan family was one of the most powerful during the Western Zhou period, Lai's lineage narrative highlighted only certain individuals. Generally, the term "patriarch" (*gong* 公) refers to the lineage head or founder. Birth order markers include "the elder" (*bo* 伯), "the second" (*zhong* 仲) "the younger (or third)" (*shu* 叔). Thus Patriarch the Younger (Gong Shu) may have been a younger brother of the original Shan Patriarch, or descendant of a younger brother. While epithets like Beneficence, Fine, and Reverence seem typical for local lords, the name New Chamber (*xinshi* 新室) is unusual. Since Zhou ceremonial activities often took place in "chambers" (*shi* 室) attached to sacred en-

---

[2] The word *wen* can mean "patterned," "cultivated," or "accomplished (in *de*)." The contrast between a ruler's using "civil" or "martial" skills to govern became an important issue during the Warring States period. During the Western Zhou period, *de* could be accrued through the cultivation of either skill. See Glossary.

[3] In the *Zuozhuan*, *li* is a vengeful spirit that appears in dreams, e.g. Legge, *The Chinese Classics*, V, 372. In medical manuscripts from Shuihudi, *li* is the name of a demon that occupies homes and causes diseases. See Harper, *Early Chinese Medical Literature*, 96.

closures or halls (*gong* 宫), and these places were often connected to the worship of specific ancestors, we can speculate that Lai's ancestor New Chamber the Second was the founder of a branch lineage that did not qualify for the name marking a secondary branch, *ya* 亞. The authority to establish a new lineage house with associated lands, peoples, and duties ultimately came from the Zhou royal house—particularly since the granting of this privilege involved the gift of sacrificial bronzes to use in an ancestral shrine that would be part of the Zhou religious network binding the state together on both the supernatural and the earthly planes. All of Lai's ancestors above his grandfather, including New Chamber the Second, were titled Brilliant High Ancestor (*huang gaozu* 皇高祖). His grandfather was a Brilliant Secondary-branch Ancestor (*huang yazu* 皇亞祖) showing that he was not the primary branch lineage heir after Elder Ling, but the head of a branch lineage. Lai's deceased father was referred to as Brilliant Deceased-father (*huang kao* 皇考), a fairly typical epithet by the late Western Zhou period. The fact that his grandfather, Yi the Younger, would use an epithet Yi ("Fine") the generation after a Zhou king's using the same epithet suggests the lack of taboo or some kind of a connection between the systems used by the Zhou kings and the Shan lineage. As in the Shi Qiang *pan* lineage narrative, Qiu eulogizes the merit that each ancestor accumulated with regard to the Zhou mission of expansion.

The inscriptions on the cauldrons and the *pan* are among the longest inscriptions belonging to the late Western Zhou (see also the Sanshi *pan* and Mao Gong *ding*, nos. 45 and 55, above). It demonstrates the urge to record lineage narratives, which may have comprised the earliest historical texts.[4] As Lothar von Falkenhausen has noted, the bronze texts were probably culled from longer archival documents originally written on bamboo.[5] Their application to vessels used in sacrifices to the ancestors and display in ancestral shrines suggests their role in satisfying the ancestral spirits. Naming the particular spirits through the recitation of the eulogy may have served to invoke their presence into the ceremony, suggesting a spiritual as well as blood relationship to Qiu.

Beyond the religious value of the bronze texts, scholars can use the full

---

[4] For a recent discussion of the competing sources that may have been used to compile the *Zuozhuan*, see Li Wai-yee, *The Readability of the Past in Early Chinese Historiography*, 29–84. For research on the Shan lineage and Western Zhou lineage relations generally, see Sena, "Reproducing Society."

[5] Falkenhausen, "The Inscribed Bronzes from Yangjiacun."

dates provided in the cauldron inscriptions to reconstruct Zhou chronology and clarify dating terminology that had never been completely understood. For example, both cauldron ceremonies, although a year apart, took place during the period of the month called "already growing brightness" (*jishengpo* 既生霸). By comparing these fully dated texts with other inscriptions, many scholars now understand that this term refers to the half of the month when the moon was waxing, and that the number of days covered by this term was flexible. The other half was called "already dying brightness" (*jisipo* 既死霸, see Glossary).

The inscription commemorates Qiu's promotion to an ancestral position of supervising borderlands around Zhou. This involved military as well as civil duties. In the *pan* inscription, Qiu supervised the forested areas that surrounded the Zhou center, providing game and wood resources for Zhou shrines and palaces. In the cauldron inscriptions, where he goes by the title Forester (*yu* 虞), he was also in charge of the local inhabitants, including new settlers. Protecting these people and the Zhou political center involved battling invaders, such as the ferocious Xianyun. King Xuan's prolonged engagement with the Xianyun is mentioned in many inscriptions from this era (e.g., Xi Jia *pan* and Guo Ji Zibai *pan*, nos. 48 and 49, above). Li Feng locates the main battleground in the upper Jing River valley, not far from the Zhou heartland in the Wei River valley.[6]

The two Qiu cauldrons cast in the forty-second and forty-third years of the king's reign provide details regarding Qiu's official career and promotion ceremonies that can be used to contextualize the information in the Qiu *pan*. In the Forty-second Year Qiu *ding* 四十二年逨鼎 inscription, Qiu's promotion took place at dawn in the Grand Chamber 大室 of the Zhou Halls for Kang and Mu 周康穆宮, who were royal ancestral spirits. The Forty-third Year Qiu *ding* 四十三年逨鼎 inscription specifies that there were two separate halls, the Kang Hall 康宮 and the Mu Hall 穆宮, and that the ceremony took place in the Zhou ancestral shrine 周廟. It is unclear whether the Grand Chamber was inside the ancestral shrine itself or simply one of many important ritual buildings in the complex. In either case, the King "took up his position," possibly on a stage facing south over a walled courtyard into which an important official would guide Qiu, the awardee, from the main gate. The awardee would then stand in the center of the courtyard, facing the King. In the Forty-second Year Qiu ding in-

---

[6] Li Feng, *Landscape and Power in Early China*, 141–92.

scription, the Supervisor of Works (*sigong* 司工, called *sikong* 司空 in the transmitted texts), a man named San 散, escorted Forester Qiu, and in the Forty-third Year Qiu *ding* inscription, it was the Supervisor of Horses (*sima* 司馬), and man named Shou 壽. In addition to the escorts, there were officers who handled the text, one who received it from the King and another who copied it for the awardee and perhaps read it out loud. In the Forty-second Year Qiu *ding* inscription, these officers were the Governor Chief 尹氏 and the Archivist 史, named Yu 淢. In the Forty-third Year Qiu *ding* inscription, they seemed to switch places, although the Governor Chief was called the Lord Governor Chief 君尹氏.[7] The "written text" (*shu* 書) is described as the "gift" (*li* 釐) in the Forty-second Year Qiu *ding* inscription and as the "command" (*ming* 命) in the Forty-third Year Qiu *ding* inscription. In either case, once the first officer "has received" (*shou* 受) the text from the King, the latter "calls" (*hu* 呼) the second officer to transcribe the "gift" or "command" onto bamboo strips (*ce* 冊).

The Qiu *pan* inscription does not include a description of the ceremony. But like the cauldron inscriptions, it includes a narrative of the King's charge, followed by documentation of Qiu's expressions of gratitude, dedication of the bronze to his ancestors, and prayers to the ancestors. The cauldron inscriptions include some unusually explicit notes regarding the ceremony of Qiu's receiving the text. We know that after Qiu clapped his hands together and knocked his head against the floor (*bai jishou* 拜稽首), a traditional act of obeisance mentioned in most inscriptions involving gifts and commands, he "received" (*shou*) the written record (*ce*) as a gift (*li*) or as something to hang from his belt (*pei* 佩), and exited the courtyard. Then he re-entered the courtyard carrying a jade staff for audiences (*jin gui* 覲圭). At this point, he expressed his gratitude to the King, addressing him as the Son of Heaven (*tianzi* 天子) in a ceremony called "extolling in response" (*dui yang* 對揚).[8] The text of Qiu's eulogy is not recorded on the cauldrons, but the *pan* begins with a eulogy to all the Zhou kings and his ancestral connections to them, so it is possible that this type of text was typical of an awardee's response.

On the *pan* inscription, the King's speech follows the eulogy. On the cauldrons, this speech follows immediately upon the reference to the cere-

---

[7] For the role of the *yin* 尹 and other scribes and officials, see Cook, "Scribes, Cooks, and Artisans."

[8] See Cook, "Education and the Way," 310; see also comments in the Introduction.

mony itself (not included in the *pan* inscription). In all three inscriptions, the King's speech begins in much the same way, suggesting a routine chant that ends with award or command details personalized for the occasion. First, the King speaks the name of gift-recipient before launching into his own eulogy of the Zhou founders and their creation of the state or possessing the Four Regions. For example, in the Forty-second Year Qiu *ding* inscription, the King says: "Qiu, the Greatly Manifest Wen and Wu took on the responsibility of receiving the Great Mandate and spreading it to the Four Regions, and since then your Former Sage Ancestor Deceased Father accompanied the illustrious former Kings, laboring for the Great Mandate and settling the Zhou state." Then, the King moves from the spirits eulogized from the Zhou ancestor to the awardee's ancestors, whose duties were being formally passed on to the awardee. Qiu directly takes on the roles of his father and grandfather (i.e. in battling the Xianyun), whom the King identifies as "sages" 聖人 on whom Qiu must continue to model himself (*xing* 型).

In each inscription, after Qiu performs the ritual of acceptance and gratitude to the King, he dedicates the sacrificial vessels to his own ancestors in order to receive their blessings. The ancestors are referred to variously as "my Brilliant Ancestors and Deceased Father," "Former Accomplished Ones" (*qian wenren* 前文人), and are sometimes named, for example, as "my Brilliant Deceased Father Gong Shu" (in the case of the Forty-third Year Qiu *ding*). As in many late Western Zhou inscriptions, the ancestors are described as "stern above, protective of those below" 嚴在上翼在下, while those below, the living descendants, go through the ritual of "gravely grasping the luminous *de*" 穆秉明德, the transmitted legacy of lineage prestige. Then the inscribed records break into onomatopoetic syllables, sets of reduplicative binomes, to describe the abundant nature and sounds of the "descent" *jiang* 降 of ancestral blessings for a healthy and wealthy long life, and endless progeny to continue the sacrifices into perpetuity.

Transcription

述曰：丕顯朕皇高祖單公，趄趄（桓桓）克明慎厥德，夾召（紹）文王、武王，達殷膺受天魯命，匍（敷）有四方，並宅厥堇（勤）疆土，用配上帝。

雩（越）朕皇高祖公叔克佐匹成王，成受大命，方狄（逖）不享，用

INSCRIPTIONS

奠四國（域）⁹ 萬邦。

雩（越）朕皇高祖新室仲，克幽明厥心，柔遠能邇，會召（紹）康王，方裹（懷）不庭。

雩（越）朕皇高祖叀（惠）仲盠父，盭龢于政，有成于猷，用會昭王、穆，盜（>到？）¹⁰ 政四方，撲伐楚荊。

雩（越）朕皇高祖零伯，炎（燅）明厥心，不墜□（厥？）服，用辟龔王、懿王。

雩（越）朕皇亞祖懿仲，往諫諫克匍（輔）保厥辟考（孝）王、夷王，有成于周邦。

雩（越）朕皇考龏叔，穆穆趩趩（翼翼），龢詢于政，明濟于德，享辟剌（烈>厲）¹¹ 王。

逨肇屍（徙）¹² 朕皇祖考服，虔夙夕敬朕死（尸）事。肆天子多錫逨休，天子其萬年無疆，耆（耇）黃耇，保奠周邦，諫辪（乂）四方。

王若諾曰：逨，丕顯文武，膺受大命，匍（敷）有四方，則繇（由）惟乃先聖祖考召（紹）先王，爵堇（勤）大命。今余惟經乃先聖祖考，䚄（申）就乃命，命汝疋（胥）榮兌，龏（兼？）嗣（司）吳（虞）四方林，用宮御。錫汝赤市幽黃（璜）、攸勒。

逨敢對天子丕顯魯休揚，用作朕皇祖考寶尊盤，用追享孝于前文

---

⁹ The earlier reference to the entire Zhou world was *si yu* 四域, which many scholars preferred to read as *si guo*, as found in this inscription (see Glossary), suggesting a clearly defined incorporated state structure rather than a more amorphous sounding "region." Since the Zhou lands presumably consisted of many more than four allied states, "region" is perhaps still more accurate.

¹⁰ Most scholars agree that the word *dao* 盜 (*dˤaw), meaning "to plunder," must be a loan for another word. Many suggest a modern homophone, such as *dao* 導 (*lˤuʔ), meaning "to guide." However, words that were closer phonetically in ancient times would include *dao* 到 (*tˤaw[k]-s) or *zhao* 朝 (*t<r>aw).

¹¹ The words represented by the graphs *lie* 烈 and *li* 厲 were originally near-homophones (*[r]at and *[r]at-s respectively).

¹² The reading as *xi* 徙 (*sajʔ) is supported if we understand that *xiao* 小 was added to *shi* 尸 (*l̥aj) to alert the reader to a different reading, a minority reading represented by the modern *sha* 沙 (*sˤraj) (小 and 少 were commonly exchanged). Alternatively we might read the graph as *shi* (*l̥aj), "to give, bestow." [CAC]. Qiu Xigui reads it as *zhuan* 篡, meaning "to succeed, to be selected," elaborating on Li Jiahao's 李家浩 earlier analysis. See Qiu Xigui, "Du Lai qi mingwen zhaji san ze" [MP].

人。前文人嚴在上，翼在[下]，豐豐彙彙（繹繹），降述魯多福，眉壽綽綰，受余康𥃟（娛）屯祐通祿，永命靈終。述眈（畯>俊）臣天子，子子孫孫永寶用享。

Translation

Qiu said: "Greatly Manifest! My Brilliant High Ancestor, the Patriarch of Shan—martial, so martial—was able to illuminate and be attentive to his *de* as an aide by the side of King Wen and King Wu. [King Wu] went as far as Yin and took on the responsibility of receiving Heaven's bountiful Mandate, and so spread it throughout the Four Regions, conquering settlements; they labored in the borderlands. With this action, King Wu matched the Deity Above's [pattern].

"Oh! My Brilliant High Ancestor, Patriarch the Younger, was able to aid and accompany King Cheng to complete his receipt of the Great Mandate, annexing and scattering those who did not offer memorial sacrifices. With this action, King Cheng settled the ten thousand states in the Four Territories.

"Oh! My Brilliant High Ancestor, New Chamber the Second, was able to make his heart both deep and luminous, weakening those far away and empowering those nearby; he joined King Kang as a helpmate, annexing and drawing in those who did not come to court.

"Oh! My Brilliant High Ancestor, Beneficence the Second, Father Li, who was diligent and harmonious in his governing campaigns, completing the [Zhou] plan; with this action, he, joined King Zhao and King Mu as a helpmate, extending the [Zhou] government to the Four Regions and pummeling the Chu-Jing peoples.

"Oh! My Brilliant High Ancestor, Elder Ling, made his heart blazing and luminous, not toppling the Mandate among those who have submitted; with this action, he aided King Gong and King Yi.

"Oh! My Brilliant Secondary-branch Ancestor, Yi the Second, forwarding proposals, was able to help protect his rulers, King Xiao and King Yi, bringing to completion the Zhou state.

"Oh! my Brilliant Deceased-Father Reverence the Younger—grave, so grave, protective, so protective (*m(r)iwk-m(r)iwk ɢ(r) əks-ɢ(r)əks)[13] —harmonious and fair in governing, luminous and dignified in [his] *de*, he presented offerings to and assisted King Li.

"I, Qiu, early on continued my Brilliant Ancestor Deceased Father's service and earnestly paid my respects from dawn to dusk in my duties as lineage representative. Thus, the Son of Heaven has given me, Qiu, many gifts. May the Son of Heaven have ten thousand years without limit to enjoy a hoary old age and to protect and settle the Zhou state, punishing and managing the Four Regions."

The King, agreeing [to Qiu's promotion], said: "Qiu, the Greatly Manifest Wen and Wu took on the responsibility of receiving the Great Mandate and spreading it to the Four Regions. From the beginning your Former Sage Ancestor Deceased Father accompanied the illustrious former Kings, laboring for the Great Mandate, so I will now, taking the model of your Former Sage Ancestor Deceased Father, extend your charge. I charge you to aid Rong Dui as well as to carry on supervising the Foresters and the woodland resources of the Four Regions for presentation at the palace. I award you crimson knee covers with a dark jade circlet, and horse reins."

I, Qiu, dared to respond to the Son of Heaven's greatly manifest bountiful gifts by extolling them and taking this opportunity to make for my Brilliant Ancestor Deceased Father a treasured basin for expressing reverence and to pursue pious behavior with sacrificial offerings to the Former Accomplished Ones. The Former Accomplished Ones are stern above and protective of those below—fruitful and mighty—they repeatedly send down to me, Qiu, bountiful fortune, extended longevity continuing on and on, and so I receive health, harmony, abundant blessings, continuous pay, eternal life without end. I, Qiu, serve the Son of Heaven as Chief Agriculturalist. May I have sons of sons and grandsons of grandsons to forever treasure and use this vessel.

---

[13] The meaning of the epithet 穆穆翼翼 is not certain; here, the best understanding is given. In this inscription, the word "to protect, protective" is spelled with 異, supporting its reconstruction as *ɢʷrək, which would create a closer rhyme with 穆 *m(r)iwk, "solemn, grave". The reconstruction of the word "wing > to shelter, to protect" is still unclear; see Baxter & Sager 2014: 107; 302–307; esp. 386 no. 30 [MP].

Further Reading

Chen Jian, *Jiaguwen kaoshi lunji,* 20-38.

Falkenhausen, "The Inscribed Bronzes from Yangjiacun."

Falkenhausen, "Royal Audience and Its Reflections."

Li Xueqin, *Wenwu zhong de guwenming,* 225–28.

Li Xueqin, *Zhongguo gudai wenming yanjiu,* 141–47.

Liu Shi'e, "Qiang pan, Lai pan zhi duibi yanjiu."

Sena, "Reproducing Society," 67–98.

Sena, "Arraying the Ancestors in Ancient China: Narratives of Lineage History in the 'Scribe Qiang' and 'Qiu' Bronzes."

"Shaanxi Meixian Yangjiacun Xi Zhou qingtongqi jiaocang."

Shaanxisheng kaogu yanjiusuo, *et al.,* "Shaanxi Meixian Yangjiacun Xi Zhou qingtongqi jiaocang fajue jianbao."

Shaughnessy, "The Writing of a Late Western Zhou Bronze Inscription."

Qiu Xigui, "Du Lai qi mingwen zhaji san ze," 74–76.

Qiu Xigui, "Bin Gong Xu mingwen kaoshi."

CAC

64. Shan Bo Hao Sheng ZHONG 單伯昊生鐘

An elder of the powerful and ancient Shan family was named Haosheng 昊生 (or Yisheng 睪生 according to some readings). While the precise date of this bell and identity of the Shan elder are not clear, we know that originally, there was a complete vessel set for a musical banquet (a late-style *dou* 豆 was known during the Song period but has since disappeared). The inscription is short and simple; it essentializes the core elements documenting that an heir (a *xiaozi*) has achieved enough merit to be promoted into the position of his ancestor (usually his deceased father). In each inscription of this sort, long or short, the ancestors are honored and testimony has to the emulation of their pattern of behavior given.

The use of "to say, to speak" (*yue* 曰) in the beginning phrase indicates that his inscription was a response to an award by the Zhou king. In this case, the he was eulogizing his ancestor's service to the Zhou kings and his own obedience to this pattern of "accumulated merit" (*de*) and subservience. He refers to himself by the self-deprecating "I, the Little One," a term that could also refer to an heir who had not completed mourning for his father. His sibling rank was *bo* "elder." In this case, Haosheng had clearly completed his mourning as he was also celebrating his own accession into the former role of his father. As with his ancestors, this role would involve military suppression of non-Zhou peoples, a requirement for "striving for the Great (or Heavenly) Mandate".[1] Rhetoric evoking the defense of the mandate would continue to be imitated by former Zhou allies, such as Qin and Jin, into the early Spring and Autumn period.

Transcription

單伯昊生曰：丕顯皇祖烈考，迷（仇）[2] 匹先王，爵堇（勤）大令（天命），余小子肇帥井（型）朕皇祖考懿德，用保奠。

Translation

Haosheng, Elder of Shan, said: "The Greatly Manifest Brilliant Ancestor Blazing Deceased Father paired himself with the Former Kings as an advisor to promote and strive for the Great Man-

---

[1] See Glossary.
[2] See Chen Jian, *Jiaguwen kaoshi lunji*, 25–26 [MP].

date. I, the Little One from the beginning followed and modeled myself on my Brilliant Ancestor and Deceased Father's refined *de*, and used it for protection and settling [the peoples]."

Further Reading
Jicheng 82.
Kimbun tsūshaku, 23.87–94.
Mingwen xuan, no. 235.

Chen Jian, *Jiaguwen kaoshi lunji*, 20–38.
Falkenhausen, *Suspended Music*, 44–45.
Sena, "Reproducing Society," 104–5.

CAC

65. Zha zhong 柞鐘

Discovered in 1960 in a hoard of bronze objects at Qijiacun 齊家村, Fufeng County, Shaanxi Province, near the Zhou royal residence on the Zhou Plain. The chime includes eight bells graduated in size from 52 to 21 cm in height. The four larger bells bear an identical inscription. Each of the smaller four bells bears one part of the same text. There are two symmetrical groups of nine bosses organized in rows of three on both sides of the vertical central panel and the intaglio design; they represent two confronted dragons with reversed heads on their lower striking areas. Such design makes the bells typical of the late Western Zhou.[1] The date indicated in the inscription corresponds to 779 B.C.E., the third year of the last Western Zhou ruler King You. In addition to Zha's bells, the Qijiacun hoard included thirty-eight other objects commissioned by various persons during the late Western Zhou period: one cooking tripod of Bo Bang Fu 伯邦父, two tureens of Zhong You Fu 仲友父, one steamer of Zhong Wo Fu 仲我父, eight bells, one plate and a ewer for washing hands of Zhong Yi Fu 仲義父, one tripod of Shu X Fu 叔 X 父, and two wine flasks of Ji Fu 季父. Some other objects were not inscribed.

It is possible that objects from the Qijiacun hoard constituted a sacrificial set commissioned collectively by brothers or cousins for their ancestral temple. As explained in the introduction to the Qiu *pan* inscription (no. 63, above), the terms *bo* 伯, *zhong* 仲, *shu* 叔, and *ji* 季 refer to the birth sequence of the members of a generation in a family or distinguish the seniority of branches in a lineage. In the present inscription, *zhong* 仲, part of the Great Captain's designation, is a kinship term of this kind. Zha, possibly a younger brother of the family or a member of a subordinated branch of the lineage that resided in Qijiacun, referred to his elder relative, who held the office of Great Captain at the royal court, using this kinship term. It is noteworthy that in several inscriptions from King Xuan's reign, Bo the Great Captain 伯大師 is mentioned (cf. Bo Ke *hu* 伯克壺, *Jicheng* 9725). Hence it is also conceivable that terms of lineage hierarchy could be used to designate the seniority of military officers, related or unrelated by blood.

Zha received the command to control the "Five Settlements" (*wu yi* 五邑), referred to elsewhere as the "Five Settlements of the Eastern Suburb"

---

[1] For the development of shank bells, see Falkenhausen, *Suspended Music*, 158ff., and So, *Eastern Zhou Ritual Bronzes from the Arthur M. Sackler Collections*, 436 and 444-47.

(*dong bi wu yi* 東鄙五邑), which were important settlements located to the east of the royal residence on the Zhou Plain. Zha was appointed to administer the Five Cities not by the Zhou king, but by another high official, who most probably was the appointee's relative. This reflects the growing autonomy of metropolitan aristocracy during the reign of King You.

Transcription

唯王三年四月初吉甲寅，仲大師右柞，柞易載（禕）、朱黃（璜）、䜌（鑾）。嗣（司）五邑佃（甸）人事。柞拜手對揚仲大師休。用乍大林鐘鈴。其子子孫孫永寶。

Translation

It was in the third year of the King, the fourth month, *chuji*, on *jiayin* day (*ganzhi* no. 51). *Zhong* the Great Captain accompanied Zha on his right-hand side. Zha was granted leather kneepads, vermillion pendants, and tinkling bells [for a banner]. He will administer the affairs of the people in the Five Settlements and their suburbs. Zha folded his hands and dared to extol in response the beneficence of *zhong* the Great Captain. I, Zha use this occasion to make this great chimed set of shank-bells and clapper-bells. May my sons and grandsons eternally use them as a treasure.

Further Reading

Jicheng 133–39.

Mingwen xuan, no. 454.

Chen Gongrou, "Ji Jifu hu, Zha zhong ji qi tongchu de tongqi."

Shaughnessy, *Sources of Western Zhou History*, 285.

Wang Hui, *Shang Zhou jinwen*, 270–72.

MKh

66. Qin Gong *bo* 秦公鎛, Qin Gong *gui* 秦公簋, and Qin Gong *yongzhong* 秦公甬鐘

Only a small number of known bronze inscriptions can be unambiguously attributed to the royal courts of the Eastern Zhou state of Qin. They all mention a "Lord of Qin" (Qin *gong* 秦公) as sponsor, albeit without specifying which particular ruler. During the reign of the Northern Song Emperor Renzong 仁宗 (r. 1022–1063 C.E.), a *bo*-bell, long since lost, appeared from an unknown place in Shaanxi; in 1919, a lidded *gui*-tureen was discovered west of Tianshui 天水, in modern Gansu; and in 1978, a set of five *yongzhong*-bells, together with another set of three *bo* bells, was found in Taigongmiaocun 太公廟村, Baoji County, in modern Shaanxi. While these vessels are the only Qin *gong* bronze artifacts to bear inscriptions of considerable length, a few more Qin *gong* bronze vessels with very brief inscriptions—simply identifying a Lord of Qin as their owner—have just recently become known: in 1993, a set of four *ding*-tripods and two *gui* tureens, inscribed with five characters on the *gui* and six on the *ding*, appeared on the Hong Kong antiquities market and is now in the Shanghai Museum. In 1994, a *hu*-vase, inscribed with six characters, was discovered in Li 禮 County in modern Gansu; and in 2008, a set of two *gui* and and another set of three *ding* vessels, each inscribed with six characters, was stated to be in the collection of Katherine and George Fan (Hu Yingying 胡盈瑩 and Fan Jirong 范季融). Finally, the longer Qin *gong* bronze inscriptions share structural features as well as a number of lines of text with a total of thirty-two fragments of apparently twenty-six chime stones that were part of at least three separate series of inscribed chime stones. These stones came to light during a multi-year excavation, concluded in 1986, of a large Qin tomb in Nanzhihuizhen 南指揮鎮, Fengxiang 鳳翔 County, Shaanxi Province.

The five *yongzhong* and three *bo* bells discovered in 1978 all bear a single text of 135 characters, which is inscribed five times: on the outside of each of the three *bo* bells and again running over one set of two, and another set of what originally were probably four *yongzhong* bells (of which three were found). The two practices of (a) repeating the same text on a series of objects and (b) spreading a text across several objects are both unexceptional and are attested with particular frequency on bells, which by their nature were regularly designed and cast in sets. Nearly half of the text on the *yongzhong* and *bo* bell sets, although with many variations of expression, can be identified with respective passages on the *bo* bell documented in Northern Song epigraphic catalogues as well as on the *gui* tureen; moreover, the inscriptions on these two objects seem to represent two versions of the same base text, with the *bo* inscription containing a longer version of 142 characters and the *gui* inscription—cast in full into the vessel and also into the lid—a shorter one of 104 characters.[1] All the inscriptions are rhymed and mostly follow the standard tetrasyllabic meter of *Shijing* poetry that gained increasing regularity in inscriptions from late Western Zhou times onwards. The same is true for the chime stones, which seem to comprise a base text of 122 characters that was repeated in at least three separate sets.

While the chime stones can be dated in the reign of Lord Jing of Qin 秦景公 (r. 576–537 B.C.E.), the dates of the bronze objects have been the subject of intense discussion. A tentative conclusion may be that both the *bo* bell and the *gui* tureen date from the reign of Lord Gong 共 (r. 608–604 B.C.E.) or Lord Huan 桓 (r. 603–577 B.C.E.), while the two sets of *bo* and *yongzhong* bells date from roughly a century earlier, namely, the reign of Lord Wu 武 (r. 697–678 B.C.E.). The bell sets were found at the site of the old Qin capital of Pingyang 平陽 (capital 714–677 B.C.E.); the other objects were discovered at a considerable distance from Pingyang, the closest being the location of the chime stones, some twenty kilometers farther north, that is, at the site of the subsequent Qin capital of Yong 雍 (capital 677–ca. 383 B.C.E.). The close intertextual relations between the earlier and the later inscriptions, together with the fact that the earlier bronzes were left behind at Pingyang when the capital was moved to Yong, suggest that the texts of the inscriptions were also preserved in another form, probably on archival stationery of bamboo or perhaps wood, and were taken to the new capital at Yong.

The textual and ritual continuity reflected in these inscriptions—evidence of a strong sense of tradition—does not end here. On the one hand, the *yongzhong* bells from around 700 B.C.E. are designed in an archaizing, almost atavistic, style that makes them indistinguishable from late Western Zhou bells; here, one may consider the fact that the state of Qin inherited the old Western Zhou homeland and its artistic traditions when the Zhou were driven eastward to re-establish themselves in 770 B.C.E. On the other hand, the *gui* tureen, in addition to its cast inscription, shows

---

[1] For issues regarding varying character counts, see Kern, *The Stele Inscriptions of Ch'in Shih-huang*, 76–77.

secondary inscriptions that were carved both on the lid and the vessel. Indicating the capacity of the tureen, these incised characters cannot predate the time of the Qin statesman Shang Yang 商鞅 (d. 338 B.C.E.) and are, in fact, believed to come from Qin imperial times (221–207 B.C.E.). Having been cast around 600 B.C.E., the *gui* vessel must thus have been kept at the Qin court for some three hundred, and possibly four hundred, years, testifying to the strength of Qin ritual traditionalism.

The traditional bent of the Qin bells and vessels is not limited to their design and their history of transmission. Both in form (observing the traditional features of rhyme and meter) and in content, the diction of their inscriptions is entirely in line with the mid- to late Western Zhou political and ritual idiom. In fact, unlike any other known bronze inscriptions of their time, they fully appropriate the prerogatives of royal Zhou rhetoric, claiming the Mandate of Heaven for the Qin Lord and explicitly placing both the Chinese realm (Xia 夏) and the regions of the non-Chinese "barbarians" (*man* 蠻) under his authority. Composed for the ancestral sacrifice, the Qin Gong inscriptions combine expressions of strong political and military power with deferential prayer toward the ancestors. Taken together, they furnish a unique political document from the Spring and Autumn period that lends expression to the aspirations of the rising state of Qin centuries before it succeeded in unifying the realm.

Transcription (*Qin Gong* bo)

秦公曰：丕顯朕皇祖。受天命，竃（奄）有下國。十有二公，不墜在上，嚴恭夤天命，保業厥秦，虩事蠻夏。曰：余雖小子，穆穆帥秉明德，叡敷明刑，虔敬朕祀，以受多福，協龢萬民，虎（吾）夙夕。剌剌（烈烈）桓桓，萬姓是敕。咸畜百辟胤士，䠗䠗（藹藹）文武。鋚（鎮）靜不廷，䰞（柔）燮百邦，于秦執事。作淑龢［鐘］，厥名曰䝁（協）邦。其音錝錝雝雝孔煌，以昭格孝享，以受屯魯多釐。眉壽無疆，畯疐在位，高引有慶，敷有四方，永寶。宜

Translation

The Lord of Qin said: "Greatly radiant are my august ancestors! They received the Mandate of Heaven and broadly possessed the state below. The twelve lords did not let it drop from their high position; solemn and reverential, in awe of the Mandate of Heaven, they have protected and ruled our state of Qin, cautiously caring for the Man and the Xia."[2]

He said: "Being a Little Son, I respectfully, respectfully obey and adhere to the shining virtuous power and brightly spread the clear punishments. I gravely and referentially perform my sacrifices to receive manifold blessings. In regulating and harmonizing the myriad people, I, from early morning to evening, act with valor and valor, awe and awe—the myriad clans, they are forced into discipline! I completely shield the hundred nobles and the hereditary officers; staunchly, staunchly they display my civilizing and martial power. I force and silence those who do not come to court; I mollify and order the hundred states so that they strictly serve the state of Qin."

"I have made these brightly harmonizing bells; their name is 'Regulating the State.' May their sound—*kˤrəj-kˤrəj q(r)oŋ-q(r)oŋ—be greatly clear to invoke [the ancestral spirits] to arrive at the sacrificial offerings, to give us accumulated happiness, multiple favors!"

"Extended longevity without limit—may the Lord [of Qin] long remain in his position! May his rewards be lofty and vast, and may he extensively possess the four quarters! May he forever treasure these bells!"

[Emblem?]

Transcription (*Qin Gong* gui)

秦公曰：丕顯朕皇祖。受天命，鼏（宓）宅禹蹟（蹟）。十有二公在帝之坏（坯），嚴恭夤天命，保業厥秦，虩事蠻夏。余雖小子，穆穆帥秉明德。剌剌（烈烈）桓桓，萬民是敕。咸畜胤士，䠽䠽（藹藹）文武。鎭（鎮）靜不廷，虔敬朕祀。作㝬（尋?）宗彞，以昭皇祖。嚴其徵格，以受屯魯多釐。眉壽無疆，畯疐在天（位?），高引有慶，寵（奄）有四方。宜

---

[2] In all three inscriptions, the division of the English translations into paragraphs follows the internal structure of the text that in most cases is marked by changes of rhyme. Based on the text on the *yongzhong* bells, I understand the voice of the final part in all three inscriptions to belong not to the Lord of Qin, but to either the ritual community present at the sacrifice or to the addressed ancestors who in response to the preceding prayer assure the Lord of Qin of his blessings. Thus I take these (and many other) inscriptions not as monologic or merely narrative but as to some extent reflecting the multivocal performances of the ancestral sacrifice.

Translation

The Lord of Qin said: "Greatly radiant are my august ancestors! They received the Mandate of Heaven and secured their residence within the realm of the merits of Yu. The twelve lords reside in the lofty heights of the Gods. Solemn and reverential, in awe of the Mandate of Heaven, they have protected and ruled our state of Qin, cautiously caring for the Man and the Xia.

"Being a Little Son, I respectfully, respectfully obey and adhere to the shining virtuous power. Through valor and valor, awe and awe—the myriad folk, they are forced into discipline! I completely shield the hereditary officers; staunchly, staunchly they display my civilizing and martial power. I force and silence those who do not come to court; I gravely and respectfully perform my sacrifices.

"I have made this vessel for the temple of (?), to invoke the august ancestors. May they solemnly and austerely arrive to give us accumulated happiness, multiple favors!

"Extended longevity without limit—may the Lord of Qin long remain in his position! [3] May his rewards be lofty and vast, and may he broadly possess the four quarters!"

[Emblem?]

Transcription (*Qin Gong* yongzhong)

秦公曰：我先祖受天命，商（賞）宅受域。剌剌（烈烈）昭文公、靜公、憲公，不墜于上。昭合皇天，以虩事蠻方。公及王姬曰：余小子，余夙夕虔敬朕祀，以受多福。克明有心，䮾（戾）龢胤士，咸畜左右。䓁䓁（藹藹）允義，翼受明德，以康奠協朕域，盜（道）百蠻，具即其服。作厥龢鐘，靈音鍺鍺雔雔，以宴皇公，以受大福，屯魯多釐，大壽萬年。秦公其畯令在位，膺受大命。眉壽無疆，敷有四方，其康寶。

Translation

The Lord of Qin said: "My ancestors of old received the Mandate of Heaven, were rewarded with a residence and received the territory. Valorous, valorous were the brilliant Lord Wen, Lord Jing,

---

[3] The inscription clearly says *zai tian* 在天, but we emend this to *zai wei* 在位 in conformity with the other texts in the series.

and Lord Hui, who did not let the Mandate drop from their high position.

Brilliantly they acted in accordance with august Heaven cautiously to care for the regions of the Man."

The lord, together with his royal wife, said: "Being the little son, from morning to evening gravely and respectfully I perform my sacrifices to receive manifold blessings. I greatly clarify my indulgent mind, restrain and harmonize the hereditary officers, and completely shield those to the left and to the right. Staunchly, staunchly, with true propriety, they reverently receive the shining virtuous power; they consolidate and regulate my territory for long, govern the hundred Man, and let them all take up their duties."

"I have made these harmonizing bells with their numinous sound (*kˤrəj-kˤrəj q(r)oŋ-q(r)oŋ) to delight the august lords, to make them give us great blessings, accumulated happiness, multiple favors!"

"Great longevity for myriad years! May the Lord of Qin for long remain in his position, receiving and obtaining the great Mandate. May he have extended longevity without limit and extensively possess the Four Quarters! Long may he keep and treasure these bells!"

Further Reading

Jicheng 262–70 (Qin Gong *yongzhong* and Qin Gong *bo*), 4315 (Qin Gong *gui*).

Kimbun tsūshaku, 34.1–34, 50.399–409, 54.109–11 and 180–81.

Mingwen xuan, nos. 917–18 (Qin Gong *yongzhong*), 919 (Qin Gong *bo*), 920 (Qin Gong *gui*).

Falkenhausen, "Ahnenkult und Grabkult im Staat Qin," 38–39.

Kern, *The Stele Inscriptions of Ch'in Shih-huang*, 59–105.

Mattos, "Eastern Zhou Bronze Inscriptions," 111–20.

Wang Hui, *Qin tongqi mingwen biannian jishi*, 13–32 and plates 8–16.

Wang Hui, *Shang Zhou jinwen*, 272–76.

MKe

67. Rong Sheng BIANZHONG 戎生編鐘

These eight bells, which are graduated in size, were purchased on the Hong Kong antiquities market in the 1990s and are presently in the collection of the Beijing Poly Museum. Each bell bears part of a continuous inscription that totals 155 words. The bells are decorated with two symmetrical groups of nine bosses that are organized in rows of three on both sides of the vertical central panel, as well as with confronted curled dragons with reversed heads, cast intaglio on the lower striking areas. As such, they display typical features of the late Western Zhou ornamental style. Recent discoveries of bells dating to the Spring and Autumn period, including Qin Gong *yongzhong* and Zifan *bianzhong* (nos. 66 and 70), demonstrate that *bianzhong* were still in use well after the end of the Western Zhou, especially in the western and northern states. The inscription on the Rong Sheng *bianzhong* also suggests an eighth-century date.

The Rong 戎 in the commissioner's name may suggest his relation to the Rong, i.e. non-Zhou, peoples. His ancient ancestor Patriarch Xian 憲, first glorified in the inscription, was charged by King Mu of Zhou to govern other non-Zhou neighbors, called Man and Rong, in an "external land" (*waitu* 外土), i.e. in the area outside of the direct control of the Zhou state. King Mu's policy of choosing and favoring the most trustworthy rulers of alien polities in order to keep the others calm with their support is also reflected in later literary sources.

Rong Sheng's father, Elder Zhao 昭伯, "assisted and joined" (*zhaopi* 召/韶匹) Wen Hou 文侯 (780–746 B.C.E.), the ruler of Jin,[1] in what is defined as "making the King's commands be respected," possibly referring to the re-establishment of the power of the Zhou royal court after its relocation to its eastern residence, Chengzhou, in 770 B.C.E.. The word *pi* 匹, used in this inscription as a verb ("to join") and referring to the relationships between Rong Sheng's father and Jin Wen Hou, signifies "pair," "companion," "equal," "mate," and even "sexual partner" as a noun. Its choice indicates that Elder Zhao had a status comparable to that of Jin Wen Hou—ruler of a small but autonomous polity. *Pi* could refer just to a political alliance, but, on the other hand, because of its sexual connotations, it could also refer to a marital alliance between Jin and Rong, achieved, for example, by

---

[1] This is not the same person as the more famous Lord Wen of Jin (671–628 B.C.E.), who bore the same posthumous name.

exchange of younger sisters, female cousins, or daughters.

The existence of such marital alliance is also suggested by the usage of the graph *sheng* 生 in Rong Sheng's name. It stands in a number of Western Zhou bronze inscriptions for the kinship term that is more fully written as *sheng* 甥. *Sheng* is one of the most complicated Chinese kinship terms, as it could designate several kinds of male relatives to which a male individual was related via females, including his maternal male cousin, his brother-in-law (wife's brother or sister's husband), and his sister's or daughter's son. It could even be applied to female relatives, particularly to a man's sister's daughter.[2] In sum, under the conditions of socially defined, patrilineal kinship, the term *sheng* was used to designate various affinal relatives. Considering that no other bells commissioned by female sponsors are currently known, it is more plausible that Rong Sheng was male. By calling himself a sheng from Rong, he emphasized his status as a relative of the ducal house of Jin, to which he himself apparently served.

Rong Sheng participated in the war against Fantang 繁湯 (later known as Fanyang 繁陽), a non-Zhou polity in the Huai 淮 River valley in present-day Xincai 新蔡 County, Henan Province, referring to it in almost the same words as the inscription on the Jin Jiang *ding* 晉姜鼎 (no. 68, below). Like Lady Jiang of Jin, the spouse of Jin Wen Hou, Rong Sheng was given a large amount of salt created by evaporating spring water (*lu* 滷). The Duchy of Jin controlled the only salt reservoir available in the entire middle Yellow River region, the Hedong Salt Lake in southwestern Shanxi province near Yuncheng 運城, from the late Western Zhou onwards.[3] Salt was hence one of the most valuable local products of Jin. In view of the fact that the gift of salt was granted in connection with the war against Fantang, it may have been used as a means to induce the rulers of other polities to join the campaign or grant passage through their territories. In Fantang, famous for its bronze trade and craftsmanship, Rong Sheng captured "its auspicious metal," which he used for casting this set of chime bells.

---

[2] Cf. Xu Chaohua, *Erya jinzhu*, 155–65 ("Shi qin" 釋親). For Chinese kinship terminology and its changes over time see also also Feng, "The Chinese Kinship System," 185–91; Kryukov, *Sistema rodstva kitaĭtsev*, 150–203.

[3] For the history of salt production in this area starting from the Paleolithic period with a reference to the Rong Sheng *bianzhong* inscription, see Li and Chen, "Cities and Towns: The Control of Natural Resources in Early States, China," 9–13.

Transcription

惟十月乙亥。戎生(甥)曰：休辝(台)皇祖憲公，趩趩(桓桓)趯趯(翼翼)，啟厥明心，廣至(經)其猷，越(臧)爯穆天子肅霝(靈)，用建于茲外土，遹嗣(司)蠻戎，用榦不庭方。至于辝(台)皇考卲(昭)伯。趩趩(還還)穆穆，懿肅不朁(僭)，召(詔)匹晉侯，用龏(恭)王命。今余弗叚(假)灋(廢)其顈(顯)光！對揚其大福。劼(嘉)遣滷責(積)，俾譖(燼)征繁湯，取厥吉金。用作寶協鐘。厥音雖雖、鎗鎗鍢鍢、袞袞鵱鵱、既龢(和)叡(且)盉(淑)。余用卲追孝于皇祖皇考，用祈綽眉壽。戎生(甥)其萬年無疆，黃老又耄畯保。其子孫永寶用。

Translation

It was in the eleventh month, on *yihai* day (*ganzhi* no. 12). Rong Sheng said: "Blessed was my august ancestor Patriarch Xian! Martial and reverent, he opened his enlightened heart. Far-reaching and thorough were his plans. He greatly relied on the ... divine power of the Son of Heaven Mu in order to establish himself in this external land so as to govern over Man and Rong, in order to deal with the countries that did not pay court. His line lasted until my august Deceased Father, Elder Zhao. Dexterous and reverent, admirably ... and not going beyond what is proper, he welcomed and joined my[4] Lord of Jin in order to make everyone abide by the King's orders. Now I do not corrupt and harm his illustrious glory! I respond to this great blessing! I was luckily given a pile of spring salt, and so exterminated and punished Fantang. I took their auspicious metal and used it to make the treasured chime of bells.[5] Their sounds are *q(r)oŋ-q(r)oŋ tsʰˤaŋ-tsʰˤaŋ toŋ-toŋ ʔˤəj-*ʔˤəj kˤrəj-kˤrəj, very harmonious and fine! I use them to welcome and to express piety to my august ancestors and my august Father, and to pray for longevity. May Rong Sheng last ten thousand years without limit, even to hoary old age and older, and will long be

---

[4] "My" here suggests that both Rong Sheng and his father assisted the same ruler of Jin, i.e. Jin Wen Hou.

[5] The last sentence parallels the inscription on the Jin Jiang *ding* (no. 68, below).

under the protection of the ancestors. May my sons and grandsons eternally use and treasure these bells.

Further Reading

Barnard, *Inscriptions*, v. 3, 1867–1924.
Li Xueqin, "Rong Sheng bianzhong lunshi."
Liu Yu and Lu Yan, *Jinchu Yin Zhou jinwen jilu*, I, 41–43.
Ma Chengyuan, "Rong Sheng zhong de tantao."

MKh

68. Jin Jiang DING 晉姜鼎

According to the Song-dynasty catalogue *Kaogu tu* 考古圖, published in 1092, the Jin Jiang cauldron came from Hancheng 韓城 (eastern Shaanxi Province, near the border with Shanxi) and was in the collection of one Mr. Liu of Linjiang 臨江. The hand-drawn illustration depicts a round three-legged cauldron with upraised loop handles and two registers of décor around the belly and monster-mask décor at the top of each leg. Generally, modern scholars use the brush copy published in 1144 in the Southern Song catalogue *Lidai zhong ding yiqi kuanzhi* 歷代鐘鼎彝器款識, rather than the earlier woodcut. Song scholars suggested that it was the widow of Lord Wen of Jin (r. 780–746 B.C.E.) who cast this cauldron. She may have originally come from the state of Qi, since her name marks her as a woman of the Jiang lineage, although it is likely that other Jiang lineage branches existed closer to Jin than the Shandong peninsula, where Qi was located; this is because Jiang women were routinely chosen as royal Zhou brides (see the Yu *ding*, no. 16, above).

Lord Wen's close cooperation with the displaced Zhou kings (he killed one Zhou contender and helped enthrone another, King Ping) benefited the Jin state. Jin Jiang brags to the Jin ancestors about the number of people who pay tribute to Jin. Scholars argue whether Lord Wen was or was not still alive at the time when this bronze vessel was cast. From the rhetoric used, it would seem that the matriarch was running the state, much as, perhaps, her mother-in-law had done before. (Wen Hou's son, Zhao Hou 昭侯, reigned only six years.) The local queen drew upon a legacy of queens, particularly Jiang-lineage brides of Zhou rulers, who ran the state after their ruler-husbands had died. Their continuation of the ruler-husband's mandate to create an ever-expanding economic network of allied and suppressed peoples copied the Zhou plan or mandate. Similar expressions can be found in other Spring and Autumn period inscriptions cast in the states of Jin and Qin, which were adjacent to each other on either side of the southward flowing section of the Yellow River (between Shaanxi and Shanxi).

Although the inscription has many rhetorical formulas recognizeable from late Western Zhou inscriptions, it employs many phrases and words that can be found in other Spring and Autumn, even Warring States, inscriptions. Although there is no mention of the Zhou king, evidence of a continued Jin allegiance to the Zhou after its fall in 771 B.C.E. includes adherence to the Zhou calendar and the fact that they title their ruler a "warrior lord" (*hou* 侯). The Jin maintained this alliance with the defunct Zhou state and King until its own demise in 349 B.C.E.

Transcription

唯王九月乙亥，晉姜曰：余唯嗣朕先姑君晉邦。余不叚（暇）妄寧經離明德。宣邲（畢）我猷，用召匹（弼）辪（台）辟。每（敏）揚厥光烈，虔不墜。魯覃京師，辪（乂）我萬民，嘉遣我賜鹵賁（積）千兩。勿灋（廢）文侯顆（顯）令，俾貫通弘征繁陽、雕，取厥吉金。用作寶尊鼎。用康柔綏懷遠邇君子。

晉姜祈綽綰眉壽。作憲（至）為極萬年無疆。用享用德，眈（畯＞俊）保其孫子三壽是利。

Translation

It was in the ninth month, on *yihai* day (*ganzhi* no. 12), of the King's [regnal year] that Jin Jiang said: "I have succeeded my Former Aunt (mother-in-law) to rule the Jin state. I am neither lax nor disruptive, but have maintained a fine and luminous *de*. Our plan has been gloriously completed, and thereby we summon divine aid to our leader. Assiduously extolling his radiant blazing aspect, we do not let the Mandate fall. At Lu, Tan, and Jing encampments, we govern our myriad peoples, who celebrate and send us gifts valued at a thousand *liang* of millet ale. Not wasting Lord Wen's continued mandate, we made continuous penetrating and vast assaults on Fanyang and Yuan (?) to take their auspicious metal, which we have used to make a treasured cauldron for expressing reverence and took the opportunity to pacify, weaken, tranquilize, and embrace rulers both near and far."

I, Jin Jiang, pray to have continuous extended longevity. Make it culminate to the point that I have ten thousand years without end. I take this opportunity and the cauldron to offer mortuary sacrifices to the ancestors and to express my *de* and so enable ancestral protection and so that we may have sons of grandsons, and the Three Long-lived Ones may thus provide benefits.

Further Reading
Jicheng 2826.
Mingwen xuan, no. 885.

Barnard, *Inscriptions*, v. 1, 361–72.
Cao Zhaolan, *Jinwen yu Yin Zhou nüxing wenhua*, 238–41.
Chen Lianqing, "'Jin Jiang ding' jiankao."
Li Xueqin, *Eastern Zhou and Qin Civilizations*, 37–39.

CAC

69. Shu Yi *bo* 叔夷鎛 and Shu Yi *zhong* 叔夷鐘

Ten bells, out of what may have originally been several sets of bells, were apparently found by peasants plowing near the ancient capital Linzi 臨淄 of the ancient state of Qi (on Shandong Peninsula) in 1123. There are slight differences in the wording among different copies of the inscriptions, particularly between the hanging-bell (*bo* 鎛) and chime-bell (*zhong* 鐘) versions, but since the bells themselves no longer exist and the inscriptions have been preserved in hand copies only, little else can be understood about the sets.

The inscriptions, by Shu Yi 叔夷, an elite member of the Qi ruling family during the late Spring and Autumn period, describe events that took place during the reign of Lord Ling 靈公 (581–554 B.C.E.). Whether the bells were cast during that time period or the subsequent reign of Lord Zhuang 莊公 (553–548 B.C.E.) is a matter of debate. The inscription's style, length, and word choice hark back to the second half of the Western Zhou and can be compared with the Mao Gong *ding* and the Qiu *pan* (nos. 55 and 63, above) by its clear literary and ceremonial continuity. There are no other late Spring and Autumn period inscriptions that document the gift-giving and response eulogies of patron and awardee that were so common in the second half of the Western Zhou. In this inscription, the announcements by the ruler were marked with the written sign for oral speech, *yue* 曰, whereas the awardee's responses were not, hence indicating not only the difference in status but also that the ruler's speech might be considered quotes within Shu Yi's narrative. The sounds of the bells themselves were also marked with a *yue*, suggesting that the music of the bells were considered voices as well as the media through which the merits of the speakers were announced to the ancestors and through which the ancestors spoke.

A major difference between Western Zhou and this Qi inscription lies in the lineage allegiances eulogized by Shu Yi. Although the Qi inscription mentioned "the King," it was only as part of the introductory dating formula. Clearly, the Qi, like the Jin, followed the Zhou calendar. Also, the ruler did not take the title of King but that of *hou*, a border-protecting lord loyal to the Zhou king. But all mention of connections to the Zhou ends there, despite Qi's longterm engagement with the Zhou and its attempt during the early Spring and Autumn to be its protector in the form of "hegemon" (*ba* 霸) over the former Zhou tribute network. In another formulaic break with Zhou practice, the eulogy to Shu Yi's ancestors and their role in state formation was placed at the end of the inscription. Even more starkly variant is the fact that Shu Yi recalled his lineage history through the rise of Shang and the Shang founder's conquest over the Xia, an event even more mythical and distant than the Zhou conquest over the Shang. It would seem that the Qi adapted the Zhou ceremony and rhetoric to legitimate a non-Zhou identity and an even more ancient authority than the Zhou founder kings, one preserved in local historical traditions on the Shandong Peninsula.

This Qi inscription includes many unique expressions found only on late Western Zhou inscriptions, such as the word represented by 黻 (and many variants, see no. 46, note 4). The language of the inscription, while including many archaic phrases, was also updated. One noticeable example is the liberal use of the causative *bi* 俾 (see also the Jin Jiang *ding*, no. 68, above) at the beginning of phrases similar to those found in the transmitted *Shi* texts and common in eastern inscriptions of the Spring and Autumn period. The Qi inscription uses reduplicated sets of words, such as *hehe* 赫赫 and *jiejie* 嗜嗜, to indicate the musicality of the performance. These sets continue oral formulas used in the earlier Qin and Jin inscriptions. The Qi inscription also shows innovation. The earlier expression *yongyong* 雖雖 was replaced by *yuyu* 譽譽 (also 與與), a northeastern expression found also in the *Lunyu*, and similar in usage to *yiyi* 翼翼, which is found in southern Spring and Autumn inscriptions and in the *Shijing*. In each case, the focus is on describing a thunderous and awe-inspiring music or dance with martial movements, with the power to unify the participants.

The musical ceremony celebrating Shu Yi's promotion during an ancestor worship ritual also reflects earlier Zhou practices and social structure. According to the *Shijing* ("Jianxi" 簡兮, Mao 38), his peers would have pranced like tigers in a dance involving a "thunderous" 赫 performance with flutes and feather-costumes while the Patriarch announced, "Award the promotions!" 錫爵. Shu Yi, like many elite heirs in similar ceremonies documented during the second half of the Western Zhou, was charged with protecting his ruler. In the Shi Ke *xu* 師克盨 and Mao Gong *ding* (no. 55, above) inscriptions, the guard composed of these elite men was called the Tiger Servants (*hu chen* 虎臣), and in many other inscriptions of the same time period, a common gift was a chariot cover made out of tiger skin lined in pale red. (See the Da Ke *ding* and related inscriptions, no. 46, above.)

Despite the evidence of Qi's literary debt to Zhou and the tendency of bronze inscriptions to retain archaic speech generally, the Shu Yi bell inscription is a clear representative of its time. As in Western Zhou inscriptions, the ruler's speeches include praise for the awardee's faithful adherence to his ancestral pattern and his success at war as well as his renewed charges and gifts. But unlike the Western Zhou concern with settling the Four Regions, the Patriarch is more concerned with controlling his own people. Also, unlike earlier Western Zhou leaders of Tiger Guards who were charged with protecting the lineage leader's person, Shu Yi had much broader responsibilities involving religious and military affairs inside and outside of the palace.

Transcription

唯王五月辰在戊寅，師于淄陲。

公曰：汝尸（夷），余經乃先祖，余既尃（傅）乃心。汝少（小）心畏忌；汝不墜，夙夜，宦執而政事。余引猒（厭）乃心。余命汝政于朕三軍，肅成朕師旟之政德，諫罰朕庶民，左右母（毋）諱。

尸（夷）不敢弗憨戒，虔卹厥死（尸）事，毀穌三軍徒遞，雩（越）厥行師，旾（慎）中厥罰。

公曰：尸（夷），汝敬共（龔）辝（台）命，汝膺㝬（歷）公家，汝𨟭褮（勞）朕行師，汝肇敏于戎攻，余賜汝釐（萊）都密劇（膠），其縣三百，余命汝嗣（司）辝（台＞以）釐（萊），㚘（陶）戜（城？）徒四千，為汝敵寮。

尸（夷）敢用拜稽首，弗敢不對揚朕辟皇君之登屯厚乃命。

汝尸（夷）母（毋）曰：余少子；汝尃（傅）余于艱卹（恤），賜休命。

公曰：尸（夷），汝康能乃又（有）事，遜乃敵寮。余用虔卹不易，左右余人。余命汝裁（職）差（佐）正卿，為大事，毀（兼？）命于外內之事，中尃（敷）盟（明）井（刑＞型？），以尃（傅）戒公家。膺卹（恤）余于盟（明）卹（恤），汝以卹（恤）余朕身。余賜汝馬車戎兵，釐（萊）僕三百又五十家，汝以戒戎作。

尸（夷）用或敢再拜稽首，膺受君公之賜光，余弗敢灋（廢）乃命，尸（夷）典其先舊及其高祖，虩虩（赫赫）成唐，又敢在帝所，尃（敷）受天命，削伐夏后，敗厥靁（靈）¹ 師，伊少（小）臣唯輔，咸有九州，處禹之堵。

丕顯穆公之孫，其配襄公之妣，而成公之女，雩（越）生叔尸夷，是辟于齊侯之所，是少（小）心恭齍，虩（靈）力若虎，堇（勤）裵（勞）其政事，又（有）共（功）于桓武靁（靈）公之所。

桓武霝（靈）公賜尸（夷）吉金鈇鎬，玄鏐鋘鋁。尸（夷）用作鑄其寶鐘，用享于其皇祖、皇妣、皇母、皇考，用旂眉壽，霝（靈）命難老，丕顯皇祖，其作福元孫，其萬福屯魯，龢協而又事，俾若鐘鼓，外內剀辟²，鍺鍺（喈喈）辥辥（嚶嚶），達而俯梟，母（毋）或承類。汝考壽萬年永保其身，俾百斯男而埶（設）斯字（子），肅肅義政，齊侯左右，母（毋）疾母（毋）已，至于世，曰武、霝（靈）、成。

子孫永保用享。

Translation

It was in the King's fifth month, when the *chen* was in *mouyin* (*ganzhi* no. 15), that the army went to the bank of the Zi River.

The Patriarch said: "You, Yi: I have taken your Former Ancestor(s) as a model, and successfully garnered your loyalty. You behave carefully and with trepidation; you do not allow the mandate to fall as you work from dawn to dusk to serve me and manage your governmental affairs. I have your unwearying loyalty. I command you to govern my three armies, speedily displaying a governing *de* in our armies, remonstrating and punishing our common peoples so that none, either on the left or the right, oppose me."

---

[1] This is an unusual way to write the word *ling* 靈. Because this inscription is preserved in a hand-written copy and the inscription elsewhere uses the more typical simplified form 霝, we will never know if the insertion of a tortoise image 龜 over fire 火 into the graph was original or not. If it was original, we might conclude that the "numinous" aspect accorded these ancestral spirits was also associated with divination.

[2] Some read these two words as the common Han-period binome *kaipi* 開闢, meaning "to devolop land for farming" or "to open, to separate," as in Heaven from Earth.

I, Yi, do not dare not to be respectful and circumspect; reverent and caring in taking over affairs (from my predecessor), I brought the soldiers of the three armies and those of the traveling army together in harmony and fitted punishments to their [crimes].

The Patriarch said: "Yi, out of respect for my command, you took responsibility over managing my house. You reined in my traveling army and made it functional. You initiated military attacks with valor. I award you the cities of Lai, Mi, Jiao, and three hundred of their appended communities. I command you to supervise my Lai holdings, and take four thousand foot soldiers from Tao City (?) for your ranked officers."

I, Yi, dare to take this opportunity to clap my hands in prayer and knock my head in obeisance. I do not dare not to respond and extol the ascendant munificent wealth of your mandate, Sovereign Brilliant Lord.

The Patriarch said: "You, Yi, did not [use the excuse and] say 'I am but a youth,'[3] but tutored me with restraint and care, wherefore I have awarded you gifts and a charge."

The Patriarch said: "You, Yi, peacefully and capably handled your duties and your ranked officers. I relied on your respectful care and unchanging loyalty, and you acted as an aid to me, the Only One. I commanded you to take on the position of associate governing minister for all major affairs, and, in addition, take on the duties of the inner and outer realms [of the royal house]. Correct our behavior and teach the Luminous Model,[4] teaching my household the proper proscriptions. You took on the responsibility of caring for how I performed the luminous rites and you made those rites work for my benefit. I award you horses, chariots, a militia, and three hundred and fifty households of Lai servants for you to use in equipping military activities."

I, Yi, take this opportunity to clap my hands together and knock my head on the ground repeatedly in honor of receiving the Lord Patriarch's awarded glory. I dare not discard your mandate as I, Yi, take as law that the way of the Former Old One and

---

[3] Possibly this refers to the fact that the period of mourning rituals for Shu Yi's father was not officially over before he took over his role as tutor for the Qi ruler and family.

[4] Ritual law as handed down from the ancestors.

High Ancestor—who with thunderous sounds, Oh, Cheng Tang, who dares to reside with the Deity!—received Heaven's Mandate and cut down the Lord of Xia, defeating his numinous army. With Young Minister Yin acting as aide, Cheng Tang then occupied the entire Nine Continents, residing in Yu's capital.

The grandson of the Greatly Manifest Patriarch Mu took as his mate the niece of Patriarch Xiang, who was the daughter of Patriarch Cheng, and who thereupon gave birth to me, Shu Yi. It is I, this Shu Yi, who manages the residence of the Lord of Qi and who cautiously advances with reverent steps and the numinous power of a tiger. I diligently labored in his government, behaving with complete reverence in the residence of the Majestic and Martial Patriarch Ling.

The Majestic and Martial Patriarch Ling awarded me, Yi, auspicious metals: smooth greenish, dark shiny, and grey hard metals. I, Yi, used them to make and cast these precious bells for use during mortuary feasts for Brilliant Ancestor, Brilliant Ancestress, Brilliant Mother, and Brilliant Deceased-father, in order to pray for an extended long life, a numinous fate in which it will be hard to age.

Greatly Manifest Brilliant Ancestors! May they send good fortune to their primary grandson; may they send such a multitude of good fortune and wealth that all affairs are unified in harmony and, just like the sounds of the bells, spread happiness throughout the inner and outer [realms of the royal house]. Harmonious! Respectful! The sounds of the bells reach them, your ranked aides and all of those who offer sacrifices. Your Aged and Long-Lived Ones shall then send down ten thousand years of life and riches, eternally protect those people of the royal household, and cause their males to number two hundred and all their sons to be set up with ranks and lands. Somberly! Somberly! May those who righteously govern, positioned to the left and right of the Protector Lord of Qi, be without affliction and no end, so throughout generations they can say: "Martial! Numinous! Accomplished!"

May sons and grandsons eternally protect the bells and use them in offering mortuary feasts.

Further Reading

Jicheng 272–85.

Mingwen xuan, nos. 847–48.

Chen Mengjia, "Shu Shi zhong bo kao."

Cook, "Auspicious Metals and Southern Spirits," 226–35.

Cook, "Scribes, Cooks, and Artisans," 242–50.

Doty, "The Bronze Inscriptions of Ch'i," 245–384.

Falkenhausen, "Ritual Music in Bronze Age China," 683, 696–707.

Falkenhausen, *Suspended Music*, 25–32, 99–101.

Hsu, "The Spring and Autumn Period," 553–56.

Li, *Eastern Zhou and Qin Civilizations*, 130–31.

CAC

70. Zifan *bianzhong* 子犯(犯)編鐘

Twelve bells dating from the early Spring and Autumn surfaced in October 1994 in the hands of a Hong Kong antiquities dealer. Further investigation established that three more bells from the same set had been acquired by a private collector in Taiwan. Together, the fifteen bells form a near-complete set of *bianzhong*, or suspended bells of differing pitches. The original set would have consisted of two matched series of eight bells, now designated simply as Set A and Set B. All eight bells presumed to belong to Set A are currently on display at the National Palace Museum in Taipei, together with the first, third, and fourth bells from Set B; the whereabouts of the second bell from this set are unknown, while the fifth through eighth bells remain in a private collection. The bells were looted from a tomb in Shanxi Province, in an area belonging to the state of Jin. Dubbed the Zifan *bianzhong* (or *hezhong* 和鐘), after the man who commissioned them and whose exploits they celebrate, the bells immediately attracted intense scholarly attention. As one of only a few intact matched sets of bells in the Western Zhou style, the Zifan *bianzhong* are very important from the perspective of art history and musicology. Of even greater significance, however, are the serial inscriptions on the bells, which document events surrounding the momentous battle of Chengpu 城濮 in 632 B.C.E., which established the state of Jin as the hegemonic power in north China and brought an abrupt halt to the northward expansion of the powerful southern state of Chu. In particular, the Zifan *bianzhong* inscriptions precisely confirm details of the epic confrontation and of the ascendancy of Jin to hegemonic status recounted in the fourth century B.C.E. narrative histories *Zuozhuan* and *Guoyu*.

The inscriptions on the Zifan *bianzhong* celebrate the achievements of Zifan (otherwise known as Hu Yan 狐偃), uncle, mentor, and chief political strategist of the famous Lord Wen of Jin (697–628 B.C.E.; otherwise known as Chong'er 重耳). Despite spending nineteen years in exile following his half-brother's elevation in Jin, Chong Er ultimately was restored to his state with Zifan's help in 636. The climax of Duke Wen's ascendancy was marked by his victory over Chu in 632, which led to his being confirmed as hegemon (*ba*) by the Zhou king. The inscriptions on the bells commemorate Zifan's leading role in these momentous events, as well as gifts awarded to him in an audience with the Zhou king shortly after the Battle of Chengpu, including the bronze used to cast the bells, donated by the lords of allied states.

The Zifan *bianzhong* is dated in terms of the Zhou royal calendar—"the King's fifth month, *chuji*, *dingwei* day" (which corresponds to April 19, 632 B.C.E.)—the same date recorded in *Zuozhuan* for the award ceremony hosted by the Zhou king. The fact that modern reconstructions of the calendar show that the *dingwei* day of the fifth month of 632 B.C.E. was either the tenth or eleventh day of the month shows that *chuji* did not refer exclusively to the first lunar quarter. (Feng Shi and Li Xueqin both argue for a date sometime after 632.)

The only serious obstacle to a serial reading of the inscriptions arises from the fact that the inscriptions on the second and third bells of Set A appear to be out of sequence. Qiu Xigui proposed that the two be read in reverse order, as presented here in the following transcription and translation. Another possibility is that the second bell actually belongs to Set B, in which case the issue might finally be resolved with the publication of the second bell, whose whereabouts are unknown. Within the text itself, there is one character whose reading remains a cipher. The inscription on the second bell begins as follows: "Great Chu lost its armies and destroyed its [?]." The last, crucial character remains undeciphered, though a leading interpretation takes the phrase to be a reference to the demise of Prime Minister Zi Yu 子玉 of Chu, who had instigated the confrontation with Jin and commanded the Chu armies.

Transcription

唯王五月初吉丁未，子犯佑晉公左右，來復其邦。者（諸）楚荊不聖（聽）令（命）于王所。子犯及晉公率西之六師，搏伐楚荊，孔休。

大攻楚荊，喪厥師，滅厥禹（渠）。子犯佑晉公左右，燮者（諸）侯得朝王。克奠王立（位）。王賜子犯輅車四、衣常（裳）、緇巿（韍）、佩（珮）。者（諸）侯羞元金于子犯之所，用為龢鐘九堵。

孔淑叀碩、乃龢叀鳴，用匽（安），用寧，用享，用孝，用祈眉壽，萬年無疆。子子孫孫永寶用樂。

Translation

It was in the King's fifth month, on *dingwei* day (*ganzhi* no. 44).

Zifan assisted the Duke of Jin as advisor, helping to restore him to his state. When Chu did not come to court to hear the King's orders, Zifan and the Lord of Jin led their Six Armies of the West, extensively attacked Chu, and achieved great merit.

The Jin Armies massively struck Chu, causing the loss of their armies and destroying their commander. Zifan assisted Duke Wen in mediating among the territorial lords, causing them to appear at court, and so was able to settle the King's throne. Therefore, King Xiang presented Zifan with a carriage and four stallions, ceremonial robes, embroidered cloth, and belt ornaments. The territorial lords brought auspicious metal to Zifan's place, with which he made nine sets of harmonious bells.

[The sound of these bells] is extremely pure and powerful; they are well-tuned and sonorous. Let them be used to allay and pacify [the spirits and ancestors], be used in ceremonial and pious ritual, and be used in praying for long life of ten thousand years without end. May sons of my sons and grandsons of my grandsons treasure them in perpetuity, and use them to make music.

Further Reading

Asahara, "Seishū kōki no henshō no sekkei."
Bai Guangqi, "Zifan bianzhong de nianfen wenti."
Barnard, *Inscriptions*, v. 1, 421–44; v. 3, 2505–37.
Chen Shuangxin, "Zifan zhongming kaoshi."
Feng Shi, "Chunqiu Zifan bianzhong jinian yanjiu."
Li Xueqin, *Xia Shang Zhou niandai xue zhaji*, 105–13.
Pankenier, "Applied Field Allocation Astrology in Zhou China."
Peng Yushang, "Ye tan Zifan bianzhong de 'wuyue chuji dingwei.'"
Qiu Xigui, "Guanyu Zifan bianzhong de paici ji qita wenti."
Wang Hui, *Shang Zhou jinwen*, 276–81.
Wu Jiabi, "Zifan bianzhong zhongming kaoshi."
Zhang Guangyuan, "Gugong xincang Chunqiu Jin Wen chengba 'Zifan he zhong' chushi."
Zhang Wenyu, "Zifan he zhong 'wuyue chuji dinghai' jie."

DWP

71. Lü Qi zhong 郘黛¹鐘

Thirteen late Spring and Autumn period bells were discovered in 1862 by the banks of a river near Houtusi 后土祠, in Ronghe 榮河 County, Shanxi Province. Six of the bells are in the Shanghai Museum, one in London, and another in the Palace Museum in Taipei, Taiwan. Scholars believe the bells were cast in Jin during the reign of Lord Dao 晉悼公 (r. 572–557 B.C.E.) by his prime minister. In transmitted texts, there is mention of a man named Lü Qi 郘錡 who worked for the Jin ruler around this time. The House of Bi founded the Wei 魏 polity, which later broke away from the Jin and established itself as a separate state. Lü was located in Wei, so the Patriarch of Bi was Lü Qi's founder ancestor. The décor of dragons and other reptiles on the bells is reflected in the imagery used for the musical instruments mentioned in the inscription below. The bells were used to entertain and communicate with the founder ancestor.

Transcription

唯王正月初吉丁亥，郘黛曰：余畢公之孫，郘伯之子。余頡岡事君，余戰釴（其）武，作為余鐘，玄鏐鑪鋁，大鐘八聿（肆），其竈（造）四者（堵），喬喬（蹻蹻）其龍，既旆（伸）㲃（暢）虐，大鐘既椿（縣>懸），玉鐔䨻鼓。余不敢為喬（驕），我以享孝，樂我先祖，以祈眉壽，世世子孫，永以為寶。

Translation

It was in the first month of the King's year, *chuji*, on *dinghai* day (*ganzhi* no. 24), that Lü Qi said: "I am a descendant of Patriarch Bi and the son of Elder Lü. I serve my lord uprightly and firmly; I have fought his battles and thus had made for myself bells of dark polished metals and smelted hard metals, with a set of eight big bells that were cast in groups of four—high, high prance those dragons; when stretched in array along the rack, the big bells are suspended and the stone chimes and alligator drums are in place. I do not dare to act arrogantly, but use them to entertain our Founder Ancestor during the presentation of our mortuary

---

¹ Read as Qi if we accept that the upper elements of the graph represented the phonetic, also written as 𢻻.

feasts and offerings so as to pray for extended longevity, and for generation after generation of descendants to eternally treat them as treasures."

Further Reading

Jicheng 230.
Kimbun tsūshaku, 35.125.
Mingwen xuan, no. 890.

Falkenhausen, "Ritual Music in Bronze Age China," 1148–55.
Falkenhausen, *Suspended Music*, 49, 179, 202–6.
Liu Yu, "Lü Qi bianzhong de chongxin yanjiu."
Wang Hui, *Shang Zhou jinwen*, 281–84.

CAC

72. Wangsun Yizhe *zhong* 王孫遺者鐘

The discovery of this bell near Yichang 宜昌, Hubei, in 1884 is mentioned in a local gazetteer (in the "Metal and Stone" 金石志 section of the *Hubei tongzhi* 湖北通志).[1] The script is delicate and ornate; the style of the bell and the rhetoric of the inscription are similar to those of many other Spring and Autumn bells and vessels produced in the late sixth century B.C.E. and distributed throughout the Yangzi River valley among elite lords who were connected to Chu.[2] The bell is now in the Avery Brundage Collection of the Asian Art Museum in San Francisco.

The sponsor, Yizhe (The One Remaining), was a member of the sublineage Royal Grandson (*wangsun* 王孫), a branch of the Chu ruling lineage located around the growing Chu metropolis of Jinancheng in Jiangling on the north shore of the upper-middle Yangzi River and in regions north and west along the Han River. This inscription was cast in honor of his founder ancestor and father, although no lineage history is recounted. Unlike inscriptions from north of Chu, such as those of the Qin and Jin, Chu inscriptions give no pretense of an ancestral link to Zhou or to Heaven and its Mandate. There is also no expression regarding military expansion or the suppression of non-Zhou peoples and control over the Four Regions that are typical of Zhou-style inscriptions. The Chu focus was on grand musical celebrations and feasts. However, Chu clearly had contact with the earlier Zhou culture and also valued the skilled performance of "Awesome Decorum" (*weiyi* 威儀) in the company of his father and older brothers as well as "fellow aides" (*pengyou* 朋友). Part of the Awesome Decorum performance involved a statement (to the ancestors) by the Royal Grandson confirming that his military and civil accomplishments and accumulated merit showed that his *de* (or inner power) was sufficient to harmonize and guide the people of his state. In this sense, the ceremony carries on the Zhou definition of social and political accomplishment apparent in the late Western Zhou inscriptions, such as that of the Mao Gong *ding* (no. 55, above).

The musical nature of this bell inscription is reflected not only in the rhyming of the text but also in the use of reduplicative binomes, many of which are found in the *Shijing*, for example: *yiyi* 翼翼, *jianjian* 簡簡, and

---

[1] See Sun Qikang, "Chu qi 'Wangsun Yizhe zhong' kaobian."
[2] Falkenhausen, *Suspended Music*, 100n.14.

huang-huang 皇皇.³ The compound *yiyi* in the *Shijing* describes beautiful movements of four fine horses, piles of things (such as sheaves of millet), or carefully performed actions, such as architectural plans or Wan dance steps. It could also describe the internalization of the physical movements in a self-cultivating meditative version of Awesome Decorum to "bring those above and below together in harmony." The reduplicative *jianjian* 簡簡 (also written 闌闌) in the *Shijing* describes the resounding sounds of the bells and drums as blessings descend from the Deity Above during the performance of Awesome Decorum (Chu inscriptions, it should be noted, however, never mention the Deity Above). The reduplicative *huanghuang* is explained in a later text, *Liji*, as expression of the bereavement after a burial, the feeling that one is looking around for someone who has not arrived. This somber interpretation is also reflected elsewhere, where it is combined with the oldest reduplicative, "grave, so grave" (*mumu* 穆穆), in prayers for rulers and their descendants. On the other hand, the original meaning of *huang*, meaning brilliant or dappled yellow, was a typical descriptor for the divine, such as Heaven, deities, ancestors, and kings, and as such was combined in Yangzi River valley inscriptions with the Zhou reduplicative *xixi* 熙熙, "glistening," also used in prayers, and descriptive of shiny bronze bells, music, and spirits. This brilliance was certainly what was implied by Chu scribes as they wrote *huang* with an extra *guang* 光 graph. The additional element had a double function, as a phonetic and as a semantic for the idea of "radiance."

This inscription uses the graph *ren* 恁 (*n[ə]m?) when referring to the inner quality of the sponsor, Yizhe. In the typical Western Zhou locution, the sponsor's heart would have gone through a process of being "broadened and opened" (*guangpi* 廣辟) by following the educational models of the former kings and receiving the ancestral *de*. This graph is often interpreted as *xin* 信 (*s-ni[ŋ]-s), but this word has a different final and appears almost exclusively in Warring States period inscriptions with the phonetic 身 (*n̥i[ŋ]). In fact, the graph in question with the phonetic 任 was phonetically closer to the more common locution *nian* 念 (*nˤim-s),⁴ a word of

---

³ See Falkenhausen, *Suspended Music*, 123.

⁴ The author thanks David P. Branner for this insight. The problem with reading this graph as either *nian* or *xin* becomes apparent in the Warring States period Zhongshan inscriptions, where these words appear with their traditional graphs but the graph 恁 is also used; see no. 80. Possibly, this is a case where phrases were handed down through time verbally and not always associated with a particular graph.

272   ANCIENT CHINESE BRONZE INSCRIPTIONS

Western Zhou times that was also used to refer to thinking about someone (or the spirits) with attention and care. The action of holding the ancestral memory and *de* in the heart was a step in the ritual practice of Awesome Decorum when one acknowledged receipt of the ancestral charge to carry on the lineage *de*. If this was the intention of the original Chu author, then we see further evidence for Chu's continuation of the Zhou ritual traditions despite the proclaimed political independence of their kings.

Transcription

唯正月初吉丁亥，王孫遺者擇其吉金，自作龢鐘，中（終）翰虡（且）揚，元鳴孔皇，用享以孝，于我皇祖文考，用旂眉壽，余圅（宏）龏獣（胡）⁵犀（遲），畏嬰（忌）趩趩（翼翼），肅忻（哲>慎）聖武，叀（惠）于政德，惄（淑）于威義（儀），誨獣不（丕）飤，闌闌（簡簡）龢鐘，用匽（宴）以喜（饎），用樂嘉賓、父兄、及我佣（朋）友。

余恁（念）台心，征（延）⁶永余德，龢䜊（引）⁷民人，余尃（敷）昀于國，皇皇趩趩（熙熙），萬年無諆（期），世萬孫子，永保鼓之。

Translation

It was in the first month, *chuji*, on *dinghai* day (*ganzhi* no. 24). I, Wangsun Yizhe, selected these auspicious metals and made for myself harmonious bells endlessly to let soar and to eulogize (the reputations of the ancestors) with primal sounds and resounding brilliance.

I use the bells when presenting memorial feasts to express my piety to our Brilliant Ancestor and Accomplished Deceased Father, and I use them to pray for extended long life. I behave with vast reverence and far-reaching equanimity, and, in awe and fear, step carefully, [being] serious and attentive, sage and martial; I am benevolent with my governing power, skilled at my awesome

---

⁵ Many read *hu* 胡 (*gˤa) as *shu* 舒 (*l̥a), "slow and easy," but it is unclear whether they were homophones in the Chu dialect. Paul R. Goldin suggests *hu* 祜 (*[g]ˤaʔ), "blessings sent down from Heaven," which appears on several occasions in the *Shijing*.

⁶ Many read this as "big," *dan* 誕.

⁷ Some read "submerge," *ni* 溺, but others "harmful," *ni* 𣵀.

decorum, amply providing sustenance (for the people) with my strategies and plans—*kˤre[n]ʔ-kˤre[n]ʔ, the harmonious bells! Use them when feasting and presenting fine ales; use them to entertain with music our fine guests, fathers, elder brothers, and our associates.

Remembering them inside my heart, I can extend eternally my *de*, bringing the people into harmony. I spread [it] throughout the kingdom—Brilliant! Glistening! (*ɢʷˤaŋ-ɢʷˤaŋ *qʰə-qʰə)—may I have ten thousand years without limit and ten thousand generations of descendants to eternally protect and strike this bell.

Further Reading

Jicheng 261.

Kimbun tsūshaku, 40.568–87.

Mingwen xuan, no. 650.

Cook, "Auspicious Metals and Southern Spirits," 212–59, 411–19.

Cook, "Scribes, Cooks, and Artisans," 242–50.

Falkenhausen, "Ritual Music in Bronze Age China," 1085.

Falkenhausen, *Suspended Music*, 25–32.

Li Xueqin, *Shang Zhou guwenzi duben*, 155–59.

Liu Xiang, "Wangsun Yizhe zhong xinshi."

Mattos, "Eastern Zhou Bronze Inscriptions," 88–91.

Sun Qikang, "Chu qi 'Wangsun Yizhe zhong' kaobian."

CAC

73. WANGZI WU DING 王子午鼎

Between 1978 and 1980, archaeologists excavated a mid-Spring and Autumn Chu burial ground in Xiasi 下寺, Xichuan 淅川, on the western edge of the Danjiang 丹江 Reservoir in southwestern Henan Province. One large tomb revealed cauldrons inscribed by a Chu prince name Wangzi Wu. Two other large tombs nearby, belonging to his wives, also contained inscribed vessels. This set of five tombs was among five sets of tombs in the Xichuan area, each separated by about 20–40 meters. The main tomb in each set was accompanied by a horse and chariot burial. The elite tombs of Prince Wu and his wives (Tomb Numbers 1, 2, and 3) dated to between 552 and 548 B.C.E. The prince's tomb (No. 2) was the largest. The wives' (Nos. 1 and 3) were to the north and south of his and also quite large. To the north and west of this burial set were sixteen human sacrificial burials. The personal name for the prince in Tomb No. 2 was Weizi Ping 薳子馮 (or perhaps Yuanzi Ping), who, according to the inscription on another cauldron (placed in Tomb No. 1), was a descendant of King Zhuang of Chu 楚莊王 (r. 613–591 B.C.E.). Because another name appears right before the final blessing where one would traditionally expect the sponsor to name himself, some scholars believe he had the style name Zigeng 子庚 to accompany his official title *lingyin* 令尹 ("commanding governor," a Chu title for the prime minister). It is unclear why a style name would use words like *geng* and *wu* which normally represent different days or numbers in the ritual calendar. The title *wangzi* means "royal son." The two names, Zigeng and Ziwu, most likely represented two different people. Zigeng was probably the name of someone whom Ziwu was commemorating, perhaps his deceased father or a more powerful official.

The other two large tombs presumably belonged to his wives, women from the smaller states of Teng 滕 and Cai 蔡. The most significant set of inscribed vessels from Tomb No. 2 (dated to 552 B.C.E.) consists of seven cauldrons with lids, identical except for their graduated sizes. Since cattle-bone chips were discovered inside and ladles were resting on top of the lids, we know that they had been filled with some sort of beef stew. The script is ornate and decorative. The lid of the vessel has the brief inscription, "Peng's (Ping's) Series of Sheng-style Cauldrons" 倗之鬻(曆)鼎. The Chu had a number of specialized terms for cauldrons (indicated with graphs made up of the basic graph for *ding* with added phonetics) that seemed to indicate their distinct shapes and functions. The Wangzi Wu cauldrons are flat-bot-tomed with extremely complex and ornate handles and decorative flanges of interwoven snake-like dragons—a Chu signature—that have led some analysts to question whether the Chu artisans had already begun to use lost-wax casting techniques in addition to the traditional clay mold techniques (as suggested for the even more ornate vessels from the 443 B.C.E. Zeng Hou Yi tomb in Suixian, Hubei). The Chu focus on musical ceremonies is reflected by the reduplicated words on a food vessel that indicate bell sounds and perhaps those of other instruments. Indeed, like all large elite tombs, the tombs in Xiasi were supplied with orchestras of bells, chime stones, and flutes. There may have been zithers (such as *qin* 琴 or *se* 瑟), drums, or other instruments as found in later Chu tombs, but these did not survive.

Transcription

唯正月初吉丁亥，王子午擇其吉金，自作䜌彝戠鼎。用享以孝于我皇祖文考。用祈眉壽。盦（宏）龏𦻚（胡）犀（遲），畏朞[1]（忌）趩趩（翼翼），敬厥盟祀，永受其福。余不畏不差，叀（惠）于政德，怒（淑）于威儀，闌闌（簡簡）獸獸，[2] 命（令）尹子庚殹（繄）[3] 民之所極。萬年無期子孫是利。

---

[1] Although many of the phrases in this inscription are the same as found in no. 72, the script forms are somewhat variable. This graph is read as a variant of 其 elsewhere (as in the Qin inscriptions, no. 66, above).

[2] Many read *shoushou* (*s.tʰu(?)-s-s.tʰu(?)-s) as *youyou* 悠悠 (*liw-liw) or 憂憂 (*?ru-?ru), the latter being closer in sound. While these words all had rounded finals, their initials were not close in pronunciation. However, the latter reading is somewhat reinforced by somewhat phonetically close binome *chouchou* 愁愁 (*[d]ru-[d]ru) found in late *Chuci* 楚辭 songs and understood to mean "sad with grief." I also suspect that *shoushou* was simplified over time and read as the graphs *dada* 憚憚 (*[d]ar-[d]ar), found in the *Shijing* and in the Warring States period Zhongshan inscriptions, see no. 80.

[3] *Yi* appears in a similar phrase regarding the governing of the people through the excution of punishments. The fact that it is on an axe head from the Chu area (Zaoyang 棗陽, Hubei) is particularly pertinent. "Elder Zeng Qi cast axes to use in making people obey the law (or "act as a model for the people"), executing punishments for crimes, and govern for the people" 曾白（伯）陭鑄戚戉（鉞），用為民贄(則? 型?),非 (罪?) 歷殹井 (刑)，用為民政(Zhong Bosheng et al., eds., *Xinshou Yin-Zhou qingtongqi mingwen ji qiying huibian*, 1203). It also appears on late Warring States period Qin tallies and is generally understood to function as a copula like *ye* 也. It is read as *yi* 繄 when at the beginning or middle of a phrase in transmitted texts, and understood to function somewhat like *shi* 是, or simply as an exclamation.

Translation

It was in the first month, *chuji*, on *dinghai* day (*ganzhi* no. 24), that Wu, Son of the King, selected these auspicious metals to make for himself *jiang*-style high-legged sacrificial vessels, cauldrons for meat offerings to present mortuary feasts. He used them to express filial piety to our Brilliant Ancestor and Accomplished Deceased-father and to pray for extended long life. With great reverence and far-reaching equanimity, full of awe and fear, I oh so cautiously express my respects to them with the luminous rite so as to receive their blessings of good fortune eternally. I am neither fierce nor lacking (in decorum), but am benevolent with my governing power and skilled at the performance of Awesome Decorum. *kˁre[n]? kˁre[n]? s.tʰu(?)-s s.tʰu(?)-s. Lingyin Zigeng is the pillar of the people! May he for ten thousand years without limit have sons and grandsons and be thus benefited.

Further Reading

Jicheng 2811.

Cook, "Auspicious Metals and Southern Spirits," 241–47, 385–96.

Cook and Major, eds., *Defining Chu*, 29, 33–34, 56, 70–72.

Falkenhausen, *Chinese Society in the Age of Confucius*, 338–48.

Falkenhausen, "Ritual Music in Bronze Age China," 1076–1116.

Falkenhausen, "The Waning of the Bronze Age," 520–23.

Li Ling, "'Chu shu zhi sun Peng' jiujing shi shui?"

Mattos, "Eastern Zhou Bronze Inscriptions," 96–100.

Wang Hui, *Shang Zhou jinwen*, 287–90.

Wu Shiqian, "Wangzi Wu ding, Wangsun Gao zhong mingwen kaoshi."

Xichuan Xiasi Chunqiu Chu mu.

Zhong Baisheng *et al.*, eds., *Xinshou Yin-Zhou qingtongqi mingwen ji qiying huibian.*

CAC

74. Cai Hou Shen *pan* 蔡侯申盤 and Cai Hou Shen *zun* 蔡侯申尊

In 1955, archaeologists discovered the tomb of Lord Shen of Cai 蔡侯申 (also known as Lord Zhao of Cai 蔡昭侯, r. 519–491 B.C.E.) in Shouxian 壽縣, Anhui Province. The tomb had been plundered, with evidence of only one north-facing occupant remaining. In the southern half of the tomb were placed the occupant, covered with jade and other jewelry, in a lacquered coffin to the east, and horse and chariot and other items to the west. In the northern half of the tomb were positioned bronze feasting vessels and musical instruments. The largest cauldron (a round, three-legged, lidded cauldron belonging to Lord Shen) was placed in the center above the tomb occupant's head. To the left of it was placed a round *jian*-basin commissioned by King Guang of Wu (no. 75, below) with a smaller round *fou* 缶 (jar) inside. To the right of it were placed two square basins also with smaller square *fou* inside. In the northwest corner of the tomb was another complete set of food, alcohol, cooking and serving vessels, including a *pan*-basin with a *zun* inside. Both vessels were dedicated by Cai Hou Shen (Cai Zhao Hou) for a woman who has been identified by some scholars as his eldest daughter and by others as his sister. The inscription commemorated her marriage to a king of Wu (which most claim must be Liao 僚) in 519 B.C.E., the first year of Cai Zhao Hou's reign.

Liu Hehui believes that this woman, Da Meng Ji ("Grand Eldest Ji-lineage woman"), was the "woman of Cai" referred to in the *Zuozhuan*. In these accounts, she was first married to King Ping of Chu, but ran back to her home in Cai when he became enamored of a young woman from Qin. Her marriage to the King of Wu would then have been a second marriage, and Liu suspects that both she and the King were in their forties. Liu believes that her dowry vessels ended up in the Cai lord's tomb for several possible reasons. One was the political disruption caused by wars between Wu and Chu that put Cai in an awkward position (bells inscribed with a loyalty oath to Chu were also found in his tomb); another was the fact that the Wu King was murdered by his successor, Guang, shortly after the marriage. So Liu speculates that either the vessels never left Cai or Da Meng Ji came home again with her vessels and buried them in Zhao Hou's tomb as a memorial.

Whoever Da Meng Ji may have been, her dowry inscription preserved some rhetoric that might reflect her marriage ritual. Like most rituals involving a change in social status, her marriage ritual may have been performed during the ancestor-worship sacrifices. An elite daughter's performance of "Awesome Decorum" involved imitating King Wen's Mother (the primal Ji-lineage woman), rather than male founder ancestors or kings, as in the case of the performance by male heirs. Her performance here suggests a languorous dance (*youyou* 遊遊). If Yu Xingwu's interpretation is correct, she did not use a Zhou melody, but sang "Shang" 商 style eulogistic, or praise, songs (*song* 頌) as preserved in the last section of the *Shijing*. One problem with this theory is that she was a woman of the Ji lineage who followed in the footsteps of the mother of King Wen, the dynastic founder of Zhou. It seems more likely that *shang* was the name of the musical mode (one of five, which happened to be connected by Qin times with divination and cosmology), rather than a specific reference to the Shang Eulogies in the *Shijing*.

Transcription

元年正月初吉辛亥，帘(蔡)侯▉(申)虔共(恭)大命，上下陟否，臘敬不惕(易)，肇差(佐)天子，用詐(作)大孟姬賸(媵)彝，禋享是以祇盟(明)嘗啻(禘)，祐受母(無)已，齋覭整肅，類文王母，穆穆亹亹，恩(聰)害(憲)訢易(暢)，威義(儀)遊遊¹，靈頌託商，康諧龢好，敬配吳王。不諱考壽，子孫蕃昌，永保用之，終歲無疆。

Translation

> It was in the first year, first month, *chuji*, on *xinhai* day [no. 48] when Lord Shen of Cai paid his respects to the Great Mandate and to the spirits above and below who ascend and descend. He performs the annual winter sacrifice respectfully without change [in his loyalty]; from the beginning, he has acted as an aide to the Son of Heaven. He takes this opportunity to make for his eldest daughter of the Ji lineage a metal basin for her sacrificial dowry vessels [that she uses] for presenting pure ale in mortuary feasts and thereby to pay her respects to the earth, perform the luminous

---

¹ Some read this as *youyou* 優優, as found in the *Shijing* and understood as "harmonious (in governing policy)," *Mao* 304. Here it describes her movements.

rites, the autumnal tasting rites, and the annual ancestral sacrifices, so as to receive divine aid without end. Purified and blessed, she is upright and serious, comparing herself to King Wen's Mother:[2] grave, so grave; diligent, so diligent; intelligent, efficient, joyful, and penetrating, her Awesome Decorum is performed langourously and saunteringly, and for her numinous praise song, she relies on the *shang* musical mode, creating peace, unity, harmony, and affection with which she expresses her respect and qualities to become the mate for the King of Wu. Do not ignore the Aged and Long-lived Ones, so that your sons and grandsons will flourish and eternally protect and use the vessels, and may your years be without end.

Further Reading

Jicheng 6010, 10171.

Mingwen xuan, no. 589.

Cao Zhaolan, *Jinwen yu Yin Zhou nüxing wenhua*, 220–24.

Chen Mengjia, "Cai qi san ji."

Cook, "Moonshine and Millet," 15.

Falkenhausen, *Chinese Society in the Age of Confucius*, 266–67.

Falkenhausen, "The Waning of the Bronze Age," 523–25.

Guo Ruoyu, "Cong you guan Cai Hou de ruogan ziliao lun Shouxian Cai Hou mu Cai qi de naindai."

Li Xueqin, *Shang Zhou guwenzi duben*, 160–65.

Liu Hehui, "Cai qi ming yu Chu Cai guanxi xintan."

Shouxian Cai Hou mu chutu yiwu.

Wang Hui, *Shang Zhou jinwen*, 290–94.

Wang Rencong, "Cai Hou X kaoyi."

Yin Difei, "Shouxian Cai Hou tongqi de zai yanjiu."

Yu Xingwu, "Shouxian Cai Hou mu tongqi mingwen kaoshi."

CAC

---

[2] Who, according to the *Shijing* song "Si zhai" 思齊 (Legge, *The Chinese Classics*, IV, 446), had a hundred sons.

75. Wu Wang Guang *jian* 吳王光鑒

Out of the five hundred bronze items discovered in Cai Hou Shen's tomb in 1955 (see no. 74, above), two late Spring and Autumn period *jian*-style high-walled basins were manufactured by artisans under King Guang of Wu 吳王光 (r. 514–496 B.C.E.), also called Helü 闔閭 (or Helu 闔廬 and Gailu 蓋廬) in transmitted texts. They are stored in the Anhui Provincial Museum. The King of Wu made dowry basins for either his daughter or other female, Shu Ji Siyu (Secondary Ji-lineage woman Siyu), to commemorate her marriage to a Cai lord. Scholars debate whether that lord was Cai Zhao Hou 蔡昭侯 (r. 518–491 B.C.E.), in whose tomb the basins were found. He had ruled for five years by the time King Guang came to power and thus was presumably already married. Others believe it had to be to his son, Shuo 朔 (titled Cai Cheng Hou 蔡成侯, r. 490–472 B.C.E.). Guo Ruoyu's analysis of the inscriptions on a poorly preserved set of bells for Shu Ji Siyu suggests that Wu may even have looted the Chu capital of bronzes in order to cast such a magnificent set of dowry vessels. He argues that the marriage was considered extremely important to the Wu state and that the groom was certainly the son, sometime before he came to power in 490 B.C.E., after his father's death. Liu Hehui does not believe that the son's vessels would be in the father's tomb and suspects that this marriage was contracted for Shuo after Wu had invaded Chu, and Lord Zhao, who was being held in Chu, escaped, perhaps around the twelfth or thirteenth year of Shuo's reign. Some scholars claim that the two marriages between Cai and Wu had to be related political events; others reject that theory.

Transcription
唯王五月，既字白（魄）期，[1]吉日初庚，吳王光擇其吉金，玄銑（磺）、白銑（磺），以作叔姬寺吁宗彝薦鑑，用享用孝，眉壽無疆，往巳（矣）叔姬，虔敬乃后，子孫勿忘。

Translation
It was in the fifth month of the King's year, *jishengpo*, on an auspicious day, the first *geng* day, when King Guang of Wu selected these auspicious

---

[1] The word *zi* 字, "to breed," is used in place of the more common 生 *sheng*, "to give birth." The words *bai* 百 (*bˤrak) and *po* 魄 (*pʰˤrak) were near homophones.

metals. With dark minerals (lead) and light minerals (tin), I make for Shu Ji Siyu a sacrificial offering basin for main shrine sacrificial vessels for her to use to present mortuary feasts and filial offerings [to receive from the ancestors] extended longevity without end. Go forth, Shu Ji, and pay your respects for your posterity; may your descendants not be forgetful.

Further Reading

Jicheng 10297–99.

Kimbun tsūshaku, 40.588–603.

Mingwen xuan, no. 538.

Behr, *Reimende Bronzeinschriften und die Entstehung der chinesischen Endreimdichtung*, 298–300.

Dong Chuping, *Wu Yue wenhua xintan*, 322–23.

Guo Ruoyu, "Cong you guan Cai Hou de ruogan ziliao lun Shouxian Cai Hou mu Cai qi de naindai."

Li Xueqin, *Shang Zhou guwenzi duben*, 166–68.

Liu Hehui, "Cai qi mingyu Chu Cai guanxi xintan."

Shouxian Cai Hou mu chutu yiwu.

Wang Hui, *Shang Zhou jinwen*, 294–96.

Yu Xingwu, "Shouxian Cai Hou mu tongqi mingwen kaoshi."

CAC

76. Guo Zuo *dan* 國佐鐕

The origin of this vessel, now kept in the National Palace Museum in Taipei, is unclear. Since a rubbing appears first in the *Xiqing gujian* 西清古鑑 catalogue (edited by Liang Shizheng 梁詩正 [1697–1763] and his colleagues in 1752), it is clear that it must have been found at a fairly early date. The massive container (ca. 12.5 kg) with four side handles, a height of 34.6 cm, and a diameter of 24.6 cm at the mouth, is practically undecorated, and, because of the absence of a foot, conveys a fairly clumsy aesthetic impression.

The inscription, found on the two upper sides of the vessel, is 53 characters long and calligraphically a reference standard for the state of Qi. The second half is rhymed, but metrically rather irregular, as shown in the following scheme (rhyme words marked in the transcription below), where each line in a rhymed sequence is headed by a Roman numeral. Each syllable is then represented by a lower-case x. At the end of a line, an upper-case letter (e.g., "A") indicates a full or perfect rhyme; a lower-case letter (e.g., "a") indicates a half- or imperfect rhyme; and an upper-case X indicates an unrhymed syllable. The different rhyming sections correspond roughly to a scheme where A = remote past, B = recent deeds of the vessel sponsor.

```
xxxxx / xxxxx / xxxxx / xxxx
   I    xxxx      A      IV   xxxxxx   X
  II    xxxxxx    A       V   xxxxxx   B
 III    xxxx      B      VI   xxxxxxx  X
```

Since the name of the person mentioned in the initial dating formula can be identified with Guo Zuo 國佐 (styled Wuzi 武子), who appears in several passages of the *Chunqiu* and the *Zuozhuan* between the years 632 and 573 B.C.E., it can be safely inferred that the vessel must have been cast before the latter date, possibly in 587. It was during this year that political reforms were introduced by Lord Qing of Qi 齊頃公 (r. 599–582), which resulted in a period of peace—albeit shortlived—among Qi, Lu 魯, and Wei 魏, in which Guo Zuo acted as negotiator and regent of Qi. The vessel sponsor, Ji 偈, is otherwise unknown, though it has been suggested that he belonged to the Tian 田 clan, which eventually ruled Qi.

The inscription contains some Qi lexical features, such as the peculiar vessel name, quoted as a dialect word in *Fangyan* 方言 (*The Topolects*), the otherwise unknown month name Xu (?), and the formula *wu jiu wu huang* 毋咎毋悗 ("become neither ill nor deranged"), as well as the rare volume measure of four *bing* 秉. According to the transmitted text *Yili* 儀禮 (*Ceremonies and Rites*), one *bing* equaled 160 *hu* 斛, and one *hu* in turn equaled ten "pecks" or *dou* 斗. But as there were roughly two liters per *dou*, the vessel would have had to contain 1,200 liters—absurd, of course, for an object that is 34.6 cm high. It has thus been suspected by some scholars that *bing* refers to the four ring handles of the vessel. The matter is not clarified by an additional inscription, probably incised before the Han dynasty and placed next to the two text sections translated below, which cryptically states: "Great official: seven pecks, three potter's wheels, three pounds" 大官七斗一鈞三斤.

Transcription

國差（佐）立（莅）事歲
咸［月］丁亥，攻（工）帀（師）
佲鑄西亭（墉）寶
䥶（甀）四秉。
用實旨酉（酒$_A$），
灰（侯）氏為福釁（眉）鑫（壽$_A$）。
卑（俾）旨卑（俾）瀞（清$_B$）。
灰（侯）氏母（毋）瘩母（毋）𤵻（悗），
齊邦貝（鼏）静安甯（寧$_B$）。
子子孫孫㑞（保）用之。

Translation

In the year when Guo Zuo assumed the services, in the Xu (?) month, on *ding-hai* day [no. 24], Master of Artisans He (?) cast a precious *dan*-pitcher for the Western Wall [of the Palace of Qi], accommodating four *bing*. Use it to be filled with sacrificial wine. May it provide blessings and long life for the Marquis and lineage head of Qi, and let it provide what is fine, provide what is clear [wine]. May the Marquis and lineage head not become ill or deranged, and the state of Qi be sheltered, tranquil, peaceful and untroubled. May sons' sons and grandsons' grandsons eternally protect and use it [this pitcher].

Further Reading

Jicheng 10361.
Kimbun tsūshaku, 38.340–48 and 52.554.
Mingwen xuan, no. 846.

Doty, "The Bronze Inscriptions of Ch'i," 206–23.
Guo Moruo, *Liang Zhou jinwenci daxi tulu kaoshi*.
Wang Hui, *Shang Zhou jinwen*, 284–87.
Yang Shuda, *Jiweiju jinwen shuo*, 264–67.

WB

77. DISHI *HU* 杕氏壺

This lidded *hu*-kettle, belonging to the collection of the Berlin Museum of East Asian Art since at least the 1920s-30s, is 37.8 cm high. It bears an inscription comprising 41 characters, spiraling around its belly, which can be divided into three sections of roughly equal length. Initially classified as a piece from the northern state of Yan and dated to the late Chunqiu period, scholars such as Li Xueqin and He Linyi have pointed to calligraphic similarities in the inscription to those from the Kingdom of Zhongshan 中山. According to sparse accounts in the early historiographical literature, this kingdom was founded by a branch of the White Di 白狄 tribes called Xianyu 鮮于, who are mentioned in this inscription as having been "outwitted" (or "overpowered," *xian* 賢) by the inscription-maker, Fuji 福及. That he himself was non-Sinitic, being from northern Yan, might, on the other hand, be borne out by the expression *qie* 契(挈) that is used for the looted container from which the kettle was cast, since *qie* is a Yan dialect word synonymous with *ping* 瓶 "vase," according to late sources such as *Jiyun* 集韻 (1037) and *Leipian* 類篇 (1039). Alternatively, one might read *qie* 契 as a loan for homophonous *qie* 挈 "to grasp, to hold," which would have designated the looted "booty" as a noun in this text.

The surprisingly insolent tone and the almost presumptuous repetition of the first person pronoun, rarely encountered in Western Zhou inscriptions, is somewhat counterbalanced by the careful employment of a strict tetrasyllabic meter carrying the following rhyme scheme:

I	xxxx	X	VI	xxxx	A
II	xxxx	A	VII	xxxx	X
III	xxxx	X	VIII	xxxx	A
IV	xxxxx	A	IX	xxxx	X
V	xxxx	X	X	xxxx	A

Each line in a rhymed sequence is headed by a Roman numeral. Each syllable is then represented by a lower-case x. At the end of a line, an upper-case letter (e.g., "A") indicates a full or perfect rhyme; an upper-case X indicates an unrhymed syllable.

Transcription

杕氏福及，
歲(歲)賢鮮于(虞ₐ)，
可(荷)是金契(鍥)，
吾台(以)為弄壺ₐ。
自頌既好。
多寡不訏ₐ。
虞(吾)台(以)匽(宴)猷(酓)，
盱(于)我家室。
罕(弋)獵母(毋)逡(後)，
籑(算)在我車ₐ。

Translation

"I, Fuji (*pək-grəp) of the Di (*dˤet-s) clan, in the year when I outwitted the Xianyu (*ser-wa), shouldered (i.e. looted) that bronze *qie*-vase. I use it to make this filigreed *hu*-kettle, to praise myself and to be loved, although its capacity is not voluminous. I use it to feast and offer food, in the abode of our family. During rope arrow chivies and hunts, do not leave it behind, and stow it in our chariot!"

Further Reading

Jicheng 9715.
Mingwen xuan, Vol. 4, 564.

Guo Moruo, *Liang Zhou jinwenci daxi tulu kaoshi*, 135–36.
Li Xueqin, "Pingshan mu zangqun yu Zhongshanguo de wenhua," 37–41.
Rong Geng, ed., *Shang-Zhou yiqi tongkao*, vol. 2, 446.
Sha Zongyuan, "Dishi hu mingwen bushi."

WB

78. Gongyu taizi Gu-fa-X-fan *jian* 工𣙇大子姑發䎽反劍

A double-edged sword bearing the present inscription was found in 1959 in Caijiagang 蔡家崗, a village in the Huainan 淮南 area of present-day Anhui province, in the tomb of Marquis Sheng of Cai 蔡聲侯 (a.k.a. Cai Sheng hou Chan 產, r. 471–452). Several other weapons were found in the same section, which was undisturbed by looters who had robbed the tomb in antiquity. The sword is 36.4 cm long and measures 3.8 cm at the point of its greatest width above the trumpet-shaped semi-hollow hilt. It is a relatively unadorned weapon and bears an inlaid inscription of 36 characters, arranged into two columns on one side. It is kept in the Anhui Provincial Museum today.

The text is one of the very rare instances of a (partially) rhymed inscription on a weapon (rhyme characters are marked with letters in the transcription below), featuring the following metrical organization:

```
xxxxxxxx / xxxx / xxxx
   I    xxxx        X        IV   xxxxx    B
   II   xxxx        A        V    xxxx     X
   III  xxxx        a        VI   xxxx     B
```

Each line in a rhymed sequence is headed by a Roman numeral. Each syllable is then represented by a lower-case x. At the end of a line, an upper-case letter (e.g., "A") indicates a full or perfect rhyme; a lower-case letter (e.g., "a") indicates a half- or imperfect rhyme; and an upper-case X indicates an unrhymed syllable. The different rhyming sections correspond roughly to a scheme where A = remote past, B = recent deeds of the vessel sponsor.

It is noteworthy for its remarkable bluntness, appreciably departing from the traditional Zhou inscriptional decorum. The names of both the sword maker, namely, the Crown Prince *kˤa-patʔ-pˤranʔ, and his state *kˤoŋ-ŋ(r)a are represented in a very peculiar orthography, offering a glimpse into the more complicated substrate language pronunciations of the same person represented as Zhufan 諸樊 (*Ta-ban) and the state known as Wu 吳 (*ŋʷˤa) in the edited literature. There are also syntactic peculiarities, such as the preposed prepositional phrase in *zhi yu xi xing* 至于西行 ("reaching out to the west I move"), which might be due to this substrate language influence, rather than an attempt to force the text into the rhyme scheme.

Zhufan succeeded the famous King Shoumeng 壽夢 on the throne of Wu in 560 B.C.E., and, to judge from his title in this inscription, namely *taizi* 大子 (Crown Prince), the sword must have been manufactured in the years before his enthronement, when he was probably stationed north of the Yangzi, in the area of present-day Fengtai 鳳台 in Anhui, as head of the Wu troops fighting against Chu.

Transcription

工𢵇(敔>吳)大子姑發𦏟反，自乍(作)元用。才(在)行之先，

㠯(以)用㠯(以)隻(獲$_A$)，

莫敢郆(御)余$_a$。

余處江之陽$_B$，

至于南，

至于西行$_B$。

Translation

> I, Crown Prince Gu-fa-X-fan (*kˤa-patʔ-pˤranʔ) of Gong-wu (*kˤoŋ-ŋ(r)a, i.e. Wu) made this superb tool on my own initiative. As the advance guard (in military undertakings), I use it to slaughter and to take captives, [so that] nobody dares to banish me. I have taken position to the north of the Yangzi, reaching down to the south, reaching to the west I move.

Further Reading

Mingwen xuan, no. 537.
Dong Chuping, *Wu Yue Xu Shu jinwen jishi*, 89–92.
Guo Moruo, "Ba Jiangling yu Shouxian chutu tongqiqun."
Li Xueqin, "Chunqiu nanfang qingtongqi mingwen de yige tedian."
Shang Chengzuo, "Gu-fa-X-fan ji Wuwang Zhufan bieyi."
Shang Chengzuo, "Gu-fa-X-fan jian busho."
Sun Zhichu, "Huainan Cai qi shiwen shangque."

Wagner, "The Language of the Ancient State of Wu."

You Rujie and Zhou Zhenhe, "Nanfang diming fenbu de quyu tezheng yu gudai yuyan de guanxi."

Zheng-Zhang Shangfang, "Gu Wu-Yue diming zhong de Dong-Taiyu chengfen."

WB

79. Piao Qiang *zhong* 驫羌鐘

The Piao Qiang *zhong* inscription is found on a set (Group A) of five *niu-zhong* 鈕鐘 bells. With the exception of minimal discrepancies in writing characteristics and ornamentation style, the inscription texts are by and large identical, but in quite different states of preservation. They are placed on the front central cartouche (*zheng* 鉦) in four columns with eight characters each, and on the back central cartouche in three columns with eight, and one with five characters, adding up to a total of sixty-one characters. This group forms a bell set with twelve further bells (Group B), usually known as the Piaoshi *zhong* 驫氏鐘, which contain short two-column inscriptions reading "*Zhong*-bells of the Piao lineage" 驫氏之鐘.

The bell set was discovered in 1931 in the vicinity of Jincun 金村, some 56 kilometers southeast of Luoyang, probably in tomb no. 7 of the eight large single Han 韓 tombs located in the area. This identification, however, is based only upon information obtained by Bishop William Charles White (1865–1943, Chinese name Huai Fuguang 懷覆光) of the Canadian Episcopalian Church mission in Kaifeng 開封, from a local artisan. One bell from each set was procured by Bishop White and is now kept in the Royal Ontario Museum in Toronto. The remaining bells belonged to the possession of Liu Tizhi 劉體智 (1879–1963) from Lujiang 廬江, whence they ended up in the Sumitomo 住友 Collection in Kyoto.

Precise sizes are only available for the twelve bells in Kyoto, while measures in Chinese publications vary considerably. Bell #1, the largest of Group A, has a height of 31.7 cm and a width of 17.7 cm between the lateral projecting rims (*xian* 銑), and weighs 4.6 kg. The smallest bell of Group B measures 12.7 x 7.1 cm, and weighs 0.5 kg.

For the better part of the twentieth century the inscription was the object of very intense dating debates, but meanwhile a consensus seems to have emerged that the initial archaizing dating formula ("twenty-second sacrificial year") is best matched with the twenty-second year of the reign of King Weilie of Zhou 周威烈王, i.e. 404 B.C.E. One year earlier, Lord Lie of Jin 晉烈公 (r. 415–389 B.C.E.) had ordered the rulers of Han, Wei, and Zhao 趙 to wage a military campaign against Qi, during which the Lord of Qi was finally taken hostage in 405 and surrendered to the Lord of Jin.

This campaign entailed an incursion by allied troops into the territory behind the long wall of Qi from the bridgehead at Pingyin, mentioned in the inscription, shortly after the territory of Qin to the west of the Yellow River had been conquered. This is, incidentally, the first mention of a "long wall" or "great wall" (*changcheng* 長城) in any datable Chinese source. During the time in question, the long wall of Qi probably ran from Langya 瑯琊 in Jiao 膠 district of today's Shandong province, along the smaller Taishan 泰山 mountain range in the east, to the area of present day Pingyin 平陰, some 35 kilometers northeast of Feicheng 肥城. The victorious campaign resulted in the regular enfeoffment of Jingzi 景子 as Marquis of Han 韓侯 in 403, who was subsequently addressed as *hou* 侯, rather than as *zhu* 主, "lineage head," as in this inscription. Han, however, played only a minor role in the campaign as compared to Wei, which continued to war against Qi and Qin under King Hui 惠王 (r. 370–319) without the help of the other two states, quickly losing its supremacy in the northeast again. The sponsor of the vessel, Piao Qiang, whose name has been suspected by some scholars of being of Central Asian provenance, is unfortunately not known from other inscriptions or the received literature.

The rhymed inscripton text features a quite regular tetrasyllabic meter, which is broken only in verses IV/V and XI. The rhyme scheme itself, on the other hand, is fairly irregular, involving possibly dialectal slant rhymes in several positions, which are typical of the phonology of late Chunqiu and early Warring States inscriptions. Lexically, the author of the inscription has already departed from the more strictly formulaic Western Zhou predecessors. Even the obligatory final dedication shows by the choice of the negative *wu* 毋 and the peculiarly augmented form of *shi* 枼 (世), "generation," and other orthographic idiosyncracies, a stylistic liberty rarely encountered in Chunqiu inscriptions, and otherwise attested only in inscriptions from Qi and Zhongshan. In the following scheme, each line in a rhymed sequence is headed by a Roman numeral. Each syllable is then represented by a lower-case x. At the end of a line, an upper-case letter (e.g., "A") indicates a full or perfect rhyme; a lower-case letter (e.g., "a") indicates a half- or imperfect rhyme, and a corresponding Greek letter an imperfect rhyme of a different rhyme class than others in the same rhyme series. An upper-case X indicates an unrhymed syllable. The different rhyming sections correspond roughly to a scheme where A = remote past, B = recent deeds of the vessel sponsor.

	xxxxx		VII	xxxx	C
I	xxxx	A	VIII	xxxx	c
II	xxxx	A	IX	xxxx	ζ
III	xxxx	B	X	xxxx	X
IV	xxxxx	b	XI	xxxxxx	D
V	xxxxx	a	XII	xxxx	X
VI	xxxx	X	XIII	xxxx	d

Transcription

(Since single characters of the inscriptions are not fully identical in the different versions, the following transcription presents an idealized form on the basis of all available rubbings.)

Front
唯廿（二十）又亝（再）祀，
鷹（鸁）羌乍（佐）戍（戎$_A$）
毕（厥）辟，旜（韓）宗$_A$，
敵（徹）逨（率）征祟（秦$_B$），
逯（迮）齊入張（長）埊（城$_b$），
先會于平陰（陰$_a$）。
武侄（鷙）寺（是）力，
壴（嘉）。

Back：
攸（奪）楚京$_C$，
賞于旜（韓）宗$_c$，
令（命）于晉公$_\zeta$，
卻（昭）于天子。
用明劑（載）^{1}之于銘$_D$。
武文咸剌（烈），
永枼（世）母（毋）忘$_d$。

---

^{1} Unlike here, this graph is routinely read as a variant of the conjunction *ze* 則, "thereupon," or the adverbial "in accordance with the regulations" (e.g., in legal contexts) elsewhere in Eastern Zhou inscriptions.

Translation

It was in the twenty-second sacrificial year. Piao Qiang supported his lord, the lineage head of Han, and stood by him in warfare. He held the supreme command during the punitive expedition against Qin, advanced against Qi, entered the territory behind the great wall [of Qi], and united the allied troops at Pingyin. Mightily employing his forces in the acts of war, he took by assault the heights of Chuqiu. He was therefore rewarded by the lineage head of Han, granted a mandate by the Lord of Jin, and illuminated by the Son of Heaven. On account of this, he records these deeds in an inscription. May his blazing warlike and civil achievements not be forgotten by generations eternally!

Further Reading

Jicheng 157–70.

Mingwen xuan, no. 889.

Behr, *Reimende Bronzeinschriften und die Entstehung der chinesischen Endreimdichtung*, 551–95.

Barnard, *Inscriptions*, v. 1, 486–518; v. 3, 2540–3574.

Chen Lianqing, "Piao Qiang zhong ming 'zheng Qin ze Qi' xin shi."

Gu Zigang, "Hanjun mu faxian lüeji."

Guo Moruo, *Jinwen congkao*, 138–61.

Karlgren, "On the Date of the Piao-Bells."

Liu Jie, "Piaoshi bianzhong kao."

Pines, "The Earliest "Great Wall"? The Long Wall of Qi Revisited."

Sahara Yasuo, "Hyōshi henshō."

Sun Zhichu, "Piao Qiang zhong mingwen huishi."

Takahashi Junji, "Hyōshi henshō ondaka sokutei."

Tang Lan, *Tang Lan xiansheng jinwen lunji*, 1–5.

Wen Tingjing, "Piao Qiang zhong ming shi."

White, *Tombs of Old Lo-yang*.

Wu Qichang, "Piao Qiang zhong bukao."

Xu Zhongshu, Piaoshi bianzhong tushi.

Zhang Weihua, "Qi changcheng kao."

Zhu Dexi, "Guanyu Piao Qiang zhong mingwen de jǐge wenti."

WB

80. Zhongshan Wang Cuo ding 中山王𫲨鼎

Beginning in the mid 1950s, farmers in Sanji 三汲, Pingshan 平山 County, Hebei Province, plowed up Spring and Autumn and Warring States period artifacts, including a tumulus in 1973. Archaeologists discovered two large tombs underneath what had once been a large architectural structure. Eventually, two royal Zhongshan burial grounds were discovered, along with many accompanying tombs, horse and chariot pits; and other sacrificial pits were discovered as well as the site of the Zhongshan capital, Lingshou 靈壽. According to contemporary and later texts, the Zhongshan people were originally non-Chinese, but it is not clear how long ago that was. Certainly by the time of the two large tombs, the late Warring States period, the Zhongshan royal family was not only very wealthy but displayed a high level of cultural knowledge common to the elite of all the Eastern Zhou states.

According to a bronze mausoleum plan, the original funerary plan for the site with the two tombs was to include five tombs. The largest of the two tombs (Tomb no. 1), in which the plan was discovered, belonged to King Cuo of Zhongshan 中山王𫲨 (r. 327–313) and was called the King's Hall 王堂; Tomb no. 2 was for his queen and was called Hall of the Mourning Queen 哀后堂. The other tombs were never built. Although all the tombs in the two burial grounds had been plundered over time, enough artifacts, many very finely crafted, remained in order to indentify tomb numbers 1 and 6 as belonging to kings. Tomb 1, the later of the two, held 90 inscribed bronzes, the most significant of which, besides the mausoleum plan, include the square hu vessels with a 448-character inscription and a round, three-legged lidded cauldron with a 469-character inscription, both of which were authorized by King Cuo. There was also a 182-character inscribed round *hu*, which had been commissioned by his son Qieci. The cauldron was cast around 316 B.C.E. to commemorate a successful battle against Yan that resulted in the acquisition of new territory. The square *hu* inscription commemorated the capture of Yan's "auspicious metal" 吉金 for use in crafting the Zhongshan vessels. Both the cauldron and the square *hu* eulogized the accomplishments of the minister who led the charge, but they also used the entire event as a warning to the royal heirs. The warning is twofold. First, there is the ostensible reason for the invasion against Yan, which is that the Yan king abdicated to a worthy minister, a proposal put forward by some literati as a noble act of self-sacrifice for the sake of a state on the part of a ruler who is less capable than the minister. The ruling elite clearly felt that this act was threatening to their own positions and must be suppressed.[1] The second aspect of the warning involved the high minister of Zhongshan, who took the initiative to attack Yan while the King was away, and hence did not formally obtain the King's permission. Such reformist (and politically threatening) behavior on the part of Zhongshan's own prime minister (Sima Zhou 司馬周) also had to be punished. So while Sima Zhou's success was lauded, he ended up paying for it with his life. Both the King and the minister were eulogized by the heir, Qieci, in the round *hu* inscription.

This philosophical and political debate addressed the question of what gives a man the greater right to rule—heredity or intelligence? In contemporary understandings, the latter consisted of a sagacity achieved through the self-cultivation of *de* and a "humane" (*ren* 仁) manner—as mentioned in the cauldron inscription. The Confucian form of this practice was supposed to result in one's transformation into a *jun* 君, a word that in Western Zhou times had referred to a ruler who was not the King, but in Confucian parlance the word possessed only moral connotations: a *jun* was someone who behaved as a *jun* ought to behave. The Zhongshan King and minister were aware of not only that debate but also popular beliefs in which the wisdom born of self-cultivation of inner energy resulted in an immortal self. The King had been out "wandering," a concept popularized by *Zhuangzi* 莊子 and representing a lack of interest in governmental affairs. On the other hand, this may be a reference to a ritual act of recreating ancient peregrinations in which the King went on military "inspection trips" just outside the state's borders in the Four Regions 四方. Also reflected in these inscriptions is a typical late Warring States concern with the proper execution of punishments and laws.

Much of the vocabulary, ideas, and pithy sayings in the inscriptions are also found in the transmitted literature. In fact, the inscription preserves little of the ancient ritual rhetoric associated with announcements to one's own ancestors, a rhetoric probably handed down orally through generations and different lineages of archivists and ministers. It survived the Spring and Autumn in the form of performed eulogies and songs, versions of which were preserved in the *Shijing*. But by the late Warring States, the typical bronze inscription was merely a note of function, with manufactur-

---

[1] See the discussion by Pines, "Disputers of Abdication."

ing signatures and designated weights and measures. Yet these remarkably long Zhongshan inscriptions hint at an archaic literary tendency in the northeast, seen early in the Shu Yi *zhong* inscription (no. 69, above), in regard to ancestor-worship ritual. The author of King Cuo's inscriptions was clearly familiar with the rhetorical tradition of modeling oneself on Heaven and one's ancestors, even though he peppered the texts with popular language and references to well known tales.

Colloquial grammatical structures such *yuhu* (or *wuhu*) ... *zai* (variously written, e.g., 於虖/烏虖 ... 哉) are found in transmitted chapters of the *Shangshu* that are seen as associated with the Zhou, also the "Daya" 大雅 and "Zhou song" 周頌 sections of the *Shijing*, *Xunzi* 荀子, and "Qi chen qi zhu" 七臣七主 chapter of *Guanzi* 管子. This confirms the likely linguistic links of those chapters to classically trained scholars of the northeast. The expression "The Altar of Soil and Millet" (*sheji* 社稷), found in the Zhongshan inscriptions, is unknown in the bronze inscription corpus but extremely common in texts like *Zuozhuan*. The similarity of expressions found in this inscription and in Warring States texts suggests a man who had access to versions, either oral or written, of songs, tales, and ritual codes that were eventually codified into classics, such as the *Shijing*, *Shangshu*, *Zuozhuan*, and *Liji*, or even the ideas of Warring States thinkers such as Mencius 孟子, Xunzi, and Zhuangzi.

The use of metaphor in the Zhongshan inscriptions also links them more closely to the contemporary literary tradition than to the transmitted ancient rhetoric we associate with the bronze inscription tradition. For example, the comment about sinking into an abyss as being preferable to losing face among men draws on common saying about fish or dragons leaping into abysses as a symbol of loss. Notions of cognitive states, such as the diametrically opposed states of "realization" (*wu* 悟) and "delusion" (*miyu* 迷惑), reflect debates about psychology and existence, such as those found in the "Mingfa jie" 明法解 of *Guanzi*.

Tales concerning the problems in Yan preserved in transmitted texts such as the *Xunzi*, *Han Feizi* 韓非子, and *Lüshi chunqiu* 呂氏春秋 contain vocabulary and sayings that are similar to language in the inscriptions, suggesting that the Zhongshan writer was helping to shape the legend of that historical event. The attempt of the ruler to abdicate in the legendary manner of Yao or Shun apparently caused the Yan war. Although it is not incidental that a bit of instability at the top allowed neighboring polities to invade and grab territory. The Zhongshan writer may also have had a hand in shaping the tale of Wu's annexation of Yue, which became a metaphor for political surprises. Moral tales about the consequences of the actions of arrogant states and rulers were popular among Confucian scholars and are even found in the Confucian *Lunyu*.

Transcription

唯十四年中山王䜣詐(作)鼎于銘曰：於虖！語不竣(廢)² 雩(哉)！寡人聞之，䢈(與)其汋(溺)於人施(也)，寧汋(溺)於淵。

昔者，郾(燕)君子噲，叡弇夫悟(悟)，長為人主，閈(閑)於天下之勿(物)矣，猶粯(迷)惑於子之而亡其邦，為天下僇(戮)，而皇(況)在於小子³君虖(乎)？

昔者，吾先考成王，量(早)棄群臣，寡人䒑䵞(幼童)未甬(通)智，隹(維)傅䋣(母)氏(是)從。天降休命于朕邦，又(有)厥忠臣賙，克順克俾，亡不率仁(仁)，敬順天德，以猻(左)右寡人，使智(知)社(社)稷之賃(任)。臣主之宜(義)，夙夜不解(懈)，以訓道(導)寡人，含(今)余方壯，智(知)天若否，侖(論)其德眚(省)其行，亡不順道考宅(度)隹(唯)型。

於虖、折(慎)雩(哉)！社(社)稷其庶虖(乎)，厥業在祗，寡人聞之，事小子女(如)長，事愚女(如)智(智)，此易言而難行施(也)，非恁⁴與忠，其誰能之？其誰能之？唯吾老賙，是克行之。

於虖攸(悠)雩(哉)！天其又(有)型于雩(茲)厥邦，氏(是)以寡人医(委)賃(任)之邦，而去之遊，亡䜣䜣(慄慄)之䜣(慮)。昔者，吾先祖桓王，卲(昭)考成王，身勤社(社)稷，行四方，以憂勞邦家，含(今)吾老賙，親率參(三)軍之眾，以征不宜(義)之邦，敓(奮)桴振鐸，闢啟封彊(疆)，方䜣(數)百里，剌(列)城䜣(數)十，克敵大邦。寡人庸其德，嘉其力，氏(是)以賜之厥命，隹(雖)又(有)死辠，及參(三)世，亡不若(赦)，以明其德，庸其工(功)，吾老賙奔走不聽命。寡人懼其忽然不可得，憚憚業業，恐隕社(社)稷之光，氏(是)以寡許之䜣(謀)䜣(慮)皆從，克又(有)工(功)，智(智)施(也)，詒死

---

² Some read this graph as *bei* 悖, "to confuse, disobey (words)," a Han usage. Although the graph is much simpler than earlier versions of *fei* 廢, the warning context regarding the King's command or words in which this graph is used has hundreds of years of tradition.

³ Some read this as the term *shaojun* 少君, a youthful ruler or young master, a Han usage.

⁴ See no. 72, note 4, above, regarding reading this graph as *nian* instead of the more common interpretation of *xin* 信. The problem with this reading is that the *nian* appears elsewhere in this inscription (but including a "mouth" semantic 念, suggesting perhaps that remembering involved reciting out loud) and *xin* appears in the Zhongshan Wang Cuo *hu* inscription (*Jicheng* 9735) in the typical Warring States form of 䜣 with the 身 phonetic.

皋之又(有)若(赦)，暂(知)為人臣之宜(義)施(也)。

於虖，念(念)之羕（哉）！後人其庸庸之，母(毋)忘尒(爾)邦。昔者，吳人幷雫(越)，雫(越)人修斅(教)備恁(任)[5]，五年覆吳，克幷之至于含(今)。尒(爾)母(毋)大而悇(肆)，母(毋)富而喬(驕)，母(毋)眾而囂，鄰邦難親，戕(仇)人在彷(旁)。

於虖，念(念)之羕（哉）！子子孫孫永定俘(保)之，母(毋)替厥邦。

Translation

It was in the fourteenth year of King Cuo of Zhongshan, when he had an inscription inscribed on a cauldron saying: "Alas! Do not discard these words! I, the Lone Man, have heard: 'It is better to sink into an abyss than to sink [in reputation and status] among men.'

"Previously, the Lord of Yan, Zikuai, knowledgeable and all-encompassing in his understanding, was a ruler of men for a long time, with a broad vision of All Under Heaven! For such as he to be deluded by Zizhi into losing his state and becoming exposed (like the corpse of a criminal) to All Under Heaven! And by a lord who was still a youth at that!

"Earlier, when my Former Aged One, King Cheng, abandoned his many ministers too early, I, the Lone Man, was a young naive child, one who followed after a nanny. When Heaven sent down its mandate as a gift to my state, there was (the deceased king's) loyal minister, Sima Zhou, who was able to obey and serve it, so that there was none who did not follow his humane government. Respectfully obedient to Heaven's power, he assisted me, the Lone Man, and made me understand the responsibility of the Altars of Soil and Millet. In the model propriety of minister and ruler, from dawn to dusk he was not lax in leading and guiding me, the Lone Man, so that now, when I am strong and grown, I can understand right and wrong according to Heaven, and discuss its power, observe its course, so that there is no moment when I do not obey the Way that is the model set up by my Aged One.

[5] Here the reading of "to think of" seems less appropriate than the sense of to "bear the burden of," but perhaps in ancient China the two inner processes were related. Earlier in the same inscription, this latter sense was conveyed with the graph 賃.

"Alas! Take care! He was close to the Altar of Soil and Millet. His duty resided in paying respects to the altar. I, the Lone Man, have heard it said: 'Serve a youth as if he were an adult; serve a fool as if he were intelligent.' This is more easily said than done! If not someone who cherishes you and is loyal, who would be capable? It was our Old Zhou (Sima Zhou) who was able to carry it out.

"Alas! How distant! Heaven has its model for us in this our state! Therefore, I, the Lone Man, entrusted the responsibility of the state to him and took off to wander about, without thought of fear or alarm. Earlier, our Former Ancestor King Huan and Lustrous Aged One, King Cheng, personally attended diligently to the Altar of Soil and Millet and traveled the Four Regions in order to express concern and to labor for state and home. Now, our Old Zhou personally led the masses of Three Armies in order to punish the state, which did not behave properly. Beating drumsticks and ringing bells, they opened the boundaries by several hundred square *li* with an array of several tens of cities, making our kingdom match the rank of a big state. I, the Lone Man, utilized his power and rejoiced in his strength, and so rewarded him with a charge. Even though he has committed a capital crime meriting execution across three generations without pardon, it was to illuminate his inner power and utilize his merit that our Old Zhou rushed around, not listening to orders. I, the Lone Man, was frightened that his rashness would receive no results—so terrified and frightened—and feared the loss of the radiance of the Altar of Soil and Millet, yet I permitted the armies all to follow his strategies and plans, enacting the merit and wisdom in them. He declined the pardon for the capital crime because he understands the propriety of acting as a minister.

"Alas! Remember it! You, descendants, employ the employable and do not forget your state. Earlier, the people of Wu annexed Yue, and the people of Yue trained and taught, prepared and entrusted themselves with the job of overturning Wu within five years and annexing it to the present day. You should not act begrudgingly when big, or arrogant when wealthy, or overpowering when there are many of you, so that neighboring states become difficult to be close to and enemies appear at your sides.

"Alas! Remember it! May sons of sons and grandsons of grandsons be eternally settled and protect it so as not to lose their state."

Further Reading

Jicheng 2840.

Mingwen xuan, no. 880.

Barnard, *Inscriptions*, v. 2, 877–945; v. 3, 2576–98.
Cook, "Chung-shan Bronze Inscriptions."
Cuo mu.
He Linyi, "Zhongshan wang qi gaishi shiyi."
Li Xueqin, *Eastern Zhou and Qin Civilizations*, 93–107.
Li Xueqin, *Shang Zhou guwenzi duben*, 183–99.
Li Xueqin, *Xinchu qingtongqi yanjiu*, 175–205.
Lin Hongming, *ZhanguoZhongshanguo wenzi yanjiu.*
Luo Fuyi, "Zhongshan wang mu ding hu mingwen xiaokao."
Mattos, "Eastern Zhou Bronze Inscriptions," 104–11.
Shang Chengzuo, "Zhongshan Wang Cuo hu, ding, mingwen chuyi."
Sun Zhichu, "Zhongshan Cuo ding, hu de niandai shishi ji qi yiyi."
Xu Zhongshu and Wu Shiqian, "Zhongshan san qi shiwen ji gongtang tu shuoming."
Yu Haoliang, "Zhongshan san qi mingwen kaoshi."
Zhang Zhenglang, "Zhongshan Wang Cuo hu ji ding ming kaoshi."
Zhao Cheng, "'Zhongshan hu' 'Zhongshan ding' mingwen shishi."
Zhu Dexi and Qiu Xigui, "Pingshan Zhongshan Wang mu tongqi mingwen de chubu yanjiu."

CAC

81. Chu Wang Yin Han *ding* 楚王酓悍鼎

The Chu royal family was pushed out of its base in 278 B.C.E. by the Qin army invading southward down the Han River valley. From that point on, the Chu government had to locate progressively farther east as the Qin forces also swept towards the eastern coastal region. In 241 B.C.E., King Kaolie 考烈 (r. 262–238 B.C.E.) built the last Chu capital, Shouchun 壽春, over the old city of Zhoulai 州來, just south of the Huai River near modern Shouxian, Anhui. King Kaolie died in 238 and Qin finally wiped out the once powerful state of Chu in 223. The tombs in Shouchun had suffered at the hands of plunderers for hundreds of years, but in the 1920s and 30s, near Lisangudui in Zhujiaji, peasants and a Swedish explorer, O. Karlbeck, stumbled upon a repository of Chu vessels and other items that were clearly from a royal tomb possibly belonging to one of King Kaolie's sons, named Yin 酓, who scholars believe was You Wang Han 幽王悍 (r. 237–228 B.C.E.). (The title *yin* 酓 was a Chu term for royal sons; it was written with the near homophone *xiong* 熊 by the Qin and in transmitted texts; see no. 59). But the "excavation" was so disorganized that the items from several tombs may have been mixed up. For example, pieces with the name of another royal son, Yin 酓 (read Ken 肯 by some), were also found (see *Jicheng* 2623). Some suggest that the second graph might be a simplified form of 蚡, the personal name for Chu King Wu (740–690 B.C.E.) mentioned in the list of Chu kings in the Tsinghua bamboo text *Chu ju* 楚居. It seems unlikely that this mystery royal son would have the same personal name as the earlier Chu King Wu.[1]

Typical of late Warring States inscriptions, the inscription is brief and functional. The focus was on identifying the artisans involved in casting each piece and the major part of the inscription is written around the lip (of the lid) or outside the vessel instead of inside the vessel and lid. Among the names of metal artisans, the Ke family had a particularly long association with the Chu royal family. In the fourth century B.C.E., members of

---

[1] For a summary of the range of earlier ideas, see Liu Hehui, *Chu wenhua de dongjian*, 198. For the "Chu Ju," see Li Xueqin, ed., *Qinghua daxue cang Zhanguo zhujian*, Vol. 1.b, 161, 187 no. 187. The personal name for King Wu in the *Shiji* is Tong 通 (*Shiji* 40.1694), but in *Chu ju* the name is transcribed with a *she* 舌 (*mə.lat) phonetic, which is somewhat close in ancient pronunciation to Da 達 (*Cə.lˤat). The *Chu ju* version also includes a "silk" 系 signifier. The graph read as Ken is missing the "mouth" aspect of the archaic graph for she as well as the "silk" element. The *Chu ju* list ends with King Dao 悼 (401–381 B.C.E.), long before King Kaolie's reign (262–238 B.C.E.).

the Ke family worked in a team of diviners and specialized in milfoil divination. The term "three Chu" may either refer to a place name or indicate the order in which it was cast. Since the vessel was cast separately from the lid, this may indicate to the artisans which lid it was to go with: "number three, for the Chu (king)."

Transcription

Lid: 楚王悍戰獲兵銅，正月吉日，室（至）鑄鐈鼎之蓋，以共（供）歲嘗。

冶師吏秦、差（佐）苛蠭為之。

集脭（廚）

Vessel: 冶師盤野、差（佐）秦丕為之。

三楚

Translation

[Lid:] King Han of Chu captured weapons, and on an auspicious day of the first month brought them to be cast as the lid of a high-footed cauldron to be used to present the annual tasting sacrifice.

Smelting Master Officer Qin and Assistant Ke Ci made it.

Chief Cook

[Vessel:] Smelting Master Pan Ye and Assistant Qin Xia made it.

Three Chu

Further Reading

Jicheng 2795.

Kimbun tsūshaku, 40.539–46.

Mingwen xuan, no. 664.

Chu wenwu zhanlan tulu.
Cook, "Auspicious Metals and Southern Spirits," 523–25.
Cook, "Scribes, Cooks, and Artisans," 256–59, 264–69, 275–77.
Cook and Major, eds., *Defining Chu*, 75, 102.
Li Xueqin, *Eastern Zhou and Qin Civilizations*, 154–56, 163–64, 167.

CAC

82. Shuo ren *jing* 碩人鏡

This bronze mirror, bearing an incomplete version of the ode "Shuo ren" 碩人 (*Mao* 57), appeared in an antique store in Wuhan 武漢 at the height of the Cultural Revolution, and was first published in 1980 by the famous palaeographer and calligrapher Luo Fuyi 羅福頤 (1905-1981). There is no reliable information regarding its present whereabouts. The mirror has a diameter of 14.8 cm and a thickness of 0.4 cm at the margin. Its back features a fairly large knob, around which several rings of creatures from the symbolic realm of *yinyang wuxing* 陰陽五行 cosmology and mythological figures, such as the popular cultic couple of the Spirit Mother of the West (*xi wangmu* 西王母) and the Spirit Lord of the East (*dong wanggong* 東王公), are densely arranged. Applying a relief fitting technique, i.e. a kind of intaglio casting, the designed mythical creatures project out of the background, and fill up the entire surface up to the conventional parallel bordure-type (*chonglieshi* 重列式) margin. The inscription, placed between this double bordure and a fine "cloud pattern" (*yunwen* 雲紋) exterior circle, was once 90 characters, but two individual characters are totally erased. It breaks off abruptly in the second line of the last stanza (IV) of the poem as known from the transmitted versions, apparently for reasons of space.

In view of several uninscribed, but stylistically comparable pieces in the posession of the Museum of the City of Ezhou 鄂州, Li Xueqin convincingly argued in 1988 that the mirror could be tentatively dated to the period between 210–240 C.E., and that it was probably manufactured in Echeng 鄂城 or the former district of Wuchang 武昌, i.e. in the area where Sun Quan 孫權 (182–252 C.E.) resided between 221 and 229 as ruler of Wu. This area, despite the conventional dating of the end of the Eastern Han dynasty to Cao Pi's 曹丕 enthronement as Emperor Wen of Wei 魏文帝 in 220, was *de facto* an independent kingdom since 196 C.E. Earlier datings of the mirror to the last two Eastern Han reign periods, namely Jian'an 建安 (196–220) and Yankang 延康 (220), seem less likely.

The text of the "Shuo ren" air, traditionally understoood as an epithalamium about the marriage between Zhuang Jiang 莊姜, daughter of the Lord of Qi, and the Lord of Wei 衛 in 757 B.C.E., was one of the most frequently quoted odes in pre-imperial and early Han literature. To give meaning to the mirror, we have to take in archaeological contexts and inscriptional contents of other Eastern Han mirrors, as well consider the quoting of this song as an admonition ascribed to Zhuang Jiang's governess in the *Lienü zhuan* 列女傳 (*Collected Biographies of Women*) in which there is a demand that the bride combine exterior pulchritude with interior sublimity even after marriage. By doing so, it is possible to say that the mirror was part of a trousseau or a wedding gift, or perhaps a farewell present from a parting husband to his wife. Lexically, it features several formulaic expressions which can be shown to form part of an earlier tradition descriptive of court dance, in which the *shuoren* of the first verse still had not undergone the literary transformation from a "stately (male) person" with prominent ritual functions to a "tall beautiful lady" on her newlywed's journey. The inscription features thirty-five deviations from the traditional edition of the *Shijing*, including loans within the phonophoric series (16), outside the phonophoric series (16), graphical mistakes (1) and true lexical variants (2). As a group, these variants are not matched by *any* of the attested traditions of the *Shijing*, nor by the fragments of the so-called Fuyang 阜陽 bamboo version of the *Shijing* discovered in 1977 in Shuanggudui 雙谷堆, Anhui Province, nor by the version preserved in the stone steles erected during the Eastern Han Xiping 熹平 reign period (172–189 C.E.).

As far as the rhyming is concerned, the present version results in an additional rhyming couplet (Ia:Ic) in one place, the loss of another in (IIf:IIg), where the bisyllabic rhyme in the *Mao* version is not corroborated by the inscription, and a possible extra impure rhyme in IIIe:IIIg. While some of these peculiarities point to a post-Qin phonology, none of them is particularly diagnostic of the Eastern Han or even later periods. Variants of the initials are more surprising, since in several cases dental sibilants of the edited versions appear as laterals or lateral cluster initials in the inscription. This phenomenon—like the secondary emergence of affricates in general— is characteristic of the earliest layers of the Wu and some Min dialects, and commonly assumed to have arisen under areal pressure from autochthonic Tai-Kadai languages in the area, to which the early northern Chinese dialects were intrusive.

If these linguistic observations are correct, they show that as late as the end of the Eastern Han period, there was still a strong oral or vocal current in the transmission of the *Shijing* in southeastern China, maybe even a floating, colloquial recension. This tiny, stylistically conventional mirror preserves a mere glimpse of that story.

INSCRIPTIONS

Transcription

Note: The following tabular transcription presents a synopsis of the mirror text and the traditional versions, along with their rhyme schemes and a phonological recostruction. The last part of the poem is missing from the tinscription. Grey shading of characters indicate variants in the mirror version.

	Mirror version			Maozhuan version*		
I	石人姬姬	dak niŋ k(r)ə.k(r)ə	A	碩人其頎	dak niŋ gə C.ɢəj	A
b	衣綿縝衣	əj-s men? kʷʰˤeŋ? ʔəj	B	衣錦褧衣	ʔəj-s k(r)əm? kʷʰˤeŋ? ʔəj	B
c	夷侯之子	ləj gˤ(r)o tə tsə-?	A	齊侯之子	[dz]ˤəj gˤ(r)o tə tsə-?	X
d	衛侯之妻	ɢʷ(r)at-s gˤ(r)o tə [tsʰ]əj	B	衛侯之妻	ɢʷ(r)at-s gˤ(r)o tə [tsʰ]əj	B
e	東宮之妹	tˤoŋ k(r)uŋ tə C.mˤət-s	X	東宮之妹	tˤoŋ k(r)uŋ tə C.mˤət-s	X
f	刑侯之夷	Gˤeŋ gˤ(r)o tə ləj	B	邢侯之姨	Gˤeŋ gˤ(r)o tə ləj	B
g	登公惟私	tˤəŋ C.qˤoŋ ɢʷij səj	B	譚公維私	lˤəm C.qˤoŋ ɢʷij səj	A
II	手如濡淒	ɲu-? na no [tsʰ]əj	B	手如柔荑	ɲu-? na nu ləj	A
b	膚如臆䏙	pra na ŋ(r)ə kij	b	膚如凝脂	pra na ŋ(r)əŋ kij	a
c	領如狩夷	Gˤəm na s-tu?-s=ləj	B	領如蝤蠐	reŋ-? na [dz]u=[dz]ˤəj	A
d	齒如會師	t-kʰə-? na m-kˤop-s-s=srij	b	齒如瓠犀	t-kʰə-? na ɢʷa=s.lˤəj	A
e	隕首娥麋	drin lu? ŋˤaj mrij	b	螓首蛾眉	dzin lu? [ŋ]ˤaj mrər	A
f	哞哄和兮	C-rˤu-? s-law-s m-sˤrə-? gˤe	xC	巧笑倩兮	kʰˤru? s-law-s [ts]ʰen-s gˤe	BB
g	美目瞋兮	mrəj? C.muk pin gˤe	xC	美目盼兮	mrəj? C.muk pʰ(r)ən-s gˤe	BB
III	石人嗷嗷	dak niŋ ŋˤaw.ŋˤaw	D	碩人敖敖	dAk niŋ ŋˤaw.ŋˤaw	C
b	稅于農郊	lot-s ɢʷa nˤoŋ kˤraw	D	說于農郊	lot-s ɢʷa nˤoŋ kˤraw	C
c	四牡有撟	s.lij-s m(r)u? ɢʷə-? kh(r)aw	D	四牡有驕	s-hlij-s m(r)u-? ɢʷə-?kh(r)aw	C
d	洙□猋猋	to □ pew.pew	d	朱幩鑣鑣	to bər prew.prew	C
e	翟□以朝	lˤewk □ lə-? m-traw	D	翟茀以朝	lˤewk pʰut lə-? m-traw	c
f	大夫宿退	lˤat-s p(r)a suk-s ŋˤəp-s	X	大夫夙退	lˤat-s p(r)a suk ŋˤəp-s	X
g	㾹使君勞	mə s-rə-? C.qur rˤaw	D	無使君勞	ma s-rə-? C.qur rˤaw	C

IV							
	河水洋洋	C.gˤaj s.turʔ ɢaŋ ɢaŋ	X	河水洋洋	C.gˤaj s.turʔ ɢaŋ ɢaŋ	X
b	北流	pˤək lu		北流活活	pˤək lu kʷˤat. kʷˤat	D
c				施眾濊濊	l̥aj kʷa qʷʰˤat. qʷʰˤat	D
d		(missing)		鱣鮪發發	tra[n] ɢʷəʔ Cə.pat.Cə.pat	D
e				葭菼揭揭	kˤra l̥ˤamʔ m-kratˑ m-krat	D
f				庶姜孽孽	s-tak-s C.qaŋ ŋr[e]t.ŋr[e]t	D
g				庶士有朅	s-ta(k)-s m-s-rə-ʔ ɢʷə-ʔ khrat	D
	TEXT	OC*	ρ	TEXT	OC*	ρ

Translation

I

a   A stately lady is she, a ravishing beauty,
b   wearing brocade beneath an unlined raiment,
c   the child of the Marquis of Yi,
d   wife to the Marquis of Wei,
e   younger sister of the "Eastern Palace" (the crown prince),
f   sister-in-law of the Marquis of Xing,
g   and the Patriarch of Deng is her brother-in-law.

II

a   Her hands are like moist sprouts,
b   her skin is glossy like lard,
c   her neck is sallow like a maggot,
d   her teeth are like pumpkin seeds,
e   finely tattooed her head, beauteous her brows.
f   Oh how flamboyant her ablated teeth,[1]
g   oh how riveting her bright eyes!

III

a   A stately lady is she, haughty,
b   resting [her cortège] in the rural suburbs.
c   Her four stallions are unreined,
d   red [bit plaques] are whirling all around.

---

[1] For the anthropological background to this practice, see, e.g., Han and Nakahashi, "A Comparative Study of Ritual Tooth Ablation in Ancient China and Japan."

e   [Her chariot] adorned with pheasant-feathers, she goes to court.
f   The great officers retire overnight,
g   so as not to exhaust the Dame.

IV
a   The waters of the Yellow River, how vast,
b   northwards they flow.

Further Reading

Behr, "Spiegelreflex."

Huber and Mittag, "Spiegel-Dichtung."

Li Xueqin, "Lun 'Shuo ren' ming shenshou jing."

Luo Fuyi, "Han Lushi jing kaoshi."

Xu Jianmei, "Dong Han *Shijing* mingwen jing."

Yang Aiguo, "Hanjing mingwen de shiliaoxue jiazhi."

Zheng-Zhang Shangfang, "Cong Shuoren jing 'qi-yi' tongjia tan shanggu jingzu shengmu de quzhi."

Zhou Shirong, "Hunan chutu Handai tongjing wenzi yanjiu."

WB

Glossary

Titles, Names, and Other Key Terms

For a comprehensive list of official titles with examples, see Li, *Bureaucracy and the State in Early China*, 305–14.

bai qi shou 拜稽首: an expression of gratitude involving the hands and lowering the head. The specifics of the act are unclear: the person may have clapped his hands together or simply placed them together in a prayer-like or other position; he may have simply bowed his head towards the floor or actually knocked his head against the floor in a more prostrate position.

baishen 百神: the Hundred Spirits; many ancestral spirits; also called Great Spirits 大神.

bang 邦: allied group under a single leader, a polity, a small state. The leaders could be termed *wang* 王, *bangjun* 邦君, or other titles. The word bang stands behind many later usages of *guo* 國, *bang* having been routinely converted to *guo* in order to avoid the taboo of using the personal name of Liu Bang 劉邦, Emperor Gaozu of Han 漢高祖 (r. 202–195 B.C.E.). (Guo itself originally referred to the fortified area of a city, as opposed to *ye* 野, "the wilds," the area beyond it.)

bo 伯: a local political leader; highest ranked sibling in the family hierarchy; elder; earl.[1]

celing (ming) 冊令 (命): a verbal commission, charge, or command that was also presented in written form, most likely on bamboo strips. The ceremony of presenting this charge is known as the "award ceremony," "appointment ceremony," or "investiture ceremony." The ceremonial actor recording and presenting the charge in one of the ritual officers in charge of creating and reading the records. For example, in the Da Ke *ding* (no. 46), after the King and the awardee have taken up their proper positions in court, "the King called the Chief Officer to give the recorded charge to *shanfu* Ke" 王呼尹氏冊令膳夫克.

chen 辰: "asterism; asterism used to mark time" (see *chen zai*). The three "Great *chen*" (*dachen* 大辰) were the Dipper (*dou* 斗, or *beidou* 北斗); Antares, the Fire Star (*huo* 火 or *dahuo* 大火); and a set of stars beneath Orion's belt representing the warrior's dagger (*fa* 伐).[2]

chen zai 辰在: "the asterism is in ..." Here, *chen* refers to a certain asterism (possibly the Dipper) in its function as an accessible (locatable) heavenly indicator

---

[1] For a recent discussion of the Western Zhou *bo* as either Zhou officers or regional leaders, see Shao Bei, "Xi Zhou bo zhi kaosuo."

that marks a specific sexagenary day in the cycle of 60, the latter often coordinated graphically with celestial divisions of different sorts. *Chen zai X [ganzhi]* is used formulaically, meaning that the chen is in the approximate vicinity of a certain Stem+Branch day. The Dipper in fact is perceivable as rotating like a dial in the sky, but how it would indicate specific days in the sixty-day cycle versus simply seasons is unclear.[3]

Cheng Tang 成湯 or 成唐: The legendary founder of the Shang Dynasty.[4] The earliest mention of this name is on an oracle bone discovered in a cache in the Zhou homeland dating to the early Western Zhou. On bronze inscriptions the earliest mention is in the late Spring and Autumn bells from the state of Qi, see no. 69.

Chengzhou 成周: "Accomplished Zhou," the administrative capital located in the modern Luoyang 洛陽 area, established by the Zhou after defeating the Shang. It represented the religious and political "center" (*zhong* 中) of the new Zhou state. Many Shang specialists were moved to Chengzhou to work for the Zhou. See the He *zun*, no. 6.

chuji 初吉: "Early Auspiciousness," formulaic dating term referring to the first few days at the beginning of the month when the moon is newly born, or to the first appearance of an auspicious *tiangan* "Heavenly Stem" day of a lunar month.[5]

da 大: a graph used to represent the word for "big" (*lˤat-s) as well as words for "grand, extreme" (*tai* 太 *lˤat-s) and "Sky, Heaven" (*tian* 天 *lˤin). Sometimes the *tai* and *tian* usages were distinguished by an extra mark, either on the "leg" or "head" of the original graph.

dafu 大服: Grand Subduer; highly ranked military guardsman; the "grand service," i.e. important duties or position.

daming; see *tianming*.

dashi; see *tianshi*.

de 德: potency, power, charisma, or merit accumulated through good service, both political and religious. During the Western Zhou, an aristocrat could accumulate merit or *de* through service to the Zhou court. This merit was accumulated by a lineage over generations and represented by material awards from the King. Lineage heirs were expected to please their ancestors by following

---

[2] See Feng Shi, "Zhongguo zaoqi xingxiang tu yanjiu," 113.

[3] Ye Zhengbo, "Lüe lun Xi-Zhou mingwen de jishi fangshi."

[4] See Fracasso, "Between Legend and History."

[5] Xu, "Using Sequential Relations of Day-Dates to Determine the Temporal Scope of Western Zhou Lunar Phase Terms."

their model and continuing to amass awards and promotions from the King. While heirs received *de* from their ancestors, it had originally derived from *shangdi* or *tian*. King Wen, the Zhou founder, received the *de* from the highest spiritual agency. Zhou kings could share the divinely authorized power through the award of bronze vessels. By the end of the Warring States period, the kings had lost all divine authority and the spiritual force was understood as something available from within all cultivated gentlemen. It represented inner virtue and the outer performance of moral behavior.[6]

di 帝: deity, (divine) lord; god; also a title for deceased Shang kings. Could refer to the "Deity Above," *shangdi* 上帝.

dizhi 地支: "Earthly branches," a later term to indicate the twelve terms combined with the ten *tiangan* ("Heavenly stems") that make up the revolving sixty-day calendar; see sexagenary cycle. See also *tiangan* and *ganzhi*.

duiyang 對揚: to respond [to the award] and extol [the gift-giver], for example, "respond and extol the King's grace (or gifts)" (*duiyang wang xiu* 對揚王休).[7] Often the verb "to dare" (*gan* 敢) is added, for example: "Duo You dared to respond and extol the Patriarch's grace" 多友敢對揚公休. Abbreviated versions using just *dui* or *yang* also occur: *dui* 對 X *xiu* 休: respond to X's grace. X is often the Zhou King in earlier inscriptions (*dui wang xiu* 對王休); "extols the Queen's grace" (*yang wangjiang xiu* 揚王姜休) appears too.

ganzhi 干支: "heavenly stems and earthly branches"; a later term applied to the sets of ten and twelve signs used in rotation to mark time. See *tiangan* and *dizhi*; see sexagenary cycle.

gong 公: a local political ruler more powerful than a *bo*; clan elder; patriarch; sire; duke; term used in epithets for deceased elite males or "honored forebear."

guansi 官司: to manage (*kwˤan-s.lə*), similar in use to *shesi* 攝司 (*kə.ŋep-s.lə*), meaning "to handle, assist" (see *Jicheng* 4287); a supervising officer, on par with "the functionary officers" (*xu* 胥) and "the invocators of the Five Settlements" (*wuyi zhu* 五邑祝) (*Jicheng* 4244, 4340, 4296–97).

hou 侯: a local lord who has pledged military allegiance to the Zhou; marquis, warrior lord.

huang 皇: brilliant, august; an epithet used for ancestors at the rank of grandfather or older; can also be applied to former kings and distant ancestors, as in

---

[6] Kryukov, "Symbols of Power and Communication in Pre-Confucian China"; Cook, "Wealth and the Western Zhou"; Cook, "Eastern Zhou Ancestor Worship"; Ai Mengfan, "'De' zai shanggu wenxian zhong de 'zhixiang' yi"; Nivison, *The Ways of Confucianism*.

[7] Kane, "Aspects of Western Zhou Appointment Inscriptions"; Wang Jing, "'Duiyang' zai shi"; Shen Wenzhuo, *Zong-Zhou liyue wenming kaolun*, 529–51.

the phrase *huangwang* 皇王 or *huangzu* 皇祖. Beginning in the Qin period, it referred to the Son of Heaven or Emperor (*huangdi* 皇帝). The term *huangdi* earlier referred to the Deity Above.

huchen 虎臣: the Tiger Guard, Corps or Servants; a clan militia that protected the King.

huo 或; also see *yu* 域: It can stand for "region," "territory"; many scholars assume 或 should be read as *guo* 國 (a graph first used in the late Western Zhou period; see the Mao Gong *ding*, no. 55).

ji 季: the youngest rank of male or female siblings.

Ji 姬: the Zhou clan name, used in women's names only.

Jiang 姜: an elite clan that intermarried with the Zhou during the Western Zhou period; a clan name used by Qi women in the Eastern Zhou period.

jijin 吉金: "auspicious metals," specially selected metals of certain colors and alloys (see nos. 69, 72) used to make bronze vessels. Since the term is most commonly used after the Western Zhou period by powerful individuals for themselves (outside of the Zhou gift-giving and award structure), the metals may have been gained through other networks (such as mines along the south bank of the Yangzi River no longer controlled by Zhou allies) or through the plunder of bronzes from destroyed ancestral shrines.

jishengpo 既生霸: "already living brightness," a formulaic dating term, most likely referring to the first half of a lunar month. The graph *ba* 霸 is usually understood as *po* 魄, and interpreted as the bright white color of the moon. In later contexts the term refers to the energy or spiritual agency that stays with the physical body after death.

jisipo 既死霸: "already dying brightness," a formulaic dating term, most likely referring to the second half of a lunar month. The graph 霸 is usually understood as *po* 魄; see *jishengpo*.

jiu 酒: ale made of millet or other grains and possibly mixed with berries, herbs, and medicinal additives such as bee pollen. By the Warring States period, numerous types and grades were produced. Sometimes translated as "wine" or "liquor."

jiwang 既望: "already fully visible," formulaic dating term, referring to a period from the sixteenth to the twenty-first day of the full moon. See also *jishengpo*.

lin zhong 林鐘: a set of chime bells; harmonious bells (*hezhong* 龢鐘). The word *lin* was written in numerous ways over the centuries, but the basic components of the ancient graph included arrangements of the phonetic elements 亩 *p.rim?* and 林 *rən* (sometimes written as 秝). Later evidence suggests that a *lin* bell actually denoted a specific tone within a gamut that formed the interval of the perfect fifth above the fundamental, and such notation may identify where the bell would have been hung within a chime set.⁸ See, for example, nos. 33, 44, 46, 51, 59, 60, and 62.

ling 令: "order, command," often used to write the cognate word *ming* 命, "command, mandate."

mei'ao 眉敖: title of a non-Zhou chief, who possibly maintained an inconstant tribute relationship with the Zhou kings; the title is no doubt related to the later title *mo'ao* 莫敖, used by certain members of the elite in the southern state of Chu (nos. 27, 42).⁹

meng 孟: the eldest rank of male or female siblings.

mieli 蔑曆 or X *mie* 蔑 Y *li* 曆: X (usually the King) rewards Y for merit accumulated through service,¹⁰ for example: "The King rewards Geng Ying's merit" (*wang mie Geng Ying li* 王蔑庚嬴曆).

qi 其: "perhaps"; later used as a pronoun for "he, she, it" (instead of *jue* 厥); used to express the tentative nature of making requests for blessings from the ancestral spirits, such as good fortune, wealth, or eternal progeny. Sometimes it indicates an optative mood, "May...," "Let..."

ruo 若: "seems"; loan for *nuo* 諾, "approve." How to read the common phrase *wang ruo yue* 王若曰 has been the source of much debate, particularly with regard to the nature of the award ceremony. The two leading interpretations are "The King says to this effect" and "The King approved, saying ...." The question revolves around whether the speech (indicated by *yue* 曰) was not intoned directly by the King, being read instead from bamboo records by an archivist, or whether the King "approved" the award narrative and permitting the ceremony to proceed.¹¹ Usually the presentation of the awards follows immediately thereafter.

sanshou 三壽: the Three Long-Lived Ones, the spirits of the first three Zhou kings; three stars in the sky.¹²

---

⁸ See Needham, *Science and Civilisation in China*, v. 4, pt. 1, 165–76; Falkenhausen, *Suspended Music*, 296–307.

⁹ See Cook and Major, eds., *Defining Chu*, 54.

¹⁰ For recent discussions, see Cook, "Wealth and the Western Zhou," 278–79; Li, *Bureaucracy and the State in Early China*, 226–29.

¹¹ See Falkenhausen, "The Inscribed Bronzes from Yangjiacun" and "Royal Audience and Its Reflections."

¹² The identity of these three stars is unknown. However, in the Han period, three stars in the vicinity of the Dipper were known as the *san gong* 三公, which Pankenier translates as "Three Eminences"; see Pankenier, *Astrology and Cosmology in Early China*, 458.

sexagenary cycle: the sixty-day cycle of ten "Heavenly stem" (*tiangan* 天干) and twelve "Earthly branch" (*dizhi* 地支) signs that rotate in pairs, resulting in a sixty-day cycle calendar. Already in use during the Shang period as a method to keep track of ritual sacrifices to ancestors, who were also named for the ten stem days.

shanfu 膳夫: a high minister who managed governmental affairs inside and outside of the court; based on later commentaries some understand his role as a steward in charge of food service; see nos. 46, 56, 62.

shangdi 上帝: the Deity Above, High Lord; the divine spirit of the sky; equivalent in Zhou bronze inscriptions to Tian.

shangxia 上下: the spirits above and below; sky and earth spirits.

shen 神: a spirit, natural or ancestral divinity.

sheng 聖: sage, an epithet for an ancestral spirit (see Yin Ji *ding*, no. 34). Also called Sage Brightness, *sheng shuang* 聖爽 (see Xing *zhong*, no. 33)

shi 師: master of ritual or military arts; teacher; captain.[13] Different types of *shi* include "grand masters" (*dashi* 大師) and "masters in chief" (*shishi* 師氏). The word *shi* could also refer to an army, a military encampment, or a garrison.

shi 史: archivist; scribe; historian; astrologer; diviner; further differentiated as "inner" or "court" scribe (*neishi*), "grand" scribe (*taishi*), or as "technician" (*yin*) or scribes of "bamboo annals" (*zuoce*).

shi 尸: "corpse"; take on the responsibility of (managing) an affair; loan for the name Yi 夷; in transmitted texts the *shi* appears as an actor in the sacrificial feast, traditionally believed to be a grandson impersonating the ancestor at the feast.

shu 叔: collateral family rank; younger brother of father.

taotie 饕餮: an Eastern Zhou term applied by later historians to the late Shang and early Western Zhou mask-like animal faces, featuring prominent horns and eyes and combining physical elements from a variety of wild animals. Historians debate the function of this prominent décor.[14]

tiangan 天干: "Heavenly stem," later term to indicate the ten primary sun signs used to mark sacrifice days to particular ancestors; also used in the solar calendar. See sexagenary cycle.

---

[13] Li Feng suggests that all *shi* at one time participated in military activities ("'Offices' in Bronze Inscriptions and Western Zhou Government Administration," 20n.60; *Bureaucracy and the State in Early China*, 229–32).

[14] See Whitfield, ed., *The Problem of Meaning in Early Chinese Ritual Bronzes*; Kesner, "The Taotie Reconsidered"; and Childs-Johnson, "The Metamorphic Image."

tianjun 天君: a reference to the Zhou queen. The title *jun* appeared as early as the Shang period and seems to have been used as a title for a ruler who was not a King. Since the King could be referred to as the Son of Heaven (*tianzi* 天子, see below), the *jun* of Heaven could be the queen. In later times, the title *jun* was adapted to refer to men who cultivated the moral qualities desired in a ruler.

tianming 天命 or *daming* 大命: Heaven's Mandate or the Great Mandate; divine authority to rule; the source of *de*. See also *de*.

tianshi 天室 or *dashi* 大室: the Chamber of Heaven or Great Hall, possibly an ancient observatory or sanctum in a palace or major shrine.

tianzi 天子: the Son of Heaven, the title used by subjects when addressing the Zhou King. Later applied to emperors. See also *huang*.

wang 王: king; hegemonic leader of an allied group of polities or of a single state. By the 4th century B.C.E., *wang* was used to refer to deceased ancestors, such as paternal grandparents.

weiyi 威儀: "Awesome Decorum," a mode of behavior displaying education in the ritual and military arts; the style of a dance performance.

wen 文: patterned, cultivated, or accomplished; a typical epithet for an ancestral spirit.

xiang 享: the presentation of sacrificial offerings and memorial feasts for the ancestral spirits, one of the primary functions of bronze vessels.

xiang 饗: a feast that, like *xiang* 享 (see above), probably included ancestral (and perhaps nature) spirits, but the scale of the invitees seems larger and the locations more public, even outdoors, and not necessarily inside a shrine. These feasts might be held (or "presented," *ni* 逆) to conclude an exchange of goods or to celebrate the harvest.

xiaozi 小子: the Little One, youth; lineage heir; scion, self-reference when addressing one's father's spirit; a son still in mourning for his father; a term of self-deprecation; a minor.

ya 亞: an office in the Shang government of unknown function; later title for a branch lineage founder. The shape of the graph ya suggests a link to mortuary ritual.[15] As with other kinship terms in late Shang society, such as "son" (*zi*) or "father" (*fu*), the *ya* could be mobilized as a group (as in the phrase "Many *ya*" 多亞).

Yin 殷: the Zhou name for the Shang polity and people; also referred to the last

---

[15] See Allan, *The Shape of the Turtle*, for a discussion how the shape of the graph reflects the shape of the *sifang* cosmos, the royal tomb, and the outline of a typical oracle plastron prepared for display rather than simply storage.

Shang capital.

yin 尹: an overseer in charge of court duties including managing the text during appointment ceremonies and engineering projects around the capital. Different types of *yin* included the "corrective overseer" (*zhengyin* 正尹), the "bamboo-document overseer" (*zuoce yin* 作冊尹), and "the overseer in chief" *yinshi* 尹氏.

yong 用: "use (the vessel, or opportunity) to (sacrifice)" (see *yongzuo*). The word *yong* often precedes a series of promises by the owner of the vessel as to its use. For example, the late Western Zhou Xi Zhong *zhong* 兮仲鐘 (*Jicheng* 71): "Xi Zhong made this greatly harmonious series of chime-bells. May he use it to pursue (in memory) and present filial sacrificial offerings to (his) Bright Deceased-father Ji Bo and use it to entertain (his) Former Accomplished Ones, so his progeny will eternally treasure and use (the bronzes) to present mortuary feasts" 兮仲作大林鐘，其用追孝于皇考己伯，用侃喜前文人，子孫永寶用享.

yong zuo 用作: "to use (materials, opportunity) to make (i.e., cast, an inscribed bronze vessel)." The phrase is translated variously depending on how the full dedication of the vessel is interpreted. For example, one issue is whether the word *yong* functioned as a full verb, perhaps even in the old Shang sense of "to use in sacrifice" or more as an auxiliary verb like *yi* 以, which was rarely used in this context during the Western Zhou. Variations of the phrase include the typical *yong zuo bao zun yi* 用作寶尊彝 "use (the gifts to commission, or this opportunity) to make a treasured sacrificial vessel for expressing reverence (to the ancestors and the gift-giver)." At times the spirit (or living bride in the case of dowry vessels) for whom the vessel is dedicated is mentioned after the *zuo*: *yong zuo que wengu bao zun yi* 用乍厥文姑寶尊彝 "use (the award or the opportunity) to make a treasured sacrificial vessel for his or her Accomplished Aunt (or mother-in-law) to express reverence." The *yong* and *zuo* were also used separately: *yong dian wang ling, zuo Zhou Gong yi* 用典王令，作周公彝 "use the occasion of recording the King's command, to make a sacrificial vessel for Zhou Gong."

yousi 有司: supervisors of governmental duties, such as of "land" distribution and management (*situ* 司土), "labor" (*sigong* 司工), and "horses" and militia supplies (*sima* 司馬). They often acted as judges in local disputes.

yu 域: "region, territory"; many scholars assume 或 should be read as *guo* 國 (a graph first used in the late Western Zhou period, see the Mao Gong *ding*, no. 55). The popular reading of *yu* 域 as *guo* 國, "state," is palaeographically possible but historically unnecessary. The "territories" were a Zhou reference for *fang* 方, an old term referring to regions considered as the far periphery of the royal sphere of influence. The *siyu* 四域 "Four Territories", like the common term *sifang* 四方, "Four Regions," had both a pragmatic meaning of "the whole sphere of political and economy influence" and also the connotation of a cosmological realm of spiritual control.[16] We know from inscriptions in no. 39 that the people in the territories were organized into confederations, or small states; see *bang*.

zhong 仲: the middle rank of male or female siblings.

Zhou *gong* 周公: Patriarch, Lord, Duke of Zhou. In later transmitted literature, Zhou Gong was famous for his moral government and for acting as regent when King Cheng was a minor. He was a younger brother of Zhou founder King Wu named Dan 旦.. In the Western Zhou bronze inscriptions there are many Zhou Gong who were obviously different people living at different times.[17]

zizi sunsun 子=(子子)孫=(孫孫): sons of sons and grandsons of grandsons, many sons and grandsons, male progeny, descendants of the awardee. The term is commonly abbreviated with the two lines of reduplication and is found in the prayer at the end of the inscription. For example, "May (the awardee's) progeny forever protect and use it (the vessel)" 其子=(子子)孫=(孫孫)永保用之.

Zongzhou 宗周: "Ancestral Zhou".

zuoce 作冊: the Document-Maker, the creator of bamboo annals, an official along with *shi* and *yin* who handled the texts of the King's commands and other archives.

Unknown Words

𦀚: "manage; carry on (inherited) duties," possibly *jian* 兼 (*kˤem), meaning "in addition, at the same time."[18] A Western Zhou term with no obvious descendant graph; see no. 46, note 4, above.

勴: "rise up"; loan for "enjoy" (*le* 樂); loan for "paying respects" (*ke* 恪)." Sometimes read as the Western Zhou version of "to celebrate" (*jia* 嘉). See no. 33, note 8.

Names of Vessel Types

For an extensive glossary including vessel names, see Falkenhausen, *Chinese Society in the Age of Confucius*, 517–55.

---

[16] See Allan, *The Shape of the Turtle*, chap. 4.
[17] See Shaughnessy, *Sources of Western Zhou History*, 201–16.
[18] Wang Hui, *Shang Zhou jinwen*, 188, note 7.

bi 匕: spatulas with long handles for serving, first cast in bronze during the Shang period.

bo 鎛: large bells that hung vertically on a wooden stand; most common during the Spring and Autumn period.

ding 鼎: cauldrons believed to be used for cooking meat stews; may be three-legged and round or four-legged and rectangular (*fangding* 方鼎); many are furnished with loop handles on the rim for lifting and moving them with poles. Cauldrons were the oldest and longest standing form, dating from the Erlitou 二里頭 period up through the Han. The largest *fangding*, ranging in height from 80 to 100 cm, belonged to Shang royalty.[19]

fangyi 方彝: square, often highly decorated, containers for storing fine ales; most common during the late Shang and early Western Zhou era.

fou 缶: storage vessels for ale with bulbous squat bodies under upright collars and paired handles; most common during the Eastern Zhou period.

fu 簠: rectangular food containers for storing grain with lids that could be reversed and used for serving dishes; most common during the Eastern Zhou period.

gong 觥: vessels for pouring alcoholic beverages; in the shape of four-legged animals with spouts and handles; most common during the late Shang and early Western Zhou era. Animals featured included tigers, dragons, and owls.

gu 觚: tall, slender vase-like drinking goblets popular among Shang elite.

gui 簋: tureen-like containers for grain cooked with herbs, legumes, or vegetables; the vessels generally have round bodies with one or two pairs of handles that sit on a ringed foot or square box that could sit over coals (called *fangzuo gui* 方座簋, occasionally with tiny bells underneath that would ring when the vessels were carried); most popular in the late Shang period up through the middle Western Zhou period.

he 盉: teapot-like vessels with spouts, lids, and handles; used for pouring liquids for drinking and bathing; popular beginning in the late Shang period and continuing through the Eastern Zhou period.

hu 壺: lidded vase-like containers for fine ale that come in round, rectangular or flask-like versions; popular beginning in the late Shang period and continuing up through the Eastern Zhou period.

jia 斝: round, flared-mouthed variations of the *jue* drinking beakers with three blade like legs that allowed the ale to be warmed before drinking. The form

---

[19] For a recent discussion, see Childs-Johnson, "Postscript on Big Ding."

dates from the Erlitou period and became extinct during the early Zhou period.

jian 鑑: large rectangular basins with two handles for bathing; most popular during the Eastern Zhou period.

jue 爵: beakers with elliptical narrow mug-like bodies, bird-like with spouts in front and tails in back that looped over a single handle attached beneath the rims. Most have two small posts on opposite sides of the cup rim, suggesting hanging décor, or perhaps a place to attach ropes. The three blade-like legs allowed alcoholic beverages to be warmed over coals. The form dates from the Erlitou period, became a signature vessel during the Shang period, and gradually was phased out during the early Zhou.

lei 罍: large tall storage vessels for alcoholic beverages with wide shoulders over narrow feet; began during the Shang period and continued through the Eastern Zhou period.

li 鬲: cauldrons for cooking with three pouch-like hollow legs that can be filled with liquid. The form was common in clay and a popular bronze vessel during the Western Zhou period.

lie 列: a term applied by modern archaeologists to a series of a single type of vessel; for example, *liegui*, *lieding*; started to appear in the middle Western Zhou period and first evident in a lineage cemetery near Baoji 寶雞, west of Xi'an.

pan 盤: low-walled basins for liquids, possibly used for ablution. The inside was often highly decorated with incised or sculptural dragons, fish, and other animal décor.

pen 盆: high walled basins for liquids, possibly for bathing.

xu 盨: rectangular round-cornered lidded vessels similar in use to *gui* vessels; popular during the second half of the Western Zhou period.

yan 甗: steamers in which a metal filter separated the lower three pouch-like hollow legs underneath the *zeng* 甑 vessels (similar to bottomless *ding*); a form cast in bronze since the Shang period and common during the first half of the Zhou period.

yi 匜: pouring vessels without lids; dated as early as Shang and continued into the Eastern Zhou period.

yongzhong 甬鐘: bells hung from a wooden bar by a shank; often used in a series as chime bells; bells in the series might be the same size or graduated.

you 卣: finely wrought round or elliptical covered containers with swing-handles for storing and transporting fine ale, particularly used for gifts of ale during the Zhou; the form was first cast into bronze during the Shang period.

zhan 盞 (or ***dui*** 敦): circular vessels with lids that, like the *fu*, could be reversed and used as a serving dish; most popular during the Eastern Zhou period.

zhi 觶: squat, round, vase-like cups, sometimes lidded, for drinking; most common during the early Western Zhou period when it might be paired with a Shang-style *jue* drinking vessel.

zhong 鐘: general term for bells, which evolved in numerous different shapes. The most common type with inscriptions included the "chime bells" (*yongzhong*) and large bells (*bo*).[20]

zhou 舟: elliptical drinking cups, sometimes with handles, feet, or lids with round knobs; most popular during the Eastern Zhou period.

zun 尊: large vase-like vessels for storing fine ale with tall beaker-like bodies, flared mouths and high ring-feet; some had lids and were cast in the shapes of animals and/or birds; the form dates to the Shang and continued up through the Eastern Zhou period.

CAC
PRG

---

[20] For the evolution, names, and quality of bells, see Falkenhausen, *Suspended Music*.

Bibliography

Ai Mengfan 艾萌范. "'De' zai shanggu wenxian zhong de 'zhixiang' yi—jian yu lunli shijia qiecuo" "德" 在上古文獻中的 "志向"義—兼與倫理史家切磋. *Shenyang Shifan Daxue xuebao* 2011.2: 48–52.

Akatsuka Kiyoshi 赤塚忠. *Kōkotsu kimbun kenkyū* 甲骨・金文研究. Tokyo: Kembunsha, 1989.

Allan, Sarah. "The Myth of the Xia Dynasty." *Journal of the Royal Asiatic Society* (84): 242–56.

———. *The Shape of the Turtle: Myth, Art, and Cosmos in Early China.* SUNY Series in Chinese Philosophy and Culture. Albany: SUNY Press, 1991.

———. "Some Preliminary Comments on the *X Gong Xu*." In Xing, *The X Gong Xu*, 16–22.

———. "On the Identity of Shang Di 上帝 and the Origin of the Concept of a Celestial Mandate (*tian ming* 天命)." *Early China* 31 (2007): 1–46.

———. "T'ien and Shang Ti in Pre-Han China." *The Culture of "Heaven" in the Former and Later Han. Acta Asiatica: Bulletin of the Institute of Eastern Culture* 98 (2010): 1–18.

Asahara Tatsurō 淺原達郎. "Seishū kōki no henshō no sekkei" 西周後期の編鐘の設計. *Tōhō gakuhō* 72 (2000): 630–56.

Bagley, Robert [W.] *Shang Ritual Bronzes in the Arthur M. Sackler Collections.* Cambridge, Mass.: Harvard University Press, 1987.

———. "Meaning and Explanation." In Whitfield, 34–55.

———. "The Prehistory of Chinese Music Theory." *Proceedings of the British Academy* 131 (2005): 41–90.

Bai Guangqi 白光琦. "Zi Fan bianzhong de nianfen wenti" 子犯編鐘的年份問題. *Wenwu shijie* 2 (1997): 53.

Baoshan Chumu 包山楚墓. 2 vols. Beijing: Wenwu, 1991.

Barnard, Noel. "A Recently Excavated Inscribed Bronze of Western Chou Date." *Monumenta Serica* 17 (1958): 12–46.

———. "Chou China: A Review of the Third Volume of Cheng Te-k'un's *Archaeology in China*." *Monumenta Serica* 24 (1965): 307–459.

———. "Records of Discoveries of Bronze Vessels in Literary Sources—And Some Pertinent Remarks on Aspects of Chinese Historiography." *Journal of the Institute of Chinese Studies of the Chinese University of Hong Kong* 6.2 (1973): 455–546.

———. *Mao Kung Ting, a Major Western Chou Period Bronze Vessel: A Rebuttal of a Rebuttal and Further Evidence of the Questionable Aspects of Its Authenticity.* Canberra: Privately published, 1974.

———. "The Nieh Ling Yi." *Journal of the Institute of Chinese Studies of the Chinese University of Hong Kong* 9.2 (1978): 585–627.

———. *Inscriptions of Chin and the San-Chin, Chung-shan, and Yen* 晉與三晉金文

及相關史事彙考. 3 vols. Taipei: SMC. 2018.

Barnard, Noel, and Wan Chia-pao. "The Casting of Inscriptions on Chinese Bronzes—With Particular Reference to Those with Relievo Guidelines." *Soochow University Journal of Chinese Art History* 6 (1976): 43–134.

Barnard, Noel, and Zhang Guangyu. *The Shan-fu Liang Ch'i Kuei and Associated Inscribed Vessels*. Taipei: SMC, 1996.

Baxter, William H., and Laurent Sagart. *Old Chinese: A New Reconstruction*. Oxford: Oxford University Press, 2014.

Behr, Wolfgang. "Reimende Bronzeinschriften und die Entstehung der chinesischen Endreimdichtung." Ph.D. dissertation, University of Frankfurt, 1997.

———. "Spiegelreflex: Reste einer Wu-Überlieferung der Lieder im Licht einer spät-Han-zeitlichen Bronzeinschrift." *Han-Zeit: Festschrift für Hans Stumpfeldt aus Anlaß seines 65. Geburtstages*. Ed. Michael Friedrich et al. Lun Wen: Studien zur Geistesgeschichte und Literatur in China 8. Wiesbaden: Harrassowitz, 2006. 333–58.

———. *Reimende Bronzeinschriften und die Entstehung der chinesischen Endreimdichtung*. Edition Cathay 55. Bochum: Projekt, 2009.

"Beijing Liulihe 1193 hao damu fajue jianbao" 北京琉璃河1193號大墓發掘簡報. *Kaogu* 1990.1:20–31.

Birrell, Anne. *Chinese Mythology: An Introduction*. Baltimore and London: Johns Hopkins University Press, 1993.

Blakeley, Barry. "In Search of Danyang." *Early China* 13 (1988): 116–52.

Cao Jinyan 曹錦炎. "Shi tu" 釋兔, *Guwenzi yanjiu* 20 (2000): 184–91.

Cao Wei 曹瑋. *Zhouyuan yizhi yu Xi Zhou tongqi yanjiu* 周原遺址與西周銅器研究. Beijing: Kexue, 2004.

Cao Wei, ed. *Zhouyuan chutu qingtongqi* 周原出土青銅器. 10 vols. Chengdu: Ba-Shu, 2005.

Cao Zhaolan 曹兆蘭. *Jinwen yu Yin Zhou nüxing wenhua* 金文與殷周女性文化. Beijing: Beijing Daxue, 2004.

Cen Zhongmian 岑仲勉. "Tian Wang gui quanshi" 天亡簋全釋. *Zhongshan Daxue xuebao: Shehui kexue ban* 1961.1: 59–64.

Chang, K[wang-]C[hih] [see also Zhang Guangzhi]. *Art, Myth, and Ritual: The Path to Political Authority in Ancient China*. Cambridge: Harvard University Press, 1983.

Chang, Kwang-chih et al. *The Formation of Chinese Civilization: An Archaeological Perspective*. Ed. Sarah Allan. Culture and Civilization of China. New Haven: Yale University Press, 2005.

Chase, Thomas. *Ancient Chinese Bronze Art*. New York: China Institute in America, 1991.

Chen Banghuai 陳邦懷. "Ke bo jianjie" 克鎛簡介. *Wenwu* 1972.6: 14–16.

———. "Yong yu kaolue" 永盂考略. *Wenwu* 1972.11: 57–59.

Chen Changyuan 陳昌遠. "Cong 'Li gui' tan youguan Wu Wang fa Zhou de jige wenti" 從《利簋》談有關武王伐紂的幾個問題. *Henan Shida xuebao: Shehui kexue ban* 1980.4: 30–37.

Chen Gongrou 陳公柔. "Ji Jifu hu, Zha zhong ji qi tongchu de tongqi" 記幾父壺，柞鐘及其同出的銅器. *Kaogu* 1962.2: 88–91.

———. "Xi Zhou jinwen zhong de 'Xinyi,' 'Chengzhou' yu 'wangcheng'" 西周金文中的"新邑"、"成周"與"王城". In idem, *Xian Qin Liang Han kaoguxue luncong* 先秦兩漢考古學論叢. Beijing: Wenwu, 2005. 33–48.

Chen Guang 陳光, ed. *Yan wenhua yanjiu lunwenji* 燕文化研究論文集. Beijingshi Wenwu Yanjiusuo keyan xilie congshu. Beijing: Zhongguo shehui kexue, 1995.

Chen Hanping 陳漢平. *Xi Zhou ce ming zhidu yanjiu* 西周冊命制度研究. Shanghai: Xuelin, 1986.

Chen Jian 陳劍. *Jiagu Jinwen Kaoshi Lunji* 甲骨金文考釋論集. Beijing. Xian zhuang shu ju. 2007

Chen Jinyi 陳進宜. "Yu ding kaoshi" 禹鼎考釋. *Guangming ribao* (July 7, 1951: appendix 增刊).

Chen Lianqing 陳連慶. "Xi jia pan kaoshi" 兮甲盤考釋. *Jilin Shida xuebao: Shehui kexue ban* 1978.4: 24–27.

———. "Piao Qiang zhong ming 'zheng Qin ze Qi' xin shi" 麤羌鐘銘「征秦迮齊」新釋. *Jilin Shifan Daxue xuebao* 1979.3: 76–81.

———. "'Jin Jiang ding' xin shi" 《晉姜鼎》銘新釋. *Gu wenzi yanjiu* 13 (1986): 189–201.

Chen Mengjia 陳夢家. "Xi-Zhou tongqi duandai (wu) 西周銅器斷代(五)," *Kaogu xuebao*. 13.3 (1956): 105–127, 157–172.

———. "Shou xian Cai hou mu tongqi" 壽縣蔡侯墓銅器, *Kaogu xuebao* 1956.2: 109–10.

———. "Cai qi san ji" 蔡器三記. *Kaogu* 1963.7: 381–84, 361.

———. "Shu Shi zhong bo kao" 叔尸鐘鎛考. *Yanjing xuebao* 1998.4: 1–24.

———. *Xi Zhou tongqi duandai* 西周銅器斷代. 2 vols. Beijing: Zhonghua, 2004.

Chen Pan 陳槃. *Chunqiu dashi biao lieguo juexing ji cunmie biao zhuanyi* 春秋大事表列國爵姓及存滅表譔異. Revised edition. Zhongyang Yanjiuyuan Lishi Yuyan Yanjiusuo zhuankan 52. Taipei: Zhongyang Yanjiuyuan Lishi Yuyan Yanjiusuo, 1969.

Chen Peifen 陳佩芬. "Fan you, Feng ding ji Liang Qi xu mingwen quanshi" 繁卣、佣鼎及梁其盨銘文詮釋. *Shanghai Bowuguan jikan* 1983.2: 15–25.

Chen Ping 陳平. "Ke lei, Ke he mingwen jiqi youguan wenti" 克罍、克盉銘文及其有關問題. In Chen Guang, 266–77.

Chen Shihui 陳世輝. "Yu ding shiwen jiao" 禹鼎釋文斠. *Renwen zazhi* 1959.2: 70–72, 88.

———. "Xun gui ji Mishu gui xiaoji" 訇簋及弭叔簋小記. *Wenwu* 1960.8–9: 78.

———. "Qiang pan mingwen jieshuo" 墻盤銘文解說. *Kaogu* 1980.5: 433–35.

Chen, Shu. "Collected Interpretations of the X Gong *Xu*." *Early China* 35–36

(2012–13): 135–55.

Chen Shuangxin 陳雙新. "Zi Fan zhongming kaoshi" 子犯鐘銘考釋. *Anhui Jiaoyu Xueyuan xuebao* 2000.1: 35–37.

Chen Sipeng 陳斯鵬. "Xi Zhou Shi Qiang pan xin shi" 西周史牆盤新釋. *Zhongshan daxue xuebao*. 2013.6.53: 69–72.

Chen Yingjie 陳英傑. "Jinwen zhong 'jun' zi zhi yiyi ji qi xiangguan wenti tanxi" 金文中"君"字之意義及其相關問題探析. *Zhongguo wenzi* 33 (2007): 107–52.

———. "Bin Gong xu mingwen zaikao" 公盨銘文再考. 2007 ms. posted on www.gwz.fudan.edu.cn, accessed October 2010.

Chen Ziyi 陳子怡. "San Shi pan Shiguwen dili kaozheng" 散氏盤石鼓文地理考證. *Yugong* 7.6–7 (1937): 141–51.

Childs-Johnson, Elizabeth. "The Bird in Shang Ritual Art: Intermediary to the Supernatural." *Orientations* 20.11 (1989): 53–60.

———. "The Metamorphic Image: A Predominant Theme in the Ritual Art of Shang China." *Bulletin of the Museum of Far Eastern Antiquities* 70 (1998): 5–171.

———. "Postscript to Big Ding and China Power-Shang Sifang." *Jinian Sun Zuoyun jiaoshou bainian danchen ji gudai Zhongguo lishi yu wenhua guoji xueshu yantaohui lunwenji* 紀念孫作雲教授百年誕辰暨古代中國歷史與文化國際學術研討會論文集. Ed. Fan Yuzhou 范毓周. Kaifeng: Henan Daxue, 2012. Pp. 191–210.

Chu wenwu zhanlan tulu 楚文物展覽圖錄. Beijing: Lishi Bowuguan, 1954.

Cook, Constance Anne. "Chung-shan Bronze Inscriptions: Introduction and Translation." M.A. thesis, University of Washington, 1980.

———. "Auspicious Metals and Southern Spirits: An Analysis of the Chu Bronze Inscriptions." Ph.D. dissertation, University of California, Berkeley, 1990.

———. "Myth and Authenticity: Deciphering the Chu Gong Ni Bell Inscription." *Journal of the American Oriental Society* 113.4 (1993): 539–50.

———. "Scribes, Cooks, and Artisans: Breaking Zhou Tradition," *Early China* 20 (1995): 241–77.

———. "Wealth and the Western Zhou." *Bulletin of the School of Oriental and African Studies* 60.2 (1997): 253–94.

———. "Moonshine and Millet: Feasting and Purification Rituals in Ancient China." In Sterckx, 9–33.

———. *Death in Ancient China: The Tale of One Man's Journey*. China Studies 8. Leiden: Brill, 2006.

———. "Ritual, Politics, and the Issue of feng (封)." *Shi Quan xiansheng jiushi danchen jinian wenji* 石泉先生九十誕辰紀念文集. Ed. Wuhan Daxue Lishi Dili Yanjiusuo. Wuhan: Hubei renmin, 2007. Pp. 215–67.

———. "Ancestor Worship during the Eastern Zhou." In Lagerwey and Kalinowski, I, 237–79.

———. "Education and the Way of the Former Kings." In Li and Branner, 302–36.

———. "Sage King Yu 禹 and the Bin Gong Xu 豳公盨." *Early China* 35–36 (2012–2013): 69–103.

———. *Ancestors, Kings, and the Dao*. Cambridge, Massachusetts: Published by the Harvard University Asia Center. 2017.

Cook, Constance Anne, and John S. Major, eds. *Defining Chu: Image and Reality in Ancient China*. Honolulu: University of Hawaii Press, 1999.

Creel, Herrlee G. *The Origins of Statecraft in China*. Chicago and London: University of Chicago Press, 1970.

Cui Hengsheng 崔恆升. "'Sui ding ke hun su you Shang' kaoshi" "歲鼎克X夙有商"考釋. *Anhui Daxue xuebao: Zhexue shehui kexue ban* 1981.1: 56–59.

Cuo mu—Zhanguo Zhongshan guo guowang zhi mu 響墓—戰國中山國國王之墓. 2 vols. Beijing: Wenwu, 1995.

Defoort, Carine. *The Pheasant Cap Master* (He guan zi): *A Rhetorical Reading*. SUNY Series in Chinese Philosophy and Culture. Albany: SUNY Press, 1997.

Deng Peiling 鄧佩玲 [i.e. Tang Pui Ling]. *Tianming, guishen yu zhudao—Dong Zhou jinwen guci tanlun* 天命、鬼神與祝禱—東周金文嘏辭探論. Taipei: Yi-wen, 2011.

A Descriptive and Illustrative Catalogue of Chinese Bronzes: Acquired during the Administration of John Ellerton Lodge. Freer Gallery of Art: Oriental Studies 3. Washington, D.C.: Smithsonian Institution, 1946.

Ding Meng 丁孟 and Jian Min 建民. "Bi Qi you de X shexian jiance fenxi" 邲其卣的 X 射綫檢測分析. *Gugong Bowuyuan xuekan* 1999.1: 83–85.

Dobson, W.A.C.H. *Early Archaic Chinese: A Descriptive Grammar*. Toronto: University of Toronto Press, 1962.

Dong Chuping 董楚平. *Wu Yue wenhua xintan* 吳越文化新探. Hangzhou: Zhejiang renmin, 1988.

———. *Wu Yue Xu Shu jinwen jishi* 吳越徐舒金文集釋. Hangzhou: Zhejiang guji, 1992.

Dong Shan 董刪, "Shi Xi Zhou jinwen de 'chenzi' he *Yi Zhou shu Huang men* de 'chenren'" 釋西周金文的'沈子'和《逸周書皇門》的'沈人', *Chutu wenxian* 出土文獻 2 (2016): 29–34.

Dong Zuobin 董作賓. "Mao Gong ding kao nian" 毛公鼎考年. *Dalu zazhi* 5.8 (1952): 3–6.

———. "Mao Gong ding shiwen zhushi" 毛公鼎釋文註釋. *Dalu zazhi* 5.8 (1952): 13–19.

Doty, Darrel Paul. "The Bronze Inscriptions of Ch'i: An Interpretation." Ph.D. dissertation, University of Washington, 1982.

Du Naisong 杜迺松. "Bi Qi san you mingwen kao ji xiangguan wenti de yanjiu" 其三 卣銘文考及相關問題的研究. *Gugong Bowu Yuan yuankan* 1985.4: 36–43, 57.

Duan Shaojia 段紹嘉. "Shi Ke xu gai kaoyi" 師克盨蓋考釋. *Renwen zazhi* 1957.3: 70.

———. "Dui Shi Ke xu gai he X ding mingwen jianbie de shangque" 對師克盨蓋和X鼎銘文鑒別的商榷. *Wenwu* 1960.8–9: 80.

Duan Yong 段勇. *Shang Zhou qingtongqi huanxiang dongwu yanjiu* 商周青銅器幻想動物研究. Shanghai: Guji, 2003.

Elman, Benjamin A. *A Cultural History of Civil Examinations in Late Imperial China*. Berkeley: University of California Press, 2000.

Eno, Robert. "Shang State Religion and the Pantheon of the Oracle Texts." In Lagerwey and Kalinowski, I, 41–102.

Falkenhausen, Lothar von [see also Luo Tai]. "Ritual Music in Bronze Age China: An Archaeological Perspective." Ph.D. dissertation, Harvard University, 1988.

———. "Ahnenkult und Grabkult im Staat Qin." *Jenseits der großen Mauer: Der erste Kaiser von Qin und seine Terrakotta-Armee*. Ed. Lothar Ledderose and Adele Schlombs. Munich: Bertelsmann, 1990. Pp. 35–48.

———. "Issues in Western Zhou Studies: A Review Article." *Early China* 18 (1993): 139–226.

———. *Suspended Music: The Chime-Bells of the Chinese Bronze Age*. Berkeley: University of California Press, 1993.

———. "Late Western Zhou Taste." *Mélanges de Sinologie offerts à Monsieur Jean-Pierre Diény (I). Études Chinoises* 18.1–2 (1999): 143–78.

———. "The Waning of the Bronze Age: Material Culture and Social Developments, 770–481 B.C." In Loewe and Shaughnessy, 450–544.

——— *Chinese Society in the Age of Confucius (1000–250 BC): The Archaeological Evidence*. Ideas, Debates and Perspectives 2. Los Angeles: Cotsen Institute of Archaeology, UCLA, 2006.

———. "The Inscribed Bronzes from Yangjiacun: New Evidence on Social Structure and Historical Consciousness in Late Western Zhou China (c. 800 BC)." *Proceedings of the British Academy* 139 (2006): 239–96.

———. "The Royal Audience and Its Reflections in Western Zhou Bronze Inscriptions." In Li and Branner, 229–70.

Fang Jicheng 方繼成. "Guanyu Zong Zhou zhong" 關於宗周鐘. *Renwen zazhi* 1957.2: 46–48.

Feng Han-yi. "The Chinese Kinship System." *Harvard Journal of Asiatic Studies* 2 (1937): 141–275.

Feng Shi 馮時. "Zhongguo zaoqi xingxiang tu yanjiu 中國早期星象圖研究." *Ziran kexueshi yanjiu* 9.2 (1990): 108–18.

———. "Chunqiu Zi Fan bianzhong jinian yanjiu" 春秋子犯編鐘紀年研究. *Wenwu jikan* 1997.4: 59–65.

Feng Yicheng 馮儀誠 [i.e. Olivier Venture, q.v.]. "Shang Zhou qingtongqi mingwen weizhi yanbian chutan" 商周青銅器銘文位置演變初探. *Renwen luncong* (2009– 2010): 117–25.

Flad, Rowan K., and Pochan Chen. *Ancient Central China: Centers and Peripheries along the Yangzi River*. Case Studies in Early Societies. Cambridge: Cambridge University Press, 2013.

Fong, Wen, ed. *The Great Bronze Age of China: An Exhibition from the People's Republic of China.* New York: Metropolitan Museum of Art, 1980.

Fracasso, Riccardo. "Between Legend and History: Notes on Cheng Tang." *Approches critiques de la mythologie chinoise.* Ed. Charles Le Blanc and Rémi Mathieu. Sociétés et cultures de l'Asie. Montreal: Presses de l'Université de Montréal, 2007. Pp. 159–206.

The Freer Chinese Bronzes. 2 vols. Freer Gallery of Art: Oriental Studies 7. Washington, D.C.: Smithsonian Institution, 1967–69.

Gao Heng 高亨. "Mao gong ding ming jianzhu" 毛公鼎銘箋注. *Wenshi shu lin* 文史述林. Ed. Dong Zhi'an 東治安. Gao Heng zhuzuo jilin 9. Beijing: Qinghua Daxue, 2004. Pp. 464–93.

Gao Zhixi 高至喜. "'Chu Gong Jia' ge'"楚公豪"戈. *Wenwu* 1959.12: 60.

Goldin, Paul Rakita. *The Culture of Sex in Ancient China.* Honolulu: University of Hawaii Press, 2002.

———. *Confucianism.* Ancient Philosophies 9. Berkeley and Los Angeles: University of California Press, 2011.

———. "The Consciousness of the Dead as a Philosophical Problem in Ancient China." *The Good Life and Conceptions of Life in Early China and Greek Antiquity.* Ed. R.A.H. King. Chinese-Western Discourse. Berlin: De Gruyter, 2015. Pp. 59-92.

———. "Representations of Regional Diversity during the Eastern Zhou Dynasty." *Ideology of Power and Power of Ideology in Early China.* Ed. Yuri Pines *et al*. Leiden: Brill, 2015.

Gu Jiguang 谷霽光. "Xun gui kaoshi zhi yi" 詢簋考釋質疑. *Shilin man shi* 史林漫拾. Fuzhou: Fujian renmin, 1982. Pp. 240–54.

Gu Zigang 顧子剛. "Hanjun mu faxian lüeji" 韓君墓發現略記. *Guoli Beiping Tushuguan guankan* 7.1 (1933): 145–49.

Guo Baojun 郭寶鈞. *Shang Zhou tongqiqun zonghe yanjiu* 商周銅器群綜合研究. Beijing: Wenwu, 1981.

Guo Moruo 郭沫若 (1892–1978). *Jinwen congkao* 金文叢攷. 1932; rpt., Beijing: Renmin, 1952.

———. "Shaanxi xinchu qiming kaoshi" 陝西新出器銘考釋. *Shuowen yuekan* 3.10 (1943): 153.

———. "Mishu gui ji Hong gui kaoshi" 弭叔簋及訇簋考釋. *Wenwu* 1960.2: 5–8.

———. "Shi Ke xu ming kaoshi" 師克盨銘考釋. *Wenwu* 1962.6: 9–14.

———. "Ba Jiangling yu Shouxian chutu tongqiqun" 跋江陵與壽縣出土銅器群. *Kaogu* 1963.4: 183.

———. "Guanyu Meixian dading mingci kaoshi" 關於眉縣大鼎名辭考釋. *Wenwu* 1972.7: 2.

———. "'Ban gui' de zai faxian" 《班簋》的再發現. *Wenwu* 1972.9: 2–13.

———. *Liang Zhou jinwenci daxi tulu kaoshi* 兩周金文辭大系圖彔攷釋. 2 vols.

Shanghai: Shanghai shudian, 1999.

Guo Ruoyu 郭若愚. "Cong you guan Cai Hou de ruogan ziliao lun Shouxian Cai Hou mu Cai qi de niandai" 從有關蔡侯的若干資料論壽縣蔡墓蔡器的年代. *Shanghai Bowuguan jikan* 1982.2: 75–88.

Guoyu 國語. Shanghai: Guji, 1978.

Hamada Kōsaku 濱田耕作 (1881–1938) and Umehara Sueji 梅原末治 (1893–1983). *Santei Sen'oku seishō* 刪訂泉屋清賞. Hyōgo-ken, Japan: Sumitomo Kichizaemon, 1934. [Also bears the title *Collection of Old Bronzes of Baron Sumitomo*.]

Han, Kangxin, and Takahiro Nakahashi. "A Comparative Study of Ritual Tooth Ablation in Ancient China and Japan." *Anthropological Science* 104.1 (1996): 43–64.

Hanshu 漢書. 12 vols. Beijing: Zhonghua, 1962.

Harper, Donald. "Natural Philosophy and Occult Thought." In Loewe and Shaughnessy, 813–84.

———. *Early Chinese medical literature: the Mawangdui medical manuscripts*. London; Kegan Paul International, 1998.

He Linyi 何琳儀. "Zhongshan wang qi kaoshi shiyi" 中山王器考釋拾遺. *Shixue jikan* 1984.3: 5–10.

He Linyi and Huang Xiquan 黃錫全. "Hu gui kaoshi liu ze" 獣簋考釋六則. *Gu wenzi yanjiu* 7 (1982): 109–22.

He Youqi 何幼琦. "Xi Zhou tongqi niandai juli" 西周銅器年代舉例. *Xueshu yanjiu* 1982.6: 108–17.

———. "'Hezun' de niandai wenti" 《何尊》的年代問題. *Zhongyuan wenwu* 1983.4: 59–61, 16.

Henan Bowuyuan 河南博物院 and Taibei Guoli Lishi Bowuguan 台北國立歷史博物館. *Xinzheng Zhenggong damu qingtongqi* 新鄭鄭公大幕青銅器. Zhengzhou: Daxiang, 2001.

Henansheng wenwu kaogusuo 河南省文物考古所, ed. *Xin Cai Geling Chu mu* 新蔡葛陵楚墓. Chengzhou: Daxiang, 2003.

Hong Jiayi 洪家義. "Guanyu 'Tian Wang gui' suo ji shishi de xingzhi" 關於《天亡簋》所記史事的性質. *Dongnan wenhua* 1987.2: 77–82.

Hou Zhiyi 侯志義. *Xi Zhou jinwen xuanbian* 西周金文選編. Xibei daxue chubanshe. 1987.

Hsu, Cho-yun. "The Spring and Autumn Period." In Loewe and Shaughnessy, 545–86.

Hsu, Cho-yun, and Katheryn M. Linduff. *Western Chou Civilization*. Early Chinese Civilization Series. New Haven and London: Yale University Press, 1988.

Huang Baoyue 黃葆戉. "San pan jin shi" 散盤今釋. *Dongfang zazhi* 27.2 (1930): 51–54.

Huang Hui 黃暉. *Lunheng jiaoshi (fu Liu Pansui jijie)* 論衡校釋 (附劉盼遂集解). 4 vols. Xinbian Zhuzi jicheng. Beijing: Zhonghua, 1990.

Huang Ranwei 黃然偉 [i.e. Wong Yin-wai]. *Yin Zhou qingtongqi shangci mingwen yanjiu* 殷周青銅器賞賜銘文研究. Hong Kong: Longmen, 1978.

Huang Shengzhang 黃盛璋. "Shi chuji" 釋初吉. *Lishi yanjiu* 1958.4: 71–86.

———. "Da Feng gui zhizuo de niandai didian yu shishi" 大豐簋製作的年代、地點與史實. *Lishi yanjiu* 1960.6: 81–95.

———. "Guanyu Xun gui de zhizuo niandai yu Hu Chen de shenfen wenti" 關於詢簋製作年代與虎臣的身分問題. *Kaogu* 1961.6: 330–33.

———. "Ban gui de niandai, dili, yu lishi wenti" 班簋的年代、地理與歷史問題. *Kaogu yu wenwu* 1981.1: 75–83.

———. "Duo You ding de lishi yu dili wenti" 多友鼎的歷史與地理問題. *Gu wenzi lunji (yi)* 古文字論集(一). Kaogu yu wenwu congkan 2. Xi'an, 1983. 12–20.

———. "Tongqi mingwen Yi Yu Ze de diwang jiqi yu Wuguo de guanxi" 銅器銘文宜 虞矢的地望及其與吳國的關係. *Kaogu xuebao* 1983.3: 295–305.

———. "Ju Fu xu gai mingwen yanjiu" 駒父盨盖銘文研究. *Kaogu yu wenwu* 1983.4: 53.

———. "Lu Bo Dong tongqi jiqi xiangguan wenti" 彔伯茲銅器及其相關問題. *Kaogu yu wenwu* 1983.5: 43–49.

———. "Fufeng Qiangjiacun xin chu Xi Zhou tongqiqun yu xiangguan shishi zhi yanjiu" 扶風強家村新出西周銅器群與相關史實之研究. *Xizhou shi yanjiu renwen zazhi congkan* 2 (1984): 278–93.

———. "Xi Zhou tongqi zhong fushi shangci yu zhiguan ji ceming zhidu guanxi fafu" 西周銅器中服飾賞賜與職官及冊命制度關係發覆. *Zhou Qin wenhua yanjiu* 周秦文化研究. Xi'an: Shaanxi renmin, 1998. 409–22.

Huber, Maria, and Achim Mittag. "Spiegel-Dichtung: Spekulationen uber einen Bronzespiegel des 3. Jahrhunderts und dessen Inschrift, das *Shijing*-Lied Nr. 57, *Shi ren*." *Chinathemen* 18 (1991): 73–110.

Idema, Wilt, and Lloyd Haft. *A Guide to Chinese Literature*. Michigan Monographs in Chinese Studies 74. Ann Arbor, 1997.

Institute of History and Philology, Academica Sinica 中央研究院歷史語言研究所. Digital Archive of Bronze Images and Inscriptions 殷周金文暨青銅器資料庫. 2020. http://www.ihp.sinica.edu.tw/~bronze/

Itō Michiharu 伊藤道治. *Chūgoku kodai ōcho no keisei: Shutsudo shiryō o chūshin to suru In Shū shi no kenkyū* 中國古代王朝の形成:出土資料を中心とする殷周史の研究. Tokyo: Sōbunsha, 1975.

———, "Shū Buō to Rakuyū—Kason mei to Itsu Shūsho doyū 周武王と雒邑—何尊 銘と逸周書度邑. *Uchida Gimpū hakushi shōju kinen tōyōshi ronshū* 內田吟風博士 頌壽紀念東洋史論集. Ed. Uchida Gimpū 內田吟風. Kyoto: Dōbōsha, 1978. 41–53.

Itō, Michiharu, and Ken-ichi Takashima. *Studies in Early Chinese Civilization: Religion, Society, Language, and Palaeography*. Ed. Gary F. Arbuckle. 2 vols. Osaka: Intercultural Research Institute, Kansai Gaidai University, 1996.

"Jiangsu Dantu xian Yandunshan chutu de gudai qingtongqi" 江蘇丹徒縣煙墩山出土的青銅器. *Wenwu cankao ziliao* 1955.5: 58–62.

Jin Hou mudi chutu qingtongqi guoji xueshu yantaohui lunwenji 晉侯墓地出土青銅器 國際學術研討會論文集. Shanghai: Shuhua, 2002. [English title: *Proceedings of the Symposium on Bronzes from the Cemetery of Marquis of Jin.*]

"Jin Hou Su zhong bitan" 晉侯蘇鐘筆談. *Wenwu* 1997.3: 54–66.

Jinguo qizhen: Shanxi Jinhou muqun chutu wenwu jingpin 晉國奇珍:山西晉侯墓群出土文物精品. Shanghai: Shanghai renmin meishu, 2002.

Jinwen jinyi leijian 金文今譯類檢. Nanning: Guangxi jiaoyu, 2003–.

Kane, Virginia. "Aspects of Western Zhou Appointment Inscriptions: The Charge, the Gifts, and the Response." *Early China* 8 (1982–83): 14–28.

Karlgren, Bernhard. "On the Date of the Piao-Bells." *Bulletin of the Museum of Far Eastern Antiquities* 6 (1934): 137–49.

———. tr. *The Book of Odes*. Stockholm: Museum of Far Eastern Antiquities, 1950.

Keightley, David N. "The Shang: China's First Historical Dynasty." In Loewe and Shaughnessy, 232–91.

———. *The Ancestral Landscape: Time, Space, and Community in Late Shang China (ca. 1200–1045 B.C.)*. Berkeley: Institute of East Asian Studies, 2000.

Kern, Martin. *The Stele Inscriptions of Ch'in Shih-huang: Text and Ritual in Early Chinese Imperial Representation*. American Oriental Series 85. New Haven: American Oriental Society, 2000.

———. "The Performance of Writing in Western Zhou China." *The Poetics of Grammar and the Metaphysics of Sound and Sign*. Ed. S. La Porta and D. Shulman. Jerusalem Studies in Religion and Culture 6. Leiden and Boston: Brill, 2007. 109–75.

———. "Bronze Inscriptions, the *Shangshu*, and the *Shijing*: The Evolution of the Ancestral Sacrifice during the Western Zhou." In Lagerwey and Kalinowski, I, 143–200.

Kesner, Ladislav. "The Taotie Reconsidered: Meaning and Function of Shang Theriomorphic Imagery." *Artibus Asiae* 51 (1991): 29–53.

Khayutina, Maria. "The Story of the He *zun*: From Political Intermediary to National Treasure." *Orientations* 50.3 (2019): 54–60.

Kominami, Ichirō. "Rituals for the Earth." Tr. Didier Davin. In Lagerwey and Kalinowski, I, 201–34.

Kong Decheng 孔德成. "Liang Qi zhong mingwen shiwen" 梁其鐘銘釋文. *Renwen xuebao* 1 (1970): 25–27.

Kryukov, Mikhail Vasil'evich. *Sistema rodstva kitaĭtsev* [*The kinship system of the Chinese*]. Moscow: Nauka, 1972.

———. "Symbols of Power and Communication in Pre-Confucian China: On the Anthropology of De." *Bulletin of the School of Oriental and African Studies* 58 (1994): 314–33.

Lagerwey, John, and Marc Kalinowski, eds. *Early Chinese Religion, Part One: Shang through Han (1250 BC–220 AD)*. 2 vols. Handbuch der Orientalistik IV.21. Leiden: Brill, 2009.

Lai Changyang 賴長揚 and Liu Xiang 劉翔. "Liang Zhou shiguan kao" 兩周史官考. *Zhongguo shi yanjiu* 1985.2: 92–108.

Lau, Ulrich. *Quellenstudien zur Landvergabe und Bodenübertragung in der westlichen Zhou-Dynastie (1045?-771 v. Chr.)*. Monumenta Serica Monograph Series 41. Sankt Augustin, Germany, 1999.

Legge, James (1815–1897), tr. *The Sacred Books of China: The Texts of Confucianism*. 4 vols. Sacred Books of the East 3, 16, and 27–28. Oxford: Clarendon, 1879–85.

———. tr. *The Chinese Classics*. 2nd edition. 5 vols. Oxford: Clarendon, 1893–95

Lewis, Mark Edward. *Sanctioned Violence in Early China*. SUNY Series in Chinese Philosophy and Culture. Albany: SUNY Press, 1990.

Li Changqing 李長慶 and Tian Ye 田野. "Zuguo lishi wenwu de you yici zhongyao faxian" 祖國歷史文物的又一次重要發現. *Wenwu cankao ziliao* 1957.4: 5–9.

Li Chaoyuan 李朝元. "Xi Zhou jinwen zhong de 'wang' yu 'wangqi'" 西周金文中的'王'與'王器'. *Wenwu* 2006.5: 74–79.

Li Fan 李幡. "X wei *jia* zheng" X為賈証. *Kaogu* 2007.11: 71–77.

Li Fang 李昉 (925–996) *et al. Taiping yulan* 太平御覽. *Sibu congkan* 四部叢刊.

Li Feng 李峰. "Ta Yū tei meibun o meguru rekishi chiri teki mondai no kaiketsu: Shū ōchō no seihoku keiryaku o kaimei suru tameni, soni ichi" 多友鼎銘文を巡る歷史地理的問題の解決：周王朝の西北經略を解明ために、その一. *Chūgoku kodai no moji to bunka* 中國古代の文字と文化. Tokyo: Kyūko, 1999. 179–206.

———. "Qinghua jian 'Qi ye' chudu ji qi xiangguan wenti" 清華簡《耆夜》初讀及其相關問題. *Chutu cailiao yu xin shiye* 出土材料與新視野. Ed. Li Zongkun 李宗焜. Taipei: Academia Sinica, in press.

———. Xi-Zhou qingtongqi mingwen zhizuo fangfa shiyi" 西周青銅器銘文製作方法釋疑, *Kaogu* 9 (2015): 78–91.

Li, Feng. "Ancient Reproductions and Calligraphic Variations: Studies of Western Zhou Bronzes with 'Identical' Inscriptions." *Early China* 22 (1997): 1–41.

———. "'Offices' in Bronze Inscriptions and Western Zhou Government Administration." *Early China* 26–27 (2001–02): 1–72.

———. "'Feudalism' in Western Zhou China: A Criticism." *Harvard Journal of Asiatic Studies* 63.1 (2003): 115–44.

———. "Succession and Promotion: Elite Mobility during the Western Zhou." *Monumenta Serica* 52 (2004): 1–35.

———. *Landscape and Power in Early China: The Crisis and Fall of the Western Zhou, 1045–771 B.C.* Cambridge: Cambridge University Press, 2006.

———. *Bureaucracy and the State in Early China: Governing the Western Zhou*. Cambridge: Cambridge University Press, 2008.

———. "Literacy and the Social Contexts of Writing in the Western Zhou", in Li and Branner, 271–301.

Li, Feng, and David Prager Branner, eds. *Literacy in Early China: Studies from the Columbia Early China Seminar*. Seattle: University of Washington Press,

2011.

Li Fuquan 李福泉. "Xun gui mingwen de zonghe yanjiu" 旬簋銘文的綜合研究. *Hunan Shiyuan xuebao: Zhexue shehui kexue* 1979.2: 58–66.

Li Ling 李零. "'Chu shu zhi sun Peng' jiujing shi shui?" "楚叔之孫倗"究竟是誰?. *Zhongyuan wenwu* 1981.4: 36–37.

———. "Chuguo tongqi mingwen biannian huishi" 楚國銅器銘文編年匯釋. *Guwenzi yanjiu* 13 (1986): 353–97.

———. "Xi Zhou jinwen zhong de tudi zhidu" 西周金文中的土地制度. *Xueren* 1992.2: 244–56.

———. *Li Ling zixuan ji* 李零自選集. Kua shiji xueren wencun. Guilin: Guangxi Shifan Daxue, 1998.

———. "Lun X gong xu faxian de yiyi" 論X公盨發現的意義. *Zhongguo lishi wenwu* 2002.6: 35–45.

———. "On the Typology of Chu Bronzes." Tr. Lothar von Falkenhausen. *Beiträge zur allgemeinen und vergleichenden Archäologie* 11 (1991): 57–113.

Li, Liu, and Xingcan Chen. "Cities and Towns: The Control of Natural Resources in Early States, China." *Bulletin of the Museum of Far Eastern Antiquities* 73 (2001): 5–47.

Li Pingxin 李平心. "Zhou dai Shang Tang xinzheng yi —'Da Feng pian ming' zhong Zhou fa Shang Tang de quezheng" 周代商唐新証(一)—《大豐簋銘》中周伐商唐 的確證. *Wenhui bao* (November 25, 1960): 3.

———. "'Da Yu ding ming' 'nü mei chen you da fu' jie" 《大盂鼎銘》"女妹辰又大服" 解. *Zhonghua wenshi luncun* 中華文史論叢 5 (1964): 194.

Li Qiliang 李啓良. "Shaanxi Ankangshi chutu Zhou Shi Mi gui" 陝西安康市出土西周史密簋. *Kaogu yu wenwu* 1989.3: 7–9.

Li, Wai-yee. *The Readability of the Past in Early Chinese Historiography*. Harvard East Asian Monographs 253. Cambridge, Mass.: Harvard University Asia Center, 2007.

Li Xixing 李西興, ed. *Shaanxi qingtongqi* 陝西青銅器. Xi'an: Shaanxi Renmin, 1994.

Li Xueqin 李學勤. "Meixian Lijiacun tongqi kao" 郿縣李傢村銅器考. *Wenwu cankao ziliao* 1957.7: 58–59.

———. "Lun Shi Qiang pan jiqi yiyi" 論史墻盤及其意義. *Kaogu xuebao* 1978.2: 149–58.

———. "Xi Zhou zhongqi qingtongqi de zhongyao biaozhi—Zhouyuan Zhuangbai Qiangjia liangchu qingtongqi jiaozang zonghe yanjiu" 西周中期青銅器的重要標尺—周原莊白強家兩處青銅器窖藏綜合研究. *Zhongguo Lishi Bowuguan guankan* 1979.1: 29–36.

———. "Pingshan mu zangqun yu Zhongshanguo de wenhua" 平山墓葬群與中山國 的文化. *Wenwu* 1979.1: 37–41.

———. "Bi Qi san you yu youguan wenti" 邲其三卣與有關問題. *Quanguo Shangshi xueshu taolun hui lunwen ji* 全國商史學術討論會論文集. Ed. Hu Houxuan 胡厚宣 et al. Yindu xuekan, zengkan 《殷都學刊》增刊 (1985). 453–63.

———. "Da Yu ding xinlun" 大盂鼎新論. *Zhengzhou Daxue xuebao* 1985.3: 51–55, 64.

———. "Yi Hou Ze gui yu Wuguo" 宜侯夨簋與吳國. *Wenwu* 1985.7: 529–60.

———. "Ban gui xukao" 班簋續考. *Guwenzi yanjiu* 13 (1986): 181–88.

———. "Lun 'Shuo ren' ming shenshou jing" 論《碩人》銘神獸鏡. *Wenshi* 30 (1988): 47–50.

———. "Ling fangyi, fangzun xin shi" 令方彝方尊新釋. *Guwenzi yanjiu* 16 (1989): 218–26.

———. *Xinchu qingtongqi yanjiu* 新出青銅器研究. Beijing: Wenwu, 1990.

———. "Yi Hou Ze gui de ren yu di" 宜侯夨簋的人與地. *Chuantong wenhua yanjiu* 2 (1993): 87–89.

———. *Zouchu yigu shidai* 走出疑古時代. Revised edition. Shenyang: Liaoning Daxue, 1997.

———. "Chunqiu nanfang qingtongqi mingwen de yige tedian" 春秋南方青銅器銘文的一個特點. *Wu-Yue diqu qingtongqi yanjiu lunwenji* 吳越地區青銅器研究論文集. Ed. Ma Chengyuan 馬承源. Hong Kong: The Woods Publisher, Tai Yip Co., 1997. 177–80.

———. "Wu Hu ding kaoshi—Xia Shang Zhou duandai gongcheng kaoguxue biji" 吳虎鼎考釋—夏商周斷代工程考古學筆記. *Kaogu yu wenwu* 1998.5: 69–71.

———. *Zhuigu ji* 綴古集. Shanghai: Guji, 1998.

———. "Rong Sheng bianzhong lunshi" 戎生編鐘論釋. *Wenwu* 1999.9: 75–82.

———. *Xia Shang Zhou niandaixue zhaji* 夏商周年代學札記. Shenyang: Liaoning Daxue, 1999.

———. "Shi Xun gui yu 'Zhai gong'" 師詢簋與"祭公". *Guwenzi yanjiu* 22 (2000): 70–72.

———. "Lun X gong xu jiqi zhongyao yiyi" 論燮公盨及其重要意義. *Zhongguo lishi wenwu* 2002.6: 5–12.

———. "Meixian Yangjiacun xinchu qingtongqi yanjiu" 眉縣楊家村新出青銅器研究. *Wenwu* 2003.6: 66–73.

———. *Zhongguo gudai wenming yanjiu* 中國古代文明研究. Shanghai: Huadong Shifan Daxue, 2005.

———. *Wenwu zhong de gu wenming* 文物中的古文明. Beijing: Shangwu, 2008.

———. "'Tian Wang' gui shishi ji youguan tuice" "天亡"簋試釋及有關推測. *Zhongguo shi yanjiu* 2009.4: 5–8.

———. *Chushi Qinghua jian* 初識清華簡. Shanghai: Zhongxi, 2013.

Li Xueqin, ed. *Qingtong qi* 青銅器. 2 vols. Zhongguo meishu quanji 中國美術全集. Gongyi meishu bian 工藝美術編 4–5. Beijing: Wenwu, 1985–86.

———. *Shang Zhou guwenzi duben* 商周古文字讀本. Beijing: Yuwen, 1989.

———. *Qinghua Daxue cang Zhanguo zhujian* 清華大學藏戰國竹簡. Vol. 1. Shanghai: Shanghai wenyi, 2010.

Li, Xueqin. *The Wonder of Chinese Bronzes*. Beijing: Foreign Languages Press, 1980.

———. *Eastern Zhou and Qin Civilizations*. Tr. K.C. Chang. Early Chinese Civilization Series. New Haven and London: Yale University Press, 1985.

Li Zhongcao 李仲操. "Shi Qiang pan mingwen shishi" 史墻盤銘文試釋. *Wenwu* 1978.3: 33–34.

Li Ziyao 黎子耀. "Shaanxi Lintong faxian de Wu Wang zheng Shang gui mingwen kaoshi" 陝西臨潼發現的武王征商簋銘文考釋. *Hangzhou Daxue xuebao: Zhexue shehui kexue ban* 1978.1: 82–84.

Lian Shaoming 連劭名. "Shi Qiang pan mingwen yanjiu" 史墻盤銘文研究. *Gu wenzi yanjiu* 5 (1981): 31–38.

———. "Shi Qiang pan mingwen yu Xi Zhou shidai de zhengtong shiguan" 史墻盤銘文與西周時代的正統史觀. *Wenbo* 1997.4: 20–24.

Lin Ganquan 林甘泉. "Dui Xi Zhou tudi guanxi de jidian xin renshi" 對西周土地關係的幾點新認識. *Wenwu* 1976.5: 45–49.

Lin Hongming 林宏明. *Zhanguo Zhongshanguo wenxi yanjiu* 戰國中山國文字研究 Taipei: Taiwan gu ji. 2003.

Lin Yun 林沄. *Lin Yun xueshu wenji* 林沄學術文集. Beijing: Zhongguo da baike quanshu, 1998.

Linduff, Katheryn M., and Yan Sun, eds. *Gender and Chinese Archaeology*. Gender and Archaeology Series 8. Walnut Creek, Calif.: Rowman & Littlefield, Altamira, 2004.

Linduff, Katheryn M. *et al.*, eds. *The Beginnings of Metallurgy in China*. Chinese Studies 11. Lewiston, N.Y.: Edwin Mellen, 2000.

Lintongxian Wenhuaguan 臨潼縣文化館. "Shaanxi Lintong faxian Wu Wang zheng Shang gui" 陝西臨潼發現武王征商簋. *Wenwu* 1977.8: 1–7.

Liu Binhui 劉彬徽. "Chuguo youming tongqi biannian gaishu" 楚國有銘銅器編年概述. *Guwenzi yanjiu* 9 (1984): 331–72.

Liu Hehui 劉和惠. "Cai qi ming yu Chu Cai guanxi xintan" 蔡器銘與楚蔡關係新探. *Dongnan wenhua* 1989.3: 22–28.

———. *Chu wenhua de dongjian* 楚文化的東漸. Wuhan: Hubei jiaoyu, 1995.

Liu Huaijun 劉懷君, Xin Yihua 辛怡華, Liu Dong 劉棟. "Sishier nian, sishisan nian Lai ding mingwen shiyi" 四十二年、四十三年逨鼎銘文試釋. *Wenwu* 2003.6: 90–93, 95.

Liu Huan 劉桓. "Duo You ding 'jing X' diwang kaobian" 多友鼎"京X"地望考辨. *Renwen zazhi* 1984.1: 125–26.

Liu Jie 劉節. "Piaoshi bianzhong kao" 䍙氏編鐘考. *Guoli Beiping Tushuguan guankan* 5.6 (1931): 35–42, 6.1: 89–93.

Liu Shi'e 劉士莪. "Qiang pan, Lai pan zhi duibi yanjiu—jian tan Xi Zhou Wei Shi, Shan Gong jiazu jiaocang tongqi qun de lishi yiyi" 牆盤、逨盤之對比研究—兼談 西周微氏、單公家族窖藏銅器群的歷史意義. *Wenbo* 2004.5: 21–27, 49.

Liu Shu 劉恕 (1032–1078). *Zizhi tongjian waiji* 資治通鑑外紀. *Yingyin Wenyuange Siku quanshu* 影音文淵閣四庫全書.

Liu Xiang 劉翔. "'Yi wushi song chu' jieshi—Du jinwen zhaji" "以五十頌處"解釋— 讀金文札記. *Zhongguo Shehui Kexue Yuan yanjiu sheng yuan xuebao* 1982.1: 79–80.

———. "Duo You ding ming liang yi" 多友鼎銘兩議. *Renwen zazhi* 1983.1: 82–85.

———. "Wangsun Yizhe zhong xinshi" 王孫遺者鐘新釋. *Jiang Han luntan* 1983.8: 76–78.

Liu Xiang *et al. Shang Zhou guwenzi duben* 商周古文字讀本. Ed. Li Xueqin. Beijing: Yuwen, 1989.

Liu Xiaodong 劉曉東. "Tian Wang gui yu Wu Wang dongtu duyi" 天亡簋與武王東土度邑. *Kaogu yu wenwu* 1987.1: 92–96.

Liu Yu 劉雨. "Duo You ding ming de shidai yu diming kaoding" 多友鼎銘的時代與地名考訂. *Kaogu* 1983.2: 152–57.

———. "Lü Qi bianzhong de chongxin yanjiu" 郘啟編鐘的重新研究. *Gu wenzi yanjiu* 12 (1985): 257–66.

———. "Xi Zhou jinwen zhong de jizu li" 西周金文中的祭祖禮. *Kaogu xuebao* 1989.4: 495–521.

———. *Jinwen lunji* 金文論集. Gugong Bowuguan xueshu wenku. Beijing: Zijincheng, 2008.

Liu Yu and Lu Yan 盧岩, eds. *Jinchu Yin Zhou jinwen jilu* 今出殷周金文集錄. 4 vols. Beijing: Zhonghua, 2002.

Liu Zhao 劉釗. "Li gui mingwen xinjie" 利簋銘文新解. *Xia da shixue* 2 (2006): 59–64.

Loewe, Michael, and Edward L. Shaughnessy, eds. *The Cambridge History of Ancient China: From the Origins of Civilization to 221 B.C.* Cambridge: Cambridge University Press, 1999.

Lu Liancheng 盧連成 and Hu Zhisheng 胡智生. *Baoji Yu guo mudi* 寶雞國墓地. 2 vols. Beijing: Wenwu, 1988.

Luo Fuyi 羅福頤. "Ke xu" 克盨. *Wenwu* 1959.3: 64.

———. "Zhongshan wang mu ding hu mingwen xiaokao" 中山王墓鼎壺銘文小考. *Gugong Bowuyuan yuankan* 1979.2: 81–85.

———. "Han Lushi jing kaoshi" 漢魯詩鏡考釋. *Wenwu* 1980.6: 80.

Luo Tai 羅泰 [i.e. Lothar von Falkenhausen, q.v.]. "Youguan Xi Zhou wanqi lizhi gaige ji Zhuangbai qingtongqi niandai de xin jiashuo: Cong shixi mingwen shuoqi" 有關西周晚期禮制改革及莊白青銅器年代的新假說：從世系銘文說起. *Zhongguo kaoguxue yu lishixue zhi zhenghe yanjiu* 中國考古學與歷史學之整合研究. Ed. Zang Zhenhua 臧振華. Zhongyang Yanjiuyuan Lishi Yuyan Yanjiusuo huiyi lunwenji 4. Taipei, 1997, II. Pp. 651–76.

———. "Xi Zhou tongqi mingwen de xingzhi" 西周銅器銘文的性質. *Kaoguxue yanjiu* 6 (2006): 343–74.

Luo Xinhui 羅新慧. "Zhoudai tianming guannian de fazhan yu shanbian" 周代天

命 觀念的發展與嬗變. *Lishi yanjiu* 5 (2012): 4–18.

Luo Xizhang 羅西章. "Shaanxi Fufeng faxian Xi Zhou Liwang shi Hu gui" 陝西扶風 發現西周厲王時㝬簋. *Wenwu* 1979.4: 89–91.

Luo Xizhang et al. "Shaanxi Fufeng chutu Xi Zhou Bo Dong zhuqi" 陝西扶風出土 西周伯䢅諸器. *Wenwu* 1976.6: 51–60.

Luo Zhenyu 羅振玉 (1866–1940). "Ze yi kaoshi" 矢彝考釋. *Shinagaku* 5 (1929): 481–85.

Ma Chengyuan 馬承源. "He zun mingwen chushi" 何尊銘文初釋. *Wenwu* 1976.1: 64–65.

———. "He zun mingwen he Zhou chu shishi" 何尊銘文和周初史實. *Wang Guowei xueshu yanjiu lun ji* 王國維學術研究論集. Ed. Wu Ze 吳澤 et al. Shanghai: Huadong Shifan Daxue chubanshe, 1983–90, I. Pp. 45–61.

———. "Jin Hou Su bianzhong" 晉侯蘇編鐘. *Shanghai Bowukan jikan* 7 (1996): 1–17.

———. "Rong Sheng zhong de tantao" 戎生鐘的探討. *Baoli cang jin: Baoli Yishu Bowuguan jingpin xuan* 保利藏金: 保利藝術博物館精品選. Guangzhou: Lingnan meishu, 1999. Pp. 361–64.

Ma Chengyuan et al. *Shang Zhou qingtong qi mingwen xuan* 商周青銅器銘文選. 4 vols. Beijing: Wenwu, 1987–90.

Ma Chengyuan, Wang Shimin 王世民, Wang Zhankui 王占奎 et al. "Shaanxi Meixian chutu jiaocang tongqi bitan" 陝西眉縣出土窖藏同期筆談. *Wenwu* 2003.6: 43–65.

Matsui Yoshinori 松井嘉德. "Seshū tochi ijō kinbun no ichi kōsatsu" 西周土地移讓 金文の一考察. *Tōyōshi kenkyū* 43.1 (1984): 1–30.

Mattos, Gilbert L. "Eastern Zhou Bronze Inscriptions." In Shaughnessy, ed., 85–123.

Mattos, Gilbert L., and Yang Hua. "The Chen Zhang Fanghu." *Orientations* 32.2 (2001): 57.

Mittag, Achim. "The *Qin Bamboo Annals* of Shuihudi: A Random Note from the Perspective of Chinese Historiography." *Monumenta Serica* 51 (2003): 543–70.

Mu tianzi zhuan 穆天子傳. *Sibu beiyao* 四部備要.

Mu Xiaojun 穆曉軍. "Shaanxi Chang'anxian chutu Xi Zhou Wu Hu ding" 陝西長安縣出土西周吳虎鼎. *Kaogu yu wenwu* 1998.3: 69–71.

Nakamura Fusetsu 中村不折 (1866–1943). *Sandai Shin-Kan no ihin ni shiruseru moji: Tsuketari rei hachibu no setsu* 三代秦漢の遺品に識せる文字: 附隸八分之說. Bijutsu Konwakai sōsho, 2nd series. Tokyo: Iwanami, 1934.

Needham, Joseph et al., eds. *Science and Civilisation in China*. 7 volumes projected. Cambridge: Cambridge University Press, 1954–.

Nivison, David S. *The Ways of Confucianism: Investigations in Chinese Philosophy*. Ed. Bryan W. Van Norden. Chicago and La Salle, Ill.: Open Court, 1996.

Nivison, David S., and Edward L. Shaughnessy. "The Jin Hou Su Bells Inscription and Its Implications for the Chronology of Early China." *Early China*

25 (2000): 29-48.

Pang Huaijing 龐懷清 et al. "Shaanxi sheng Qishan xian Dongjiacun Xi Zhou tongqi jiaoxue fajue jianbao" 陝西省岐山縣董家村西周銅器窖穴發掘簡報報. *Wenwu* 1976.5: 26-44.

Pankenier, David W. *Astrology and Cosmology in Early China: Conforming Earth to Heaven.* Cambridge: Cambridge University Press, 2013.

Peng Yushang 彭裕商. "Yetan Zi Fan bianzhong de 'wuyue chuji dingwei'" 也談子犯編鐘的"五月初吉丁未". *Zhongguo wenwu bao* (February 11, 1996): 3.

———. "Yelun xinchu Hu gui gai de niandai" 也論新出虎簋蓋的年代. *Wenwu* 1999.6: 57-62.

Pham, Lee-Moi 范麗梅. "You cong 'nie' zhu zi lun jinwen 'li' yu chujian X zi" 由從「卒」諸字論金文「盭」與楚簡「X」字. *Zhongguo wenxue yanjiu.* 2006.6: 1-28.

Pines, Yuri. *Foundations of Confucian Thought: Intellectual Life in the Chunqiu Period, 722-453 B.C.E.* Honolulu: University of Hawaii Press, 2002.

———. "Disputers of Abdication: Zhanguo Egalitarianism and the Sovereign's Power." *T'oung Pao* 91.4-5 (2005): 243-300.

———. "The Earliest "Great Wall"? The Long Wall of Qi Revisited," *Journal of the American Oriental Society* 138 (2018) 4: 743-762.

Qi Guiyan 戚桂宴. "Yong yu ming canzi kaoshi" 永盂銘殘字考釋. *Kaogu* 1981.5: 448.

Qian Boquan 錢柏泉. "'Shuo Tian Wan gui wei Wu Wang mei Shang yiqian tongqi' yi wen de jidian shangque" "說天亡簋為武王滅商以前銅器"一文的幾點商榷. *Wenwu cankao ziliao* 1958.12: 56-57.

Qiu Xigui 裘錫圭. "Shi Qiang pan ming jieshi" 史墻盤銘解釋. *Wenwu* 1978.3: 25-32.

———. *Gudai wenxue yanjiu xintan* 古代文史研究新探. Jiangsu guji chubanshe, 1992.

———. *Guwenzi lunji* 古文子論集. Beijing: Zhonghua, 1992.

———. "Shuo 'Puyong'" 說僕庸. In idem, *Gudai wenshi yanjiu xintan* 古代文史新探. [Nanjing]: Jiangsu guji, 1992.

———. "Shuo Yinxu buci de 'dian': Shilun Shangren chuzhi fushuzhe de yizhong fangfa" 說殷墟卜辭的"奠"—試論商人處置服屬者的一種方法. *Zhongyang Yanjiuyuan Lishi Yuyan Yanjiusuo jikan* 64.4 (1993): 659-86.

———. "Guanyu Zi Fan bianzhong de paici ji qita wenti" 關於子犯編鐘的排次及其它問題. *Zhongguo wenwu bao* (October 8, 1995): 3.

———. "X gong xu mingwen kaoshi" X 公盨銘文考釋. *Zhongguo lishi wenwu* 2002.6: 13-27.

———. "Du Lai qi mingwen zhaji" 讀逨器銘文札記三則. *Wenwu* 2003.6: 74-77.

Qiu, Xigui. *Chinese Writing.* Tr. Gilbert L. Mattos and Jerry Norman. Early China Special Monograph Series 4. Berkeley: Society for the Study of Early China, 2000.

Rawson, Jessica. *Chinese Bronzes: Art and Ritual*. London: British Museum, 1987.

———. "Statesmen or Barbarians? The Western Zhou as Seen through Their Bronzes." *Proceedings of the British Academy* 75 (1989): 71–95.

———. *Western Zhou Ritual Bronzes from the Arthur M. Sackler Collections*. 2 vols. Ancient Chinese Bronzes from the Arthur M. Sackler Collections 2. Washington, D.C.: Arthur M. Sackler Foundation, 1990.

———, ed. *Mysteries of Ancient China: New Discoveries from the Early Dynasties*. New York: George Braziller, 1996.

———. "Western Zhou Archaeology." In Loewe and Shaughnessy, 352–449.

Ren Song 韌松. "Ji Shaanxi Lantian xian xin chutu de Ying Hou zhong yi wen buzheng" 記陝西藍田縣新出土的應侯鐘一文補證. *Wenwu* 1977.8: 27–28.

Ren Song and Fan Weiyue 樊維岳. "Ji Shaanxi Lantian xian xin chutu de Ying Hou zhong" 記陝西藍田縣新出土的應侯鐘. *Wenwu* 1975.10: 68–69.

Ren Zhoufang 任周方. *Guobao jishi* 國寶紀事. Xi'an: Shaanxi renmin, 2003.

Rong Geng 容庚 (1894–1983), ed. *Shang-Zhou yiqi tongkao* 商周彝器通考. 2 vols. (*Yanjing Xuebao* zhuanhao 燕京學報專號 17). Beiping: Hafo-Yanjing Xueshe 哈佛燕京學社, 1941.

———. "Mishu gui yu Xun gui kaoshi de shangque" 弭叔簋及訇簋考釋的商榷. *Wenwu* 1960.8–9: 78.

Ruan Yuan 阮元 (1764–1849). *Jiguzhai zhongding yiqi kuanshi* 積古齋鐘鼎彝器款識. Yangzhou: Ruanshi, 1842. Reprint Taipei: Yiwen, 1970.

Sahara Yasuo 佐原康夫. "Hyōshi henshō" 鼏氏編鐘. *Sen'oku Hakkokan kiyō* 1 (1984): 65–93.

Sanmenxia Guoguo mudi 三門峽虢國墓地. Beijing: Wenwu, 1999.

Schaberg, David. *A Patterned Past: Form and Thought in Early Chinese Historiography*. Harvard East Asian Monographs 205. Cambridge, Mass., and London: Harvard University Asia Center, 2001.

Schunk, Lutz. "Dokumente zur Rechtsgeschichte des alten China: Übersetzung und historisch-philologische Kommentierung juristischer Bronzeinschriften der West-Zhou-Zeit (1045–771 v.Chr.)." Ph.D. dissertation, Westfälische Wilhelms-Universität Münster, 1994.

Sena, David M. "Reproducing Society: Lineage and Kinship in Western Zhou China." Ph.D. dissertation, University of Chicago, 2005.

———. "Arraying the Ancestors in Ancient China: Narratives of Lineage History in the 'Scribe Qiang' and 'Qiu' Bronzes." *Asia Major*. 2012. 25.1: 63–81.

Serruys, Paul L-M. "Fang Yen IV, 5 and 31. Knee Covers and Apron." *The Bulletin of the Institute of History and Philology, Academia Sinica* 39 (1969) 2: 245–66.

Sha Zongyuan 沙宗元. "Dishi hu mingwen bushi" 杕氏壺銘文補釋. *Anhui Daxue xuebao* 2001.4: 52–55.

"Shaanxi Ankangshi chutu Xi Zhou Shi Mi gui" 陝西安康市出土西周史密簋. *Kaogu yu wenwu* 1989.3: 7–9.

"Shaanxi Fufeng chutu Xi Zhou Bo Dong zhuqi" 陝西扶風出土西周伯威諸器. *Wenwu* 1976.6: 51.

"Shaanxi Fufeng Qiangjia yihao mu" 陝西扶風強家一號墓. *Wenbo* 4 (1987): 5–20.

"Shaanxi Fufeng Zhuangbai yihao Xi Zhou qingtongqi jiaocang fajue jianbao" 陝西扶風莊白一號西周青銅器窖藏發掘簡報. *Wenwu* 1978.3: 1–18.

"Shaanxi Hancheng Liangdaicun yizhi M27 fajue jianbao" 陝西韓城梁帶村遺址 M27發掘簡報. *Kaogu yu wenwu* 2007.6: 3–22.

"Shaanxi Meixian Yangjiacun Xi Zhou qingtongqi jiaocang" 陝西眉縣楊家村西周青銅器窖藏. *Kaogu yu wenwu* 2003.3: 3–12.

Shaanxisheng kaogu yanjiusuo 陝西省考古研究所, Baojishi kaogu gongzuodui 寶雞市考古工作隊, Yangjiacun lianhe kaogudui 楊家村聯合考古隊, and Meixian wenwuguan 眉縣文物館. "Shaanxi Meixian Yangjiacun Xi Zhou qingtongqi jiaocang fajue jianbao" 陝西眉縣楊家村西周青銅器窖藏發掘簡報. *Wenwu* 2003.6: 4–42.

Shan Zhouyao 單周堯. "Qiang pan X zi shishi" 墻盤X字試釋. *Wenwu* 1979.11: 70.

Shang Chengzuo 商承祚. "Gu-fa-X-fan ji Wuwang Zhufan bieyi" 姑發X反即吳王諸樊別議. *Zhongshan Daxue Xuebao* 1963.3: 67.

———. "Gu-fa-X-fan jian busho" 姑發X反劍補說. *Zhongshan Daxue xuebao* 1964.1: 93.

———. "Guanyu Li gui mingwen de shidu—Yu Tang Lan, Yu Xingwu tongzhi shangque" 關於利簋銘文的釋讀——與唐蘭、于省吾同志商榷. *Zhongshan Daxue xuebao* 1978.2: 78–79.

———. "Zhongshan Wang Cuo hu, ding, mingwen chuyi" 中山王䰠壺、鼎銘文芻議. *Shanghai Bowuguan jikan* 1982.2: 62–74.

Shanxisheng kaogu yanjiusuo 山西省考古研究所 and Taiyuanshi Wenwu guanli weiyuanhui 太原市文物管理委員會. "Taiyuan Jinshengcun 251 hao Chunqiu damu ji chemakeng fajue jianbao" 太原金勝村251號春秋大墓及車馬坑發掘簡報. *Wenwu* 1989.9: 59–86.

Shao Bei 邵蓓. "Xi Zhou bo zhi kaosuo" 西周伯制考索. *Zhongguo shi yanjiu* 2008.2: 3–12.

Shaughnessy, Edward L. [i.e. Xia Hanyi, q.v.]. "The Date of the Duo You ding and Its Significance." *Early China* 9–10 (1983–85): 55–69.

———. "Historical Geography and the Extent of the Earliest Chinese Kingdoms." *Asia Major* (third series) 2.2 (1989): 1–22.

———. *Sources of Western Zhou History: Inscribed Bronze Vessels.* Berkeley: University of California Press, 1991.

———. *Before Confucius: Studies in the Creation of the Chinese Classics.* SUNY Series in Chinese Philosophy and Culture. Albany, 1997.

———, ed. *New Sources of Early Chinese History: An Introduction to the Reading of Inscriptions and Manuscripts.* Early China Special Monograph Series 3. Berkeley, Calif.: Society for the Study of Early China and the Institute of East Asian Studies, 1997.

———. "Western Zhou Bronze Inscriptions." In Shaughnessy, 57–84.

———. "Western Zhou History." In Loewe and Shaughnessy, 292–351.

———. "New Sources of Western Zhou History: Recent Discoveries of Inscribed Bronze Vessels." *Early China* 26–27 (2001–02): 73–98.

———. "Toward a Social Geography of the Zhouyuan during the Western Zhou Dynasty: The Jing and Zhong Lineages of Fufeng County." *Political Frontiers, Ethnic Boundaries, and Human Geographies in Chinese History*. Ed. Nicola Di Cosmo and Don J. Wyatt. London and New York: Routledge Curzon, 2003. Pp. 16–34.

———. "The Bin Gong Xu Inscription and the Origins of the Chinese Literary Tradition." *Books in Numbers: Seventy-Fifth Anniversary of the Harvard-Yenching Library*. Ed. Wilt L. Idema. Cambridge, Mass., 2007. Pp. 3–21.

———. "The Writing of a Late Western Zhou Bronze Inscription," *Asiatische Studien* 61.3 (2007), 845–77.

———. "The Dowager v. the Royal Court: A Ninth-Century B.C. Case of Family Law Recorded in Chinese Bronze Inscriptions." *Structures of Power: Law and Gender across the Ancient Near East and Beyond*. Ed. Ilan Peled. Chicago: The Oriental Institute, 2018.

Shelach, Gideon, and Yuri Pines. "Secondary State Formation and the Development of Local Identity: Change and Continuity in the State of Qin (770–221 B.C.)." *Archaeology of Asia*. Ed. Miriam T. Stark. Blackwell Studies in Global Archaeology. Malden, Mass.: Wiley-Blackwell, 2006. Pp. 202–30.

Shen Wenzhuo 沈文倬. *Zong-Zhou liyue wenming kaolun* 宗周禮樂文明考論. Hangzhou: Hangzhou Daxue, 1999.

Shengshi jijin: Shaanxi Baoji Meixian qingtongqi jiaocang 盛世吉金：陝西寶鷄眉縣青銅器窖藏. Beijing: Beijing chubanshe, 2003.

Shi Yan 史言. "Meixian Yangjiacun dading" 眉縣楊家村大鼎. *Wenwu* 1972.7: 3–4.

Shiji 史記. 10 vols. Beijing: Zhonghua, 1959.

Shim, Jaehoon. "The 'Jinhou Su bianzhong' Inscription and Its Significance." *Early China* 22 (1997): 43–75.

Shirakawa Shizuka 白川靜. *Kimbun tsūshaku* 金文通釋. 56 vols. Kobe: Hakutsuru bijutsukan, 1962–84.

———. *Kōkotsu kimbungaku ronshū* 甲骨金文學論集. Kyoto: Hōyū shoten, 1974.

———. *Jinwen tongshi xuanshi* 金文通釋選釋. Wuhan: Wuhan Daxue, 2000.

Shouxian Cai Hou mu chutu yiwu 壽縣蔡侯墓出土遺物. Kaoguxue zhuankan 2.5. Beijing: Kexue, 1956.

Skosey, Laura A. "The Legal System and Legal Tradition of the Western Zhou (ca. 1045–771 B.C.E.)." Ph.D. dissertation, University of Chicago, 1996.

Škrabal, Ondřej. 石安瑞 "You tongqi mingwen de bianzuan jiaodu kan Xi-Zhou jinwen zhong 'bai shou qi shou' de xingzhi" 由銅器銘文的編纂角度看西周金文中 "拜手稽首" 的性質, *Qingtongqi yu jinwen* 1. Shanghai buji chubanshe (2017): 541–559.

———. "Writing Before Inscribing: On The Use Of Manuscripts In The Production Of Western Zhou Bronze Inscriptions." *Early China* 42 (2019): 273–332.

Smith, Adam D. "The Chinese sexagenary cycle and the ritual foundations of the calendar," *Calendars and years II: Astronomy and Time in the Ancient and Medieval World.* Ed. John M. Steele, Oxbow Books (2011): 1–37.

———. "Rejoinder To Jonathan Smith, Research Note On Shun 舜." *Early China*, 41 (2018): 423–433.

———. "'What Difficulty Could There Be?' The Composition of the Guodian Qiong Da Yi Shi 窮達以時 from Memorized Performance Cues." In Wolfgang Behr and Lisa Indraccolo eds. *Warp, Woof, Wen / Phoneme, Pattern, Pun - Structural Approaches to Early Chinese Texts.* Leiden: Brill. Forthcoming.

So, Jenny [F.]. *Eastern Zhou Ritual Bronzes from the Arthur M. Sackler Collections.* Ancient Chinese Bronzes from the Arthur M. Sackler Collections 3. [Washington, D.C.]: Arthur M. Sackler Foundation, 1995.

———. "Chu Art: Link Between the Old and New." In Cook and Major, 33–47.

Song Huanwen 宋煥文. "Anzhou liu qi bianzheng" 安州六器辨正. *Jianghan kaogu* 1989.2: 72–73.

Song Lingping 宋玲平. *Jinxi muzang zhidu yanjiu* 晉系墓葬制度研究. Beijing Daxue Zhendan Gudai Wenming Yanjiu Zhongxin xueshu congshu 13. Beijing: Kexue, 2007.

Sterckx, Roel, ed. *Of Tripod and Palate: Food, Politics, and Religion in Traditional China.* NY: Palgrave Macmillan, 2005.

———. *Food, Sacrifice, and Sagehood in Early China.* Cambridge: Cambridge University Press, 2011.

Sun Bingjun 孫秉君. *Ruiguo Jinyu xuancui: Shaanxi Hancheng Chunqiu baozang* 芮國晉玉選粹：陝西韓城春秋寶藏. Xi'an: San Qin, 2007.

Sun Changxu 孫常敘. "'Tian Wang gui' wen zi yi nian" 《天亡簋》問字疑年. *Jilin Shida xuebao* 1963.1: 27–58.

———. *Sun Changxu guwezi lunji* 孫常敘古文字學論集. Shanghai: Shanghai guji chubanshe. 2016.

Sun Qikang 孫啟康. "Chu qi 'Wangsun Yizhe zhong' kaobian" 楚器《王孫遺者鐘》考辨. *Jiang Han kaogu* 1983.4: 41–46.

Sun Zhichu 孫稚雛. "Huainan Cai qi shiwen shangque" 淮南蔡器釋文商榷. *Kaogu* 1965.9: 467–69.

———. "Zhongshan Cuo ding, hu de niandai shishi ji qi yiyi" 中山王䰜鼎、壺的年代史實及其意義. *Gu wenzi yanjiu* 1 (1979): 273–305.

———. "Tian Wang gui mingwen huishi" 天亡簋銘文匯釋. *Guwenzi yanjiu* 3 (1980): 166–80.

———. "Piao Qiang zhong mingwen huishi" 㝬羌鐘銘文彙釋. *Guwenzi yanjiu* 19 (1992): 102–14.

———. "Ban gui mingwen shidu de yixie wenti" 班簋銘文釋讀的一些問題. *Guwenzi yanjiu* 20 (2000): 98–105.

———. "Qiang pan mingwen jinshi" 墻盤銘文今釋. *Guwenzi yanjiu* 24 (2002): 217–19.

Sun Zuoyun 孫作雲. "Shuo 'Tian Wang gui' wei Wuwang mie Shang yiqian tongqi" 說天王簋為武王滅商以前銅器. *Wenwu cankao ziliao* 1958.1: 29–31.

———. "Zai lun 'Tian Wang gui' er san shi" 再論"天亡簋"二三事. *Wenwu* 1960.5: 50–52.

Takahashi Junji 高橋準二. "Hyōshi henshō ondaka sokutei" 䗊氏編鐘音高測定. *Sen'oku Hakkokan kiyō* 1 (1986): 94–107.

Takashima, Kenichi. "Settling the Cauldron in the Right Place: A Study of ting in the Bone Inscriptions." *Wang Li Memorial Volumes: English Volume*. Ed. Chinese Language Society of Hong Kong. Hong Kong: Joint Publishing, 1987. Pp. 405–21.

Takigawa Kametarō 瀧川龜太朗. *Shiki kaichū kōshō* 史記會注考證. Rpt. Taipei: Hongshi, 1977.

Tang Lan 唐蘭. "Zhou wang Hu zhong kao" 周王猷鐘考. *Guoli Beiping Gugong Bowuyuan niankan* 國立北平故宮博物院年刊 1936: 1–16.

———. "Zhen gui" 朕簋. *Wenwu cankao ziliao* 1958.9: 69.

———. "Yi Hou Ze kaoshi." 宜侯矢簋考釋. *Kaogu xuebao* 1965.2.

———. "Yong yu mingwen jieshi" 永盂銘文解釋. *Wenwu* 1972.1: 58–62.

———. "Yong yu mingwen jieshi de yixie buchong: Jian da duzhe laixin" 永盂銘文解釋的一些補充:兼答讀者來信. *Wenwu* 1972.11: 54–55.

———. "Xi Zhou shidai zuizao de yi jian tongqi Li gui mingwen jieshi" 西周時代最早的一件銅器利簋銘文解釋. *Wenwu* 1977.8: 8–9.

———. "Guanyu Da Ke zhong" 關於大克鐘. *Chutu wenxian yanjiu* 出土文獻研究. Beijing: Wenwu, 1985. 121–25.

———. *Xi Zhou qingtongqi mingwen fendai shi zheng* 西周青銅器銘文分代史徵. Beijing: Zhonghua, 1986.

———. *Tang Lan xiansheng jinwen lunji* 唐蘭先生金文論集. Beijing: Zijincheng, 1995.

Thomas, Rosalind. *Literacy and Orality in Ancient Greece*. Key Themes in Ancient History. Cambridge: Cambridge University Press, 1995.

Thorp, Robert L. "Erlitou and the Search for the Xia." *Early China* 16 (1991): 1–38.

———. *China in the Early Bronze Age*: Shang Civilization. Encounters with Asia. Philadelphia: University of Pennsylvania Press, 2006.

Thote, Alain. "The Double Coffin of Leigudun Tomb No. 1: Iconographic Sources and Related Problems." *New Perspectives on Chu Culture during the Eastern Zhou Period*. Ed. Thomas Lawton. Washington: Smithsonian Institution, 1991. Pp. 23–46.

———. "Shang and Zhou Funeral Practices: Interpretation of Material Vestiges." In Lagerwey and Kalinowski, I, 103–42.

Tian Xingnong 田醒農 and Luo Zhongru 雒忠如. "Duo You ding de faxian ji qi mingwen shishi" 多友鼎的發現及其銘文試釋. *Renwen zazhi* 1981.4: 115–18.

Underhill, Anne P., and Hui Fang. "Early State Economic Systems in China."

Archaeological Perspectives on Political Economies. Ed. Gary M. Feinman and Linda M. Nicholas. Foundations of Archaeological Inquiry. Salt Lake City: University of Utah, 2004. Pp. 129–44.

Venture, Olivier [see also Feng Yicheng]. "Visibilité et lisibilité dans les inscriptions sur bronze de la Chine archaïque (1250–771 av. notre ère)." *Du visible au lisible: Texte et image en Chine et au Japon.* Ed. Anne Kerlan-Stephens and Cécile Sakai. Arles: Philippe Picquier, 2006. Pp. 67–81.

Vogt, Paul Nicholas. "Between Kin and King: Social Aspects of Western Zhou Ritual." Ph.D. dissertation, Columbia University, 2012

Wagner, Donald B., "The Language of the Ancient State of Wu." *The Master Said: To Study and ...: To Søren Egerod on the Occasion of His Sixty-seventh Birthday.* Ed. B. Arendrup, B. Heilesen, and J. Østergård Petersen. Festschrift S. Egerød, East Asian Institute, Occasional Papers 6. Copenhagen, 1991. Pp. 161–76.

Wang Guowei 王國維 (1877–1927). *Guantang jilin, fu bieji* 觀堂集林附別集. 4 vols. in 2. Beijing: Zhonghua, 1959.

Wang Hui 王輝. *Qin tongqi mingwen biannian jishi* 秦銅器銘文編年集釋. Xi'an: San Qin, 1990.

———. *Shang Zhou jinwen* 商周金文. Zhongguo guwenzi daodu. Beijing: Wenwu, 2006.

Wang Jing 王晶. "'Duiyang' zai shi" "對揚"再釋. Beifang luntan 2007.3, 4–6.

Wang Rencong 王人聰. "Cai Hou X kao" 蔡侯▓考. *Gu wenzi yanjiu* 12 (1985): 321–26.

———. "Jizai Wu Wang fa Shang shishi de Zhou chu zhongqi—Li gui" 記載武王伐商史實的周初重器—利簋. *Zhongguo wenwu shijie* 1986.8.

Wang Shenxing 王慎行 and Wang Hanzhen 王漢珍. "Yimao zun mingwen tongshi lun" 乙卯尊銘文通譯論. *Guwenzi yanjiu* 13 (1986): 209–25.

Wang Tao. "A Textual Investigation of the *taotie*." In Whitfield, 102–18.

Wang Wenxuan 王文轩. "Yi Hou Ze gui ji qi xiangguan wenti yanjiu zongshu." 宜侯夨簋及其相关问题研究综述. Suzhou wenbo luncong 2016.7: 34–40.

Wang Zhankui 王占奎. "Guanyu Jing fangding de jidian kanfa" 關於靜方鼎的幾點看法. *Wenwu* 1998.5: 89–90.

Wang Zhongwen 汪中文. "'Bo Dong' yu 'Lu,' 'Lu Bo Dong' zhuqi xilian wenti zhi jiantao" "伯戜"與"彔"、"彔伯戜"諸器間系聯問題之檢討. *Dalu zazhi* 79.3 (1989): 43–48.

Wang Zichu 王子初. "Jin Hou Su zhong de yinyuexue yanjiu" 晉侯蘇鐘的音樂學研究. *Wenwu* 1998.5: 23–30.

Watson, William. *Ancient Chinese Bronzes.* 2nd ed. The Arts of the East. London: Faber & Faber, 1977.

Wen Tingjing 溫廷敬. "Piao Qiang zhong ming shi" 𪊵羌鐘銘釋. *Zhongshan Daxue shixue zhuankan* 1.1 (1935): 195.

White, William Charles. *Tombs of Old Lo-yang.* Shanghai: Kelly & Walsh, 1934.

Whitfield, Roderick, ed. *The Problem of Meaning in Early Chinese Ritual Bronzes.*

Colloquies on Art & Archaeology in Asia 15. London: School of Oriental and African Studies, University of London, 1993.

Wu Hong 巫鴻 [see also Wu Hung]. "'Mingqi' de lilun he shijian—Zhanguo shiqi liyi meishu zhong de guannianhua qingxiang" "明器"的理踐和實踐—戰國時期禮儀美術中的觀念化傾向. *Wenwu* 2006.6: 72–81.

Wu, Hung [i.e. Wu Hong, q.v.]. *The Wu Liang Shrine: The Ideology of Early Chinese Pictorial Art.* Stanford: Stanford University Press, 1989.

———. *Monumentality in Early Chinese Art and Architecture.* Stanford: Stanford University Press, 1995.

———. "Art and Architecture of the Warring States Period." In Loewe and Shaughnessy, 651–744.

———. "On Rubbings: Their Materiality and Historicity." *Writing and Materiality in China: Essays in Honor of Patrick Hanan.* Ed. Judith T. Zeitlin *et al.* Harvard-Yenching Institute Monograph Series 58. Cambridge, Mass., and London: Harvard University Asia Center, 2003. Pp. 29–72.

———. *The Art of the Yellow Springs: Understanding Chinese Tombs.* Honolulu: University of Hawaii Press, 2010.

Wu Jiabi 武家璧. "Zi Fan bianzhong zhongming kaoshi" 子犯鐘鐘銘考釋. *Zhongyuan wenwu* 1998.2: 61–65.

Wu Qichang 吳其昌. "Piao Qiang zhong bukao" 驫羌鐘補考. *Guoli Beiping Tushuguan guankan* 6 (1931): 43–52.

Wu Shiqian 伍仕謙. "Wangzi Wu ding, Wangsun Gao zhong mingwen kaoshi" 王子午鼎、王孫誥鐘銘文考釋. *Guwenzi yanjiu* 9 (1985): 275–94.

Wu Zhenfeng 吳鎮烽 and Luo Zhongru 雒忠如. "Shaanxisheng Fufengxian Qiangjiacun chutu de Xi Zhou tongqi" 陝西省扶風縣強家村出土的西周銅器. *Wenwu* 1975.8: 57–61.

Wu Zhenwu 吳振武. "Shishi Xi Zhou X gui mingwen zhong de 'xin' zi" 試釋西周 X 簋銘文中的"馨"字. *Wenwu* 2006.11: 61–62.

Xi Hanjing 席涵靜. *Zhoudai shiguan yanjiu* 周代史官研究. Taipei: Fuji wenhua tushu youxian gongsi, 1983.

Xia Hanyi 夏含夷 [i.e. Edward Shaughnessy, q.v.]. "Shi 'Yufang'" 釋御方. *Guwenzi yanjiu* 9 (1984): 97–110.

———. *Wengu zhixin lu: Shang Zhou wenhua shi guanjian* 溫故知新錄—商周文化史管見. Taipei: Daohuo, 1997.

———. "Fu bu fu, zi bu zi: Shilun Xi Zhou zhongqi Xun gui he Shi You gui de duandai" 父不父,子不子:試論西周中期詢簋和師酉簋的斷代. *Zhongguo guwenzi yu gu wenxian* 1 (1999): 62–64.

Xia Shang Zhou duandai gongcheng 1996–2000 nian jieduan chengguo baogao: Jianben 夏商周斷代工程 1996–2000 年階段成果報告:簡本. Beijing: Shijie Tushu, 2000.

Xichuan Xiasi Chunqiu Chumu 淅川下寺春秋楚墓. Beijing: Wenwu, 1991.

Xie Wenming 謝文明. *Shangdai jinwen de zhengli yu yanjiu* 商代金文的整理與研究. Doctoral Dissertation. Fudan University, 2012.

Xing, Wen, ed. *The X gong xu: A Report and Papers from the Dartmouth Workshop*. International Research on Bamboo and Silk Documents Newsletter 3.2–6. Hanover, N.H.: Dartmouth College, 2003.

Xu Chaohua 徐朝華. *Er ya jin zhu* 爾雅今注. Shanghai: Guji, 1987.

Xu, Fengxian. "Using Sequential Relations of Day-Dates to Determine the Temporal Scope of Western Zhou Lunar Phase Terms." *Early China* 33–34 (2010–2011): 171–98.

Xu, Jay. "The Cemetery of the Western Zhou Lords of Jin." *Artibus Asiae* 56.3–4 (1996): 193–222.

Xu Jianmei 徐鑒梅. "Dong Han Shijing mingwen jing" 東漢詩經銘文鏡. *Jiang Han Kaogu* 1985.4: 77.

Xu Shaohua 徐少華. *Zhoudai nantu lishi dili yu wenhua* 周代南土歷史地理與文化. Wuhan: Wuhan Daxue, 1994.

Xu Tianjin 徐天進. "Riben Chuguang Meishuguan shoucang de Jing fangding" 日本出光美術館收藏的靜方鼎. *Wenwu* 1998.5: 85–87.

Xu Tianjin *et al.*, eds. *Jijin zhuguo shi: Zhouyuan chutu Xi Zhou qingtongqi jingcui* 吉金鑄國史: 周原出土西周青銅器精粹. Beijing: Wenwu, 2002.

Xu Tongbo 徐同柏 (1775–1854). *Conggu tang kuanshi xue* 從古堂款識學. [Shanghai]: Tongwen, 1886. Reprint Hong Kong: Xianggang ming shi wen hua guo ji, 2004.

Xu Xichen 徐喜辰. "'He zun' ming zhong de 'wang' dang zhi Zhou Gong shuo" 《何尊》銘中的"王"當指周公說. *Xizhou shi yanjiu renwen zazhi congkan* 2 (1984): 308–16.

Xu Zhongshu 徐中舒. *Piaoshi bianzhong tushi* 鷹氏編鐘圖釋. Beijing: N.p. 1932.

———. "Jinwen guci shili" 金文嘏辭釋例. *Zhongyang Yanjiuyuan Lishi Yuyan Yanjiusuo jikan* 中央研究院歷史語言研究所集刊 6.1 (1936): 1–44.

———. "Yu ding de niandai jiqi xiangguan wenti" 禹鼎的年代及其相關問題. *Kaogu xuebao* 1959.3: 53–66.

———. "Xi Zhou Qiang pan mingwen jianyi" 西周墻盤銘文箋釋. *Kaogu xuebao* 1978.2: 139–48.

———. "Xi Zhou Li gui mingwen jianshi" 西周利簋銘文箋釋. *Sichuan Daxue xuebao* 1980.2: 109–110, 93.

Xu Zhongshu and Wu Shiqian 伍仕謙. "Zhongshan san qi shiwen ji gongtang tu shuoming" 中山三器釋文及宮堂圖說明. *Zhongguo shi yanjiu* 1979.4: 85–98.

Yakobson, Alexander. "Political Rhetoric in China and in Imperial Rome: The Persuader, the Ruler, the Audience." *Extrême-Orient, Extrême-Occident* 34 (2012): 195–208.

Yan Yiping 嚴一萍. "He zun yu Zhou chu de niandai" 何尊與周初的年代. *Dong Zuobin xiansheng shishi shisi zhou nian jinian kan* 董作賓先生逝世十四周年紀念刊. Taipei: Yiwen, 1978. Pp. 1–8.

———. "Cong Li gui ming kan fa Zhou nian" 從利簋銘看伐紂年. *Zhongguo wenzi* 8 (1983): 1–22.

Yang Aiguo 楊愛國. "Hanjing mingwen de shiliaoxue jiazhi" 漢鏡銘文的史料學

价值. *Zhongyuan wenwu* 1996.4: 84–88.

Yang Kuan 楊寬. "Shi He zun mingwen jianlun Zhou kaiguo niandai" 釋何尊銘文兼論周開國年代. *Wenwu* 1983.6: 53–57.

Yang Mingzhao 楊明照. *Zengding Wenxin diaolong jiaozhu* 增訂文心雕龍校注. Beijing: Zhonghua, 2000.

Yang Shaoxuan 楊紹萱. "Zong Zhou zhong, San Shi pan, yu Mao Gong ding suo jizai de Xi Zhou lishi" 宗周鐘、散氏盤與毛公鼎所記載的西周歷史. *Beijing Shifan Daxue xuebao* 1961.4: 25–36.

Yang Shuda 楊樹達. *Jiweiju jinwen shuo* 積微居金文說. Kaoguxue zhuankan A.1. Beijing: Zhongguo Kexueyuan, 1952.

Yang Wenshan 楊文山. "Qingtongqi 'Mai zun' yu Xingguo shifeng" 青銅器"麥尊"與邢國始封. *Wenwu chunqiu* 59.3 (2001): 1–9.

———. "Xi Zhou qingtongqi Xinghou gui tongshi" 西周青銅器邢侯簋通釋. *Xingtai Shifan Gaozhuan xuebao* 2002.3: 23–28, 2005.3: 5–9.

Yates, Robin D.S. "The City State in Ancient China." *The Archaeology of City-States: Cross-Cultural Approaches*. Ed. Deborah L. Nichols and Thomas H. Charlton. Washington, D.C.: Smithsonian, 1997. Pp. 71–90.

Ye Zhengbo 葉正渤. "Lue lun Xi-Zhou mingwen de jishi fangshi" 略論西周銘文的記時方式. *Xuzhou Shifan Daxue xuebao* (Zhexue shehui kexue ban) 26.3 (2000): 48–52.

———. "Ershi shiji yilai Xi-Zhou jinwen yuexiang wenti yanjiu zongshu" 20世紀以來西周金文月相問題研究綜述. *Xuzhou Shifan Daxue xuebao* (Zhexue shehui kexue ban) 30.5 (2004): 9–13.

Yi Peiji 易培基. "San shi pan shiwen" 散氏盤釋文. *Guoxue congkan* 1.1 (1923): 91–92. Yin Difei 殷滌非. "Shilun Da Feng gui de niandai 試論大豐簋的年代. *Wenwu* 1960.5:53–54.

———. "Shouxian Cai Hou tongqi de zai yanjiu" 壽縣蔡侯銅器的再研究. *Kaogu yu wenwu* 1984.4: 60–62.

Yin Shengping 尹盛平 et al., eds. *Xi Zhou Wei shi jiazu qingtongqi yanjiu* 西周微氏家族青銅器研究. Beijing: Wenwu, 1992.

Yin Weizhang 殷瑋璋. "Xin chutu de taibao tongqi jiqi xiangguan wenti" 新出土的太保銅器及其相關問題. In Chen Guang, 253–65.

Yin Zhou jinwen ji qingtongqi ziliaoku 殷周金文暨青銅器資料庫. [See Institute of History and Philology, Academica Sinica.]

Yin Zhou jinwen jicheng 殷周金文集成. Currently 18 vols. Kaoguxue tekan. Beijing: Zhonghua, 1984–.

Yin Zhou jinwen jicheng shiwen 殷周金文集成釋文. 6 vols. Hong Kong: Chinese University, 2001.

Yinxu Fu Hao mu 殷墟婦好墓. Beijing: Wenwu, 1980.

You Rujie 游汝傑 and Zhou Zhenhe 周振鶴. "Nanfang diming fenbu de quyu tezheng yu gudai yuyan de guanxi" 南方地名的區于特徵與古代語言的關係. *Jinian Gu Jiegang xueshu lunwenji* 紀念顧頡剛學術論文集. Ed. Yin Da 尹達 et al. Chengdu: Ba-Shu, 1990. Vol. 2. Pp. 709–24.

Yu Haoliang 于豪亮. "Zhongshan san qi mingwen kaoshi" 中山三器銘文考釋. *Kaogu xuebao* 1979.2: 171–84.

———. "Qiang pan mingwen kaoshi" 墻盤銘文考釋. *Guwenzi yanjiu* 7 (1982): 87–101.

———. *Yu Haoliang xueshu wencun* 于豪亮學術文存. Beijing: Zhonghua, 1985.

Yu Xingwu 于省吾 (1896–1984). "Jing Hou gui kaoshi" 井侯簋考醳. *Kaogu shekan* 1936.4: 22–26.

———. "Guanyu Tian wang gui mingwen de jidian lunzheng" 關於「天亡簋」銘文的幾點論政. *Kaogu* 1960.8: 34–36, 41.

———. "'Shi Ke xu ming kaoshi' shu hou" 《師克盨銘考釋》書後. *Wenwu* 1962.11: 56–57.

———. "Li gui mingwen kaoshi" 利簋铭文考釋. *Wenwu* 1977.8: 10–12.

———. "'Guanyu Li gui mingwen de shidu' yi wen de jidian yijian" 《關於利簋銘文的釋讀》一文的幾點意見. *Zhongshan Daxue xuebao* 1978.5: 21–22.

———. "Shouxian Cai Hou mu tongqi mingwen kaoshi" 壽縣蔡侯墓銅器銘文考釋. *Guwenzi yanjiu* 1 (1979): 40–54.

———. "Qiang pan mingwen shier jie" 墻盤銘文十二解. *Guwenzi yanjiu* 5 (1981): 1–16.

Yu Yongliang 余永梁. "Ji san Shi pan" 記散氏盤. *Guoli Diyi Zhongshan Daxue Yuyan Lishixue Yanjiusuo zhoukan* 1.5 (1927): 111–13.

Yu Xingwu 于省吾. *Jiagu wenzi shilin* 甲骨文字釋林. Beijing: Zhonghua shuju. 1979.

Zeng hou Yi mu 曾侯乙墓. 2 vols. Beijing: Wenwu, 1989.

Zhang Binglin 章炳麟 (1868–1936). "Lun San Shi pan shu er zha" 論散氏盤書二札. *Guoxue congkan* 1.1 (1923): 92–94.

Zhang Changshou 張長壽 and Wen Guang 聞廣. "Wen You xiansheng Luozhaotang cang Da Yu ding moben ba" 聞宥先生落照堂藏大盂鼎墨本跋. *Wenwu* 2008.10: 88–91.

———. "Ba Luozhaotang cang Mao gong ding taben—Luozhaotang cang ta zhi er" 跋落照堂藏毛公鼎拓本—落照堂藏拓之二. *Wenwu* 2009.2: 44–52.

———. "Mao Gong ding chutu nianfen de yi ze ezhuan" 毛公鼎出土年份的一則訛傳. *Wenwu* 2012.4: 46–49.

Zhang Enxian 張恩賢 and Wei Xingxing 魏興興. "Zhouyuan yizhi chutu Dan Shu Fan yu" 周原遺址出土丹叔番盂. *Kaogu yu wenwu* 2001.5: 89–90.

Zhang Guangyu 張光裕 [i.e. Cheung Kwong-yue]. "Lantian xin chutu de Ying Hou zhong yu shudao cangqi de fuhe" 藍田新出土的應侯鐘與書道藏器的復合. *Dongfang wenhua* 15.2 (1977): 203–5.

———. "Hu gui jia, yi gai ming hexiao xiaoji" 虎簋甲、乙蓋銘合校小記. *Gu wenzi yanjiu* 24 (2004): 183–93.

Zhang Guangyuan 張光遠. "Xi Zhou zhongqi Mao gong ding: Bolun Aozhou Bana boshi wuwei zhi shuo" 西周重器毛公鼎: 駁論澳洲巴納博士誣偽之說. *Gugong jikan* 7.2 (1973): 1–69.

———. "Gugong xincang Chunqiu Jin Wen chengba 'Zi Fan he zhong' chushi" 故宮新藏春秋晉文稱霸 "子犯和鐘" 初釋. *Gugong wenwu yuekan* 13.1 (1995): 4–31.

Zhang Guangzhi 張光直 [i.e. Kwang-chih Chang, q.v.]. *Zhongguo qingtong shidai* 中國青銅時代. 2 vols. Taipei: Lianjing, 1983–90.

Zhang Maorong 張懋鎔. "Jing fangding xiaokao" 靜方鼎小考. *Wenwu* 1998.5: 88, 90. Zhang Maorong et al. "Ankang chutu Shi Mi gui jiqi yiyi" 安康出土的史密簋及其意義. *Wenwu* 1989.7: 64–71.

Zhang Peiyu 張培瑜. "Lai ding de yuexiang jiri Xi Zhou niandai" 逨鼎的月相紀日西周年代. *Wenwu* 2003.6: 78–84.

Zhang Peiyu et al. *Zhongguo gudai lifa* 中國古代曆法. Beijing: Zhonguo kexue lishu, 2008.

Zhang Weihua 張維華. "Qi changcheng kao" 齊長城考. *Yugong* 7.1–3 (1946): 121–48.

Zhang Wenyu 張聞玉. "Zi Fan he zhong 'wuyue chuji dinghai' jie" 子犯和鐘"五月初吉丁亥"解. *Zhongguo wenwu bao* (January 7, 1996): 3.

———. "Hu guigai ming jianshi" 虎簋蓋銘簡釋. *Kaogu yu wenwu* 1997.3: 78–80.

Zhang Xiaoheng 張筱衡. "Shao Yu ding kaoshi" 召禹鼎考釋. *Renwen zazhi* 1958.1: 63–81.

———. "San pan kaoshi" 散盤考釋. *Renwen zazhi* 1958.3: 68–81, 88; 1958.4: 81–98.

Zhang Yachu 張亞初. "Zhou Li Wang suo zuo jiqi Hu gui kao—Jian lun yu zhi xiangguan de jige wenti" 周厲王所作祭器䵣簋考—兼論與之相關的幾個問題. *Gu wenzi yanjiu* 5 (1981): 151–68.

———. "Tan Duo You ding mingwen de jige wenti" 談多友鼎銘文的幾個問題. *Kaogu yu wenwu* 1982.3: 64–68

———. "Lun Chu Gong Jia zhong he Chu Gong Ni bo de niandai" 論楚公豪鐘和楚公逆鎛的年代. *Jiang Han kaogu* 1984.4: 95–96.

Zhang Yachu and Liu Yu 劉雨. *Xi Zhou jinwen guanzhi yanjiu* 西周金文官制研究. Beijing: Zhonghua, 1986.

Zhang Yongshan 張永山. "Li gui 'sui ding ke wen' buzheng" 利簋"歲鼎克聞"補證. *Qinghua Daxue xuebao (Zhexue shehui kexue ban)* 16.4 (2001): 42–44.

Zhang Zhenglang 張政烺. "He zun mingwen jieshi buyi" 何尊銘文解釋補遺. *Wenwu* 1976.1: 66–67.

———. "Li gui shiwen" 利簋釋文. *Kaogu* 1978.1: 58–59.

———. "Zhongshan Wang Cuo hu ji ding ming kaoshi" 中山王䦒壺及鼎銘考釋. *Gu wenzi yanjiu* 1 (1979): 208–32.

———. "Zhou Li Wang Hu gui shiwen" 周厲王胡簋釋文. *Gu wenzi yanjiu* 3 (1980): 104–19.

———. "Bi Qi you de zhenwei wenti" 矤其卣的真偽問題. *Gugong bowuyuan xuekan* 1998.4: 1–5. [Also articles in the same issue by Zhang Guangyu 張光裕, Sun Zhichu 孫稚雛, Lian Shaoming 連邵名, and Zhu Fenghan 朱鳳瀚, 6–16.]

Zhao Cheng 趙誠. "'Zhongshan hu' 'Zhongshan ding' mingwen shishi"《中山壺》《中山鼎》釋文試釋. *Gu wenzi yanjiu* 1 (1979): 247-72.

———. "Qiang pan mingwen bushi" 墻盤銘文補釋. *Gu wenzi yanjiu* 5 (1981): 17-26.

Zhao Ping'an 趙平安. *Jinwen shidu yu wenming tansuo* 金文釋讀與文明探索. Shanghai: Shanghai guji, 2011.

Zheng Wei 鄭威. "Liang Zhou zhi jigao dengji guizu mu qingtongqi zuhe xintan" 兩周之際高等級貴族墓青銅禮器組合新探. *Kaogu* 2009.3: 57-63.

Zheng-Zhang Shangfang 鄭張尚芳. "Gu Wu-Yue diming zhong de Dong-Taiyu chengfen" 古吳越地名中的侗台語成份. *Minzu yuwen* 1990.6: 16-18.

———. "Cong Shuoren jing 'qi-yi' tongjia tan shanggu jingzu shengmu de quzhi" 從碩人鏡 "齊夷" 通假談上古精組聲母的取值. *Yinshi xin lun: qingzhu Shao Rongfen xiansheng bashi shouchen xueshu lunwenji* 音史新論:慶祝邵榮芬先生八十壽辰學術論文集. Ed. Dong Kun 董琨 and Feng Zheng 馮蒸. Beijing: Xueyuan chubanshe, 2005. 71-77.

Zhengzhou Shang cheng—1953-1985 kaogu fajue baogao 鄭州商城—1953-1985考古發掘報告. 3 vols. Beijing: Wenwu, 2001.

Zhong Bosheng 鍾柏生 et al., eds., *Xinshou Yin-Zhou qingtongqi mingwen ji qiying huibian* 新收殷周青銅器銘文暨器影彙編. Taibei Shi: Yi wen yin shu guan, Minguo 95, 2006.

Zhong Fengnian 鐘鳳年 et al. "Guanyu Li gui mingwen kaoshi de taolun" 關於利簋銘文考釋的討論. Wenwu 1978.6: 77-84.

Zhongguo tianwenxue shi 中國天文學史. Beijing: Kexue chubanshe, 1981.

Zhou Baohong 周寶宏. *Jinchu Xi Zhou jinwen jishi* 近出西周金文集釋. Tianjin: Guji, 2005.

———. *Xi Zhou qingtong zhong qi mingwen jishi* 西周青銅重器銘文集釋. Tianjin: Guji, 2007.

Zhou Shirong 周世榮. "Hunan chutu Handai tongjing wenzi yanjiu" 湖南出土漢代銅鏡文字研究. *Guwenzi yanjiu* 14 (1986): 69-175.

Zhou Xifu 周錫䘂. "Tian Wang gui ying wei Kang Wang shi qi" 天亡簋應為康王時器. *Guwenzi yanjiu* 24 (2002): 211-16.

Zhou Xunchu 周勳初 and Tan Youxue 譚優學. "Yu ding kaoshi" 禹鼎考釋. *Nanjing Daxue xuebao: Renwen kexue* 1959.2: 65-71.

Zhou Yan 周言. "Li gui mingwen 'sui ding' bushi" 利簋銘文"歲鼎"補釋. *Huadong Shifan Daxue xuebao* (Zhexue shehui kexue ban) 32.5 (2000): 121-22.

Zhou Yuan 周瑗. "Ju Bo, Qiu Wei liangjiazu de xiaochang yu Zhouli de benghuai" 矩 伯、裘微兩家族的消長與周禮的崩壞. Wenwu 1976.6: 45-50.

Zhu Dexi 朱德熙. "Guanyu Piao Qiang zhong mingwen de jige wenti" 關於䥯羌鐘銘文的幾個問題. *Zhongguo yuyan xuebao* 2 (1985): 55-58.

Zhu Dexi and Qiu Xigui 裘錫圭. "Pingshan Zhongshan Wang mu tongqi mingwen de chubu yanjiu" 平山中山王墓銅器銘文的初步研究. *Wenwu* 1979.1: 42-52.

Zhu Fenghan 朱鳳瀚. *Gudai Zhongguo qingtongqi* 古代中國青銅器. Tianjin: Nankai Daxue, 1994.

———. "Ying Hou Jiangong zhong" 應侯見工鐘. *Baoli cang jin, xu: Baoli Yishu Bowuguan jingpin xuan* 保利藏金, 續: 保利藝術博物館精品選. Guangzhou: Lingnan meishu, 2001. 122–27.

———. "X gong xu mingwen chushi" X公盨銘文初釋. *Zhongguo lishi wenwu* 2002.6: 28–34.

———. "'Shao gao,' 'Luo gao,' He zun yu Chengzhou" 《召誥》、《洛誥》、何尊與成周. *Lishi yanjiu* 2006.1: 3–14.

Zou Heng 鄒衡. *Tianma Qucun, 1980–1989* 天馬曲村1980–1989. 4 vols. Beijing: Kexue, 2000.

CAC
PRG

Index

Terms in bold have dedicated entries in the Glossary.

agriculture, xix-xxi, 198. *See also* Houji, she.
altar of soil. *See she.*
ancestors. *See* rituals, of ancestor worship.
animal-facedécor, xxiv, xxviii, lvii, 5. *See also panchi.*
animal-shaped vessels, xxiv, 80
Ankang 安康, 144
Anyang 安陽, xxii-xxv, 3, 5, 117
Anzhou 安州, 39, 53
archery. *See* rituals, of archery.
archivist. *See shi* 史.
army. *See shi* 師.
astrology, 10. *See also* divination.

ba 霸, xxxiii, 258, 256
Ba 巴, xlvii
Baijiacun 白家村, 148
bamboo as a medium for writing, xix, xxii, xliii-xlvii, 246, 301
Baoji 寶雞, 16, 86, 93, 187, 243
Baoshan 包山, xliv
Barnard, Noel, lvi, 172
bells and chimes, xix-xxiv, xxviii, xxxi, xxxv, xli-li, 94, 147-48, 221, 268-73; onomatopoeia in inscriptions, lxi-lxii, 121, 151-53, 223 n.2, 236, 258-59, 270-72; tuned sets of, 115, 120-24, 147-53, 166-67, 172-74, 192-94, 213-17, 221-29, 243-53, 258-59, 290. See also music and musical instruments, onomatopoeia.
benediction. *See guci.*

biyong 璧雍, 42-44, 55. *See also* rituals.

Cai 蔡, 195-96, 274, 277-79
Caijiagang 蔡家崗, 287
Cao Pi 曹丕, 303
captain. *See shi* 師.
ceming 冊命, 19, 21
chang 鬯, xxx
Chang, K.C., lvi
Chen Banghuai 陳邦懷, 66
Chen Jieqi 陳介祺, 204 n.1, 221
Chen Yongren 陳詠仁, 204
Chen Zhang fanghu 陳璋方壺, xv
Cheng, King of Zhou 周成王, lviii, 16-17, 19-20, 24-26, 28, 36, 42, 94-98, 129-30, 232, 236-38
Cheng, Lord of Cai 蔡成侯, 280
Chengpu 城濮, 256-66. *See also* Chu, Jin.
Chengzhou 成周, xxxiii, 16-17, 42-43, 68-69, 81, 108-10, 118, 182, 185-86, 193, 213-17, 251; as the seat of government, 46-47. *See also* Luoyang.
Chu 楚, xxxvi-xl, xlii-xlvii, lvi-lviii, 74, 87, 144, 160-62, 219-22, 238, 265-66, 270-75, 280, 287, 301-02
Chuci 楚辭, 275 n.2. *See also* transmitted texts.
Chu ju 楚居, 301
Chunqiu 春秋 (text), 214, 282. *See also* transmitted texts.
coins, xxiii
Confucius, lx-lxi
cosmology, 278, 303

Danfengxian 丹鳳縣, 74
Dao, King of Chu 楚悼王, 301 n.1
Dao, Lord of Jin 晉悼公, 268
dates in inscriptions, xii, xxv, xxxiii-xxxiv, 201, 232-33
Dayuancun 大原村, 5
de 德, xxvii, xxix, xlii, lvi-lviii, 31-32, 61 n.5, 101-2, 112-13, 120-23, 177-78, 198-200, 205-6, 227, 235-39, 256, 261-62, 272. *See also*, Heaven, Mandate of.
Deity Above. *See di*.
di 帝 (*shangdi* 上帝), xxi, 13, 43, 95-98, 112-13, 123, 152, 197, 259-61, 269; above and below (*shangxia di* 上下帝), 28; court of (*diting* 帝廷, home of ancestral spirits), 148-51. *See also* Heaven, Mandate of; spirits.
di 禘, xxvi, 36, 78, 101. *See also* rituals
Di Xin, King of Shang 帝辛, lviii, 3
Di Yi, King of Shang 帝乙, 3
Dian 滇, xlvii
Diantoucun 店頭村, 255
ding 鼎, xxiii-xxiv, xxviii-xxxi; as symbols of political power, lvi-lix; in the sense of "to correct," 10; sets of, called *lieding* 列鼎, xxx-xxxii, xxxvii-xl, xlv-xlvi
Ding, King of Zhou, 周定王, lvii-lviii
divination, xix, xxii, xxv, 94, 129-31, 181. *See also* astrology, omens, oracle-bone inscriptions, shi 史.
Dong wanggong 東王公, 303
Dong Zhongshu 董仲舒, lxiii
Dongjiacun 董家村, 84, 136
Duan Fang 端方, xl n.62, 204 n.1
duiyang 對揚, xiii, lxii-lxiii, 120, 148 n.2, 245

E 噩/鄂, 53-54, 154-56
Echeng 鄂城, 303
Erligang 二里崗, xxi, xxiii-xxv

Erlitou 二里頭, xxi, xxiii, 198. *See also* Xia dynasty.
Falkenhausen, Lothar von, xiii, xlix, 233
Fan, George, 245
Fangyan 方言, 283
Fantang 繁湯, 252-53
Fen River 汾河, 198
feng ritual 豐, xxx, 13, 16-17, 42-43, 126. *See also* rituals.
feng 封, 87-88, 201-2. *See also* law and legal decisions, relating to land.
Feng and Hao 豐鎬, 43, 105, 137 n.1. *See also* Wei River.
Feng Shi 馮時, 266
Fengtai 鳳台, 288
Four Regions. *See sifang*.
Fu Hao 婦好, xxiv
Fu Sheng 伏勝, lix
Fufeng 扶風, xxxii, 64, 84, 93, 101, 115, 119, 139, 147-48, 172, 210, 223, 227, 243

Geng Ying. *See* Ying of Geng.
gods. *See* spirits.
Gong, King of Zhou 周共/恭王, 77, 86, 93-94, 101, 105, 108, 112, 173, 177-78, 182, 232,, 236-38
Gong, Lord of Qin 秦共公, 244
Gongsun Hong 公孫弘, lxiii
government, xxvii, 46, 105, 141, 157, 210, 290-95. *See also* law and legal decision.
Guai 乖, 160-62. *See also* Chu.
Guanzi 管子, 291. *See also* transmitted texts.
guci 嘏辭, xiii-xiv
gui 簋, xxiv, xxviii-xxxii, 118-20; sets of, called liegui 列簋, xxx-xxxi, xxxvii
Guo 虢 lineage, 101-4, 163-67, 187-88
Guo Ruoyu 郭若愚, 280

INDEX

Guoyu 國語, 96 n.4, 265. *See also* transmitted texts

Han 韓, 290-93

Han 漢, xiv

Han Feizi 韓非子, 296. *See also* transmitted texts.

Han River 漢江, xliii, 21, 53, 109, 270, 301

Hancheng 韓城, xxxvii, 255

He Linyi 何琳儀, 285

Heaven, xxi, lviii; Chamber of (*tianshi* 天室), 13-14, 16-17, 43; Mandate of (*tianming* 天命), xxvi-xxix, xl, lviii, 16-18, 28, 31-32, 112-13, 150-52, 161-62, 175-76, 197-200, 204-7, 235-39, 245-50, 259-63

Hefu 龢父, 223-24

hegemon. *See ba*.

Helü, King of Wu 吳王闔閭, 277, 280

Hongxing 紅星, 192

Houji 后稷, xxx, 95-98, 198. *See also* agriculture.

Houma 侯馬, xl

Houtusi 后土祠, 268

Huai River 淮河, 64-65, 68, 144, 154-55, 195-96, 252, 301

Huan, Lord of Qin 秦桓公, 246

Huang Shengzhang 黃盛璋, 60

Huangtupo 黃土坡, 19

Hubin 湖濱, 105

huchen 虎臣, 64-65, 74-75, 108-12, 172, 175-76, 205-8, 257-58. *See also* war.

Hui, King of Wei 魏惠王, 291

hunting, xix-xx

Ji 姬 lineage, 56, 64, 94, 108, 117, 277-78

Ji 姞 lineage, 126-28

Jiang 姜 lineage, xxxv, 72-73; Jin Jiang 晉姜, 252, 255-56; Wang Jiang 王姜, Queen of Zhou, 49, 51; Zhuang Jiang 莊姜, 303-04; You Jiang 幽姜 139, 142

Jie 桀, lviii

Jin 晉, xxix, xxxvi-xxxvii, xl, 150, 213-17, 252-56, , 265-68, 270, 290-93

Jinancheng 紀南城, 270

Jincun 金村, 290

Jing, Lord of Qin 秦景公, 245

Jing River 涇水, 157, 160-61, 173-74, 234

Jiyun 集韻, 285

Jupiter. *See sui*.

Kang, King of Zhou 周康王, 24, 28, 30, 42, 78, 96-98, 232-38

Kaogu tu 考古圖, 255

Kaolie, King of Chu 楚考烈王, 301

Karlbeck, Orvar, 301

Ke, Lord of Yan 匽侯克, 19-20

King Father of the East. *See* Dong wanggong.

Kunbi 昆疕, 219-21

Langya 瑯琊, 291

Lantian 藍田, 105, 108, 192

law and legal decisions, xiii, xxvi, xxxiii, liii, 57-59, 131-42; relating to land, 84-88, 105-7, 139-42, 163-65, 168-71, 201-3; relating to perjury, 136-38; relating to theft, 133-35. *See also* government.

Leipian 類篇, 285

li 醴, xxx n.37

Li Feng, 190, 243

Li, King of Zhou 周厲王, 136, 147-57, 168, 201, 213-14, 221, 223, 231, 235-37

Li Shannong 李山農, 72

Li Xueqin 李學勤, 60, 266, 285, 303

Liang Shizheng 梁詩正, 282
Liao, King of Wu 吳王僚, 277
Licun 禮村, 30
Lidai zhong ding yiqi kuanzhi 歷代鐘鼎彝器款識, 255
Lie, Lord of Jin 晉烈公, 290
Lienü zhuan 列女傳, 304. See also women.
Liji 禮記, xiv, liii, lv-lvi, 271, 296. See also rituals.
Lijiacun 李家村, 80
lineages, xix, xxix; emblems of, xxii, xxv, 3-5, 8-9, 66, 117; names of (*shi* 氏), 25; recorded histories of, xxxi-xxxiii, l-li, 120, 231-36. See also rituals of ancestor worship.
Ling, Lord of Qi 齊靈公, 258
Lingshou 靈壽, 294
lingtai 靈台, 43
Lintong 臨潼, 10
Linzi 臨淄, 258
Lisangudui 李三弧堆, 301
literacy, xix-xxii
Liu Hehui 劉和惠, 277, 280
Liu Tizhi 劉體智, 290
Liu Yu 劉雨, 197
Lixian 禮縣, 245
Lu 魯, 20, 282
Lu 彔, 64-67
Lü 旅 lineage, 84
Lunyu 論語, 120, 259, 297
Luo Fuyi 羅福頤, 303
Luo Zhenyu 羅振玉, 219
Luo[yang] 雒/洛陽, xxxiii, lvi, 8, 16-17, 28, 36, 290. See also Chengzhou.
Lüshi chunqiu 呂氏春秋, 296

Man 蠻, 96-98, 195, 245-51
Mao 毛 lineage, 60, 204-8
Mao Shu Zheng 毛叔鄭, 60 master. See *shi* 師.
mei'ao 眉敖, 87, 90-91, 160-61
Meixian 眉縣, xxix, xxxii, lii, 30, 49, 80, 231
Mengzi 孟子, lix. Mengzi 孟子 296. See also transmitted texts.
Mi 芈 lineage, 160
Mi 弭 lineage, 109
mieli 蔑歷, xxix, 39-40, 126
mingqi 明器, xxxi, xxxvii, xliii, xlvi
mingtang 明堂, 13, 43
Mu, King of Zhou 周穆王, 55, 57, 60, 64, 72, 74, 80, 94-98, 101, 126, 232-38; reforms of, 210; relations with Man and Rong, 251
music and musical instruments, xix, xxxi, xli-xlvii, liii, 172-73, 273. See also bells and chimes.
Mu tianzi zhuan 穆天子傳 60

Nangong Zhong 南宮中, 39-40
Nanzhihuizhen 南指揮鎮, 245

oaths, 164, 168-71
omens, xxvi, lx-lxi. See also divination.
onomatopoeia, xix, lx-lxii. See also bells and chimes.
oracle-bone inscriptions, xx-xxiv, 14. See also divination.

Pan Zuyin 潘祖蔭, 51
panchi 蟠螭, xxxviii, xliv
Pangjing 蒡京, 42-43, 55
paper, xxii
philosophy, xvi
Ping, King of Chu 楚平王, 277
Ping, King of Zhou 周平王, 39
Pingdingshan 平頂山, 192
Pingyang 平陽, 246
Pingyin 平陰, 290-93

Qi 齊, xvi, xxxvi, xli-xlii, 14, 144-45, 255, 258-63, 282-84, 290-93
Qi 杞, 144-45
Qiangjiacun 強家村, 101
Qianlong Emperor 乾隆, 60
Qicun 齊村, 147
Qijiacun 齊家村, 243
Qin 秦, xxxiii, xxxvi, xl-xlii, 39, 150, 190, 221, 245-50, 259, 270, 275 nn.1, 3, 277-80, 291-93, 301-02, 303; First Emperor of, lix
Qing, Lord of Qi 齊頃公, 282
Qishan 岐山, 13, 84, 136, 154, 198, 204
Qiu Xigui 裘錫圭, 266
Qizhen 齊鎮, 223
Qucun 曲村, xxix, xl, 213
Queen Mother of the West. *See* Xi wangmu.

Rawson, Jessica, xlix
ren 仁, 295-97
Renjiacun 任家村, 154, 172, 177, 227
Renzong, Emperor of Song 宋仁宗, 245
respondeat superior, 58, 134, 163. *See also* law and legal decisions.
rhetoric of bronze inscriptions, xii-xiii, xxxiii-xxxv, l-liv, 19-21, 59, 66, 147, 149, 181-82, 210-11, 245-47, 255, 259 270, 277
rhyme, xix, lii, 13, 31-32, 96, 102, 150, 198, 227-28, 246-47, 282-88, 291, 304
rituals, xiii-xiv; of ancestor worship, xiv-xv, xix-xxvii, xxxii-xxxiii, xxx-vi, xli, xlvii-l, 3, 24, 36, 46, 123-24, 172; of archery, 42, 55-56; bathing, xxx; drinking, xix, xxiv, xxvii-xxix, 31, 116; exorcistic, 8; feasting and banqueting, xix, xxiv-xxviii, xxxi, xli, liii, 16; harvest, xxx, 55; military, 30; mourning, 148, 195. *See also di* 禘; divination, feng, lineages, mingtang, she, xiangli.
Rong 戎, 65, 69, 190, 195, 251-52. *See also* war, against the Rong.
rong 肜, lxix-lx, 3-4. *See also* rituals, drinking.
Rong Geng 容庚, 57 Rui 芮, xxxvii
Ruo 若 lineage, 8

Sanji 三汲, 294
Sanxingdui 三星堆, xlvii
Shan 單 lineage, xxxii, 80, 231-41
shanfu 膳夫, 172-79, 201-3, 210-11, 215-17, 227
Shang Yang 商鞅, 247
Shangcai 上蔡, 195
Shangshu dazhuan 尚書大傳, lix-lx, 17. *See also* Shu.
Shaughnessy, Edward L., lxi
she 社, 24, 296-99. *See also* agriculture, rituals.
Shen 沈, 36-38
Shen, Lord of Cai 蔡侯申, 277-78
Sheng, Lord of Cai 蔡聲侯, 287
Shi 詩, *Shijing* 詩經 xli, lii-liii, lxi, 31, 49, 150-52, 181, 184, 195, 198, 246, 259, 270-71, 275 n.2, 278, 295-96; Mao 1, lx-lxi; Mao 38, 259; Mao 57, 298-303; Mao 131, lx-lxi; Mao 205, 85 n.4; Mao 259, 19; Mao 245, 65, 95; Mao 261, 19, 21; Mao 262, 21; Mao 263, 196; Mao 300, 184. *See also* transmitted texts.
shi 師, 11, 54, 68, 108-09, 172-75, 190-91; *bashi* 八師, 58, 81, 155, 174; *dashi* 大師, 78, 103; *liushi* 六師, 81; *shi shi* 師氏, 68, 109. *See also* war.
shi 史, 94, 181, 225-26; *neishi* 內史, 72, 89-90, 181, 203 n.6, 235; *shi xiaochen* 史小臣, 173. *See also* zuoce.
Shiji 史記, 5, 14, 19, 31, 60, 147, 198, 214, 221, 223. *See also* transmitted

texts.
Shouchun 壽春, 301
Shoumeng, King of Wu 吳王壽夢, 288
Shouxian 壽縣, 277, 301
Shu 書, 16, 31, 95, 120, 181, 198, 204, 296; "Gaozong rongri," lx n.105; "Gu ming," 95; "Jiugao," 95; "Luogao," 16; "Shaogao," 16; "Yaodian," 120. See also Shangshu dazhuan, transmitted texts.
Shu 蜀, xlvii
Shuanggudui 雙谷堆, 304
Shun 舜, 296
si 祀, xxv-xxvi, 101
Si River 泗水, lix
sifang 四方, xxvi-xxix, xxxvi, xlii, 31-33, 42, 62, 95, 112-13, 123, 148-51, 155, 175-79, 205-7, 236-39, 245-48, 260, 270, 290-95, 299
silk as a medium for writing, xxii, xlvii
Sipocun 寺坡村, 108
spirits and ghosts, xiv-xv, xxi-xxiii, xxxi, xxxv, li, liii, 95, 233-35. See also di; Houji; rituals, of ancestor worship.
Sufang 蘇坊, 195
sui 歲, 10-11
Suixian 隨縣, 275
Sun Quan 孫權, 303

Tai Wang 太望, 13
Taigongmiaocun 太公廟村, 245
Taiping Rebellion 太平天國, 129
Taiyi 太一, xxiii
Tang, King of Shang (Cheng Tang 成湯), xxv, lix, 260-63
taotie 饕餮. See animal-face décor. ten-day week. See xun.
Teng 滕, 274
tian 天. See Heaven.
Tian 田 lineage, 282
tianshi 天室. See Heaven, Chamber of.

Tianshui 天水, 245
Tiger Corps. See huchen.
tin, xxiii
transmitted texts, xix, 28, 53. See also Chuci, Chunqiu, Guanzi, Guoyu, Han Feizi, Liji, Lunyu, Lüshi chunqiu, Mengzi, Shi, Shiji, Shu, Xunzi, Yi Zhoushu, Yili, Zhouli, Zhuangzi, Zuozhuan.

Wang Chong 王充, lix n.101
Wang Jiang 王姜. See Jiang lineage.
Wang Mang 王莽, 43
Wangsun Man 王孫滿, lvi-lviii
war, xxi, xxvii, xxxviii, xliii, 30-34, 51, 60, 187-89; against the Hu 胡, 68-69; against the Hu 虎, 53; against the Rong 戎, xxxiii, lvi, 60-65, 69, 157, 160, 190; against the Yi 夷, xli, 58-59, 68, 96-98, 108, 144-45, 154-55, 213-17; against the Xianyun 獫狁, 84, 157-59, 184-91, 234; against Xu 徐, 195-96. See also huchen; rituals, military; shi 師; Zhao, King of Zhou, southern expeditions of.
Wei 魏, 268, 282, 290-91
Wei 微 lineage, xxxii, 94-96, 115-24
Wei River 渭河, xxii, xxix, 23, 43, 51, 81, 84-87, 105-6, 154, 157, 161, 168, 187-88, 193, 219, 233
Weilie, King of Zhou 周威烈王, 290
Wen, King of Zhou 周文王, xxvii, 13-14, 16-18, 60, 94-98, 109-13, 120, 150-52, 232, 236-39, 276-77. See also Heaven, Mandate of.
Wen, Lord of Jin 晉文侯, 249-50, 251-55; Chong'er 重耳, 265-67
White, William Charles, 290
women, xiii, xv, 39-40, 49, 117-18, 126-28, 255-56, 277-81, 298-99; as lineage matriarchs, 139-40; buried with lords in tombs, xliv-xlv, 272, 294
Wu 吳, 280-81, 287-88, 298-99

Wu Ding 武丁, xxiv, lix-lx

Wu Family Shrines, lix

Wu, King of Chu 楚武王, 301

Wu, King of Zhou 周武王, xxvii, xxxii, 10-11, 13-20, 24-26, 46, 60, 94-98, 109-13, 120, 123, 150-52, 231, 236-38; sons established as regional lords, 192. See also Heaven, Mandate of.

Wu, Lord of Qin 秦武公, 246

Wu Shifen 吳式芬, 51

Wuhan 武漢, 53, 184, 303

Xi wangmu 西王母, 303

Xia 夏, xxi-xxii, lvi-lvii, 197, 259-63; general term for Chinese culture, 247-49

Xian, Lord of Jin 晉獻侯, 214

xiangli 饗醴, 55, 116, 126. See also rituals.

Xianyu 鮮于, 285-86

Xianyun. See war, against the Xianyun.

Xiao, King of Zhou 周孝王, 115, 126, 136, 154, 173, 225, 232, 235-37

Xiaoganxian 孝感縣, 53

xiaozi 小子, 17, 55, 78, 82, 88-91, 101-3, 112, 148-50, 190-91, 225-26, 239, 248-50, 297-99

Xiang, King of Zhou 周襄王, 265-66

Xiaquancun 下泉村, 157

Xiasi 下寺, xxxviii-xxxix, 274-75

Xing 邢, 28, 129-35, 173

Xingtai 邢台, 28

Xinzheng 新鄭, xxxviii-xxxix

Xiong Zhi Hong 熊摯紅, 221. See also Chu.

Xiping shijing 熹平石經, 299

Xiqing gujian 西清古鑑, 282

Xu 徐. See war, against Xu.

Xuan, King of Zhou 周宣王, 139, 157, 163, 182, 195, 201, 210, 213, 223, 231, 241; military campaigns of, 184-91, 195-96. See also war, against the Xianyun.

Xujiazhai 徐家寨, 201

Xunzi 荀子, 296. Xunzi 荀子 xxxi, 296. See also transmitted texts.

Yan 燕/匽, xvi, 19-22, 285, 294-95

Yandunshan 煙墩山, 23

Yangjiacun 楊家村, xxix, xxxii, lii, 49, 231

Yangzi River 揚子江, xxiv, xxxvi, xlii-xliii, xlv n.71, xlvii, 5, 23, 53, 154, 219, 221, 231, 270-71, 287-88

Yao 堯, 291

Ye Gongchuo 葉恭綽, 204

Yellow River 黃河, xx-xxiv, xxxvi-xxxvii, xl-xlii, xlvii, 5, 106, 168, 212-13, 252, 255, 291

Yi 夷 (ethonym), xli, 51, 55, 95, 112-13, 144, 147 n.1; Huai Yi 淮夷, 58, 184-86, 195-96. See also war, against the Yi.

Yi 宜, 23-25

Yí, King of Zhou 周夷王, 223, 232, 238-39

Yì, King of Zhou 周懿王, 112, 115, 129, 232, 238-39

Yi, Lord of Zeng 曾侯乙, xliii-xliv, 275

Yi Zhoushu 逸周書, 16. See also transmitted texts.

Yichang 宜昌, 270

Yili 儀禮, liii, 283

Ying of Geng 庚嬴, xiv, 39-40

Ying 嬴 lineage, 39

Ying 應 lineage, 192-93

Yong 雍, 246

You, King of Chu 楚幽王, 301-02

You, King of Zhou 周幽王, 136, 243-44

Yu 虞, 24-25

yu 虞 (Forester), 233-34
Yu 禹, 102, 197-200, 259-61
Yu Xingwu 于省吾, 57, 278
Yue 越, xli, 297
Yuncheng 運城, 252

Ze 夨, 127, 168-71, 219
Ze, Lord of Yi 宜侯夨, 23-26
Zhao 趙, xl, xlv, 290
Zhao, King of Zhou 周昭王, xlix, 49, 51, 80, 94, 117, 232, 235-38; southern expeditions of, 39, 53-55, 57, 60, 149-52, 210
Zheng 鄭, xxxviii
Zhi, Lord of Yan 匽侯旨, 21-22
Zhongshan 中山, xvi, xlv-xlvii, 271 n.4, 275 n.2, 285, 291, 294-300
Zhou 舟, 144-45
Zhòu 紂. *See* Di Xin.
Zhoulai 州來, 301

Zhouli 周禮, liii, 55, 181
Zhuang, King of Chu 楚莊王, lvi-lviii, 274
Zhuang, Lord of Qi 齊莊公, 258
Zhuangbai 莊白, xxxii, 64-66, 93, 115
Zhuangzi 莊子, 295. Zhuangzi 莊子 296. *See also* transmitted texts.
zhuhou 諸侯, 39
Zifan 子犯, 265-67
Zi Yu 子玉, 266
Zongzhou 宗周, xxxiv, 22, 31-32, 43, 49, 61-62, 72, 174, 177-79, 182, 198, 213-16
zuhui 族徽, xxii. *See* lineages, emblems of.
Zuo Zongtang 左宗棠, 77
zuoce 作冊, 42, 51, 181, 201. *See also shi* 史.
Zuozhuan 左傳, xxxvi, lvi-lviii, 19, 31, 265-66, 277, 282, 296. *See also* transmitted texts.

www.ingramcontent.com/pod-product-compliance
Lightning Source LLC
Chambersburg PA
CBHW030601230426
43661CB00053B/1801